RELIGION, FAMILY, AND COMMUNITY
IN VICTORIAN CANADA

MCGILL-QUEEN'S STUDIES IN THE HISTORY OF RELIGION

Volumes in this series have been supported by the Jackman Foundation of Toronto.

SERIES TWO In memory of George Rawlyk
Donald Harman Akenson, Editor

1 Marguerite Bourgeoys and Montreal, 1640–1665
  Patricia Simpson

2 Aspects of the Canadian Evangelical Experience
  Edited by G.A. Rawlyk

3 Infinity, Faith, and Time
  Christian Humanism and Renaissance Literature
  John Spencer Hill

4 The Contribution of Presbyterianism to the Maritime Provinces of Canada
  Edited by Charles H.H. Scobie and G.A. Rawlyk

5 Labour, Love, and Prayer
  Female Piety in Ulster Religious Literature, 1850–1914
  Andrea Ebel Brozyna

6 The Waning of the Green
  Catholics, the Irish, and Identity in Toronto, 1887–1922
  Mark G. McGowan

7 Religion and Nationality in Western Ukraine
  The Greek Catholic Church and the Ruthenian National Movement in Galicia, 1867–1900
  John-Paul Himka

8 Good Citizens
  British Missionaries and Imperial States, 1870–1918
  James G. Greenlee and Charles M. Johnston

9 The Theology of the Oral Torah
  Revealing the Justice of God
  Jacob Neusner

10 Gentle Eminence
   A Life of Cardinal Flahiff
   P. Wallace Platt

11 Culture, Religion, and Demographic Behaviour
   Catholics and Lutherans in Alsace, 1750–1870
   Kevin McQuillan

12 Between Damnation and Starvation
   Priests and Merchants in Newfoundland Politics, 1745–1855
   John P. Greene

13 Martin Luther, German Saviour
   German Evangelical Theological Factions and the Interpretation of Luther, 1917–1933
   James M. Stayer

14 Modernity and the Dilemma of North American Anglican Identities, 1880–1950
   William H. Katerberg

15 The Methodist Church on the Prairies, 1896–1914
   George Emery

16 Christian Attitudes towards the State of Israel
   Paul Charles Merkley

17 A Social History of the Cloister
   Daily Life in the Teaching Monasteries of the Old Regime
   Elizabeth Rapley

18 Households of Faith
   Family, Gender, and Community in Canada, 1760–1969
   Edited by Nancy Christie

19 Blood Ground
   Colonialism, Missions, and the Contest for Christianity in the Cape Colony and Britain, 1799–1853
   Elizabeth Elbourne

20 A History of Canadian Catholics
   Gallicanism, Romanism,
   and Canadianism
   Terence J. Fay

21 The View from Rome
   Archbishop Stagni's 1915 Reports
   on the Ontario Bilingual Schools
   Question
   Translated and edited by John Zucchi

22 The Founding Moment
   Church, Society, and the
   Constructing of Trinity College
   William Westfall

23 The Holocaust, Israel, and
   Canadian Protestant Churches
   Haim Genizi

24 Governing Charities
   Church and State in Toronto's
   Catholic Archdiocese, 1850–1950
   Paula Maurutto

25 Anglicans and the Atlantic World
   High Churchmen, Evangelicals, and
   the Quebec Connection
   Richard W. Vaudry

26 Evangelicals and the Continental
   Divide
   The Conservative Protestant
   Subculture in Canada and the
   United States
   Sam Reimer

27 Christians in a Secular World
   The Canadian Experience
   Kurt Bowen

28 Anatomy of a Seance
   A History of Spirit Communication
   in Central Canada
   Stan McMullin

29 With Skilful Hand
   The Story of King David
   David T. Barnard

30 Faithful Intellect
   Samuel S. Nelles and Victoria
   University
   Neil Semple

31 W. Stanford Reid
   An Evangelical Calvinist in
   the Academy
   A. Donald MacLeod

32 A Long Eclipse
   The Liberal Protestant Establishment
   and the Canadian University,
   1920–1970
   Catherine Gidney

33 Forkhill Protestants and Forkhill
   Catholics, 1787–1858
   Kyla Madden

34 For Canada's Sake
   The Centennial Celebrations,
   Expo '67, and Religious Construction
   of Canada in the 1960s
   Gary R. Miedema

35 Revival in the City
   The Impact of American Evangelists
   in Canada, 1884–1914
   Eric C. Crouse

36 The Lord for the Body
   Religion, Medicine, and Protestant
   Faith Healing in Canada, 1880–1930
   James Opp

37 600 Years or Reform
   Bishops and the French Church,
   1190–1789
   *J. Michael Hayden and
   Malcolm R. Greenshield*

38 The Missionary Oblate Sisters
   The Spirit of the Congregation and
   Struggles over Vision and Mission,
   1904–1929
   Rosa Bruno-Jofré

39 Religion, Family, and Community in
   Victorian Canada
   The Colbys of Carrollcroft
   Marguerite Van Die

SERIES ONE
G.A. Rawlyk, Editor

1 Small Differences
  Irish Catholics and Irish Protestants,
  1815–1922
  An International Perspective
  Donald Harman Akenson

2 Two Worlds
  The Protestant Culture of
  Nineteenth-Century Ontario
  William Westfall

3 An Evangelical Mind
  Nathanael Burwash and the
  Methodist Tradition in Canada,
  1839–1918
  Marguerite Van Die

4 The Dévotes
  Women and Church in
  Seventeenth-Century France
  Elizabeth Rapley

5 The Evangelical Century
  College and Creed in English
  Canada from the Great Revival
  to the Great Depression
  Michael Gauvreau

6 The German Peasants' War and
  Anabaptist Community of Goods
  James M. Stayer

7 A World Mission
  Canadian Protestantism and the
  Quest for a New International
  Order, 1918–1939
  Robert Wright

8 Serving the Present Age
  Revivalism, Progressivism, and the
  Methodist Tradition in Canada
  Phyllis D. Airhart

9 A Sensitive Independence
  Canadian Methodist Women
  Missionaries in Canada and
  the Orient, 1881–1925
  Rosemary R. Gagan

10 God's Peoples
   Covenant and Land in South Africa,
   Israel, and Ulster
   Donald Harman Akenson

11 Creed and Culture
   The Place of English-Speaking
   Catholics in Canadian Society,
   1750–1930
   *Edited by Terrence Murphy and
   Gerald Stortz*

12 Piety and Nationalism
   Lay Voluntary Associations and the
   Creation of an Irish-Catholic
   Community in Toronto, 1850–1895
   Brian P. Clarke

13 Amazing Grace
   Studies in Evangelicalism in
   Australia, Britain, Canada, and the
   United States
   *Edited by George Rawlyk and
   Mark A. Noll*

14 Children of Peace
   W. John McIntyre

15 A Solitary Pillar
   Montreal's Anglican Church and
   the Quiet Revolution
   John Marshall

16 Padres in No Man's Land
   Canadian Chaplains and
   the Great War
   Duff Crerar

17 Christian Ethics and Political
   Economy in North America
   A Critical Analysis of U.S. and
   Canadian Approaches
   P. Travis Kroeker

18 Pilgrims in Lotus Land
   Conservative Protestantism
   in British Columbia, 1917–1981
   Robert K. Burkinshaw

19 Through Sunshine and Shadow
   The Woman's Christian Temperance
   Union, Evangelicalism, and Reform
   in Ontario, 1874–1930
   Sharon Cook

20 Church, College, and Clergy
A History of Theological Education
at Knox College, Toronto, 1844–1994
Brian J. Fraser

21 The Lord's Dominion
The History of Canadian Methodism
Neil Semple

22 A Full-Orbed Christianity
The Protestant Churches and Social
Welfare in Canada, 1900–1940
Nancy Christie and Michael Gauvreau

23 Evangelism and Apostasy
The Evolution and Impact of
Evangelicals in Modern Mexico
Kurt Bowen

24 The Chignecto Covenanters
A Regional History of Reformed
Presbyterianism in New Brunswick
and Nova Scotia, 1827–1905
Eldon Hay

25 Methodists and Women's Education
in Ontario, 1836–1925
Johanna M. Selles

26 Puritanism and Historical
Controversy
William Lamont

Religion, Family, and Community in Victorian Canada

The Colbys of Carrollcroft

MARGUERITE VAN DIE

McGill-Queen's University Press
Montreal & Kingston · London · Ithaca

Erratum: page 32, lines 7 and 8, should read (in 1776 under the Association Test all 46 adult male Colbys in New Hampshire had supported the Revolution)

© McGill-Queen's University Press 2005
ISBN 0-7735-2959-4 (cloth)
ISBN 0-7735-3028-2 (paper)

Legal deposit fourth quarter 2005
Bibliothèque nationale du Québec

Printed in Canada on acid-free paper that is 100% ancient forest free (100% post-consumer recycled), processed chlorine free.

This book has been published with the help of a grant from the Canadian Federation for the Humanities and Social Sciences, through the Aid to Scholarly Publications Programme, using funds provided by the Social Sciences and Humanities Research Council of Canada.

McGill-Queen's University Press acknowledges the support of the Canada Council for the Arts for our publishing program. We also acknowledge the financial support of the Government of Canada through the Book Publishing Industry Development Program (BPIDP) for our publishing activities.

Library and Archives Canada Cataloguing in Publication

Van Die, Marguerite
  Religion, family and community in Victorian Canada : the Colbys of Carrollcroft / Marguerite Van Die.

(McGill-Queen's studies in the history of religion 39)
Includes bibliographical references and index.
ISBN 0-7735-2959-4 (bnd)
ISBN 0-7735-3028-2 (pbk)

1. Colby family. 2. Family–Religious aspects–Canada–Case studies. 3. Evangelicalism–Canada–History–19th century. 4. Religion and sociology–Canada–Case studies. 5. Stanstead (Québec)–Biography. I. Title. II. Series.

FC2949.S72Z49 2005   280'.4'097109034   C2005-903268-5

Typeset in New Baskerville 10/12
by Infoscan Collette Québec, Quebec City

To my mother
Margaretha Helena Van Die de Klerk

Contents

Illustrations xiii

Acknowledgments xv

Map of Stanstead County and the wider world of the Colbys xviii

Genealogical Table: The Stanstead Colbys in the Nineteenth Century xix

Introduction 3

1 A World in Transition: God, Identity, and Family 15
2 Redefining Family Identity: The Convergence of Moral Philosophy, Romanticism, and Evangelical Religion 42
3 Faith, Hope, and Charity: Religion, Women, and the New Economic Order 61
4 Time, Faith, Energy: Religion and the Spirit of Capitalism 83
5 Nurture and Education: The Christian Home 101
6 Family, Community, and Religion 125
7 Protestants, Social Harmony, and Moral Order 149

Conclusion 181

Notes 191

Index 271

Illustrations

Dr Moses Colby, c 1830   28
Lemira Colby, c 1830   28
Charles Carroll Colby in 1847   46
Harriet (Hattie) Child Colby, 1859   62
Hattie Colby reading   64
Emily Strong Colby, c 1861   70
William T. White and son Charles, 1866   73
William Benton Colby with daughter Mary, c 1864   78
Carrollcroft, home to four generations of Colbys   86
Hattie Colby and Harriet Alice, c 1870   95
Colby and Child family picnic, 1910   113
Abby, Charles William, Jessie, and John Colby, c 1885   119
Methodist Centenary Church, Stanstead, rebuilt after
    the 1883 fire   139
The Village of Stanstead Plain, c 1905   145
Charles Carroll Colby, 1867   152
Charles Carroll Colby, 1890, attired as president of the Privy
    Council   174
Family group in the garden of Carrollcroft, 1890   175
Celebrations for Charles on his appointment to the Privy Council,
    Coaticook, 1889   176
Melvina Colby, with daughters Martha and Mary, 1890   177
Hattie and Charles Colby, 1895   182
Tea at Carrollcroft, 1910   183
Tombstones of Charles and Hattie Colby   187

Acknowledgments

In keeping with a book on religion, my acknowledgments include both confession and words of gratitude.

Leaving absolution to the discretion of the reader and reviewer, I confess that this book was far too long in the making. An Evangelical Scholar Fellowship in 1993–94 awarded by the Pew Charitable Trusts funded initial research for a study on religion and the family in Victorian Canada in which the Colby story was to play only a minor part. Ultimately I found it necessary to revise the original plan, and I thank Don Akenson for suggesting that the rich collection of Colby papers deserve an entire monograph. Although it took some time for me to refocus, the new approach made it possible to penetrate beyond the prescriptive and predictable and to examine religion as lived in daily life. The earlier research, consisting of an examination of denominational literature and a quantitative study of religious change over time within a single community, has since been published in articles.

In the course of this lengthy trajectory I have incurred many debts. Susan Stanley first alerted me to the existence of the Colby Papers and introduced me to Helen Lovat Colby (d. 1998), whose generosity opened the family home and its archives to the public. John Colby, great-grandson of Moses Colby, graciously read and offered commentary on a final draft of the manuscript, as did his relative, John Nicholas Wickenden. Archivist Elizabeth Brock, her successor Kathy Curtis, and their staff provided informed, consistent, and cheerful assistance and turned research visits to the former Colby home in Stanstead into sheer pleasure. Stephen Moore's intimate knowledge of nineteenth-century local history and his extensive familiarity with land transaction records made him the ideal researcher to help unravel the business world of Moses Colby and his sons. At Queen's University, graduate students Christopher Currie, Sandra Hewton, Julie Godkin, and Darren Schmidt delved into census records and parliamentary debates to shed light on how religious affiliation found political expression in the early decades of Confederation. In the final stage of the manuscript, Stéphane Vermette's computer skills came to the rescue of an electronically challenged and overextended writer. A six-month sabbatical given by Queen's Theological College and the Department of History at Queen's University in the fall of 2003 provided the opportunity to bring the project to a close.

During the ebb and flow of confidence that accompanies the completion of a book, one becomes greatly reliant on the support of colleagues and friends. The enthusiasm of Nancy Christie and Michael Gauvreau was crucial in getting me started; later, Elva McGaughey and Ruth Compton Brouwer offered unfailing understanding and encouragement. Jack Little and Jane Errington kindly read sections of the manuscript related to their area of expertise. I consider myself especially fortunate in having as friends and candid critics Bob Gidney and Wyn Millar, each of whom took time out of a busy research schedule to read a penultimate draft of the entire manuscript and offer invaluable advice on its improvement.

The team at McGill-Queen's University Press who took this work under their wing – Don Akenson, Kyla Madden, and Joan McGilvray – have provided a reassuring combination of professional and personal assistance that greatly helped smooth the hurdles of the publication process. I am grateful also to them for putting me into contact with Michael Pacey, a skilled and versatile cartographer, and with Carlotta Lemieux, a gracious and dauntingly competent copyeditor. Her skills, along with the helpful feedback of two anonymous readers, have strengthened the book and saved me more than once from embarrassment. I thank Gillian Griffith for assistance in preparing the index. Although the many people listed here remind me of the pleasure of belonging to a community of scholars, in the end I take sole responsibility for all errors of omission or commission that may be present in the book.

Finally, I would like to acknowledge the loyal presence of my canine companions, Ben and his successor Morely, two black labs who with infinite patience each day awaited the moment when the computer was shut off and they could claim their entitled walk. Last of all, but chief among my reasons for gratitude, is my mother, whose longevity rivals that of the Colby women and whose avid letter writing over the decades emulates their efforts to remain connected with a far-flung family. I am delighted to be able to dedicate this book to her.

Marguerite Van Die
Kingston, Ontario

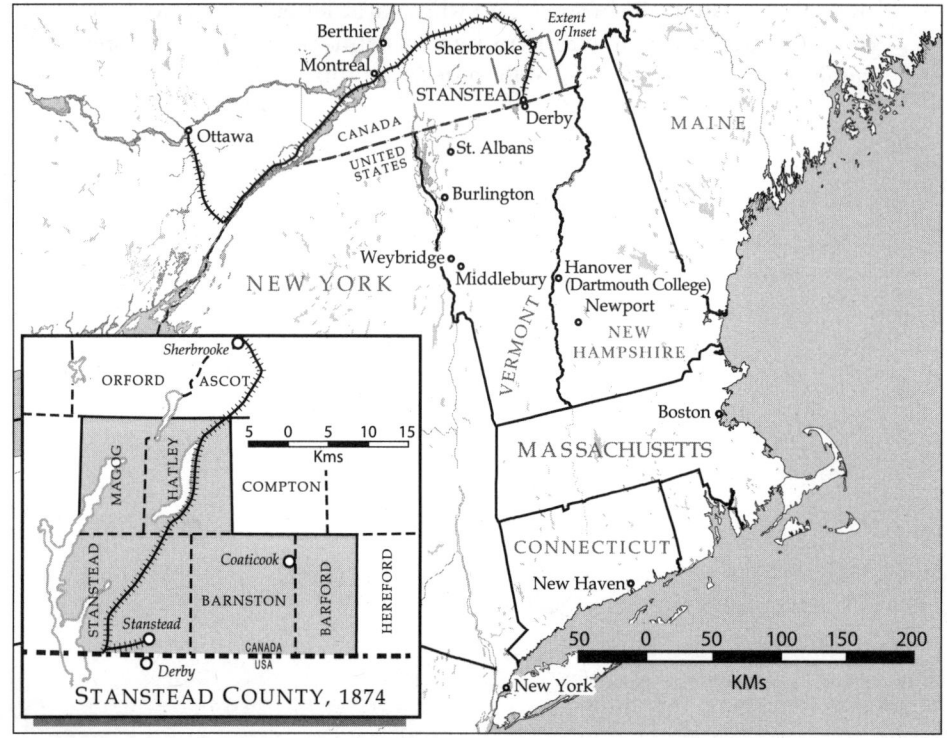

Map of Stanstead County in 1874 and the wider world of the Colbys, showing the railway from Stanstead Plain to Ottawa

GENEALOGICAL TABLE
THE STANSTEAD COLBYS IN THE NINETEENTH CENTURY

Moses French Colby
1795–1863 b. Thorton, N.H.

m. 1826 Lemira Strong
1806–1889 b. Pawlet, Vt

- Charles Carroll
  1827–1907

  m. 1858 Harriet
  Hannah Child
  1838–1932

  - Abby Lemira
    1859–1943
    m. Somerset Aikins
    1850–1911
  - Jessie Maud
    1861–1958
  - Emily Stewart
    1864–1865
  - Charles William
    1867–1955
    m. Emma Frances Cobb
    1866–1945
  - Carroll Child
    1869–1869
  - Harriet Alice
    1870–1871
  - John Child
    1873–1926
    m. Mary Spafford Williams
    1877–1921

- Emily
  1830–1832

- William Benton
  1833–1884

  m. 1862 Melvina
  Wallingford
  1832–1899

  - Mary French
    1862–1931
    m. James M.A. Aikins
    1851–1929
  - Martha Stoddard
    1865–1951
    m. Rev. Walter A. Cooke

- Emily Strong
  1836–1866

  m. 1861 William T. White
  1836–1925

  - Infant Son
    1862
  - Charles Carroll
    1866–1866

RELIGION, FAMILY, AND COMMUNITY
IN VICTORIAN CANADA

Introduction

"The family is essential, as without it the world would be a mere chaos of human beings. The domestic state is indispensable to the health and comfort of mankind ... Not for Adam and Eve only, and their posterity ... but for the human race in all time, was the family state ordained, that every man and woman might share and enjoy its blessings. How else shall the people of our land and the world have homes? How else shall the tender and endearing relations of kindred be perpetuated? How, without the family, can domestic happiness be preserved in the earth?"[1]

Written by a local historian in the early 1870s as introduction to a chronicle of some five hundred families in Stanstead County in Quebec's Eastern Townships, these are sentiments that many Canadians appear to have long since abandoned. Universals have been replaced by particulars, the burden for human happiness has shifted from God and the family to the state and the economy, and individual rights are challenging and eroding collective responsibilities. At a time when the definition of marriage is in the process of being rewritten to include two people of the same sex, and when a high rate of separation and divorce is again making single-parent or blended families the norm, the family has moved sharply from this nineteenth-century construction. Far from seeing it as the much-vaunted haven in a heartless world, Canadians today, according to opinion polls, are placing a higher value on friendships and relationships than on family life.[2] In such a context, why would anyone write, let alone read, a book on religion and family life in Victorian Canada?

The reader who expects such a study to express nostalgia for a simpler, purer time will be disappointed. As historians have been careful to point out, the Victorian family, more often than not, failed to live up to its rhetorical construction. "We want to believe that families past were less fragmented, discontinuous and divided than families now," reads one such admonition, "but historical reality is anything but reassuring on this point."[3] With the high rate of maternal and infant mortality, the remarriage of young widowers and widows, and separation caused by immigration and frequent relocation, people in Victorian Canada, as elsewhere in the Anglo-American world, experienced their own variations of family breakup.[4] Thus, reading about past habits and beliefs as they relate to family life raises our awareness of the continuities between our own time and earlier generations. It can, however, do more. Although the family has always faced challenges to its happiness and continuity, the cultural resources on which people draw in such circumstances have varied from one period to the other. Looking at the family in an earlier time and in a different context can serve to deepen our understanding of human versatility and creativity in the face of socio-economic and intellectual change.

Some of the main cultural resources on which individuals and communities have drawn in the past to provide meaning and reshape identity as they negotiated transformations in their experience of space and time are the symbols, rituals, and beliefs offered by religious traditions. In so doing, they have also ensured that in order to remain meaningful to its practitioners, religion has itself become part of the maelstrom of change. This has been especially true for Western Christianity, which since its early days has been deeply implicated in social and political life. Accordingly, as part of a new interest in the historical family, scholars have offered compelling analyses of how the Christian religion, in contexts as varied as medieval France, Reformation Germany, and Puritan New England, helped individuals, families, and communities to shape meaningful new forms of identity.[5]

The Victorian period, on the other hand, has been seen as an era of marked change and discontinuity in the ability of religion to act as a sacred cosmos that legitimated and formed family structures. Basing their research primarily on the Protestant middle classes of Britain and the United States, historians have argued that under the combined force of the commercial and technological revolution, industrialization, and urbanization, the family underwent major alterations in gender roles and class expectations.[6] Although the impact of these changes on religion has generally not been their primary focus, their conclusions have been far-reaching for religion. Instead of continuing to draw on traditional beliefs and practices for their self-understanding, families began to relocate the myths, rituals, and images of religion from the church to the home. Central to this relocation of the sacred was the role of the mother, upon whom were divested the expectations of spirituality, morality, and nurture previously assigned to the institutional church. Accompanying this shift from institutional to domestic religion was the increasingly sacred character assigned to the home.[7] While earlier periods, such as the Puritan, had emphasized the importance of the home as a site of Christian socialization, it had never been presented as a redemptive site, and thus the sacralization of home and family was a break culturally and theologically with Christian tradition.[8]

As a result, the Victorian fascination with domestic religion has been seen as an important step in the gradual secularization of Western society. Leonore Davidoff, for example, has concluded, "It is the tie between parents and children which has been imbued with ever more poignancy as people's relationship to the transcendental realms of religion, folk belief and magic has gradually disappeared."[9] In such a reading, the implications of relocating the source of morality from a transcendent God, sacred Scriptures, and ancient traditions to the family are extensive. Not only did the shift leave people with a sharply contracted symbolic universe by which to negotiate their daily lives and family arrangements, but the burden of making moral and spiritual decisions was now displaced from communal traditions to the individual. In the words of historian John Gillis in an aptly entitled study, *A World of Their Own Making*, "to the challenge of sustaining the material basis of family life was now added the awesome task of providing for its spiritual requirements."[10]

Such a conclusion may resonate with today's individualism and sense of anomie, but it creates a puzzle for the historian of religion. Although there have been dissenting voices, historians have on the whole seen the Victorian period as a thriving time for Christianity in Britain and North America. This was true in particular in Canada, which, in the conclusion of one observer, deserved the title "Christian" more than Britain or the United States, shaped as it was by two very activist forms of Christianity, evangelical Protestantism and ultramontane Roman Catholicism.[11] Neither form can be fully understood without acknowledging the presence of the other, but for the purpose of exploring Victorian domestic religion, the focus will be on evangelical Protestantism, since in ultramontanism the dynamic force of religion was not the home but the institutional church, centred in Rome.[12] Before proceeding to examine domestic religion in Victorian Canada, the term "evangelical," therefore needs to be defined, and the movement must be set within an institutional and national context.

During the nineteenth century, various Protestant denominations – primarily Methodists, Congregationalists, Presbyterians (especially

Secessionist and Free Church), Baptists, and to a lesser extent Anglicans, or Episcopals – began to take on the added name "evangelical."[13] The term drew attention to a set of related beliefs and practices which with varying degrees of emphasis they held in common (and which they assumed were characteristic of all Protestants). Compressed in four code words widely used by historians of evangelicalism, these shared emphases were "biblicism," "conversionism," "crucicentrism," and "activism."[14] Each of these captures an important evangelical understanding of the nature and means of Christian salvation. First, the Bible, not church tradition or the sacraments, was seen as the foundation of faith. Secondly, faith was to be personal and experiential: all people were sinners, and thus all needed to be called to repentance. Thirdly, God offered redemption and forgiveness to all who trusted not in themselves but in Christ's atoning death on the cross. Finally, those who were converted and underwent "a new birth," as it were, were called to a new way of life that was focused not on themselves but on the needs of others. Although often mistakenly seen as the essence of evangelical Protestantism, religious revivals were nonetheless one of the most important means by which evangelical Protestants increased their numbers. To sustain their strength and to ensure that individuals and communities remained surrounded by "godly" influences, they further availed themselves of the pulpit, the press, and an ever-increasing number of voluntary societies, from temperance groups to Sunday schools.[15]

By taking such an experiential, activist position, evangelicals helped dissolve older corporate forms of faith. This process was accelerated by the fact that churches lost their status and privileges as established institutions and became dependent on the laity for financial support, first in the newly formed United States and by 1854 throughout British North America.[16] More research is needed into the class background of evangelicals in nineteenth-century Canada, but evidence points to a similar development to that in the United States, where a dynamic entrepreneurial middle class assumed religious leadership. Turning religion into a flourishing activity, people strengthened its public role as they sought to reform society to reflect their evangelical understanding of reality.[17] All of this has been well documented. However, although there have been a number of insightful studies of religion at a community level, much remains to be learned about the way evangelical religion functioned in the private realm.[18] Specifically for this study, how do we account for the apparent discontinuity between the pervasive, assertive presence of evangelical religion in the public sphere and the loss of meaningful religious discourse and practice noted by family historians of the Victorian era?

Here the wider cultural context is important. The latter part of the nineteenth century saw revolutionary changes in a wide number of areas. In addition to large-scale socio-economic restructuring brought about by new modes of transportation and communication, Victorians faced formidable intellectual challenges to the Christian faith in the form of Darwinian evolution and the new historical approach to the Bible known as the higher criticism. The impact of these changes upon evangelical Protestantism has been a matter of considerable historical debate. Some historians, especially in Canada, have seen the final decades of the nineteenth century as a time of religious decline, in which evangelical Protestants grew increasingly liberal and accommodated their faith to a secularizing culture.[19] This view is shared by those for whom the term "liberal" in reference to religion has taken on a negative connotation. Evangelicals in the Victorian period, on the other hand, generally saw "liberal" as a badge of honour and as evidence that theirs was a faith that, while maintaining essential beliefs, was also in tune with the progressive spirit of the age.[20] This self-understanding is reflected in the work of another group of historians who, rather than seeing liberal evangelicalism as a form of declension, have depicted it as an expression of religious revitalization, especially in its early-twentieth-century mutation, "the social gospel."[21] Their approach finds support in a recent study of liberal Protestantism in the United States. Its definition, which also informs the present study, sees the movement as "a genuine form of Christianity not based on external authority" but characterized "by its openness to the verdicts of modern intellectual inquiry, especially the natural and social sciences; its commitment to the authority of individual reasons and experience; its conception of Christianity as an ethical way of life; its favoring of moral concepts of atonement; and its commitment to make Christianity credible and socially relevant to modern people."[22]

What should by now be clear is that anyone interested in understanding the nature and place of religion in Victorian family life in Protestant Canada is confronted with a contested interpretive framework. While the argument of family historians that Victorian domestic religion was an important turning point towards today's "secular city" fits well with one reading, it raises questions for those who argue that mainline Protestant denominations retained significant cultural authority well into the first half of the twentieth century.[23] How, indeed, did religiously minded people confront socio-economic and intellectual changes within the family and in the wider church and society? Was there a discontinuity between the religion practised privately in the home and its public presence? Did gender shape religion differently in the family from that in the church and the community?

Even to begin to answer such questions, one has to look beyond the sermons, theological treatises, personalities, and ecclesiastical institutions whose study has shaped much of what one Canadian historian has rightly called "the strained and somewhat inclusive debate over 'secularization.'"[24] Such sources, as well as the debate, should not be overlooked, for ultimately they form part of the metanarrative of religious history. The study of domestic religion, however, calls for a quite different definition and approach, one that goes beyond church participation or the articulation of creed and doctrine to include concepts of salvation, sacred experience, and participation in a sacred community through liturgy, symbols, and ceremony.[25] This change in method is needed all the more since historians can no longer assume familiarity with Christian thought and practice on the part of their audience. Thus they have to cast about for new ways to decode the thought of ministers and theologians into the idiom of lay experience. Here, historians of French Canada have blazed a trail. Through a wide range of creative methods and new questions, their work has provided insight into the ways in which Roman Catholic belief and rituals helped shape family life, and how an ecclesiastical presence accompanied such rites of passage as marriage, birth, and death in nineteenth-century Quebec society.[26]

Informed by the growing interest in social history and cross-disciplinary research, and drawing on the concept of "lived religion," American historians have begun to take a similar approach.[27] Attention has shifted from institutions and theology to studying religion as a living and mutating phenomenon that allowed people to deal with the contradictions and tensions inherent in their culture as they made connections between their own family situation, the wider society, and God. Increasingly using cultural and anthropological approaches, historians of religion are raising new questions that are less defined by assumptions of modernity.[28] As a result, earlier analytical categories, including those of "declension" and "secularization," are giving way to understandings that are more fluid and open-ended. No longer simply associated with theological belief and institutional structures, nineteenth-century religious idioms are being explored in a wide range of material forms, from holy water and Victorian Bibles to church architecture and suburban cemeteries.[29] The study of new sites of religious experience has brought long-overlooked groups to the centre of historical investigation. An examination of the intergenerational family as a place of religious change in Puritan New England, for example, has made us more aware of the ways in which parents' strategies to provide both economic and spiritual security for their children helped influence theological pronouncements and church practice.[30]

As a "lived" experience – rather than as something that exists "out there" in sermons and theological discourses – religion, in the words of historian Robert Orsi, "comes into being in an ongoing, dynamic relationship with the realities of everyday life."[31] One of the main exponents of the new approach, Orsi offers a helpful fourfold approach aimed at setting religious practice in a densely configured context. First, he notes, in placing religion within its own time and place, it is important to have a sense of the idiomatic possibilities and limitations in a culture – the limits of what can be desired, fantasized, imagined, and felt. Secondly, we need to examine the "knowledges of the body in the culture" – the ways in which religion has been embodied in people's corporeality, what it is that their tongues, skin, ears "know." In the case of nineteenth-century evangelical religion, for example, this would include not only paying attention to such practices as singing hymns, listening to Scripture and sermons, participating in liturgy, and kneeling in prayer, but also, in an age of ecclesiastical growth, changes in the material setting of worship. A third consideration when exploring lived religion are the structures of social experience such as marriage and kinship patterns, moral and legal obligations and expectations, and the allocation of valued resources. Finally – and here the dynamic nature of religion comes to the fore – attention needs to be directed to the types of tension that erupt within these particular structures.[32] How, for example, might increased wealth and social status among church members place pressure on long-standing denominational teachings of sobriety of dress and frugal lifestyle?

Innovative and especially promising for a study of family and religion in Victorian Canada, this new approach does not neglect more traditional religious scholarship, and it engages the work of scholars in other fields. For example, the role of money and fundraising in evangelical Protestantism, which has a direct bearing on family life, has been receiving considerable historical attention.[33] Related to this is the move away from earlier interpretations of religion as a form of social control to a more complex understanding of the relationship between evangelical Protestantism and the middle class.[34] As well, sophisticated research into the nature of cultural hegemony has raised the need to re-examine the dominance of Protestantism in the nineteenth century with a view to understanding more clearly its role in shaping power relationships. Emphasizing legitimization and validation of beliefs and values, rather than manipulation and social control, the concept of hegemony nuances insight into how a ruling class rules, an important concern when examining the interface between the religion, the family, and socio-economic change.[35] Also pertinent are the parallels between religious belief and intellectual thought drawn by historians such as Mark Noll and Daniel Walker Howe for the antebellum United States. Among the most important agents in relocating the source of Christian morality from God and the Scriptures to the individual, they have identified the nineteenth-century common-sense philosophy that held sway in the universities of Scotland, the United States, and Canada until the final quarter of the nineteenth century.[36] The conjunction between economic concerns and moral values has in turn become the subject of a growing literature on evangelical participation in Anglo-American political life in the nineteenth century. Recent work (for example, by Richard Carwardine, Howe, and others) has drawn attention to the shared moral values of evangelicals and American Whigs and their expression in antebellum political culture.[37]

These studies, along with new methodological approaches, raise important questions for the study of Victorian domestic religion in Canada. Building, for example, on existing research on the prevalence of common-sense thought in Canadian colleges, we need to know more about the connections that college-educated middle-class Protestants made between the world in which they lived and their perceptions of God.[38] Did those perceptions change as people began to experience time and space differently under the impact of new technologies, new communications systems, and increased consumerism? What motivated lay people to invest so heavily in religious and moral institutions once they were no longer supported by the state through religious establishment? Did religious concerns have any influence on the economic and political strategies of middle-class families to ensure their well-being and continuity? It has been observed that in Canada "Confederation was an offspring of secular statesmanship, born of political and economic necessity, fathered by politicians and railway promoters. Its purpose was not to create a covenant people or to hasten the coming of the kingdom of God."[39] We know little, however, about the ways in which evangelicals made connections in private and public life between their moral convictions and the economic policies of the new Canadian nation.[40] In short, how did religion interact with other aspects of people's lives – the day-to-day demands of keeping a house and caring for one's family, coping with death and loss, advancing a family's economic and social interests, and shaping individual and family identity in the local community and the nation?

As historians, we ask such questions of the past but realize that the answers we come up with of necessity are provisional and are contingent on the available sources. One major problem concerning the sources is the heavily prescriptive nature of Victorian domestic religion. Nineteenth-century evangelical publishers, facilitated by such technological innovations as steam-run presses and the stereotype plate, rolled out a seemingly endless supply of denominational journals, tracts, and other prescriptive literature. While much of this has been well mined by historians, the nagging question remains: To what extent did the family that Victorian rhetoric constructed as ideal actually reflect the experience of real people?[41]

The study that follows is an entry – a kind of "preliminary probe" – into these and related questions.[42] It is a case study of three generations of an evangelical and unabashedly middle-class family, the Colbys of Stanstead, Quebec. Members of Canada's emerging economic elite, they were active contributors to their local community and, through elected political office, to public life in early post-Confederation Canada.[43] Stanstead, a border village adjacent to Vermont, was in the St Francis district in Quebec's Eastern Townships and was settled in the 1790s by Americans attracted to its potentially fertile farmland and rich forests. Among the Americans who followed the pioneers was Moses Colby (1795–1863) who, with his wife Lemira Strong (1806–89) and their infant son Charles Carroll, moved across the border from Derby, Vermont, in 1832 to begin a medical practice in Stanstead. A man of strong republican sympathies, who named his first-born after Charles Carroll, the sole surviving signatory of the Declaration of Independence, Moses soon found that his interests on British soil lay with the local Conservatives and briefly, in 1837–38, represented his riding in the Legislative Assembly of Lower Canada.[44]

By 1859, after several moves, the couple established what became the ancestral home for four generations of Colbys, until it was deeded by the family as a museum to the Stanstead Historical Society in 1992. During these many years – through material objects, renovations, and, above all, in a voluminous correspondence exchanged among family members – the Colbys invested the home with a unique identity that was closely related to their own evolving self-understanding. Fashionably invested with the name Carrollcroft in the late 1880s, this was the place to which they returned after personal and business trips to Europe and the United States. It was the place to which they brought newly acquired friends and marriage partners, and into which they inducted their offspring. Their enthusiastic research into their family tree, the many boxes of letters, diaries, and other personal papers collected in the house, and the home's carefully selected furnishings and *objets d'art* all bear witness to the fact that this was a family consciously constructing its own identity in the well-documented fashion of the period.[45] In so doing, the Colbys left behind a wealth of historical data, including, thanks to their own limited but helpful genealogical research, a family tree whose origins on both parents' sides stretched back to New England's first Puritan settlers.

While Moses and Lemira and their two younger children, William and Emily, made some contribution to the accumulated family correspondence, the bulk of it documents the lives of their elder son Charles Carroll Colby (1827–1907), his wife Hattie Child (1838–1932), and their four children: Abby Lemira (1859–1943), Jessie Maud (1861–1958), Charles William (1867–1955), and John Child (1873–1926). A prominent though often financially insecure member of the middle class, who in 1872 was forced to declare insolvency, Charles Colby was a respected lawyer, an active entrepreneur and railway and mining promoter in the St Francis district, and from 1867 to 1891 the county's representative to the dominion parliament (first as an Independent and then, after 1872, as a Conservative).[46] During his years in Ottawa and his innumerable and generally disappointing business trips in pursuit of a financially secure livelihood, Charles kept in constant touch by letter with his closely knit family. Thanks to the completion of an extensive railway network by the early 1870s, the children too were often on the move, making annual visits to their maternal grandparents, aunts, uncles, and cousins in Weybridge, Vermont. Later, the daughters – in search of distraction, improved health, and matrimonial prospects – began to make extended visits to family in Chicago and Kansas, and also spent time with their father in Ottawa. Throughout these travels the volume of correspondence kept pace.

In the course of the latter half of the nineteenth century, the family's increased mobility, education, and growing prominence refashioned its self-identity. Although Charles Colby's wealth was often based more on hopes and financial speculation than on real assets, his prominence as a member of parliament enabled him to forge important contacts with leading Canadian businessmen, and the family began to move in prominent social circles in Ottawa and, later, in London, England. The eldest son, Charles William, became a noted Canadian historian at McGill, while the couple's elder daughter, Abby, in 1887 married Somerset Aikins of Winnipeg, son of Sir James Cox Aikins, lieutenant governor of Manitoba. Even more brilliant was the match made in 1890 by Abby's Stanstead cousin Mary, daughter of William Colby, to Somerset's brother James Albert, who in 1916, recently knighted, succeeded his father as lieutenant governor. Although Mary experienced serious family turmoil and economic insecurity in her youth, her parents managed to give her a good education, allowing her to take up school teaching and, as Lady Aikins, to fulfill with much acclaim and general affection her role as Manitoba's first lady.

Religion was part of the complex mix that helped shape the family's changing identity. While Moses and Lemira remained true to the

Congregationalist faith of their ancestors, though with some tensions, their two sons married Methodists and in time took an active role in church life. The Winnipeg Aikins, too, were known for their strong allegiance to the Methodist Church, as were a number of the Colbys' other prominent contacts, including the families of political colleagues and local ministers. Elected to Parliament to represent his region's economic interests, Colby during his lengthy tenure experienced first-hand the ways in which economic, political, and religious concerns frequently intersected in public and private life in Ottawa.

Viewed through the lens of a single family, this was a world in dynamic flux, where fortunes were made, lost, and remade, where people whose ancestors had never moved beyond the confines of their village found themselves travelling great distances by rail and steamship. The people studied here were, to be sure, relatively few in number, but in many ways we can look back on them as grappling with issues that have shaped our own growing identification with a global society. What makes them so fascinating is that while they forged ahead and embraced new concepts of time and place, they also sought to maintain their older identity as members of a family who shared a specific house, a religious faith, and a community. Their travels, brilliant marriages, and growing affluence – all products of the 1890s – are not, however, the focus of this study. Rather, the pages that follow will examine how in the preceding period, during a time of considerable socio-economic strain, religion helped shape and reshape family identity, the local community, and, through the eyes of Charles Colby, MP for Stanstead County, life in Canada's new federal capital.

As a case study, therefore, this is not intended to be a history of the Colby family, nor is it the study of a "representative" evangelical family. Rather, this microhistory is a search for meaning, a probing into the dynamic relationship of religion with everyday life in order to understand how the two influenced and changed one another. Like examining a small detail on a broad canvas, the study of the domestic, religious, and social relations of a single family has its own intrinsic interest, but it can also help us see more clearly the intricate interplay and interconnectedness of line and colour in the larger framework. In so doing, as a miniature but also as part of a larger picture, this study makes the emphatic claim that the history of Protestant belief and practice in Victorian Canada cannot be pursued in isolation from concerns of family and gender, social relations, economic activity, and politics. Conversely, our understanding of daily life in this period will be markedly flattened without an awareness of the presence of religion. In pursuing these goals, I will also make a number of connections between the Canadian and U.S. experience of evangelical religion and will seek to shed more light on its liberal form. With these brief comments firmly in mind, we turn to the world of the first generation, Moses and Lemira Colby, as they lived and brought up their three young children.

CHAPTER ONE

A World in Transition: God, Identity, and Family

"My trust is in Providence. If we go down – it will be His will – and let us all be prepared to say sincerely His will be done." In the unlikely eventuality that his ship would sink, Charles Colby, en route from Liverpool to New York early in January 1884, telegraphed his family in Stanstead to advise them not to be concerned when they received news that, shortly after embarking on its eighty-third voyage, the Royal Mail Ship *Germanic*, on which he was a passenger, had broken its propeller shaft. When a long sixteen days later the disabled ship arrived off Waterford, Ireland, he presented a commendation on behalf of the passengers to the captain and crew, expressing "gratitude to Almighty God for having brought us safely through the perils of the sea."[1] Though conventional rhetoric, these words, like his allusion to Providence, echoed the sentiments of his Puritan ancestors, who two and a half centuries earlier had made their own perilous voyage across the ocean. Unlike the heroic Calvinism and political resistance that had led to the Great Migration of his distant forebears, a much more mundane background was the setting for Charles Colby's words of faith and reassurance. His was a Late Victorian world of unparalleled change, where technology and human ingenuity were reconfiguring space and time in ways that profoundly affected social relations and, ultimately, even the once inscrutable ways of Providence. Thanks to the marvels of the telegraph, the news of the *Germanic*'s mishap was conveyed almost instantly to a small village in Quebec's Eastern Townships, and when Colby later disembarked in New York City, he faced less than a half day's journey by train to be reunited with his family.

Not long before his trip, he had reread the 1817 journal that his father Moses Colby had written as a young man, detailing a twenty-five-day journey by colt, foot, and wagon from Derby, Vermont, to New Haven, Connecticut, in pursuit of medical studies at Yale. At the time, Charles had made thoughtful note of Moses' dislike of the intense and excitable revivalism he had encountered as he traversed a religiously volatile "burned-over" district. Charles concluded that his father, at age twenty-one, had already evinced that reverence for the God of Revelation and the God of Nature that informed his lifelong pursuit of medical practice and research.[2] Since New England's earliest days, and now in Late Victorian Canada, generations of Colbys had been faced with changing patterns of space and time. Consistently they had drawn on the symbols and language of the Christian religion as they negotiated their way across what one historian has aptly called "the unfamiliar geographies of their new experiences and hopes."[3] By the time young Moses made his cumbersome journey to New Haven in pursuit of knowledge and a livelihood capable of sustaining a family, the moral and material ambiguities and possibilities had increased. Those who centuries earlier had arrived in New England had sought security in the Congregational way, a series of covenants with God and one another, mutual promises that had joined church, town, and commonwealth into a single chain of order, including as its smallest component the household of parents, children, and servants.[4] Well before the time of Moses' birth, the Congregational way had begun to unravel, as conversion – that deeply transforming work of God's Spirit – began to elude the children of the saints, thereby jeopardizing the social web of church membership, access to the Lord's Supper, and the right to present one's child for baptism.[5]

As members of the second generation in the post-revolutionary United States, Moses and his wife Lemira saw the last gasps of this covenantal society. First as newlyweds in Derby, Vermont, and then across the border in Stanstead (in what was then Lower Canada) in a community of largely transplanted Americans, they encountered sweeping and complex socio-economic and intellectual changes that profoundly affected their sense of self and family and the Puritan religion that had sustained their ancestors. Born into a society that was overwhelmingly rural, they had already begun to witness change by the time of their marriage in 1826. As they raised into adulthood their young family in the 1840s and 1850s, they saw this change accelerate, thanks to an expanding commercial market economy in the northeastern United States and the neighbouring Eastern Townships.[6] At the same time, new attitudes such as republican individualism, along with the extension of the genteel ideal of the companionate marriage to middle-class circles and an enhanced understanding of woman's role as mother, all worked together to reshape the traditional patriarchal family.[7] An even more swiftly dismantled hierarchy was church establishment, which by the mid-1850s had disappeared in British North America. As the revivals of the early-nineteenth-century Second Great Awakening had moved north from New England and swept into the Eastern Townships, church membership had been reconfigured in favour of new evangelical groups such as the Baptists, Methodists, and Millerites, recasting the definition of religion from formal church allegiance to individual experience.[8]

Taken together, these changes not only unsettled old patterns of life but also expanded the opportunity for men and women to weave family and religion together in new ways that were congruent with their changing circumstances and sense of self. The lives of Moses and Lemira Colby, despite the scattered and fragmentary sources available, offer a glimpse into the emerging reconstruction of the relationship between the family and religion, the contradictions and anxieties they faced as laypeople, and the ambiguities they left unaddressed. It is their in-between world and their God that form the focus of this chapter.

MIGRATION, FAMILY, AND RELIGIOUS CHANGE IN RETROSPECT

When Moses in 1832 decided to bring his wife Lemira and their infant son Charles from their home in Derby, Vermont, to the nearby village of Stanstead in Lower Canada, where he had set up a medical practice the previous year, his migration was part of a much larger demographic dislocation in the transatlantic world, which would eventually reorient the Eastern Townships, turning them away from the United States and towards Britain.[9] For the Colbys, however, such a reorientation merely reconnected the circle in a well-trodden path of family migration. While Moses knew little about his ancestors beyond the two most recent generations, his grandchildren would learn that they were the descendants of Anthony Colby, who had left his native Lincolnshire and gone as part of John Winthrop's company to Massachusetts Bay in 1630, and who not long thereafter was one of the founders of Amesbury, Massachusetts.[10] Lemira, who unlike her husband was well versed in her family's history, also traced her American roots to Puritan ancestors. On her father's side was Elder John Strong, who had arrived in 1630 from Plymouth with another party of Calvinists and had become one of the founders of Northampton, Massachusetts; and on her mother's side was Anthony Stoddard, whose offspring included two of New England's most influential ministers who recast the Congregational way: Solomon Stoddard and his grandson, the theologian Jonathan Edwards.[11]

Known like their forebears for their strong civic and church involvement, the successors of these early Puritans soon faced further migrations. By the time of the third generation, the pattern of landowning, kinship, and inheritance, which had been characteristic of New England since the seventeenth century (and is described by Philip Greven and others) had begun to unravel, and Colbys with such stalwart biblical names as Enoch and Samuel began to look north to New Hampshire for new land.[12] Initially, the relocation was cautious, first to Chester, only ten miles from the Massachusetts frontier; then, with the next generation, ten miles farther, to Candia; and with the sixth generation, ninety miles farther still to Thornton, New Hampshire. It was here in 1795 that Moses Colby was born to Samuel Colby and his wife Ruth French, the daughter of a prominent Candia family, also of Puritan extraction.[13] Demographic pressure and the need to provide for their young family compelled the couple to cast about for more land, and two years after Moses' birth, drawn by news of a recently opened and promising farm settlement, Samuel and Ruth, riding together on a single horse, made an exploratory trip to Derby, Vermont, five miles south of the Canadian border. Although moving one hundred miles from Thornton entailed the effective loss of kinship ties, the couple returned for their three infant children and made Derby their permanent home. In so doing, they were part of a larger post-revolutionary thrust of American settlers into Vermont, a portion of which spilled over into the St Francis district of the recently created province of Lower Canada.[14]

Unlike the property of some of Derby's earliest families, the Colby homestead was too small to provide a living for both the stem family and two sons, not to mention dowries for the three daughters. The elder son, Nehemiah, supplemented his income for a while with store keeping in Rock Island, a hamlet adjacent to Derby on the Canadian side of the border, while Moses, who had an unusually keen and inquiring mind, became apprenticed at age seventeen to a local doctor.[15] No doubt recognizing his ability and the fact that without further education his opportunities to earn a decent living would be limited, the family cobbled together a financial plan that enabled Moses to attend lectures at Yale College from November 1817 to April 1818. Financing for these studies was a collaborative effort, with Moses borrowing a hundred dollars, presumably on the basis of future earnings, and his father supplying a colt, which was to be sold in New Haven, Connecticut, on his arrival there, the proceeds paying all college expenses during the academic term, which then extended from 1 November to 1 April. In frontier communities in the early decades of the nineteenth century, such family strategies to concentrate scarce financial and emotional resources on the care and education of their sons were still relatively novel.[16] At the same time, they can be seen as part of a wider process of change telescoped in only two generations – from an older primitive home economy, with its strong community base, to the more specialized and individualistic trade network that was emerging. It was as a member of these two worlds that the twenty-two-year-old Moses, with a companion, set off on his colt from northern Vermont to seek an education in New Haven, carefully noting his impressions along the way in a daily journal.[17]

A YOUNG MAN'S JOURNEY

As the two men slowly travelled along the rough roads of southwest Vermont and the banks of the Connecticut River, often on foot to save their burdened colt, they moved in and out of various village cultures, all of which received assiduous attention. Time, place, and people were the basic framework that provided meaning to this rural society in obvious flux. Beginning in mid-June, Moses kept a daily record of weather conditions, periodically noting their effect on the crops, with such comments as: "The season here is very backward and discouraging to farmers and the prospect of corn coming to maturity is small indeed." In this agricultural society there was a community network on which the two travellers were able to rely for their basic needs, sometimes staying with friends or kin, as arranged in advance, and on rare occasions simply knocking on the doors of strangers and being taken in for the night. Such reliance for hospitality on friends, kin, and even strangers fell within long-established traditions that marked an agricultural society.[18]

Alongside this rhythm there was another, which reflected the expanding commercial marketplace, whose signs of growing prosperity and successful entrepreneurship invariably caught Moses' eye.[19] "The prospect of the farmer on the Connecticut River is extremely flattering," he appreciatively observed, noting that though the corn harvest might be small, the foresight of the early English settlers to plant grain and also apple trees, which were now upwards of one hundred and fifty years old, was paying off abundantly. Similar scenes of agricultural prosperity inspired equally approving entries, each reflecting Moses' understanding of time as progress, with improvements brought about by obvious human skill and ingenuity rather than simply by responding to the cyclical working of nature.[20]

Part of a wider spectrum of changing attitudes, young Moses' belief in progress reflected the flourishing ideal of self-development in the newly created American republic. By 1817 this new republican ideal of a balanced life of self-development and self-discipline, encouraged by evident signs of material prosperity, was already sufficiently familiar to a studious young American such as Moses to form a template with which to evaluate unfamiliar places and experiences.[21] Interesting medical cases, for example, such as the report of a hemophiliac family, were noted by Moses with exacting detail, while thriving village economies brought forth his hearty approval. The Fourth of July, "sacred in the memory of the American people" (which was celebrated near the end of the journey with a boat excursion to Long Island), gave rise to such rhetorical staples of republican patriotism as mention of "tyrants" who had been toppled and "the immortal Washington and his wise legislators," who had succeeded in planting and cultivating a new laurel in American soil. On the other hand, Moses' encounter with an astrologist holding a village population in his thrall evoked his exclamation, "O, when will the people of this enlightened country be wise enough to spurn such imposters from our land." Whereas in the popular religion of his seventeenth-century Puritan ancestors, portents and astrology had been part and parcel of the Calvinist theology of "special providences," in his own enlightened age such superstitions evoked only contempt.[22] Alongside this still tenacious folk culture, but calling for pity rather than contempt, was the evidence of a vanishing aboriginal people, who despite their decision "to espouse the cause of freedom and justice" were now "but few and dissipated." Once portents of divine judgment upon wayward New Englanders, the Native people had been reconstructed into sad victims of the march of progress.[23]

When it came to assessing how economic and intellectual changes were affecting religion, Moses' diagnosis was more ambivalent. These were years when the fires of revivalism were sweeping through the "burned-over district" of western Vermont and New York.[24] Moses' response as an aspiring doctor and a young man educated in the Puritan tradition of sound biblical knowledge and a healthy awe of the wisdom and reasonableness of the Creator was both critical and thoughtful. Called on to give his medical diagnosis of a young woman who in the course of a revival meeting had experienced a complete loss of strength for three days, he mused, "These ignorant people consider it as the effect of the power of God upon their souls whether it is or not – perhaps I ought not to judge. God treats his creatures as reasonable beings ... How then can the excitement of the passions which is no less than the privation of reason, be a compliance with the request of the Almighty or the effect of his power upon us, acting contrary to his mandate."

For unknown reasons, Moses' parents had not presented their infant son for baptism, but he had, according to the conventional phrasing of the time, been trained in religion by a "godly mother," who in keeping with the Congregationalist understanding of salvation had taught him a deep respect for the ways of God detailed in the Scriptures. Accordingly, like those Congregationalist clergy and laity who frowned on any effort to equate true scriptural religion with the New Light revivals of the eighteenth and early nineteenth centuries, Moses mistrusted those who pointed to the emotions as a sign of their conversion.[25] As he observed in his diary upon giving his medical diagnosis of the young woman incapacitated by religious revival, "True Christianity I think evinces itself in a humiliating sense our own imperfection and a continued sorrowing for our own varied transgressions – embraces gravity as a virtue indispensable to our gaining admittance into the kingdom of perfect day."

In his view, such seriousness was entirely absent in the revivalist preaching that he encountered during his journey, where the goal was to bring individuals to a sudden highly emotional conversion experience. Since repentance and conversion were the work of an omnipotent and inscrutable God, not the work of an individual, the new revivalism could only be suspect as a way of true salvation. While at New Haven, Moses attended the Congregational meeting house on Sunday mornings and the Episcopal church in the evening. Although the latter offered fine preaching, he had reservations about "the formalities of their ceremonies, which contradicted the living nature of religion."[26] As the work of an omnipotent and inscrutable God, living religion could not be expressed only in human ceremonies, but as his Puritan forebears had taught, neither could it simply be conjured up at will.[27] Commenting on what he considered to be an excellent sermon one Sunday morning in the meeting house, Moses was quick to catch himself with the thought: "Excellent did I say. Why should I be capable of judging while I sit insensibly and as it were inanimate beneath the sound of the gospel triumph – the doctrines of revelation are mysterious to me – Is it because I am enveloped in a cloud of darkness – If so may the light of revelation illumine my mind and dispel the mists thereby enabling one to perceive and know aright."

Returning to Derby after a term of study he set up a practice, and in 1820 he took further lectures, this time at the Medical Department of Dartmouth College in Hanover, New Hampshire, from which he graduated in 1821.[28] It was shortly after resuming his practice that he experienced, in the conventional terms of the time, some measure of "lifting of his spiritual darkness." This occurred under the preaching of a scholarly Methodist minister, Wilbur Fisk, who was stationed in nearby Craftsbury in 1822 and later became president of Wesleyan University in Middletown, Connecticut.[29] However, Moses did not at that time seek baptism or become a member of a church. "Illumination," or conversion, which was the work of God's Spirit, eluded him until just before his death, when finally he sought baptism and asked to take part in the Lord's Supper.

As many historians have pointed out, conversion presented difficulties for other educated middle-class members of his generation.[30] Among the factors influential in undermining their ability to undergo conversion, much attention has been devoted to the impact of Scottish common-sense philosophy. Intended to undermine the dangers of skepticism and unbelief by upholding the practical wisdom of "common sense," this was an eighteenth-century synthesis of two seemingly antithetical visions of human nature and human capacity: Calvinism and the Enlightenment.[31] The revivals of the early nineteenth century had encouraged the more hopeful Arminian acceptance of human agency in the process of salvation. Common-sense thought further undermined the Calvinist sense of divine providence and human impotence by making a strong case for individual moral responsibility. Flourishing in North America, where the potential for human agency seemed especially promising, this philosophy shaped theological discourse in colleges and universities in Canada and the United States during the first three-quarters of the nineteenth century. Enamoured of science, and convinced that reason and religion both pointed the mind to God, educators relied on common-sense thought to ensure that, if rightly educated, young men would remain devoutly religious while at the same time being open to new scientific and intellectual thought.[32]

The common-sense belief in the unity of knowledge was also the cornerstone of Baconian science, as taught by devout professors such as Benjamin Silliman and Jonathan Knight at Yale, whose courses Moses had attended and whose patronage he had successfully sought immediately on arriving at Yale, armed with an introductory letter solicited en route from Dr Smith of Dartmouth.[33] Since the God of Nature was also the God of Revelation, the mind – through the right use of reason – was led from the study of nature to contemplate the wonders of nature's God. If humankind were to advance, it was imperative that reason keep the emotions under control and not permit religion to degenerate into enthusiasm. Thus, when young Moses noted in his travel journal his abhorrence of astrology and emotional revivalism, he was implicitly reflecting the common-sense position on the need to keep the right balance between authority and experience, between reason and emotion. It was not at all clear, however, where in this balance conversion fitted. For Moses, there seemed to be only two spiritual alternatives at the time. The first, in keeping with his forebears' Calvinist emphasis on a sovereign God, was to wait until the day when he could personally testify to the work of God's Spirit in his heart. The second, which his reason and upbringing resisted, was to experience the new intense revivalism, which everywhere, in the words of historian Nathan Hatch, was "storming heaven by the back door."[34] In summary, in theological terms, Moses Colby found himself caught between traditional Calvinism's theology of a sovereign God, who controlled the timing of conversion, and the new and increasingly prevalent Arminian emphasis on the cooperation of the human will in the process of salvation.

The work of theologians and the impact of economic and social change resolved this tension for the next generation in favour of the Arminian position.[35] On the level of university life – as Yale's principal Noel Porter realized a few decades later, in the 1860s – reason and religion required more conscious integration if young scholars, raised in devout homes, were to undergo conversion.[36] However, clergy and educators often followed where devout laypeople, faced by the contradictions of their situation, had already led the way.[37] If the Colby family story is any indication, important social changes – especially a shift from an agrarian to a commercial economic base of livelihood and a growing emphasis on the affections as the basis of family identity – in time resolved the tension. Although these took several generations to work themselves out, Moses' decision at age thirty-one to marry Lemira Strong laid the foundations in his own small world.

THE COMPANIONATE MARRIAGE AND RELIGIOUS CHANGE

During his 1817 journey, while enmeshed in a network of kin and community that provided nightly accommodation and daily food, Moses had jotted down a few thoughts on the pleasures of home. Unlike the republican imagery of progress that shaped his observations of social and economic change, his few comments here looked back to an earlier idealized and idyllic state. At the conclusion of a short boat trip that left him decidedly unwell and unattracted to the dangers of a life at sea, he had opted for "a humble cottage in a lonely country village where the tempestuous storms will pass without me listing and where friendship and benevolence actuate the heart of the peasant diffusing charity around the humble circle." Some years afterwards, the issue of "woman's sphere" became a topic of interest. Still a bachelor and probably a member of one of the popular young men's moral improvement societies, Moses tried his hand at public speaking on the subject "Female Influence and its Appropriate Sphere."[38] Although he had to confess to limited knowledge and could muster none of the minute observation typical of his scientific discourses (in fact, the composition was abandoned in midstream), his views were enlightened and modern. They were, in fact, decidedly advanced, for he chose to give his talk a more idealized title, "The Supremacy of Woman." In tune with the emerging emphasis on woman's perceived spiritual and moral superiority, the concept led him to move far beyond his usually precise medical field of observation into the more dangerous and slippery terrain of spirit and sentiment. In the flowery rhetoric of the period, he proclaimed, "Like the great forces of Nature, like the atmosphere we breathe, like the never ceasing attractions that roll their Planets in their spheres, her influence is silent and insensible, but all powerful in its effects." Nature's God, it seems, had taken on a feminine face, for though Moses made no explicit comment to this effect, the apparent transcendence of woman's spiritual nature placed her unequivocally within the realm of religion.[39]

In its conventional hyperbole, his views on womanhood also fitted well with the new ideal of the companionate marriage. This concept can be traced to at least the eighteenth century in Britain, where historians have noted its prevalence among the English gentry and its growing attraction among "the middling sort." Although economic concerns continued to be a significant factor in selecting a spouse, intellectual and spiritual compatibility – as part of the growing emphasis on self-development – had taken on a new importance and was one of the essentials of the companionate marriage. To the north in French Canada, at least among the elite, young people were not given free rein in selecting a spouse, but this was less the case in British North America and in the American republic. There, as in Britain, the companionate marriage retained the importance of shared class concerns, which now included as patrimony not only property but also education for women as well as for men.[40]

For Moses, the ideals of womanhood and home were realized in 1826 when he married twenty-year-old Lemira, the daughter of Timothy Strong, a well-to-do sheep farmer in Pawlet, Vermont, who had caught his attention while she was visiting her aunt in Derby.[41] Like the Colby family, Lemira's paternal relatives, the Strongs – and on her mother's side, the Stoddards – had been caught up in the centrifugal pressures of family and land, and from Massachusetts they had spread out to Connecticut and Vermont. Reserved by nature, Lemira left little direct documentation, but her fine handwriting, excellent use of English, and the love of reading and household skills evident in her correspondence all witness to a genteel, middle-class upbringing, which allowed her to share many of her husband's interests. In all probability, she also brought a substantial dowry into the marriage, for in 1828, less than a year after the birth of their first child, Moses travelled to Boston for further graduate study at Harvard's School of Practical Anatomy, where he combined regular coursework with further research at the General Hospital, as well as offering medical services to the city's penal and charitable institutions.[42]

The companionate ideal of their marriage found strong expression in the only surviving letter to his "dear Lemirey," which was written during this time at Harvard.[43] While describing his new work environment and noting his concern about the welfare of their infant son, he also took care to describe an item obviously of feminine interest – the dress of Boston's female society: plaid cloaks which "might be mistaken in Derby for bed blankets." The sharing of gossip and professional and family matters between husband and wife were not simply formalities; they were expressions of an existing bond or, in Moses' words, a "friendship," which, as he elaborated, had become integrated into the very warp and woof of his identity. "Today is thanksgiving and not being much engaged I have often thought of home – of you and Charles," he began the letter, but added: "Not because I feel discontented. No it is a different feeling that presents you to my mind. It is a friendship or rather an affection interwoven into my existence and which cannot be dissolved till the principle by which I move this pen shall become extinct. Revolution may take place in Governments and nature itself may be convulsed but friendship itself will exist till its connection with organized matter ceases." While the laws of "organized matter" were the physician's area of investigation, friendship was governed by moral faculties which, in his words, were "held amenable to the laws of revelation."

Despite the conventional formality of discourse, Moses' letter offers a glimpse into a middle-class world in transition, a world that was changing from the patriarchal household with its hierarchical structures of authority to a more egalitarian relationship of mutual interest between husband and wife. In time, the connection between the love of husband and wife and God's moral law would find expression in a new understanding of religion, one that was more congruent with familial imagery and growing egalitarian relationships.[44] For Lemira and Moses, however, there remained a dissonance between the language used to describe the love between husband and wife and that describing the relationship between an individual and God. Raised in the Congregationalist tradition, both continued to adhere to the Calvinist theology of an omnipotent, inscrutable deity, to be addressed in awe and reverence, not unlike the patriarchal family structure in which they had been raised.

There is evidence that for both Lemira and Moses, the religious legacy they inherited from an earlier generation carried with it tensions for those growing up in the increasingly egalitarian and individualistic early republican period. In the early days of New England Puritan piety, church membership – which included partaking in communion, or the Lord's Supper, and the right to present one's infant for baptism – had been open only to those who were able to give a testimony of God's saving work in their lives, and who thereby "owned the covenant" which God had made with sinful humanity. As testified by much recent research, such spiritually rigorous conditions for church membership became increasingly difficult for those Puritan young people who, despite being unable to experience conversion, nevertheless did want to transmit to their children the benefits of baptism.[45] A more lenient position emerged, known as the "half-way covenant," whereby even the offspring of unconverted parents, and hence non-members, though refraining from taking communion, could receive infant baptism in the hope that at some future date they would express a desire "to own the covenant." It was Lemira's ancestor Solomon Stoddard – the minister of Northampton, Massachusetts, between 1665 and 1729 – who, influenced by ongoing lay scruples, had gone even further and instituted a form of "open communion" without any membership requirement. Such compromises did not go uncontested, especially during the revivals of the 1730s and 1740s, and in particular by Stoddard's grandson Jonathan Edwards, who succeeded him in the ministry at Northampton. Under Edwards's preaching and the New Light movement of the First Great Awakening in the mid-eighteenth century, the call to conversion and strict conditions for membership had again become insistent.[46]

Thus, members of the generation that preceded Moses and Lemira had encountered much uncertainty about what could arguably be the central question of family identity: their own eternal safety and that of their children. Moses' parents, who had failed to seek baptism for their infant son, may well have been among them. Lemira's father, who despite having asked for the reading of the apostle Paul's hymn to Charity in 1 Corinthians 13 on his deathbed, had died without giving clear evidence of a personal experience of saving grace, much to the distress of his children. In Lemira's final years, a similar inability to claim such an experience for herself caused her much anxiety and became a matter of great concern to at least one of her sisters, whose entreaties pursued her well into old age. Failure to testify to a conversion experience of saving faith did not mean, however, that a person did not believe in God, read the Scriptures, and attend church on a weekly basis. All this Lemira faithfully did throughout her long life, in which her favourite reading consisted largely of devotional literature and the biographies of devout prominent individuals. Nor did her failure to testify prevent her from presenting her children for baptism. But what she would not and could not do was answer affirmatively to her sister's entreaty that she openly commit her life to Christ.[47] Moses, who unlike his wife had not received baptism as an infant, shared both her scruples and her religiosity. However, in the course of his years in Stanstead as a medical doctor, landholder, and politician, he played a part in bringing about changes in social and economic conditions that ultimately led to a new configuration of the old covenantal relationship between church, town, the family, and God.

These far-reaching changes originated with the need to make provisions for one's children's material well-being. Studies of early-nineteenth-century New England and Vermont inheritance practices underscore the care with which parents planned the economic future of their children.[48] This included the practice of birth control to limit family size, which for Lemira and Moses would have been facilitated by Moses' medical knowledge and by the long absence from home brought about by his desire to seek further training.[49] At the age of thirty-one Lemira ceased bearing children, having given birth four times, at regular three-year intervals, to Charles in 1827, Emily in 1830 (who died two years later), William in 1833, and finally a second daughter, Emily, in 1836.

The practice of birth control to limit family size was accompanied by carefully designed financial sacrifices to lay the foundation for economic support for their children. To supplement his medical practice and his ongoing research, farming was the most obvious option for Moses, and since uncleared but potentially fertile land just to the north in Stanstead County was half the price of that in the Derby area, a move north across the border made sound economic sense.[50] Accordingly, armed with an MA from Harvard, and after passing an examination before the Medical Board of Lower Canada, Moses set up a practice in December 1831 in the village of Stanstead Plain, filling a vacancy created by the death of one of the village's two physicians. Shortly thereafter he was joined by Lemira and their son Charles.[51]

SOCIAL CHANGE AND MORAL VALUES IN A BORDERLAND COMMUNITY

Although only a small village, Stanstead Plain functioned as the urban centre to a large agriculturally fertile area, which three decades after

Dr Moses Colby, c 1830, painted shortly before his immigration to Canada with his young wife Lemira and infant son Charles (courtesy of the Stanstead Historical Society Collection, Colby Curtis Museum, Stanstead, Quebec [CCM])

Lemira Colby, c 1830, the matriarch of the family (CCM)

its initial settlement was beginning to shed its pioneer conditions. The establishment in 1822 of a customs station in the village and, the following year, the region's first weekly newspaper, the *British Colonist*, under its fiery republican editor Silas Dickerson, as well as an improved mail system – which by 1833 was able to carry news and information on a semi-weekly basis to and from the United States, Montreal, and Quebec City – all worked to move the village out of its earlier isolation. With a population of 10,248 by the time of the 1831 census, Stanstead County, created only three years earlier and containing the villages of Stanstead Plain, Hatley, Barnston, Barford, and Bolton, was the most populated county of the English-speaking Eastern Townships of Lower Canada. Still predominantly American, with close economic ties to Vermont and New England thanks to the poor transportation system to Montreal and Quebec, its inhabitants worked primarily in agriculture, as landowners or day labourers, or as small merchants servicing the area. Although some of its founding families moved elsewhere (and outmigration continued throughout the 1830s and 1840s), already by the time of Moses Colby's arrival, Stanstead Plain had become home to a core of well-to-do landowners, active in improving the village's services to allow them to compete more effectively in a growing agricultural market. Because of the scarcity of money, credit and payment in kind were still the norm. Nonetheless, in 1830 a number of these affluent old-timers had tried to create a regional bank, but their efforts to obtain a charter were frustrated by the suspicions on the one hand of Louis-Joseph Papineau and his Reformers and on the other hand by the vested anglophone banking interests of Montreal and Quebec City. Persistence paid off, however, and in 1836 Montreal's City Bank opened branches in Sherbrooke and Stanstead Plain, though primarily for deposits and to facilitate land transactions.[52]

While some of the new institutions such as banks, a land registry office (1830), and an agricultural society (1824) clearly advanced the interests of commercial capitalism, a budding system of voluntary societies and religious denominations functioned to maintain an earlier sense of a classless community in which, in the nostalgic words of one old-timer, people were "thrown together" and "every man was as good as his fellow."[53] Beginning in 1796, when Congregationalists started to meet in the log barn of one of the first settlers, church gatherings served as a locus for community in providing an opportunity for social gathering and worship.[54] This communal ideal was maintained by the erection in 1816 of a privately funded union meeting house capable of seating 1,500. It was built as an exact replica of the First Church of Christ Congregational Meeting House in East Haddam, Connecticut, and originally was shared by the two other main denominations, the Free Will Baptists and the Methodists.[55] The latter group, who will receive more detailed attention in chapter 6, had been present in the area since 1804, first under American and then, after 1821, under British Wesleyan leadership. In 1829, owing to disagreements with the Congregationalists over their shared ministerial appointments, they built their own brick meeting house. The initial dreams of religious unity had floundered, but the Methodists did for some time continue to share the new building with the Congregationalists, though meeting at a different hour.

Given a long tradition of lay leadership in these earliest denominations, there gradually emerged a consensus on religious behaviour and values, which served as a force in redefining community identity. Under the efforts of the British Wesleyan preachers, the older form of revivalism – comparable to that religious enthusiasm that had offended young Moses Colby in rural Vermont – now became replaced by a more orderly, sober expression. The more exuberant expression in the meanwhile increasingly became associated with new sectarian groups, such as the Millerites, who by 1842 had become a regular feature on the religious landscape.[56] Always a potential cause of communal division, the Millerites and their successors, the Adventists, made inroads primarily among the area's relatively small group of Baptists, while facing a common front among Stanstead's Congregationalists, Methodists, and Anglicans. This consensus reflected the move away from a frontier society to a more ordered community and helped ensure that the more revivalist minded began to worship elsewhere, joining the large Baptist church in nearby Hatley village or, after the 1870s, attending services at the new Christian Adventist campgrounds at Beebe, three miles west of Stanstead.[57]

Strengthening the emerging sense of community founded on social order and material progress were a growing number of schools and an academy (founded in 1829) all reflecting the high rate of literacy that was characteristic of the early New England population. There were also several voluntary societies, primarily of American origin, some of which went back to the town's pioneer days.[58] They included such usual agents of evangelical moral reform as a Bible society, to disseminate religious tract literature, and a variety of temperance societies, which were organized to combat the pervasive problem of intemperance in a society where, until the coming of the railroads in the early 1850s, distilling remained the cheapest way to make a profit from the area's large crops of wheat, potatoes, and hops.[59] During the 1840s and 1850s an agricultural society and a masonic Golden Rule Lodge, founded in 1821 by its sister in Derby, Vermont, further brought together a number of the town's modest middle class as well as several of its wealthier men: landowners, politicians, and professionals.[60] This latter group included Moses Colby who, thrust into this developing community, soon found himself taking a leading role in civic life. Besides joining the Masons and the agricultural society, he became a member of the Bible society and the Independent Order of the Rechabites, an American-based society dedicated to temperance and moral reform.[61]

In religion, on the other hand, Moses chose to follow his own independent leanings, and while he was known for his assiduous private Bible study, he remained largely on the outside of church life.[62] Given the fact that the town's elite at the time was not identified with any particular denomination, there was little social penalty for making such a choice. When he arrived in Stanstead, the Congregational church was weak and leaderless, but the Methodists were beginning the construction of their new brick church in the midst of a successful cycle of revival, and Moses displayed his civic leadership by subscribing thirty dollars to their building fund in 1833. Three years later, in 1836, possibly with an eye to running in the forthcoming political election, he rented a pew in the new church.[63] Although this proved to be only a one-year arrangement – he remained a Congregational adherent all his life – Moses' relationship with the town's Methodists was defined by shared communal interests. Not least of these were the hard economic times endured in the 1840s, which inevitably resulted in failure to pay ministerial salaries. Moses' own circumstances were extremely straitened, yet he managed to offer his medical services without fee to the family of the Methodist minister in 1849, thereby incurring the deep appreciation of the district quarterly meeting.[64] This was not an isolated example: "Every poor man who left the country owed him," his elder son later recalled as he described how Moses used his own supplies to relieve those in need.[65] In such ways, in a society where church pew rents, such as in the new Methodist chapel, continued to be paid largely in goods and services, the bonds of community were strengthened.[66]

While as a physician Moses attended to the needs of poor and rich alike, socially and politically he became identified with the region's well-to-do landowners. Already by 1837, a year after the birth of their youngest daughter, he had as the result of a series of judicious land purchases become the owner of some 530 acres of fertile agricultural land, which was favoured by river access and included a valuable sugar bush.[67] His interest in advanced farming techniques in the cultivation of hops and grain, and also his prize-winning cattle, led to participation in the county agricultural society that was founded in 1845.[68] This moved him into sharing the concerns of Stanstead's more substantial farmers and businessmen, in particular their growing economic and political grievances. Here the situation was less straightforward than in Upper Canada, where the desire of the middle class for economic and political change allied them with the Reformers against the government. In Lower Canada the Reformers, under Louis-Joseph Papineau's leadership, were resistant to changes that were seen to benefit primarily the colony's anglophone elite.[69] Moses stemmed from republican roots (in 1776, under the Association Test, all forty-six adult male Colbys in New Hampshire had refused to bear arms against Britain's king), and initially he was drawn to the Reformers, who had much sympathy in the Stanstead area.[70] But Papineau's desire to extend the seigneurial system of landholding into the area recently reclaimed from the British American Land Company forced the issue. Colby, who had observed the inequity and meagre results of tenant farming in parts of New York State, now shifted his support to the other side.[71]

Allying himself with the town's merchants and gentlemen farmers, he agreed to serve as the Tory candidate for Stanstead County in a by-election in 1837; and after his successful election, he was one of the minority on the final address that closed the legislature of Lower Canada the following year.[72] Following the 1837–38 rebellions and the Act of Union, he ran in the 1841 election campaign. Although these were years of economic depression, his election speeches glowed with the same optimism that had informed his observations during his 1817 journey through New England, a sentiment entirely in step with the economic aspirations of his middle-class Stanstead supporters. Offering electors a vision of prosperity in the new age that was dawning, he confidently proclaimed, "The invincible power of steam will impart new life and vigor to every department of labor and every enterprise of trade, and thus an incalculable benefit will accrue to the agricultural, commercial and mechanical interests of the community."[73]

Unfortunately for Moses, the election went to the rival Reform candidate, Marcus Child, and the next few decades challenged his optimism greatly. In 1839, shortly after the rebellions in Lower Canada, in which he had acted as surgeon to the government forces, he became the victim of a costly drawn-out lawsuit instigated by one of the rebellion's leaders, Dr Robert Nelson. Nelson, who had fled to Derby, Vermont, had encouraged a local man, William Nelson, to sue Colby for malpractice in the case of his wife, whom Colby had treated for a fractured leg five years earlier. According to Nelson's allegations, which were upheld by a Vermont court, the break had never healed properly and had led Mrs Nelson to suffer from the religious delusion that she had "committed the unpardonable sin." Given Colby's political stature and the strength of anti-Tory feeling in the area, there was every incentive for the Nelsons to embarrass him; but for Colby the costs of collecting evidence to support his contention of innocence, along with lost time from his practice, proved to be extremely expensive.[74] Although he was ably defended by his nephew Stoddard Colby, a promising young Derby lawyer (son of his brother Nehemiah) who in 1841 was elected a state senator on the Democratic ticket, the case went through three trials, all decided in favour of the plaintiff.[75] Not until 1857, after Mrs Nelson's death, followed by an autopsy on the bone in question, was he finally vindicated, and the plaintiff ceased litigation.

Completely exonerated, Colby continued his fruitless campaign to seek financial compensation, noting with some bitterness that the entire incident had cost him a thousand pounds.[76] In a largely cashless economy, with little income from his medical practice and with most of his remaining assets in land, he found himself casting about for a means to support his family. As a result, Moses and Lemira, who shared the back-breaking work of harvesting and hop picking, found the need to increase their workload in 1844 with the purchase of a tavern in Stanstead. Intended to alleviate their cash flow (but leading to conflict with the local temperance forces), the hotel could also later be a potential source of employment for their second son, William (then age twelve).[77]

By the mid-1840s William and his brother Charles were entering adolescence, and provision had to be made for their future support and also, eventually, for that of their young sister. Although both sons were able to receive a grammar school education at the recently established Stanstead Seminary, family means permitted the acquisition of higher education only for the older son, Charles. As with young Moses a generation earlier, this called for major family planning and a willingness to postpone the purchase of needed domestic items. Charles later noted with gratitude the memory of his father going "thinly clad" in order to make his education possible. In addition, community resources were utilized: in order to receive at minimal cost a good academic preparation, Charles spent two winters in the home of a family friend, the Scottish theological graduate and former principal of Stanstead Seminary, Hugh Elder.[78] Accordingly, in 1843, a year when the family's finances were stretched to the limit, Charles, at age sixteen, under the accompaniment of Elder, registered at Dartmouth, his father's alma mater, which at the time was the seat of higher education for the anglophones of the Eastern Townships. Studies at Dartmouth, to be followed by entry into law, were part of a larger middle-class family strategy, which would be useful in an era of growing litigation and land and mining speculation in the Eastern Townships. In a lively correspondence with his son concerning mineral deposits in the Dartmouth area, Moses was already anticipating subsequent mining development in the Stanstead area.[79] Upon Charles's graduation in 1847, Moses was able to draw on his earlier political connections to negotiate a legal apprenticeship for his son with John Sanborn, Sherbrooke's influential politician lawyer.[80]

YOUTH, SOCIAL CHANGE, AND MORAL TENSION

While this patronage would in due course be of great help in launching Charles's professional career – a point to be developed in the next chapter – there are signs that the 1850s were a troubled decade for the two sons of Moses Colby and that some of this turmoil was intimately related to their precarious position in the period's volatile economy. By the mid-1850s Moses Colby's health, because of his ceaseless overwork, had begun to deteriorate, while his estate was still suffering the impact of the 1839 lawsuit.[81] Poor health and economic loss were only part of his concern, however. Increasingly, he was becoming aware that just when social and economic change had accelerated and he had reached a certain level of economic well-being, his sons no longer seemed to adhere to the moral values that had guided his generation, and they were putting at risk all that he had so carefully built up.

In the summer of 1855 he became gravely ill, and it was at this time that he attended to his own spiritual welfare by requesting baptism.[82] Performed privately by a Congregational minister and family friend, the sacred rite of baptism attested to the fact that finally, in advanced age, Moses Colby accepted the divine grace of forgiveness. Promised by God's covenant to generations of his forebears who had confessed their sinful condition and relied on Christ's atonement for sin, this had eluded him years earlier when, as a young man listening to the solemn preaching in New Haven's Congregational meeting house, he had felt only nothingness. His reception of baptism in turn led to a request to participate in the Lord's Supper. And so, formally and openly, Moses Colby returned to the faith of his Puritan ancestors.[83]

Shortly after receiving baptism, he attended to the material welfare of his family and made a will.[84] Here, too, he found himself guided by the wisdom of the past. An eight-page document, it reflected the considerable thought he had put into safeguarding the future of his family. It also gave evidence of the values that guided men of his generation whose property consisted entirely of land and who wished to transmit both to their children.[85] Modesty and sobriety of lifestyle led Moses to eschew all ostentation and to request to be buried in a simple manner with as little ceremony as possible. A request to his family members to become life members of the Bible society reflected both his own assiduous reading of the Scriptures and his conviction that this was the one voluntary society of ultimate social significance. Finally, and implicitly related to these two communal concerns, he tried to ensure the stability and continuity of the family by safeguarding his landed estate through a judicious system of checks and balances.

As testified by the land transaction records and the details of his will, his estate at this time amounted to eight hundred acres, ninety of which constituted a farm known as the Badger Place.[86] While the farm was specifically bequested to his younger son William, the rest of the estate was to be encumbered with provisions that were intended to maintain its integrity and ensure adequate care for Lemira and their daughter Emily. Following New England practice, one-third of the yearly income of the estate was to be Lemira's during her lifetime, and she was to receive from her sons in their home "a good comfortable support and maintenance ... according to the custom of the country and her rank and station in life ... (without her being held or bound to contribute in the least by her work and labour toward the said support)." Emily, then nineteen years old, was to be given similar care in her brothers' home, as well as receiving the family piano, and upon marriage she was to be provided with a dowry equivalent to $2,000, along with whatever outfits of clothing might be considered appropriate.[87] The land itself, with the exception of William's farm, was to be divided between the two sons, but again with major encumbrances. Besides having to support their mother and sister through its proceeds and giving their mother an additional one-third as income, they were not to sell without her consent.

In making these conditions, Moses allowed himself to be guided by an older system of land distribution, based on a covenant of social obligations rather than on the more recent move to contract. With the passing of the 1841 Registry Ordinance in the new united Province of Canada, the generous dower rights which Lower Canadian women had enjoyed under the Coutume de Paris had been curtailed in order to meet growing middle-class criticism that such rights constituted an impediment to the exchange of land in a capitalist society. Prior to 1841, unless the couple had agreed otherwise in their marriage contract, widows in Lower Canada had had the right to a proportion (usually one-half) of their husband's land during their lifetime. Under the new law, dower's rights were no longer automatic but had to be registered by the husband in order to have precedence over other claims to his estate. Historians have seen this legislation as part of a wider curtailment of women's rights in Britain and America in the early nineteenth century. In the words of Bettina Bradbury, referring specifically to Lower Canada, "men's rights to freedom of contract minimized older socially based claims like those of a widow on her husband's property."[88] Moses' will made no mention of dower rights, but his provisions for his wife followed the traditional New England form of assigning one-third of the estate to go to her support. More significantly, by insisting that no land could be alienated without Lemira's consent, he placed in her hands both the power to protect the land from any debts incurred by his sons and to ensure their cooperation in looking after her and her daughter. In this way a companionate marriage could act as a powerful tool to ensure the continuity of patriarchy after a father's death until both sons could convince their mother that they could responsibly fulfill their responsibilities as landowners. At the same time, by appointing his sons as trustees, Moses implicitly indicated his trust in their ability to work together for the common good of the family.

Less than two weeks later, Moses suddenly drew up a second will to replace the first.[89] This time, patriarchal power to ensure filial obedience asserted itself even more strongly. Possibly caused by the news of several recent dubious land transactions by Charles, the new will, which contained only a few changes, was intended to protect the estate from any possible destructive impact of the elder son's behaviour.[90] Demoting Charles from his position as executor and trustee, the new will appointed his younger brother William and Matthew Dixon, a local customs officer. The two were to hold in trust any income derived from Charles's portion of the estate until "the said Charles Carroll Colby shall have become of confirmed steady habits, to the full and entire satisfaction of both of the said trustees or of the survivors of them and of his mother the said testator's said wife."

This shaming of his elder son must have had the desired effect. At some unspecified date not too long thereafter, the conditions were removed, and the earlier will again became operative. Although Moses lived until 1863, he became increasingly bedridden and had to look to his two sons to carry on the management of the estate. In a climate of acute economic and social change, it was precisely on them that his anxieties converged. In 1853 rumours were rife that Stanstead would finally receive a railway link with the building of a second line in the Eastern Townships: the Stanstead, Shefford, and Chambly Railway.[91] A decade earlier, as an eager politician, Moses had spoken eloquently on the bright future in store for Stanstead County through the help of just such revolutionary technology. Now, older and weakened in health, he observed with increasing alarm the changes in social and economic life brought about by the railways and by the region's accompanying shift from small artisan to capitalist production in the new railway, mining, and pulp and paper industries.[92] With the prospect of the large American market facilitated by the 1854 Reciprocity Treaty and the completion of the major canals, a third generation stood poised to reap the benefits of the work of the earliest settlers.

As Jean-Pierre Kesteman has demonstrated in a detailed analysis of the formation of entrepreneurial capitalism during this period, the financial resources required meant that those with the deepest roots who had prospered by agriculture, inheritance, or commerce were best placed to avail themselves of the new economic opportunities.[93] Although agriculture continued to be the main economic base of the region, banking was beginning to replace old communal ways of labour with the individualism of monetary compensation. Payment in kind had dominated in farming societies ever since the days when the first Colby in seventeenth-century New England had bought his house "by a mare fole at 10£, 3£ in bonds and income, 12 or 14£ in money, the rest in pipe staves or hogshead staves, cattle, all at prices current; Indian corn at 3s., wheat and barley, 5s."[94] But now Moses, who had previously been able to pay his hired hands with cattle, could no longer do so; thanks to the entry of banks into the county, cash had become the norm. In this changed environment, it became clear that Moses, like other fathers of the period, had been unsuccessful in transmitting to his sons the economic practices and values that had served his own generation so well.[95]

Where he pleaded caution, Charles and William saw only economic opportunity. Emblematic of their aspirations and the focal point of Moses' anxiety was the large stone house he began to build for his family in 1858 – primarily, he insisted, out of concern to provide a warm house for his increasingly arthritic wife.[96] Forced by ill health to leave the management in his sons' hands, he saw the building grow in grandeur as costs escalated. They were the ones who jointly had purchased the building lot, the first such land purchase, it would seem, after Charles's ill-advised land transactions of the early 1850s. Situated in a choice location in the village on the main road to Derby, the land at $600 had not been cheap, but almost immediately after the purchase the brothers had begun to use it as security against a number of high mortgages for land purchases which totalled at least $3,000 in the next two years.[97]

Although the conditions of Moses' 1855 will ensured that the estate could not be divided without parental consent, this did not prevent his sons from writing promissory notes against it. Their apparent willingness to sign these notes and their failure to keep an accurate account of debts raised their father's anxiety to the utmost. By this date, his major anxiety had moved from his elder son to the younger. In 1853 the hotel intended as a livelihood for William had been sold, and after his brief stint at running this tavern/hotel – which regrettably set him on a lifelong battle with alcoholism – William had turned to working on the family farm.[98] Known for his conviviality, which made him the friend of all he met and one of the most popular members of Stanstead's Golden Rule Lodge, he appears to have signed promissory notes with abandon, thereby seriously compromising the estate. As Moses pointed out in a lengthy letter to William, written after the financial impact of the escalating costs of the new home was beginning to become apparent, the enterprise seemed out of control. In his estimation, the estate had already been thinned by $5,000 as a result of William's and Charles's spending. The fact that at a time of anticipated railway construction, when the value of land was increasing, his sons were letting property go at a fraction of its prospective value and that neither son kept accurate records only increased his anxiety.[99]

Although over the years Moses had tried to establish a medical business in pills, this had never covered the family's expenses. Economic stability, in his view, lay not with commerce but with agriculture, with the kind of patient, careful planning for the crops of each successive year, a process that he now described in painstaking detail for William's benefit. And so, in the face of the economic speculation that was sweeping up his sons, Moses fell back on the wisdom of his ancestors: always to know the amount of one's liabilities and to be very careful about acting as security for another. Since William's convivial habits made him especially in need of the latter advice, Moses warned that in these volatile times, unless a person's wealth was almost all in cash, he was liable to lose all. For those like him whose wealth was in real estate, the possibility of bankruptcy loomed ahead. One could easily be forced to sell "at a vast sacrifice so that every person who finds himself as security for others above what he has means to pay if his friend fails, is liable to become poor in a moment and the one who has ruined him becomes his worst enemy. A very young man should read the Proverbs of Solomon often." The biblical book of Proverbs, with its view of life as a moral probation in which both good and evil acts received their reward from a righteous God, was a favourite of many of his generation.[100]

In a brilliant study, *The Age of Atonement: The Influence of Evangelicalism on Social and Economic Thought, 1795–1865*, Boyd Hilton has subtly and persuasively shown the congruence between this economic approach and the prevailing theological system, which emphasized human sinfulness, the need for personal conversion by completely trusting in the atonement of Christ, and the pursuit of a blameless life, including in one's business dealings.[101] Despite his inability to experience conversion, Moses Colby had articulated this theology many years earlier, as a young student at Yale, and he continued to uphold it in his later years. In depicting life to his sons as a time of moral probation, he had drawn on the classical Protestant view that there exists a sharp discontinuity between this world and the next, that God transcends the world and provides for it, that God is clearly revealed in Scripture and in the natural world, and that all humans are sinful and in need of redemption.[102]

It was a view shared by others of his generation, such as his friend Malcolm MacDonald, the Wesleyan minister of Presbyterian background who regularly visited Moses in his final days and who, after the latter's death, openly criticized the economic practices of his son Charles.[103] In a world where misfortune and death could strike without notice, it was also a theology held by Lemira, even when she was unable to experience it in the form of a personal conversion. Among her few remaining writings are the words of a hymn sung in 1866 at the funeral of her daughter Emily, who died at the age of thirty after giving birth to a son, who himself died a month later:

… And must this body die?
This well-wrought frame decay?
And must these active limbs of mine
Lie mouldering in the clay? …

God my redeemer lives
And ever from the skies
Looks down and watches all my dust
'Till he shall bid it rise.[104]

Hers was a world where home was the site of death, where no camouflage of its ravages was possible, and where not even the hope of resurrection could allow one to ignore the bitter reality of the present.[105] Even so, in the face of death, religion could provide meaning to life. Shortly before his own death on 4 May 1863, Moses Colby, whose mind had been wandering for some time, was heard to utter as his final words, "My gracious Saviour" – the confession that assured those surrounding his bedside that he had finally found eternal safety. Short in length, the words of the burial service that followed, which consisted mainly of biblical texts as stern as they were grim, intoned the age-old words: "We brought nothing into this world, and it is certain we can carry nothing out" … "Man that is born of woman hath but a short time to live, and is full of misery." Comfort was offered in the liturgy, not by reflecting on the good life of the deceased but in the hope of the resurrection of the body committed to the earth.[106]

Yet those who read the eulogy that appeared a few days later in the *Stanstead Journal* could not but notice, in the midst of the glowing testimony to Moses Colby's biblical and evangelical faith, that this same faith had allowed him to penetrate beyond the veil of traditional piety. "In the physical sciences especially he took delight in marking the wisdom, the power, and the love of that Great Being who formed and fashioned all great things for his own glory and for the good of man," his eulogist noted, picking up a thread which many years earlier had compelled an aspiring medical student to criticize some of the physical manifestations observed in the religious revivals so prevalent at the time.[107] As a medical doctor he had continued to make note of the psychosomatic impact of religious enthusiasm and, as part of his research, had conducted experiments whose findings were published in a number of articles in the *Boston Medical and Surgical Journal*.[108] Moses, like many devout scientists of his generation, was motivated in such research by respect for the God of Nature and the God of Revelation, but his research ultimately contributed to a larger process of disenchantment, which historian Leigh Eric Schmidt has termed "the pathologizing of religious excitements and various forms of devotional intensity."[109] Although even in his medical treatises Moses took pains to emphasize that everything emanates from God, he was also part of a longer nineteenth-century trajectory that approached religious experience through analysis of the mind, culminating in the psychology of religion and writers such as Willam James.[110]

Some four decades earlier, not long after a youthful Moses Colby chronicled an account of his travels to Yale College, Timothy Dwight, Yale's former president, was publishing similar observations of New England society. What Dwight portrayed was a New England that, though changing, remained knit together by family and friendship, a society where, in his words, "a general spirit of good neighborhood" and mutual aid were "part of the established manners" of town life.[111] And while Moses' and Dwight's travel accounts were evidence that people were on the move, theirs was still a society in which, as historian Thomas Bender notes, one's primary identity remained communal. A locality-based pattern of community continued well after Moses' death, but in the final decades of his life the bonds that defined a younger generation's sense of community were becoming more complicated.[112] With the help of a host of legal and political reforms in the united Canadas in the course of the 1840s and 1850s, Moses' own local community was moving from preindustrial conditions to becoming increasingly dominated by capitalist relations.

The old communal ways were being redefined by new forms of communication such as the telegraph and the railway, by the dismantling of seigneurial tenure, the establishment of a state-run land registry system, improved mail and banking systems, and the greater availability of financial resources for mining and industry. Intellectually as well, some of the old ways and beliefs no longer seemed self-evident. "God, our Creator is the 'truth, the life, and the light' – all emanates from Him," Moses could still confidently proclaim in a published abstract announcing a forthcoming treatise on the functions of the digestive tract.[113] Yet by the time of its publication in 1860, because of such unsettling concepts as Darwinian evolution and the new biblical criticism, which underscored the historical and literary nature of the Scriptures, some no longer saw the God revealed through the study of nature and the Scriptures as awesome and omnipotent.[114] In economic and social life as well as in religion, old certainties were crumbling. The world which parents such as Moses and Lemira hoped to bequeath to their children was not the one the children inherited.

CHAPTER TWO

Redefining Family Identity: The Convergence of Moral Philosophy, Romanticism, and Evangelical Religion

"Biology by itself is incapable of providing us with a habitable world," family historian John Gillis has observed. "Unlike animals, humans must be born twice, once physically and a second time culturally, for only culture can provide us with the sense of security and direction that to animals is instinctual."[1] At the core of this reading of life are the concepts of space and time, for these determine the particular form that culture will take. Religious revivalists were calling for yet a third birth, the evangelical "new" birth, but there were also those who, like Moses and Lemira Colby, held the view that this was unnecessary, since God redeemed people within the culture. Culture, however, was not static. In more than one way, space and time were changing, and it was in the family, the site of one's birth into the culture, that new meanings would be mediated. If religious symbols, language, and practice were to continue to articulate ultimate priorities and be a meaningful resource in shaping self- and family identity, these too would have to reflect people's changing sense of time and place.

The task of integrating self-identity, family, and religion in new ways would fall to the next generation. As men and women who in their youth had already encountered anomalies between behaviour and belief, they would now address these as they faced the adult responsibilities of courtship, marriage, and family formation. Unlike those of Moses and Lemira Colby, the courtship, marriage and family life of their son Charles and his wife Hattie Child have been amply documented, and thus we are able to give greater attention to the gendered dimensions of social and religious restatement than was possible in the previous chapter. Middle-class women participated in their own way in the changing experience of time, and though their legal and political rights remained curtailed, new possibilities for self-improvement opened up through formal education, the training of their children, and material improvements in the home. In the many letters the young Colbys exchanged with one another and with other family members, and in Hattie's personal diaries, a new sense of male and female agency becomes evident. In theological terms as well, this sense of agency found expression in a shift from Calvinism to Arminianism. Many Congregationalist, Presbyterian, and Baptist clergy continued to preach the Calvinist understanding of salvation, in which humankind was totally dependent on the work of an all-powerful and inscrutable God. Nevertheless, under the combined impact of new economic and social opportunities and of religious revivalism, especially by the Methodists, the Arminian emphasis on individual human agency in the process of salvation (leading critics to call it a "theology of self-help") increasingly prevailed.[2] The ways in which all these developments coalesced to refashion individual and family identity during the courtship and marriage of Charles Colby and his young wife Hattie will be the focus of this chapter.

INTELLECTUAL CHANGE AND SELF-IDENTITY

The free enterprise in commerce, which had already begun to redefine Moses' and Lemira's world and which shaped the economic activity of their sons, found a parallel expression in new opportunities for self-development expressed through education, manners, leisure, and consumer goods.[3] When Charles Colby commenced his studies at Dartmouth College, New Hampshire, in March 1843, his father may well have marvelled, as he read his enthusiastic letters, at the possibilities for personal improvement which had been unavailable when he had attended that institution in 1821. These novelties varied from a popular concern with bodily hygiene (conveyed in a detailed description of how Moses and Lemira might install a crude outside shower) to an avid commentary on the economic and technological progress of the Eastern Townships, culled from the weekly paper received by Charles's roommate Edward Brooks, son of a prominent Sherbrooke lawyer and politician.[4] Fuelled by Moses' recent political involvement as an MLA, Charles found at Dartmouth his own political mentor, Daniel Webster, one of its most illustrious alumni, who continued to be revered by faculty and students long after his assumption of the Whig Party leadership. For Charles, who years later prominently displayed an engraving of Webster in his office, the influence was as much moral as political. Webster's rhetorical style and conservative values resonated well with the high moral ideals intended to prevail at Dartmouth in the 1840s through its student life and curriculum.[5] Founded in 1769 by a Congregationalist New Light preacher, Dartmouth was a well-established institution with a strong church presence by the time of Charles Colby's enrolment. Academic life was punctuated by daily chapel attendance at 6 AM, and the sight of some two hundred young men streaming across campus in the grey dawn reinforced for young Colby his father's teachings that reason and religion were indeed natural partners.[6]

Although his religious formation had been largely left to the efforts of his parents and the teachings of a Union Sunday school, the college curriculum to which Charles was now exposed in no way contradicted the beliefs he had thus far learned. One of its major goals was to counteract the challenges of "free thought" and "religious skepticism," which college educators commonly considered to be the two perils to intellectual life and the moral integrity of their nation in the 1830s and 1840s. Against these dangers they marshalled the full arsenal, with some revisions, of the Scottish Enlightenment and common-sense thought. The latter, drawing heavily on eighteenth-century faculty psychology for its educational theory of mental discipline, shaped the standard curriculum in American and Canadian Protestant denominational colleges and thus a generation of civic leaders, until at least the 1870s.[7] Moses Colby had been exposed in a less systematic way to its main premises, but by the time his son entered Dartmouth its crown had become a formal course in moral philosophy, which was usually given by the college president.[8] Here, through a reasoned question-and-answer approach, students were taught the importance of strengthening the higher faculties at the expense of the passions and ensuring that the moral sense, or conscience, became and remained the supreme regulator of their conduct.[9] Because the course did not simply describe and analyse human nature but also moved into prescribing right action, it was an important force in encouraging individual self-development. Through didactic children's literature, sermons, conduct manuals, and tasteful fiction, this moralistic approach was in turn disseminated into popular self-understanding by college-trained educators and ministers.[10]

For sons like Charles Colby, whose middle-class families had often made significant sacrifices to further their education, self-improvement naturally became a moral imperative. Giving a careful account of his expenses to the smallest item, offering elaborate justifications when additional funds were needed, and providing a detailed schedule of his study and class hours, his letters to his parents faithfully lived up to the moral expectations imposed by family, society, and the college curriculum. In 1845, for example, in his second-last year at Dartmouth – at a time when the Colby finances were especially straitened – Charles seized the opportunity to help the family budget by doing a brief stint at schoolteaching in Georgeville, a village near Stanstead.[11]

A year later, back at Dartmouth and about to finish his studies, he assured his mother, "It gives me pleasure that in a few more months I shall be able to provide for myself & I hope in some measure remunerate you for the kindness & expense which you have lavished upon me."[12] His closing comment, "May I become the prop of your old age as you have been of my boyhood," captured well the teaching of the moral philosophers that self-improvement was never an individualistic enterprise but was embedded in family concerns. In the words of Colby's college text, *Elements of Moral Science*, written by Francis Wayland, a Baptist minister and the president of Brown University, "There can be no doubt that we were created to find a large part of our earthly happiness in domestic society." As Wayland further reminded his youthful readers, "Parents themselves, in advanced age, frequently need the care of their children, and are greatly dependent for their happiness upon them."[13] Young Colby's own visual image of family members acting as props to one another was apt in an economy where families could survive or improve their circumstances only through mutual dependency. Implicit in this image was another, however – the expectation of a sturdy individual reliability.

Such contradictions presented a distinct if unacknowledged challenge for serious young men. In the view of faculty psychology, conscience – or the moral sense – which ought to be the guide to conduct, was by nature considerably weaker than the passions. In the fluctuating feelings of adolescence there were indeed times when a twenty-year-old male like Charles Colby met Wayland's high moral expectations, but there were also many less comfortable occasions of confusion and self-doubt. Where Roman Catholics could find release in confession and absolution, the only recourse for a college-educated Protestant was to struggle to regain control of his "unregulated" moral faculty.[14] Confiding shortly before his graduation one such instance to his parents (and apparently trusting they would not share his self-rejection), he revealed how thoroughly the teachings of moral philosophy had come to shape his self-definition: "In a moral view I stand in a dim twilight midway [between] truth and error a state of all others the most vague and uncertain. For a time I walk studiously & soberly before my Maker & the world with an unspotted reputation & above all with *self-approbation*. Then turned away by some sudden impulse or vagrant passions or blinded by some false

Charles Carroll Colby, elder son of Moses and Lemira, in 1847, around the time of his graduation from Dartmouth College (CCM)

theory, reckless of consequences I rush into what I would wish darkness would forever conceal."[15]

Evangelical educators were careful to point out that a life guided by passion was a perversion of the natural order or, as Colby put it, was marked by "intervals of *insanity*," which could only be overcome by the will to do better.[16] When some years later, in the late 1850s, Moses admonished his sons that their actions were subverting family life and the natural order of a stable agrarian society, it was through the lens of moral philosophy that he criticized their behaviour. While moral philosophy did not use the language of sin and salvation that revivalist preachers evoked in their impassioned pleas to the unconverted, both forms of rhetoric reflected in parallel ways an understanding of reality in which present actions were inherently connected to future outcomes.[17]

Although his brother William's actions were less encouraging, by 1857 there was every indication that Charles, at the age of thirty, had reached the desired level of moral self-regulation. Upon graduation in 1847 and in need of the patronage of prominent "friends" in order to advance, he had been fortunate to have as mentors two of the area's most prominent lawyer politicians. Working first in Sherbrooke with John Sanborn, brother-in-law of Edward Brooks, his Dartmouth roommate, in 1851 he entered the office of Hazard Bailey Terrill, a promising Stanstead politician and lawyer.[18] After Terrill's sudden death of asiatic cholera in 1852 – a loss that had a devastating impact on his young colleague – Charles again taught school. A year later, in 1855, he was admitted to the bar, becoming one of only two practising attorneys in the county.[19]

For a young ambitious lawyer, rumoured to be Terrill's natural political successor, such prospects called for greater civic prominence. Possibly jolted into a new self-awareness by his father's illness and by the parental discipline in Moses' last will and testament, Charles Colby, with a view to their communal significance became conspicuous in local religious events. In 1856 he became a financial contributor to the Wesleyan Methodist church as well as continuing to worship in the Congregational church and on occasion being an invited speaker at Congregational social and fundraising events. In December 1857 he began to rent a pew in the Wesleyan Methodist church, though he continued to retain his family's Congregational affiliation.[20] Such a public expression of support for another denomination was not unusual – his father had done the same in his quest for political office some two decades earlier. For the son, however, the fruits of visibility in a Methodist pew were in the first place personal. It gave him the opportunity to see and be seen by the attractive new school preceptress, nineteen-year-old Harriet Hannah Child, who had recently been hired by the Stanstead Seminary to teach French and English.[21]

CHANGING SELF-IDENTITY AND COURTSHIP

Hattie, as she was commonly called, later recalled her initial shyness as an outsider in Stanstead, but her lively letters to her parents in Weybridge, Vermont, show her to have quickly made contacts with the village's community. Boarding with the young family of Dr Cecil Cowles (Moses Colby's medical partner in Stanstead) and on affectionate terms with his wife and their two young children, she was included in visits to their extended family just across the border in Derby, Vermont. A devout Congregationalist household, the Cowles family each morning convened for family prayers with their boarders, who besides Hattie included the new Methodist principal and his young wife. At the seminary, founded by Methodists and now nonsectarian, each day also began formally with devotional exercises. Raised in a Methodist home, Hattie was accustomed to such practices and to the corporate forms of worship, which consisted of Wednesday evening prayer meetings and Sunday morning church worship. For a single and sociable young woman, Sundays offered a good opportunity to make new acquaintances, so she also accompanied the Cowleses to their afternoon Congregational service and then, at 5 PM, attended evensong with the Episcopals. A pianist with a lively interest in song, she joined both the Methodist and the Congregational choirs. Such religious observances did not appear to have been burdensome, and their lively description in her letters home rounded out a weekly routine of school preparation, reading, and visiting – activities which helped integrate her into the social fabric of Stanstead life.[22]

In a social world where single young working women and men were no longer under the watchful eye of family and community, one of the advantages of this proliferation of church organizations and voluntary societies was the opportunity they provided to meet a potential marriage partner.[23] A young woman, who according to her own admission to her parents had in the past caused significant family discord "in consequence of my ill-chosen and multi-numerous attachments," Hattie Child was well aware of such possibilities.[24] Charles Colby, who happened to be the town's most eligible bachelor at the time, settled all earlier suits, and by 1 April, at a Moose Dinner held as a fundraiser for the Episcopal church, he had proposed marriage. Hattie accepted without a thought. As she pointed out years later in a letter to Charles, "'The love that *admits of question* is not love.' I had *deliberated* upon several matches before I knew you – but when I knew you there was *no more questioning* – there was certainty like that flash of doom."[25]

Fate might indeed be invoked, but her decision was also part of a wider opening up of choices and opportunities of self-development for young middle-class women that had been unavailable a generation earlier. In the succinct observation of one women's historian, "Simply stated, a woman began to make choices about her life, including the identity of the man she would marry, clearly the most important single choice of all in a society where divorce was rare and 'careers' unheard of."[26] Ten years younger than Charles, Hattie was the daughter of John Child, a hard-working substantial farmer, who wished to provide every available advantage for his children.[27] After his wife died in childbirth, leaving him with five children, he had remarried, and the eleven-year-old Hattie soon became very close to her stepmother Mahala, a recent widow with no surviving children. A devout woman and the sister of a Methodist clergyman, Mahala had not, by the evidence of her letter writing, received more than a rudimentary education, and she was remembered by her more refined grandchildren in Stanstead as having had the quaint habit of puffing on a clay pipe.[28] She was, however, a member of a religious denomination that encouraged female education, and she was extremely fond of her young stepdaughter. When it became apparent that Hattie, an avid reader, was eager to pursue higher education, Mahala threw her full support behind her husband's decision to send Hattie to a boarding school after graduation from the district elementary school. Boarding with the family of an erudite clergyman, Rufus Wendell, who later taught at Harvard, Hattie received a college "preparatory" education, first at the Fort Edward Institute (located midway between Weybridge and Saratoga) and then at the Fort Plain Seminary and Female Collegiate Institute, near Albany, where the Wendell family had relocated.[29]

Family finances prevented Hattie from taking the full four years for a degree, but in her studies she had taken avidly to romantic thought, especially poetry, and was sufficiently accomplished to have three of her poems published in 1858 in *Poets and Poetry of Vermont*.[30] The decision to come to teach at Stanstead had been motivated by the financial need to help a younger brother, Jack, who was now beginning his secondary education. An advertisement sent to her by a college friend whose father was stationed in Stanstead as its Wesleyan preacher alerted her to an opening in the primary department at the Stanstead Seminary, and here in September 1857, at a salary of $75 per term with board at a weekly rate of $2.25, she commenced teaching.[31]

An articulate young woman, Hattie displayed in her poetry and in her letters home an independence of mind, a love of family, and a facility in conveying on paper the bonds of intimacy that shaped her relationships and friendships. By training and temperament she therefore reflected many of the aspirations seen to be part of a companionate marriage. By 1857 this concept had become firmly entrenched and codified in a wide range of marriage and etiquette books, as well as in novels.[32] Even Francis Wayland's college text, while emphasizing to its male readers that in the family it was man's lot to rule and woman's to obey, nevertheless underscored that mutual affection lay at the basis of marriage.[33] By the time of Hattie's courtship it was generally agreed that, for both sexes, the choice of a spouse was to be guided more by romantic inclination than by economic and social advantage, and most young middle-class women were able to make their own matrimonial choices.[34] Even so, in a society where the web of family relations provided a key component of self-identity, it was essential (and also required by the Methodist Discipline) to have the approval of one's parents before making a public pronouncement.[35] When a woman argued her choice before her parents, it was prudent, therefore, to look beyond romantic inclination to economic and social advantage.

Nine days after Charles's proposal, the mail between Stanstead and Weybridge suddenly shifted from its earlier focus on family gossip and community events to the subject of matrimony, first as Hattie informed her startled father and stepmother of a new admirer in her life and then as Charles wrote pressing his suit. In seeking approval, the young couple drew attention to their romantic inclinations but also gave practical reasons for their choice. Hattie, insisting that she was quite capable of making up her own mind, firmly dismissed any further thought of a suitor favoured by her parents – a professor at the Fort Edward Institute – and was unequivocal about her decision, arguing that this was "precisely the person you have always selected for me in ideal. 1st Talented 2nd Educated 3d A Lawyer 4th Popular." The following day she elaborated her case by reminding her parents of the worries her love life had thus far caused them: "It would I dare say, take a load off your mind, and a burden of care off your hearts, dear Father and Mother, to have me happily and honorably married." Well aware of her father's reputation as a "canny farmer," she took pains to note that the Colbys owned a farm not far from Stanstead "containing more acres than Papa's land all counted together ... The family live well, dress well, appear well."[36]

Charles Colby, in an enclosed letter addressed to Mr Child, professed his admiration for the latter's daughter and gave a brief account of his educational and professional attainments. He, too, drew attention to his family's "respectable" place in society and – possibly having in mind that one of John Child's sons had been named Andrew Jackson – casually dropped a reference to his cousin, the Democratic state senator Stoddard B. Colby, Esq., "an eminent lawyer" living in Montpelier, Vermont.[37] More restrained than Hattie, he was careful, when outlining his economic situation, to emphasize that although he had no wealth, he hoped that "with health" he would "be enabled to retain a respectable position in society." Such aspirations, like the reference to prominent connections, were important to young men whose economic prospects lay not in land but in finding their way in the marketplace of commercial capitalism. As Daniel Howe has observed, the expanding economies not only allowed for more scope in personal freedom but also provided new possibilities for self-reconstruction, an ideal understood primarily in terms of character development.[38] Since Charles could claim no financial assets, character was a crucial asset in convincing his future in-laws that he would be both a responsible husband and a good provider for their daughter.

Despite the inherent individualism of the expanding commercial marketplace, the couple's efforts to win parental approval indicate how important family and community remained as marks of identity. Following Hattie's cue, Charles tried to walk a narrow line between acknowledging traditional authority and claiming individual freedom. While he informed the Childs that he did not feel it was a parent's right to dictate absolutely in matrimonial matters, he added, "I could not deem it consistent with honor or propriety to urge her acceptance of proposals until first I had solicited your permission to make them." When in their response the Childs agreed to leave the matter to their daughter, Charles was quick to voice his satisfaction, saying that "in submitting the determination of so important a question to her unbiased decision, you have not only exhibited your love and confidence in your daughter but have taken the only course which wisdom and prudence could sanction."[39] John Child had made it clear that for the foreseeable future there would be little chance of offering a dowry or "appurtenances" to accompany his daughter into matrimony. All he could offer was his daughter. Nor, because of Moses' will, could Charles expect any economic assistance from his father.[40] Hence, the proposed marriage broke with a traditional and much-documented middle-class inheritance pattern of passing wealth at marriage from one generation to the next.[41] While under such conditions there might be greater freedom in selecting a spouse, a growing emphasis on shared sentiment in shaping family identity ensured that Hattie's happiness remained dependent on her parents' approval of her choice. Without the latter, Charles sagely observed, one faced "not only the estrangement of parent and child but also the unhappiness of both for years if not for life."

The full impact of the continued social influence of the network of family, kin, and community became evident only a month later. An impetuous announcement by Hattie of her intention not to renew her teaching contract and instead to spend the next six months in the francophone town of St Hyacinthe (some thirty miles from Montreal), in order to prepare for marriage to an ambitious young lawyer in a bilingual province, elicited her father's stern disapproval. Although the efficient mail system between Weybridge and Stanstead usually kept Hattie within parental reach, in this case, because of a slowdown, news of Mr Child's opposition arrived belatedly, and the Stanstead Seminary had already hired her successor. In the heated correspondence that ensued, Charles bristled at the suggestion that the decision had been influenced by his family's low view of school teaching. It was community values and not individual preference that had dictated the decision, he insisted, pointing out the delicate situation in which Hattie found herself in Stanstead once their engagement had become common knowledge (though this had not prevented the young couple from enjoying en route a romantic tour of Montreal's Mount Royal).[42] As a compromise, Hattie was allowed to remain at St Hyacinthe for the summer at her own expense, but she was then to terminate her stay in "the French country" and step on the train to spend the months before her marriage in her girlhood home in Weybridge, Vermont.[43]

Such conventions of courtship, historians have noted, fulfilled an important function for society and individuals alike in ensuring that private affections would ultimately be channelled into stable married life.[44] For the sake of social convention and to appease her parents, Hattie therefore found herself that autumn in Weybridge, eagerly awaiting the mail each day and the intended arrival of Charles, two weeks before the December wedding date.

During this period, with the bride to be relocated to the safety of her family home and the groom exiled to his workplace, religion emerged to add yet another dimension to the anticipated marriage. In October the mail from Stanstead suddenly brought a lengthy letter addressed to Hattie's stepmother, Mahala, in which Charles Colby elaborated on a religious conversion he had recently experienced. Although his letter did not say so explicitly, it is clear that his courtship and proposed marriage had played no small part in bringing him to conversion. For this reason, before examining its nature and implications, some attention should be directed at the religious sentiments of his future wife.

HEART RELIGION AND ROMANTICISM

Although there had been little mention of religion in the initial correspondence between Charles and Hattie and her parents, once Hattie was home she and her stepmother often spoke of it. Brought up in a devout Methodist home, Hattie appears not to have undergone a conversion. As is becoming evident from research into evangelical female spirituality during and after the revivals of the first half of the nineteenth century, the evangelical doctrine of the new birth, as articulated by male ministers, seems to have had little resonance with the experience of many young women. Socialized since childhood into bending their will to meet the needs and expectations of family and friends, they experienced a more gradual form of conversion – an affirmation of their religious nurture rather than the searing breaking of the will which revivalistic preaching demanded of the potential convert.[45] References to religious practice and trust in God surface regularly in Hattie's letters, but the traditional language of Methodist piety is almost wholly absent. Having lost her mother at an early age, she had responded with moral earnestness and had tried to live in a way pleasing to the deceased, whom she pictured now in heaven looking down on her. This sentiment also found its way into a birthday poem for her father, written the year she commenced teaching in Stanstead. Using a favourite female image for family relationships, she compared her mother's death to a cord splitting apart: "We little orphan strands remained – She went to heaven!"[46]

Writing these words to her father appears to have come easily, for both of them shared a love of poetry. Poetry and hymns had been the medium of Hattie's earliest religious nurture, as they were for many young evangelicals, and years later she recalled how as a child she was woken on Sunday mornings by hearing her father singing through the open window: "Lord in the morning / Thou shalt hear my voice ascending high, / To Thee will I direct my prayer, / To Thee lift up mine eye."[47] Rather than reading to his children the didactic and moralistic poetry in vogue in evangelical publications, John Child had turned to earlier Quaker writers, whose references to "the inner light" were conducive to seeing religion and life as part of a seamless whole. As studies of childhood religion have demonstrated, this approach helped to develop a child's sense of self and helped build healthy relations with others.[48]

This is apparent in the poetry Hattie wrote as a student. For her, rather than pointing to her unworthiness, religion seems to have played an important part in what Glenna Matthews has called the valorization of self – a concept that functioned for women not unlike the way the republican ideal of self-construction functioned for men.[49] For young women, as for men, the development and strengthening of their inner identity and sense of agency was a necessary precursor to participation in the host of gendered religiopolitical organizations that emerged after the 1860s. But unlike the more competitive, individualistic male model, women's valorization of self found natural expression in familial terms and symbols. Hattie's writing abounded with such language. Her poem to her father on his birthday concluded: "Say thine only daughter lives / Deep in thy heart meanwhile."

Such intertwining of religious and relational imagery also reflected the increasingly popular affinity between romanticism and evangelical religion. Both placed a strong emphasis on feeling. The comment by historian Lenore Davidoff that early-nineteenth-century romanticism "took the male protagonist outside society into a No Man's Land of individuality and genius" is equally applicable to dramatic evangelical accounts of male conversion.[50] The latter had initially been largely the work of ministers, but women, through novels and poems, were beginning to make their contributions to the genre, and in her lengthy poem "Contemplating Ruins," which Hattie had declaimed at a public college function in 1855, she gave her own impassioned rendition. After offering her audience the well-trodden comparison between a misspent life and a ruined castle, she exhorted the unnamed profligate "to sue for pardon at the Saviour's feet." Grafting an aesthetic sensibility to the familiar tropes of sin and repentance, she deftly moved to the customary climax of the conversion tale:

> And when perchance at yonder glowing portal,
> The spirit-lyre to heavenly strains may chime,
> Thine ivy wreath, shall be a *crown immortal*,
> Far, far above the wasting wrecks of Time![51]

This growing affinity between romanticism and evangelical religion (of which her writing is but one example) offers insight into the parallels between religious and social change that were recasting the revivalism of an earlier era. As Anne Braude has so brilliantly argued, the metanarrative of religious change in the nineteenth century, invariably presented as a process of declension and secularization, has largely been a story in which women are absent.[52] It may well be, however, that through their affective writings and discourse, evangelical women – rather than the much-analysed treatises and sermons of ministers and theologians – were in the vanguard of the shift from the experiential revivalism of the camp meeting to religious socialization within the family, the school, and the church.[53]

Less controversial is the evidence that although women dominated as converts, men had long been the primary targets of revivalism. Gender historians have drawn attention to the difficulties that men faced in earlier revivals, for even those who were raised in godly homes were not considered to be naturally devout as their mothers and sisters were. Expected to be self-reliant in the market, when it came to salvation they were exhorted to abandon any form of self-reliance and to rely totally on God's grace for forgiveness. It is not surprising, then, that the limited research probing the complex nature of male piety in the latter part of the nineteenth century indicates that traditional evangelical revivalism, with its emphasis on sin and repentance, had little resonance among young men, whose education and family environment had been shaped by the tenets of middle-class morality.[54]

Charles Colby was no exception. Besides the usual impediments to male conversion, he was a member of a doctor's family that had strong reservations about revivalism. Prompted by their father's scientific research into its physical aberrations, Charles and his siblings were inclined to see revivals as little more than a display of irreverent emotionalism on the part of preacher and convert. His sister Emily, writing to her family as a young bride in Quebec City, captured this attitude in her usual witty way when she gave a scathing description of a revival service conducted by the famed American Methodist preacher, James

Caughey. Noting that some of the three hundred people allegedly converted that evening had probably been frightened into repentance by this "very excitable" revivalist, who had confronted his audience with fear of damnation, she had nothing but scorn for his presumptuous ways: "He is very intimate with the *Lord* – according to his own story ... I heard him say – 'I wish to remind you O Lord that at two O'Clock this morning, I was pacing my room – meditating on thy goodness.'"[55] Yet in the face of this well-entrenched family bias against revivalism, there suddenly arrived that October, in Hattie's Weybridge home, Charles's letter to Mrs Child, in which he described in considerable detail his recent profound religious conversion. In the existing historical record, such descriptions by an articulate layman and professional are rare, so the letter is worth examining in some detail.[56]

Unlike the clergy-authored accounts of male conversion of an earlier period, Charles's letter contained no reference to repentance from a sinful life or to any breaking of his will.[57] Instead, he began his account by describing to his future mother-in-law his early religious formation within the family, his father's diligent reading of the Bible, and his mother's lesson to her children that religion "transcended all things in importance." Reinforced by Sunday school attendance, this Christian socialization, he emphasized, had been sufficiently strong to assure him that "the eternal truths of the Gospel, or that repentance, regeneration and sanctification were essential to salvation." "Never have I failed to recognize in the Savior the very impersonation of all purity, holiness, and love," he wrote confidently. While he made no explicit reference to his college education, it was apparent that as an adult he had continued in this intellectual acceptance of the Christian faith. He took pains to note that he had always tried to defend religion against its critics, and he said that even when not personally living up to the moral expectations of the biblical commandments, he had kept a distance from "infidels, blasphemers or the revilers of good men and good things."

Rather than intellectual doubts, the obstacle to true religion had been experiential. As he phrased it, "The other part which teaches us how to love God, I have studiously avoided." Real prayer had been impossible, he confessed and (in tones reminiscent of young Moses' awe of God's holiness forty years earlier) he felt that to come before God "with any feelings short of absolute submission to his righteous requirements – was the bitterest mockery, the deepest insult, the most unpardonable affront that could by possibility [sic] be offered to the Majesty of Heaven." Suddenly, however, all had changed: "When the flood gates were once opened, the pent up feelings of years burst out with a resistless force which broke down all barriers separating me from the Savior." The result was a new sense of self and of God, who was apprehended not through the intellect, as had previously been the case, but through the emotions. As a result of this recentring, Charles said that for the first time he was able to enter into prayer as an intimate dialogue with God. "I have lived long enough and seen enough of the world to know the vanity of many things which formerly dazzled the Imagination and captivated the heart," he concluded, in an attempt to summarize how this experience of divine love had changed his priorities.

Charles made no reference in his letter to the time and circumstances of his conversion, but its timing suggests that it was part of a much wider, well-documented revival movement. In one of Hattie's letters to her family in April 1858 she had made brief reference to a series of union revivals taking place in the Stanstead-Derby area.[58] The couple's courtship had intersected with widespread interdenominational revivals in urban centres in the northeastern United States and British North America. These had departed in several ways from earlier revivals by directing their appeal largely to middle-class men and by adopting a sober and systematic style of revival, one more in tune with middle-class values than the earlier emphasis on emotional manifestations. Commencing in April 1857 at a time of severe economic downturn, which was followed in August by the failure of the stock market, this urban revival movement was quickly dubbed the "businessmen's revival." The significance of its economic context will receive more attention in the fourth chapter, when examining the relationship between nineteenth-century evangelical religion and the marketplace, but here we need to note the role played by family and community.

In the first place, among the convergent strands shaping the revivals there was the pervasive urban presence of well-established churches and voluntary institutions, which by the late 1850s had already played a role in socializing the revivals' middle-class converts to religion. At the time of the flowering of the companionate marriage ideal, revival accounts drew attention to and applauded the assisting role of wives, mothers, and sisters as agents in revival. This widespread involvement of women has led the most recent historian of the movement to underscore "the deep relational character of the movement," noting further that at the grassroots level it was a spiritual event of "family and friends."[59]

The formal leadership, however, came from a number of ministers and revivalists of genteel middle-class background. Among the most prominent participants, especially in the later stages, was the American Methodist revivalist Phoebe Palmer. With her husband Walter, a retired homeopathic doctor, Mrs Palmer had since the early 1850s made a number of revivalist visits to Canada from her native New York

City, and in the summer of 1858, around the time of Charles Colby's conversion, she had passed through Montreal after a highly successful visit to major Maritime urban centres.[60] In his letter to Mahala, Charles had used two traditional Wesleyan terms to describe his experience: a "new birth" in which, like a child, he had again to learn to walk, and a "Baptism of the Holy Spirit." In traditional Wesleyan theology the two terms designate distinct experiences, the former referring to the initial conversion and the latter (known alternatively as sanctification, holiness, or Christian perfection) signifying a second work of grace. After having fallen into some oblivion after Wesley's time, this latter doctrine had become a dominant theme in Palmer's preaching, though with some revision.[61]

Palmer's work, and the 1857–58 revival in general, received sustained attention in the *Christian Guardian*, the Wesleyan paper in the Province of Canada. But despite Charles's use of Wesleyan terms, his conversion experience seems to have been informed more by a liberal shift in evangelical theology than by classical Methodist doctrine and spirituality.[62] A second strand of the urban revivals – the interdenominational businessmen's prayer meetings, which began in New York City's Fulton Street Dutch Reformed Church – was a more probable link. Their astounding impact and their spread to other urban centres in the northern United States had received considerable attention in religious and secular publications, including the *Stanstead Journal*.[63] One of the main centres was New York's Plymouth Congregational Church, under its talented preacher Henry Ward Beecher, where Charles sometimes worshipped when on business in New York. Beecher's sister, novelist Harriet Beecher Stowe, had used similar perfectionist language when describing her own conversion in 1843, and the prevalence of this language in Congregationalist piety has been well documented.[64]

In his discovery that God's nature was love and that religion was primarily a matter of the heart rather than the head, Charles Colby had articulated one of the dominant teachings of liberal Protestantism. Introduced early in the century by the German theologian Friedrich Schleiermacher and eventually finding its way into the preaching of a number of American ministers – in particular, Henry Ward Beecher – this theology sought to persuade "the cultured despisers of religion" (to use Schleiermacher's well-known term) that religion was not an intellectual or moral system.[65] Although it contained elements of both, religion was in essence a sense of relationship to the divine. According to Beecher, "the work of the Spirit is not to supersede, but help our faculties." God, far from being the stern judge of sinful humankind, had taken on human form in a Christ who breathed goodness and kindness: "The moment that you realize this goodness of Christ, his helpfulness to you, his lenient, forgiving, sympathizing spirit, then you know what faith in Christ means. If such a Savior attracts you and you strive all the more ardently, from love toward him, and trust in him, then you are a Christian: not a religious man merely, but a Christian."[66] Conversion, therefore, was a simple, natural experience; the way a man could become a Christian was not through an arduous striving to be perfect, an anxious waiting for God to work in his soul, but simply by deciding to accept God's love, a love as simple as caring for and cherishing one's own family: "Any man who knows enough to love his children, his father, mother, brother or sister, has theological knowledge enough to know the Lord Jesus Christ."[67]

The assertion that turning to Christ was qualitatively similar to the love of wife and family would have resonated with Charles Colby's own aspirations as he contemplated marriage. In the 1860s and early 1870s (until the notorious scandal of 1874–75 concerning Beecher's relationship with a female parishioner), the preacher was much sought after as a speaker by civic leaders in American and Canadian urban centres, including Stanstead.[68] His sermons, first published as a series of newspaper articles during the dramatic religious awakening of 1857–58, were intended to further the work of revival, and they quickly became available in book form under the title *New Star Papers*. Hot off the press, the *New Star Papers* were one of Charles's first gifts to his young wife.[69]

Charles's conversion intersected with his recent experience of falling in love and forming plans to marry and begin a family. His future wife, who since infancy had been taught to correlate religion with familial love (and who as an older sister showed considerable concern for the spiritual welfare of her brothers), may well have played a role in preparing the ground for his conversion.[70] A second influence was more intellectual in nature. At Dartmouth, while it was made clear that religion was more than a system of morality, the moral philosophy taught in the college curriculum predisposed young men to make a connection between divine nature and human relationships. The liberal shift to religion as an experience of God as divine love dovetailed with the ideal of the companionate marriage, and thus it spoke not simply to women but also to men, who like Charles were now finding traditional concepts of God and religion inaccessible to their self-understanding and experience. The wide media dissemination of the accounts and sermons of the revivals of 1857–58 offered the companionate marriage yet a further religious dimension. Where earlier a couple such as Charles and Hattie would have been able to point to similar educational backgrounds, physical attraction, and socio-economic compatibility, religion had now become the means to forge an even more intimate link.

Religion was also a shared public link with Hattie's kin and community. At an unspecified date close to the time of his marriage, Charles made the public gesture of presenting the Methodist Episcopal Church in Weybridge with a set of communion service. It was, he told his bride's home congregation, a symbol of his pride and joy that he had "formed connections" among them, and it was an expression of his "strong desire to be pleasantly remembered by ... all."[71] Such a gesture might be expected of an aspiring civic leader, but Charles's choice of an ecclesiastical rather than a secular setting was part of a larger male middle-class pattern linking religion, family, and community. Similar statements – from active involvement in church building projects and moral reform societies, to large charitable donations to voluntary associations such as the YMCA – became the hallmark of other men swept up in the 1857–58 revivals.[72]

We know less, however, about the ways in which religion became part of the more private domestic sphere and how it was able to enrich the companionate marriage. While a wedding liturgy defined a couple's legal status as husband and wife, a companionate marriage could only flourish on shared love and interests. For Charles and Hattie, the actual wedding ceremony was a very modest event, possibly because of its precipitous nature but also because, in a domestic economy heavily reliant on the annual spring sheep shearing, finances were scarce in the month of December.[73] Neither of Charles's parents was able to be present, but Lemira had written a warm letter to the Childs, in which she excused the Colby family's attendance because of William's "fragile health," as she tactfully phrased it. On Tuesday, 21 December 1858, the marriage ceremony was performed in Weybridge, the witnesses being Hattie's oldest brother John A. Child, his wife Sarah L. Child, and her maternal grandfather Samuel Wright.[74] The humble nature of the event evoked an angry letter from Hattie's absent younger brother, Jack. Although Charles and Hattie were married in December, they always considered 1 April, the date of the proposal, to be their real anniversary date.

In this way, family rituals supplemented and subtly recast the meaning of public ecclesiastical rites. The Methodist Episcopal Church's liturgy for the "Solemnization of Matrimony" contained little of the rhetoric and symbolism of romantic love that was so important to the companionate marriage. Largely unchanged from its predecessor in the Anglican Book of Common Prayer, its sober, earnest wording continued to reflect a time when the union of church and state, not the family, was seen as the basis of social stability. Given that humankind had lost its original state of innocence, the requirement of fidelity was the liturgy's central theme. Built upon a mutual oath of faithfulness, marriage was a covenantal relationship, with each partner promising to "have and to hold, from this day forward, for better for worse, for richer for poorer, in sickness and in health, to love and to cherish till death do us part."[75] The inclusion of the words "to obey" in the wife's vows further ensured that the hierarchical structuring of society, entrenched in law and hallowed by the Christian Church, remained firmly in place. Nevertheless, as was noted in the previous chapter, this was also a society where property rights were increasingly leading the state to play a role in defining marriage.[76] John Child had in the end been able to promise a modest monetary gift after the spring sheep sales, but with little dowry, the new contractual understanding of marriage, like the old ecclesiastical one, had little immediate personal meaning for Hattie.

Between covenant and contract, however, stood the companionate marriage, and it was this construct, strengthened by the new liberal theology and by Charles's recent conversion, which defined for Hattie and Charles the marriage on which they were embarking. Here, unlike the wedding liturgy, the focus was not on humankind's fall into sin but on the love shared by husband and wife. Fragile by nature, love was supported by religion. In the words of one clerically authored marriage manual, "The objects, then, of marriage are altogether religious, and the duties it brings and the joys it gives should be considered in a religious light."[77] It was a task for which Hattie was well prepared and in which her husband, after his recent religious experience, was happy to support her. How the ideals of religion and the companionate marriage translated themselves into woman's confining place in the home and the uncertain male world of business are the subjects of the next two chapters.

CHAPTER THREE

Faith, Hope, and Charity: Religion, Women, and the New Economic Order

The companionate marriage on which Charles and Hattie Colby embarked in 1858 was shaped not only by affection and shared interests but also by the religious influences and the changing economic and social structures of the latter half of the nineteenth century. While the advice manuals which the evangelical presses directed at newlyweds tended to place the emphasis on the moral influence of religion to the neglect of the influence of the marketplace, in real life the two were inextricably connected, as Hattie and Charles Colby soon realized. Together they experienced financial worries, which eventually led to insolvency, followed by the forced sale of the large stone house they had so confidently entered as newlyweds. In the economically trying times that immediately followed this loss, when Charles was often away for long periods on business, Hattie collected the letters exchanged during their courtship and the early years of their marriage, placing them in a volume, which she read and reread. The title she assigned to the collection, "Faith, Hope, Charity," had over the years become her motto. Her husband, significantly, chose to supplement it with another, which reflected his world of business: "Time, Faith, Energy."[1] This implicit distinction between the lives of middle-class men and women gradually became part of their own self-identification as a couple. The fact that Hattie and Charles used these gendered tropes and that each decided to include the term "faith" in the motto suggests that more may be at stakehere than formulaic rhetoric.

Like the worlds that the tropes sought to portray, the lives of husband and wife were both interdependent and distinct. In his first letter to

Harriet (Hattie) Child Colby, 1859, shortly after her marriage to Charles Colby (CCM)

his in-laws after his marriage, Charles reassured his mother-in-law (now addressed as Mama) of his complete faith in his and Hattie's future happiness, noting, "My moderation will correct her sensibility – and her ambition will stimulate my insensibility and inactivity."[2] A complementarity between the sexes was considered one of the foundations of the nineteenth-century companionate marriage. As Suzanne Lebsock has observed of this institution, and as Charles and Hattie discovered, such a marriage "when it worked, worked wonderfully well."[3]

Even when a marriage did not work well, complementarity was assumed. This concept lay at the heart of the Victorian domestic doctrine of the "separation of spheres," which distinguished between a middle-class woman's place in the home as wife, consumer, and nurturer, and her husband's role as family provider in the brave new world of commercial and industrial capitalism. Where middle-class men derived their identity from success in the capitalist marketplace by accumulating wealth and power, women, according to this separation, retreated into the private world of home and piety, commonly referred to as "the cult of domesticity."[4]

Gender historians have recently drawn attention to the limitations of this dualism. With a growing awareness of the multiplicity of ways in which gender has been constructed, they have analysed the complex and varied power relations inherent in the metaphor of "separate spheres."[5] They have argued that while this concept did hem in a woman's life with constraints, it also offered her new opportunities for self-definition, especially in the area of religion.[6] These insights must be taken into account as we examine Hattie Colby's self-understanding and her place in the new economic order of commercial and industrializing capitalism (leaving until the next chapter the description of how her husband's motto "time, faith, energy" reflected its challenges to male identity, family, and faith).

In the letter to his new family in Weybridge, Charles had lightheartedly pointed out that these were new times in conjugal relations. "Immediately after our arrival here," he wrote, Hattie "was promoted to a very important post – that of Trustee Visitor and Director of Stanstead Seminary." However, he felt compelled to add, "The appointment had to be given in my name of course, for women can't vote or hold office here, but we all knew what was meant."[7] Had he elaborated on what precisely was the status of a married woman in Quebec (or Canada East, as it was then known) in the new economic order, he would have had to point out that there, as elsewhere in many North American jurisdictions, a wife's identity had become more closely integrated into that of her husband.[8] For example, in an effort to make the alienation of land easier and to relieve it from the customary entitlements, the Registry Ordinance of 1841 had made dower rights dependent on registration by the husband. In addition, in 1849, propertied women, especially widows who had earlier voted in the colony's elections, lost the right to vote. Culminating in the Civil Code of 1866, the old communal and customary obligations in Quebec accorded by the Coutume de Paris were giving way to relationships that were defined increasingly by contract and by gender. The civil law reformers and codifiers of the 1860s, Brian Young has observed, were guided by a strongly gendered sense of the relations between men and women: men were to provide leadership and order in the family and in society at large, while obedience and domesticity were women's virtues.[9] Quebec was not alone in linking the new economic liberalism and the patriarchal family. Its social conservatism was enhanced by the fact that 84.8 per cent of the population claimed allegiance to the Roman Catholic Church, whose pontiff in 1854, amidst

Woman Reading [Harriet Colby], by Wilbur A. Reaser, 1910.
Photo François Lafrance (CCM)

an expanding cult of the Blessed Virgin, had entrenched the ideal of female purity in the new dogma of the Immaculate Conception.[10]

As a recently married middle-class woman, Hattie therefore found herself within two intersecting social orders. On the one hand, her identity continued to be shaped by a wide and fluid network of family and friends. At the same time, by the law of church and state, and by such parallel constructs as the companionate marriage, her relationship to her husband became the primary one. As a married woman, she was dependent on her husband for her social position. In a society driven by the prospects of fast wealth and upward mobility, she experienced first-hand, in the succinct words of historian Stuart Blumin, that "the middle-class escalator was at least as likely to go down as up."[11]

The tensions resulting from these changes affected husband and wife in different ways. A husband might roam far and wide in the search of financially lucrative investments. It was the wife who provided stability by staying at home and by serving as a moral compass in an economic world where the old rules no longer seemed to hold and where individualist acquisitiveness threatened communal values.[12] For

Roman Catholics, the Blessed Virgin became the symbol of woman's moral role in a heartless acquisitive society, but Protestants had rejected such religious constructs as Mary and the saints. In their place, educators and clergy inserted an even more pervasive symbol, idealizing and essentializing woman herself. "Woman is properly regarded as the love-element of humanity," the Reverend George S. Weaver rhapsodized in *The Christian Household: Embracing the Christian Home, Husband, Wife, Father, Mother, Child, Brother and Sister* – a slim manual which Hattie read "nearly through" on a rainy Sunday early in her marriage.[13] Largely authored by male clergy writing with sublime rhetoric and lofty aspirations, such literature offered little insight into how a woman might actually live out her high spiritual mission in the realities of household chores and family responsibilities, not to mention meeting her own needs.

Thus, middle-class women, like their husbands in the marketplace, had to find their own way to give meaning to their lives. It was in the spaces in between, in the interstices between woman's world in the home and the male world of unrelenting drive for a livelihood, that new religious symbols, meaningful to a changed time and space, began to appear. Articulated in the home and initiated by women, these symbols did not at first show a sharp discontinuity with the past, but over time the world as conceived by religion came to resemble more closely the world of middle-class lives.

RELIGION, WOMEN, AND THE RITUALS OF "HOME"

On the first day of 1859, married less than two weeks, Hattie began a new diary, entering the following: "The New Year dawned brightly. It found me in a new home, with new friends, but in a home I love, with friends I trust, and therefore was I happy."[14] The short entries she continued to make for a year with remarkable regularity offer some insight into how her place reconfigured itself into "home" and the ways in which religion helped in this. Reflective of the transiency which historians have noted to mark family life prior to the mid-nineteenth century, the couple's initial housing consisted of rooms in the home of a local widow, Mrs Wallingford, the mother of brother William's future bride, Melvina.[15] "Home" however, meant more than a house, for it encompassed a person's most intimate relationships. Hattie continued to use the term interchangeably for her family in Weybridge, for the space she initially occupied with her husband, and for the household of which she became a part when the couple in mid-October moved into the stone house, which was still only partially completed.

From its beginning, the new house became home to two families: Moses and Lemira Colby, with their adult children William and Emily, and Charles and Hattie. By 1863, when both William and Emily had married and left and Moses had died, the allocation of space, already inherent years earlier in the provisions for Lemira in Moses' will, took on the multigenerational contours that remained in place for the next twenty-five years. During this time Lemira maintained separate quarters upstairs until her failing health caused her to move to the main floor.[16] In addition, at various intervals, relatives and friends formed part of the household. A number of young cousins from Weybridge stayed for extended periods, and in 1862 sister-in-law Lizzie came to Stanstead while her husband, Jack (Andrew Jackson), did his year of military service in the U.S. federal army. In the mid-1870s the household included the matronly Mrs Bailey, a companion to Hattie and a nurse to the children.[17] Although money remained scarce until the final years of the century, the family also employed one to three servants, including a handyman and a household help. After a number of unsuccessful attempts at finding and keeping a young woman in the country, the family's servant problems subsided with the hiring of a young French Canadian, Rosalie, who became a valued member of the Colby household, serving until well into old age.[18]

This collection of individuals formed not only the household; as Hattie had intimated in the opening line of her 1859 diary, these were the friends who constituted a woman's home.[19] Like the words "home," "household," and "family," the term "friends" retained an elasticity that allowed it to encompass the wide range of relationships which together shaped female identity.[20] Where a man's friends were defined primarily through educational and career contacts, for a woman biological and social ties were paramount. In addition to Moses and Lemira and Charles's siblings Emily and William, these included a large network of extended family and acquaintances. Several quickly became Hattie's intimate friends – for instance, Martha Pierce, daughter of Wilder Pierce, Stanstead's wealthiest commercial farmer, and Melvina Wallingford, who in 1862 married William. As a young middle-class woman in a small village, Hattie was part of an astoundingly wide social network. A count of the names mentioned in her 1859 diary (not taking into account the Colbys and her Weybridge family, whom she visited in June) yields ninety-eight residents of Stanstead and surrounding area, eight shopkeepers and hotelkeepers with whom she was in regular contact, and twenty-six individuals residing elsewhere. These figures reveal the extent to which a young wife's identity was not simply dependent on a relationship with a husband or even his immediate family; servants, tradespeople, visitors, and neighbours ensured that one was never isolated from human contact.

At the same time, Hattie's identity among this new network of friends was in good part dependent on her status as the wife of Charles Colby. The religious rite of marriage had legalized this dependency, and religion continued to play a role in shaping her identity as a woman, but slowly and subtly her sense of self began to reflect the construct of the companionate marriage. Where an earlier generation of evangelicals had addressed their fellow church members as "brothers" and "sisters," these terms were increasingly being directed inward to the home, which was replacing church and religious society as the site of one's deepest religious experience and most intimate contacts.[21] Central among these practices were family devotions.

Family prayers, under the leadership of the head of the household, had been a staple in Puritan piety since its earliest days and were intended to be an essential building block of a godly society. Evangelical clergy in the nineteenth century were no less assiduous in promoting this family ritual – though, more often than not, they lamented its perceived waning rather than applauding its practice.[22] Accustomed to family prayers in her parental home and in her temporary lodgings as a schoolteacher with the Cowles family, Hattie Colby saw it as her task to ensure that this ritual would be part of her new relationship with her husband. "How sweet are our home devotions!" she sighed in her diary in the second week of her marriage.[23] The tradition of family prayers just before retiring to bed opened up an additional space of intimacy. Here one could express aloud one's anxieties, fears, and hopes, directing the words not only to God but also indirectly to one's partner. On one occasion, early in the marriage, when Hattie was dreading her husband's absence on a business trip the next day, she finally dried her tears and sought the mutual comfort of religion: "We prayed & rested & slept."[24] For a young woman who since childhood had been taught to kneel before her bed and voice her concerns in prayer, the inclusion of a husband in such a ritual assured continuity even as it helped define her new identity as a married woman.

Like prayer, the rituals of the Sabbath were important in ensuring both continuity and redefinition. Roman Catholics in the weekly mass found themselves in the presence of the holy family and the maternal presence of Mary, but familial symbolism took on a different form in the hallowed Protestant Sabbath. Here, old and young, week after week, sat together in a family pew under the preaching of a God whose fatherly attributes reminded them of their connectedness to one another and to the assembled congregation. A newly married, young couple could draw on this symbolism to shape their own distinct family identity. Until they became members of the Methodist church in 1867, the young Colbys retained for census purposes their original church affiliations, Charles remaining Congregational, while Hattie and the children were entered as Methodist.[25] During these years, their usual pattern of attending the Wesleyan Methodist service in the morning and the Congregationalist chapel in the afternoon was periodically adjusted to allow morning attendance with other members of the Colby family and, on occasion, the substitution of a 6 PM Episcopal service. Where their place in the Colby family pew continued to symbolize Charles's filial status, the pew which he had first rented in 1857 in the Methodist church now set them apart as a couple. It also offered a space where, from time to time, visiting Child relatives could make a public appearance. In addition to the maintenance of a family pew, a second Sunday ritual – roast beef dinner with the Colby family, followed by visits to kin in the area – further defined Hattie's new status as wife in a wider network of family and friends.

By mid-1859, when she made an extended visit to her Weybridge home, she was well on the way to anticipating yet another role, that of motherhood. "We are never likely to know much about the sexual lives of Victorian couples, because they alluded to it so little themselves," historian John Tosh has sagely observed, and despite their voluminous and affectionate correspondence, Hattie and Charles Colby are no exception.[26] Expressing herself with due discretion on the matter of sexual intimacy, Hattie wrote in her diary several weeks after the wedding, "What a marriage! Courtship made easy!"[27] Thereafter, brief phrases in French, such as "J'aime mon mari" or "A very happy *Soir et Nuit*," made veiled reference to nocturnal activity that a young Victorian woman could not possibly articulate, not even in the pages of a private journal."[28] Pregnant by mid-January, she was soon busy sewing baby clothes with the help of "Sis Em." The pregnancy was difficult, and though historians have discerned a prevailing shift, in writings, from "humours" to sensibility when defining the female sex, this had not yet translated itself into the medical care that Hattie received. Moses Colby on occasion found it necessary to bleed her, as well as offering her morphine to control pain, while Lemira and Hattie's "own, own husband" spent anxious nights at her bedside as the event approached and the pain increased.[29] On 27 September Hattie was able to record the birth of a daughter, named Abby Lemira after her late mother and her mother-in-law.

In her foray into motherhood, Hattie remained emotionally and physically dependent on the two older mothers, Mahala and Lemira, especially Lemira, who became a valued caregiver. Although the period saw a new emphasis on the biological mother as the moral centre of a nuclear family, the term "mother" was fluid. Four days after Abby's birth, Charles wrote to tell Mrs Child, "Mother suffers the greatest anxiety when anything goes wrong, for she has all a mother's tendencies and love and she feels a degree of responsibility that would not exist in case of her own children even."[30] A month later, shortly after the move to the new and still unfinished house, the Childs came in person to Stanstead. A regular mail service and good roads (though still calling for a twenty-seven-hour journey) ensured that in critical times families need no longer be separated physically.[31]

Alternatively fretting over her baby's health and coddling her, Hattie appeared to enjoy motherhood without losing any of the attention her husband had previously showered on her. "How precious to know that we are necessary to his happiness," she confided to her diary upon receiving a letter from her husband in Weybridge, where he was attending to business matters.[32] Such comments were part of a wider process of female valorization, whose complexities were largely overlooked in the didactic literature with its well-worn theme that women were to find their value in their role as mother and wife. Like his clerical colleagues, the author of Hattie Child's marriage manual, *The Christian Household*, chose not to mention the spacing of childbirth – the one way by which a woman might realistically balance the high expectations of being a wife and mother. Evident already in the family arrangements of Moses and Lemira a generation earlier, the practice of birth control continued to be motivated by economic concerns. However, middle-class women were now also expressing a sense of self that was congruent with new female educational opportunities by expecting a greater say over their own bodies in the matter of conception.[33] Several months after Abby's birth and just before their first wedding anniversary, Hattie had lightheartedly told her husband, "I shall offer you baby as a giftie on the 21st! Will that do?" But she had also playfully added, "By the way you won't expect such a present every wedding anniversary?"[34]

During the next fourteen years, at roughly two-year intervals, she bore seven children, ending her childbearing at the relatively young age of thirty-five. A two-year space separated the birth of Abby from that of the second infant, again a daughter, named Jessie Maud, born prematurely on 11 November 1861 and weighing only five and a half pounds. A third daughter, named Emily, born on 1 February 1864, died the following September. Charles William Colby, the couple's first son, was born on 25 March 1867 and would rival his two oldest sisters in longevity. He was followed on 7 September 1869 by a stillborn boy, Carroll Child, and a year later by a girl, Harriet Alice, whose fragile

Emily Strong Colby, daughter
of Moses and Lemira,
c 1861, the year of her
marriage to Quebec lawyer
William T. White (CCM)

condition culminated in death on 30 August 1871. With a second surviving son, John Child, born 25 November 1873 while the family was staying in Weybridge, Hattie's childbearing came to an end.

In spacing births, a woman might exercise some control over fertility, but as the high incidence of infant deaths during the century testifies, family formation continued to be an awesome endeavour for which ultimately only religion could provide meaning and security. For young women of childbearing age such as Hattie, marriage, birth, and death were part of an inseparable continuum that left them at the mercy of forces beyond their control or, as the marriage liturgy phrased it, "for better for worse ... till death do us part." An educated, religiously minded woman, Hattie crafted her own religious symbolism with which to interpret the experience of wife and mother, rather than relying entirely on the theological formulations of an institutional church.

After giving birth to her second child, and while being cosseted by a nurse as well as her mother-in-law, she shared some of her experience in a letter to her sister-in-law Emily, who had moved with her husband to Quebec City and was now experiencing her first pregnancy. By mid-century, as a reflection of the increased importance that the family was beginning to assume in middle-class identity – and fuelled by sentimental literature – it had become desirable for middle-class husbands to show their solicitude by being present at the birth.[35] Implicitly acknowledging her husband's presence, Hattie offered her sister-in-law her own definition of childbirth: an event shared by both husband and wife "in which it would be hard to say whose part is the most severe." As she connected husband and wife together in a more intimate way, childbirth became "a sacrament – as solemn and more sacred than your marriage if possible – It is the baptism of suffering. God bless and sanctify these days to you both – to your present and eternal good."[36]

In Protestant theology, while marriage was a covenant, only communion and baptism were considered sacraments, and no liturgical status was accorded to giving birth. By contrast, Roman Catholics did consider marriage to be one of their seven sacraments, though not childbirth. In the Anglican tradition, childbirth was accompanied by a lesser ritual, "churching," or reincorporation into the community, signifying the resumption of sexual relations between husband and wife and the restoration of normal domestic order.[37] However, Hattie's symbolism, in keeping with the construct of the companionate marriage, emphasized the love of husband and wife rather than the role of priest or minister. The religious groundwork for such rearticulation of ecclesiastical tradition to the family setting had already been evident during the couple's courtship, both in Charles's conversion experience of God as the source of human and divine love, and in the affective sentimental poetry she had written.

This liberalizing of religious symbols was increasingly being made available to a literate audience in the writings of prominent urban preachers such as Henry Ward Beecher and in popularized renditions of the new theology on the historical Jesus. After reading Beecher's *New Star Papers* shortly after her marriage, Hattie noted in her journal that she had also finished "that German life of Christ" – the romanticized *Leben Jesu* written by D.F. Strauss in 1835–36 and recently translated into English by George Eliot, whose novels became favourites of hers.[38] At a later date she read Beecher's *Life of Jesus, the Christ* as well as the more scholarly *Life of Christ* by the "Broad Church" Anglican theologian, Frederic Farrar. She also eagerly followed in *Scribner's* the account of the Chicago heresy trial of David Swing, whose poetic approach to Scripture and theology had led him to reject all doctrines that seemed out of keeping with God's loving nature.[39] Such reading was more than a diversion to fill a middle-class woman's free hours; it helped her recast the language and beliefs of ecclesiastical Christianity into forms that structured and gave meaning to life's most uncertain – and hence awesome and frightening – events.

All did not share her symbolic discourse, however. Hattie's homily on childbirth called forth a gentle but firm rebuke from her brother-in-law, who begged her to refrain from exciting his highly strung and nervous young wife. Sadly, the need to surround childbirth with the comfort of religious symbols became all too evident only a short while later when Emily gave birth. Her experience of motherhood followed a tragic pattern similar to that of Hattie's mother and of so many other women of the time. Emily's first child, a son, was born on 25 April 1862 only to die after four months. During his brief life, his prospects of survival had been so poor that his christening and naming had been deferred.[40] Four years later, about to give birth to a second child, this time in the security of her ancestral home, Emily was in such poor health that it was deemed advisable for her to make a will. A heart-wrenching document, composed with the advice and help of her lawyer husband, it underscored the fragility of life for women of child-bearing age.[41] Shortly thereafter, on 25 April 1866, she gave birth to a second son, Charles Colby White, but she died on 12 July and was survived by her infant son for only seven months. At times of death, it was important for the survivors to cling together as part of a wider family network, and Emily's husband, William White, remained with the Colby's for several months after her death.

Marriages, births, and deaths were carefully recorded in Hattie's Bible, as was the custom. There were times in the 1860s and 1870s when in the Colby household death seemed to be everywhere. Besides the death of Emily and her two infant sons, there had been Moses' death in 1863, the death of Charles and Hattie's three babies, and in 1872 that of Hattie's father, John Child, who died suddenly in Weybridge while unloading a wagon.[42] Death was frequent, unexpected, and impervious to distinctions of age or class. The pages inserted in the centre of every Victorian family Bible witnessed to the fact that despite the socio-economic changes revolutionizing communal relations, the family remained the site of life's holiest events, those that fragmented or augmented happiness and wholeness.

Rituals of home and friends, and of marriage, birth, and death, helped shape a woman's identity. These were inseparable, however, from their menfolk's unrelenting and often frantic pursuit of material gain and security. After her husband's death, Lemira played a frantic part in trying to retain an economic base in land for her younger son William. By contrast, Hattie's role as consumer, nurturer, and moral sustainer identified her with the new order. The improvements in travel and communication that expanded a husband's business opportunities – and also heightened his anxieties and increased his absence from his family – affected a wife's life in quite different ways. The timing of Charles and Hattie's marriage coincided with a developing consumerism, which became an important factor to middle-class women in shaping their identity.[43] By the 1860s the entry of the

William T. White, recently widowed, and son Charles
Carroll, 1866, shortly before the infant's death (CCM)

railway into the Eastern Townships and an enhanced mail system were beginning to make available a limited number of new goods in the shops of Stanstead and in nearby Derby, Vermont. As the wife of a prominent professional in the Stanstead area, Hattie Colby had certain assumptions about the style of life she expected, and she accepted as natural her dependence on men to meet these assumptions. Entries in her diary during the first year of their marriage make clear her unabashed pleasure in material things and her distress at their absence.[44]

Stanstead's limited number of stores formed part of a much wider mercantile system wherein a journey to the well-stocked shops of New England or Montreal gave women the opportunity to expand their taste and fashions. In the first two decades of her marriage, Hattie made relatively few such visits, and at times a tinge of envy surfaced in her letters as she described the trips and vacations indulged in by Stanstead's female elite. For those not able to afford such a lifestyle, much of the developing consumerism consisted of vicarious participation. Thus, references to the displays of female headgear, the elegant apparel of visiting cousins, and the travel plans of community residents regularly found their way into Hattie's correspondence with her husband.[45] At the same time, while her husband was borrowing thousands of dollars in an effort to improve the family's material future, Hattie's letters were peppered with the gnawing worry over small sums of money: a five-dollar subscription to the Congregational minister's salary, a few dollars to pay the village dressmaker, or a small sum to buy a child's gift. All of this was part of the need to keep up appearances, a need that was as great for the wife of one of the town's leading families as for the husband who was intent on building assets with limited and legally encumbered resources.

The need to make do with less also expressed itself in the running of the household, and here women of the middle class were able to help their husbands in a significant and often mutually supportive way. During Charles's frequent absences, it was Hattie who had to assume responsibility for the hired man, whose regular drinking binges severely curtailed his ability to do the butchering, woodcutting, and other farm chores.[46] With servants handling the heavy work and Lemira Colby doing the cooking, Hattie was primarily in charge of the spiritual, moral, and material needs of her children. This included sewing their clothing, a task facilitated by a sewing machine that was acquired during her first year of marriage. Scraps of material (often selected by her husband while on business trips) regularly found themselves in letters to family and friends as part of a sharing in this material women's culture.[47] Despite her love of attractive clothing, it was some time before Hattie was consistently able to transfer her own standards of taste and suitability to the appearance of her children, and when she failed to do so, her mother-in-law was quick to rebuke her.[48] Pride in the clothing of one's children was an obvious expression of middle-class success; its failure, a cause of censure.

Material goods were more than a means of meeting needs; they were also an expression of affection between husband and wife. In the early years of their marriage, before their children's needs consumed much of the family budget, the purchase of a parasol, books, gloves, and other such gifts was a regular occurrence.[49] Though enjoyed and displayed as part of a wife's middle-class identity, they could recede from one's reach when finances floundered. Then, into the breach, entered moral values as the true bedrock of family happiness. On their first Christmas, when their material prospects were still very promising, Hattie had set the tone for this with her diary entry: "New shoes, new gloves … etc. Dearest Husband, We agreed that costliness is not happiness."[50] Celebrative rituals such as birthdays, the anniversary of their engagement and wedding, and Christmas were marked sometimes with material gifts, but always with letters. Writing from Boston three days before Christmas 1864, and anxiously awaiting the closing of a business transaction, Charles regretted he could only afford to send a few books for their three infant daughters: "The children will remember me Christmas eve although I am a poor contributor to the elegant tree which will be erected in the parlor."[51]

Throughout the family's financial troubles, Hattie remained supportive, though on occasion she drew on the constructed role of the moral wife, whose task was to remind a husband caught up in the antithetical demands of the marketplace of the eternal verities of correct Christian behaviour. Her business advice to her husband, though veiled, was always of a moral nature. "If you fix the gold mine business in Providence – I need hardly say do it safely & prudently & honourably …" she counselled in 1865.[52] In their correspondence, as their economic circumstances deteriorated, affirmations of love for one another took on a heightened role in a world of delayed gratification where one looked to future success in the midst of disappointment. Writing after one such disappointment, Hattie declared with emphasis, "Je vous aime – *tout le temps*," leading her husband to respond that those "very dear words" had become his last reading at night and first in the morning for the remainder of his business trip.[53] A little later, after yet another business reversal, he was again reassured: "The externals are not the main thing; we are so rich we can afford to be poorer if need be. You are my boundless unchanging, unalienable wealth – now & ever more. In this view how dwarfed all considerations of money seem. They are accidental, irrelevant."[54]

Material deprivation was not new to a woman whose entry into Stanstead as a teacher had been motivated by the need to supplement her family's income in order to allow a younger brother to have his chance at higher education.[55] Like her husband, Hattie had been exposed in her youth to the material constraints of a farming family in a cash-strapped economy, and she took pride in such domestic skills as her sewing ability.⁵⁶ The few times when complaints did surface in her letters to her husband they related not to material things but to fissures in family wholeness. These invariably centred around the impact, especially on Lemira, of brother-in-law William's increasing alcoholism and were always retracted immediately with an apology for her "unchristian" words.⁵⁷

Implicit in these relatively few "lapses" into criticizing a family member was Hattie's knowledge that the careful provisions in Moses Colby's will, intended to make family members mutually dependent, had in the new age of land and mining speculation actually hemmed in her husband's ability to manoeuvre financially. In late 1869, when the family's economic well-being was fast reaching its nadir, she confided to Charles: "To think how much hard work and anxiety your life might have been free from, could you only have had a fair start, instead of carrying the burden of a past generation in addition to the daily bread to be won for those dependent on you!"⁵⁸ The understanding of the family as part of a larger kinship unit, which had been at the core of Moses' will, now played a central part in the couple's weal and woe. "'Bearing one another's burdens' seems to be a tolerably steady business for Christian people here below," was Hattie's summary when William was again missing and her husband was delayed on business. "So the family will meet again," she concluded, "this time with a mixture of the joy & sorrow which goes up to make up the world and life itself."⁵⁹

The potential for economic reversals to destroy a home and family was indeed great, and for all three Colby women – Lemira, Hattie, and William's wife Melvina – maintaining family cohesion came at a high price. As noted previously, among the legal changes of the 1840s, a married woman was allowed to renounce the dower given in her marriage contract if her husband wished to sell the land.⁶⁰ Already in 1862, while Moses was still alive, Hattie and her sister-in-law Melvina had been asked to renounce briefly their right of dower on the stone house and property which the brothers had jointly bought.⁶¹ In 1863, when Charles bought out William's portion and assumed all accumulated debts, Melvina again agreed to renounce her rights to her husband's half of the stone house, and the following year she renounced her rights to the remainder of his half of his father's estate.⁶² When Charles began to mortgage portions of this land, it had been Hattie's turn to renounce her rights, in 1868 and 1869, followed by her renunciation of the entire remaining estate when in 1872 he was forced to declare insolvency.⁶³

Lemira was trapped in the same maelstrom as her daughters-in-law.⁶⁴ With her older son's insolvency and the sale of the house, she had to leave her "dear home" – the home financed by Moses Colby in which, as she tersely noted on the day of departure, she had expected to spend her last days.[65] During this period, apparently drawing on an independent source of income, she worked frantically to ensure some form of livelihood for her younger son and his family. She purchased several small parcels of land close to the family home and deeded them to William and Melvina, only to have to bail him out again when he continued his habit of signing promissory notes against the land.[66] Despite her willingness to engage in land transactions for over a decade for the benefit of her younger son, she was unable to succeed in helping him remain on his feet and to stop the spiral of misery, which culminated in bankruptcy in 1874 and led to his premature death ten years later.

All of this also took its toll on Melvina, who like her sister-in-law a few years earlier had to face the shame of seeing all the household furniture and other chattels seized and sold. In her limited extant correspondence, and in references in Hattie's letters, Melvina gives every indication of being a woman whose life had become cramped with disappointment. The daughter of an old and respected Stanstead family that moved west soon after her wedding, she had not married until the age of thirty, whereupon she bore two daughters, Mary French in 1862 and Martha Stoddard in 1865. Although the Colby connection figured prominently in their naming, and although William appears to have been a caring father and uncle and was seemingly much troubled by the grief he caused his wife, his alcoholism marred the marriage almost from its beginning. Melvina's response was to devote herself to temperance work and other charitable causes. Outwardly, the relationship with Hattie was cordial, but disappointment sometimes reared its head in barbed criticisms of her more fortunate sister-in-law.[67]

At a distance, Hattie's life may appear to have been easier, but the demands of "woman's work" – the cooking, washing, ironing, and house cleaning that were part of running a household – were far from light, and they increased as the family's economic circumstances deteriorated. Initially, the transition from young bride to mother had been eased by a dependency on Lemira to help with household work, and as Hattie went through the childbearing years, much of the household work had continued to devolve on her mother-in-law. In the face of an unreliable supply of servants, it was Lemira who did all the cooking, much of the cleaning, and took charge during the summer intervals when Hattie and the children went off to visit her Weybridge family. By the time of the insolvency, however, Lemira had begun to suffer from ill health, leaving Hattie to shoulder more of the housework.

William Benton Colby, younger son of Moses and Lemira, with daughter Mary French, c. 1864 (CCM)

Despite the straitened finances, the family continued to employ a hired man and a female servant, and though for a while in the early 1870s Mrs Bailey joined the household as female companion and nanny, her bouts with ill health often made her presence a mixed blessing.[68] The household continued to welcome long-term guests, usually relatives, including Hattie's widowed stepmother. All this took its toll on a woman who loved to read books and whose domestic duties in the early years of marriage had consisted largely of nurturing the children, sewing, visiting, and receiving guests. Writing to her husband, who was away in Washington on business in 1874, she noted how much more time she was now spending downstairs – in cooking and bread making – and how her wrist was shaking from ironing. At times, as the demands of the housework drained her of all her time and energy, she apologized for the dullness of her letters.[69]

Such self-deprecation was part of female epistolary convention, but for Hattie there was a deeper undercurrent of anxiety that sapped her self-esteem.[70] Always nagging at her was a concern for her husband. Beginning in 1867, when he was elected to the new dominion parliament, his absences from home as he fulfilled his government duties and pursued additional sources of income increased in length, and they remained a continual element of family life until 1891, when his political career ended. In addition, there was the constant anxiety about the health of their children, especially the two surviving daughters, Jessie and Abby, who as children did not enjoy a robust constitution and were sent to relatives for extended periods for rest and renewal.[71] Not surprisingly, Hattie's own health began to be affected, and references to chronic headaches, toothache, and fatigue surfaced regularly in the correspondence. Her love of reading began to exact a toll: the headaches, which she had had since youth, now became accompanied by such a deterioration of her eyesight that by the 1890s she required a special opaque lampshade and dark glasses as a shield from bright light.[72]

In 1874, when their financial situation continued to be grim, the need for rest and renewal found a suitably religious outlet. Where her Methodist ancestors had once found a measure of spiritual strength in camp meetings held in sylvan settings, Hattie and her children spent a number of weeks at a French Canadian pension in Berthier-en-Haut. Recommended by one of Charles's parliamentary colleagues, it was run by the daughters of Calvin Amaron, a Swiss Protestant evangelist.[73] Being a part of this cultured evangelical household offered Hattie an opportunity for French conversation, rest, and participation in community events, and the experience was sufficiently rewarding to be repeated several summers in succession.[74] In the winter of 1879–80 she and her eldest daughter Abby spent six weeks in Colorado on the sheep farm of her brother Dan. Notwithstanding her fondness of her brother, Hattie soon found herself at odds with her less educated sister-in-law, whose suitability as a wife for her brother had from the beginning been a source of concern. The latter now criticized her non-paying guest for "eating the bread of idleness" instead of helping with household tasks.[75] The previous decade's penury exacted its revenge in another way as well. A handsome woman, Hattie had by age thirty-five lost her teeth, and having put off getting proper dental attention in Stanstead, she was now shocked to discover that the cost in Colorado would be even higher.[76]

Such experiences confirm what feminist historians have noted concerning the internal conflict experienced by middle-class women. While didactic literature and social expectations extolled their moral power, their legal and personal identity was subsumed into that of wife and mother.[77] Hattie Colby's breakdown in energy and health reflected the tensions brought about by an economic order that proclaimed high ideals such as the companionate marriage and self-valorization but at the same time placed women in a state of dependency and deferred gratification. Her experience was replicated in the accounts of many middle-class women's lives. Among the best known are the novelist Harriet Beecher Stowe and her equally published sister, Catharine Beecher, whose brother Henry Ward Beecher had influenced Charles and Hattie theologically and spiritually early in their marriage. Both of the Beecher women sought to find a place for women in the new economic order. Of Stowe, Jane Tompkins has noted that she "relocates the center of power in American life, placing it not in the courts of law, nor in the factories, nor in the marketplace, but in the kitchen. And that means that the new society will not be controlled by men, but by women."[78] Such proclamations of woman's power in the home were belied, however, by the contradictions in Stowe's own private life as she struggled to balance her roles as writer and mother.[79]

Just as conflicted was the life of Stowe's sister Catharine. Like her brother, Catharine sought to ensure the ongoing influence of religion in the new capitalistic society – in her case, by claiming a role for women to make home and school a moral buttress against the individualism of the marketplace. While in this way she found a divinely ordained place for women beyond the confines of home and family, she, like her sister, overlooked women's legal and social limitations. It was not without reason that Catharine, a single woman, embarked on a recurring search for physical and spiritual cures as she struggled with the contradictions between the role she proclaimed and the practical realities of a woman without money or power.[80] Spiritually exalted but materially dependent on the efforts of their husbands or fathers, women remained stationed in the home. Thus, while time and space were redefining the lives of middle-class men, for women self-definition had to take place within the static world of the home.

Not surprisingly, religious faith was affected. The revivals of the early nineteenth century in which women for a brief time had prophesied – and had experienced intensely, in a flash, the searing fire of divine love – these were events of the past, and in any case they were looked at askance in the Colby household. For middle-class women who, like the Beecher sisters and Hattie Child Colby, had been nurtured since infancy in a Christian home, conversion in the earlier sense had become either problematic or unnecessary.[81] This did not mean that women did not at times undergo a crisis of faith. In a society where religious symbols provided meaning to everyday existence, such a crisis might well occur when a woman's emotional and physical resources had become depleted through anxiety, illness, or unrelenting family demands. The contemporary term of "burnout" symbolically captures the essentials of such a crisis.

In 1875 Hattie Colby underwent her own brief crisis of faith. Unlike the crises documented for a number of well-known Victorian males, hers did not arise out of an intellectual struggle with new biblical or scientific thought, though she was familiar with some of its current expressions. For her, the catalyst appears to have been a loss of respect for Stanstead's Methodist minister, which was brought about by his apparent neglect of his sickly wife and thereafter by his internal political wrangling as the newly appointed moral governor of Stanstead College.[82] Hattie's resulting loss of faith, not surprisingly, was expressed not in abstract spiritual terms but in a family concern, her constant anxiety for her husband's safety. In its timing, the distress was all the more acute, for Stanstead as a border community was the site that spring of efforts at religious revival under the auspices of the American YMCA.[83] In a fit of panic, when the mail failed three days in a row to bring one of the expected letters that had become her emotional mainstay, her resources collapsed, and she dashed off a frantic note:

O My dear Charles. What can I do? No letter from you yet. I fell in a despairing kind of wonder. I couldn't *believe* Charley hadn't brought me one to day and yesterday and the day before. Tomorrow those special service people are to preach and hold forth. All worship seems a mockery and "the bottom has fallen out of the universe" when I am in doubt about your safety. I can't always even pray prayers but sit dumb and confounded.[84]

Later, she would thank Charles for guiding her theologically through her spiritual difficulties, but in practical terms, his safe arrival home soon after her letter was probably of at least as much help. Significantly, when it came to asking for intellectual help, she had turned not to a theologically trained minister but to her husband.[85] Family relationships mattered in more ways than one. Her crisis of faith again underscores the extent to which religion for middle-class women was integrated into the warp and woof of everyday life. More than a summary of conventional gender expectations, Hattie Colby's motto "faith, hope, charity" revealed how deeply religion had become embedded in her family affections and relationships. In this way her motto would be one of the threads through which the symbolic universe of traditional Protestantism merged into the religious construct of the Victorian family. The pattern will become more clearly discernible as we turn to the world of her businessman husband.

CHAPTER FOUR

Time, Faith, Energy:
Religion and the Spirit of Capitalism

Where middle-class women such as Hattie Colby were consigned to the private world of home and piety, their husbands, it is generally argued, derived their identity from success acquired by accumulating wealth and power in the capitalist marketplace. Unlike its female counterpart, the male gender construct, variously referred to as "marketplace manhood" or "the myth of the self-made man," has been presented as an entirely secular ideal. Religion, it is assumed, belonged in the private sphere – that increasingly marginalized world in which women and the clergy who extolled and inflated woman's role sought mutual consolation. For men, participation in religious activity was a remnant of the old order, at best only a stepping stone in the march to political and cultural dominance in a de-enchanted brave new world.[1]

As in the analyses of women's lives – though here in different ways – historians of gender and religion have begun to challenge earlier constructs typifying the world of Victorian middle-class men. Dualism and dichotomy are giving way to a more integrated understanding of gender and religion as part of a web of social relations, structured by family, community, and legal networks.[2] Thus, for the Victorian period, the evangelical concept of Christian manhood has been added to the "self-made man," secular counterpart to the "pious female."[3] Here, nineteenth-century religious writing is instructive. Already by mid-century, ministers were not only extolling the virtue of the praying mother but were also writing a new form of literature, in which they drew attention to the Christian virtues to be expressed in the world of commerce. Appearing at a time when denominational expansion called for increased lay involvement in time and money, this new construct of masculinity, the "Christian businessman," figured prominently in the columns of denominational papers and in evangelical prescriptive and biographical literature, most of which was authored by ministers.[4] The construct itself has been traced to a clearly defined period, the 1857–58 "businessmen's revivals" – those that had led to Charles Colby's religious conversion shortly before his marriage.[5]

From newspaper accounts, it is clear that in places as distant from the New England urban epicentre as the village of Stanstead, these revivals were seen as a turning point in which God's time was being reconfigured in ways more congruent with economic time. While radical revivalist groups such as the Millerites and the Children of Peace proclaimed a world whose secular time would be transformed into a divinely inaugurated millennium, the accounts of the 1857–58 revivals underscore that the divine had become immanent in the secular world of business. "There are times when an altogether new set of spiritual activities are evolved in society, and the old are immeasurably quickened and strengthened – when the veriest infidel can hardly help recognizing that a divine spirit is being poured out, bringing the human spirit into subjection," rhapsodized the *Stanstead Journal* in one of its accounts.[6] Where agrarian rhythms had set the timing of the camp meetings and millenarian movements of the previous decade, the new revivals were noonday events held in large churches in the heart of urban commercial districts. In their sober style, and in calling upon the cooperation of wives and sisters, they targeted men who were active in the new commercial and industrializing marketplace, in the world where "time is money."[7] In so doing, new revival leaders such as Henry Ward Beecher and Phoebe Palmer were forging positive links between God's time and economic time. Historians have noted, therefore, the congruence between the timing of the revivals and the subsequent expansion of the mainline Protestant denominations, as businessmen invested their time, skills, and funds into church-building projects and benevolent societies. At the same time, the new compatibility between religion and the commercial world has been viewed with considerable ambivalence as undermining the integrity of the faith. In the view of the businessmen's revivals' foremost historian, Kathryn T. Long, "during the revival some of the tension that most American Protestants historically felt between the convictions of their faith and the practices of free-market capitalism became relaxed."[8]

In a similar vein, Mark Noll has noted that during this period clergy showed little interest in critically analysing the conventional means of gaining wealth but instead were concerned that wealth be used wisely, benevolently, and for the good of others.[9] While the resulting systematic benevolence has been well documented and its contradictions extensively critiqued, we still know little about the tensions that middle-class men may have experienced between their faith and the demands of the marketplace.[10] That these tensions helped shape Hattie Colby's female world of "faith, hope, and charity" is evident, but how did they shape the identity of her husband? On the surface, like the trope of the Christian businessman, his motto "time, faith, energy" offers an entry into how one male convert of the 1857–58 revivals tried to place within the framework of family and religion a marketplace in which time and energy dominated. Charles Colby's experience is of special interest for two reasons. It underscores the centrality of the family in motivating his relentless and often unsuccessful business transactions; and it departs from the customary pattern of revival accounts. Colby did not immediately take a prominent role in church life; not until 1867 did he and Hattie apply for church membership and become actively involved in providing financial and social leadership in Stanstead's Wesleyan Methodist congregation. Conversion found its initial field of activity not in the church but in the family. The focus in this chapter, like the previous one, will be on religion within the family, leaving for a later chapter its place in church and community life.

CHANGING ECONOMIC AND SOCIAL STRUCTURES: THE 1860S AND 1870S

Early in their marriage, writing late at night to his wife in Weybridge, Charles reminded her of the bewildering demands placed on the life of a businessman: "Dearest, you who have not coppermines, law, wool, pills and ticker beds to think of beside house building etc. do you ever think of him who longs to be with you again?"[11] Then, as today, it was the need to provide for self and family that moved men into the public world of business. What distinguished the latter half of the nineteenth century was the heightened significance given to the home as the unifying centre to the individualistic life in the marketplace.[12] "The world is full of staying-places, but not so full of homes," one writer aptly summarized the importance of home life for the peripatetic businessman.[13]

For Charles Colby, business and home were inextricably connected to the family's large stone house, which had been built amidst much controversy with his father and which by mid-October 1859 was ready for occupancy. The timing of its construction coincided with a new interest in domestic architecture that was reflective of the growing wealth of segments of the middle class in North America and the increased interest in creating a controlled living space separate from the vagaries of the business world. Taking on a personal nature, houses

Carrollcroft, the stone house completed in 1859, home to four generations of Colbys (photo by John Mahoney, which includes the sunporch added after 1888)

were increasingly considered to be an integral part of a family's identity and acquired a perceived personality of their own, signified by the new custom of providing them with personal names.[14] Hattie's Weybridge home, perched on a high hill, went by the name of the Mountain House, while Sunny Home, a clapboard Gothic mansion recently built by her Stanstead friend Martha Pierce, was already becoming a local landmark. It would not be until 1887, however, that the Colby stone house received the name Carrollcroft (after Charles's second name) and became the living space of a single family.

Designed by Charles, who also did much of the finishing work during the summers of 1859 and 1860, it boasted an impressive front made of local granite, while the back, as was often the case, was of wood.[15] The simple exterior, with its central porch, reflected Charles's interest in the Neoclassical style dating back to his days at Dartmouth, and the house became a distinctive landmark on Stanstead's main street, a contrast to the village's other notable homes with their variations of Victorian Gothic. A central hallway and two storeys, plus a spacious attic, simplified the necessary divisions into office space, located at the front, domestic space, with a shared kitchen and pantry at the back, and servants' rooms at the top of the house. After Lemira's death, the house took on the contours of a single family dwelling, but during its first thirty years it was a multigenerational living space as well as both home and office.[16]

Its statement of solid middle-class comfort seemed well suited to the progressive spirit that was then evident in the Eastern Townships. As capitalist relations began increasingly to drive the regional economy, legal reforms intended to facilitate the transfer of property rights helped ensure a steady round of legal business for an energetic lawyer. Area residents who were engaging in a booming real estate market regularly sought Charles Colby to represent their interests, more frequently as plaintiffs than as defendants.[17] Economic change and communication improvements accompanied legal reform. The strong agricultural base built in the Eastern Townships in the first half of the nineteenth century began to reap rewards in the next few decades, providing the financial resources needed to expand the communications system and develop the area's mineral resources, along with manufacturing and industry. As late as 1875 it still took six hours to reach Montreal from Stanstead by train, but the building of railways in the area, begun in the early 1840s, the introduction of the telegraph, and an improved mail system were already revolutionizing a businessman's sense of space and time.[18] Greater and more frequent communication by mail and train also strengthened family ties and made possible regular visits with Hattie's Weybridge family, as well as ensuring a steady flow of mail among separated family members.

In the world of business, on the other hand, developments such as the establishment of the Eastern Townships Bank in 1859 began to place traditional person-to-person contacts on a more impersonal footing. Where Moses Colby and his generation had paid their hired help in kind and had often rendered services through a barter system, his sons were part of the new cash-based commercial economy. Known for its fine farms, the Stanstead area, whose population by the 1860s was well into its third generation, had seen its land values increase dramatically as a result of transportation improvements. Moses Colby's concerns about his sons' accumulation of debts against the estate had therefore been justified. While agriculture remained the mainstay and claimed the largest number of large landholders, a number of them had by the 1860s built up sufficient capital through commercial farming, especially in sheep and cattle, to invest in the growing mining and manufacturing industries. In Quebec, mining rights (with the exception of gold and silver) belonged exclusively to the owner of the land surface rather than to the Crown. A promising piece of property could be bought outright and developed, or the mining rights could simply be rented out, making the possibilities for speculation considerable.[19] Speculation, which included other natural resources such as granite and oil, brought a new element of risk and stress, one quite different from the activities traditionally associated with agriculture and the professions. Travel in order to solicit funds made increased demands on a man's time and led to a sense of impermanence. This seemed a small price to pay when economic times were good, as they were in the years 1854–66, thanks to American reciprocity and the northern states' insatiable need of food and equipment during the Civil War.[20] But when the economy contracted after the war or collapsed as it did in 1875, a businessman's peripatetic lifestyle was no longer the means to an achievable goal but was simply a way of life that called for seemingly endless separation from home and loved ones.

All of this Charles Colby experienced during the 1860s and 1870s. A constant refrain in the correspondence that often passed daily between himself and his wife and children was a longing for "the good times coming" when he would finally be able to remain permanently at home.[21] To supplement his income, he seized the opportunity to branch out from law and farming into railway and mining speculation.[22] Along with a number of local entrepreneurs of various means, he was soon caught up in developing the rich veins of copper that were being opened up in nearby Ascot Township in 1858.[23] In 1860 he began to invest in mining prospects in the area around Stowe, Vermont, and in October 1862 he secured the rights for mineral exploration on a 350-acre tract in Potton Township, to the west of Stanstead.[24] A month later, in partnership with a local entrepreneur, Ozro Morrill, he received further mining rights on half the area, formed a company called Canadian Copper Mines, and by January was in New York City advertising company shares to "a dozen gentlemen of wealth."[25] By the time of his father's death in May 1863, Charles had virtually ceased his legal practice.[26] From this time on, mining speculation, based on hopeful prospects but mounting debts, became a constant and obsessive theme in his letters to Hattie. Not all of his land transactions were notarized, but the paper trail left in its wake show that the land purchases he made with Morrill and several other partners in nearby Cleveland, Hatley, Brome, and Ascot townships between 1863 and 1866 amounted to an outlay of about $26,800.[27]

Although, on Moses' death, Charles inherited half of the family land and home, his means remained limited because of the need to keep the estate intact and pay off its encumbered debts. Meanwhile, one-third of the proceeds of the estate had to go to support his mother, as stipulated in the will, and in 1861 a dowry had to be found for his sister. In addition, his brother William's chronic dependence on alcohol was already causing problems, as were his debts. The 90-acre farm which his father had left to William disappeared from the record of land transactions after Moses' death and was in all probability sold to pay debts. When a year after the reading of the will, Charles, with the consent of his mother, bought his brother's share of the house and property, he assumed sole responsibility for the mortgages with which the two brothers had encumbered the estate as far back as 1857.[28] This, in addition to his ongoing land speculation in mining, oil, and railways, increased his economic worries.[29] He mortaged parts of the estate and sold others, and immersed himself fully in the region's apparently promising industrial development.

In such economic volatility, religion offered limited guidance and solace. As noted earlier, the new economic order challenged the sacred sense of time that had found expression in such signposts as restful Sabbaths, lengthy church sermons, and midweek prayer meetings. For businessmen time was money, but religious restrictions on any kind of Sabbath work remained unchanged. Shortly after their marriage, Charles and Hattie had made a mutual decision to assume the responsibilities of church membership, but this fell by the wayside in the following weeks, when various factors intervened, including Charles's frequent absences due to business.[30] As adherents rather than members, both continued to attend the Methodist church on Sunday mornings and could often be found in the Colby pew in the Congregationalist chapel at the afternoon (and, later, evening) service. Financially contributing to the salaries of both ministers, they carried on this dual allegiance at some personal cost as their financial situation worsened.[31]

From time to time, the difficulty of holding together the expectations of the life of a converted sinner with the demands of his business life surfaced in Charles's writings. "I must seek to keep business off my back," he recorded with chagrin in his journal when on a Sunday he found himself catching up on his journal entries.[32] At the same time, though it might be impossible to devote the entire day to religious pursuits, Sundays did offer an anchor and a place of stability in the chaotic world of business demands.[33] When he spent Sunday on the road, he invariably attended church, and in his choice of pulpit and congregation, he made an effort to sample preaching that was practical in content and plain in style, in keeping with the generally observed taste of laymen.[34] A sermon he heard at the Congregationalist meeting house at St Alban's in 1862, for example, evoked the response that "though full of vigor and warmth," it seemed more of a moral essay than a sermon and was "severely correct enough for insertion in the *Atlantic*."[35] Sharing such insights and tastes with his wife in the letter writing that formed their Sunday ritual when separated became a way to deepen their relationship and to refine a layman's theological understanding.

Often alone on Sunday evenings in an inhospitable hotel room, and missing his wife and young children, Charles looked to religious faith and love of family to provide some meaning to the individualistic lifestyle of a businessman in pursuit of reward. In such instances, the moral conviction that divine providence rewards those who have pursued their goals with diligence and tenacity provided a meaningful framework by which to understand his often futile travels. "This is another instance of what faith and perseverence [sic] will accomplish under difficult circumstances when aided by the great disposer of events," he was able to write at the successful completion of a mining contract with Boston investors in January 1864, one of the rare occasions when a venture reached a desirable conclusion.[36] This assumption that providence aided the efforts of disciplined individuals gave buoyancy to business life in good times and allowed for dogged persistence in adversity.[37]

"Even in an age of expanding markets, God still ruled economic life, as well as other spheres of existence," one scholar has summarized the traditional modes of thinking that continued to guide evangelical thought on economic questions.[38] However, the agency through which God ruled was not an impersonal force but consisted of the decisions and investments of fallible men, caught in market forces which they at best apprehended and rarely controlled. Such men were also heads of families that were dependent on them for a livelihood as well as for their social standing. It was within this anxiety-ridden economic environment that Charles and Hattie Colby had to shape their identity as a family – but also as evangelicals.

For Charles, the swing between boom and bust, which characterized the business world of the late 1860s and the 1870s, made the possibility of financial collapse an ever-present reality.[39] The catalyst to economic risk and ultimately to insolvency turned out to be a Vermont mining partnership with two of Hattie's brothers. As with his ventures with local businessmen, family partnerships provided an opportunity to pool limited resources for major financial investments. An unprofitable sheep-raising partnership with his brothers-in-law shortly after his marriage to Hattie had set the stage. As one of her brothers confidently assured him, "Your reputation is such that they say 'any thing that *Colby* will put money into or advise you to go in, we will go in from $1000 to $10,000.'"[40] This investment was followed in 1866 by a second and much more grandiose venture, the mining of a recently discovered marble site at Belden's Falls, near Middlebury, Vermont. Convinced that it contained a financial bonanza, since it held a new type of marble that promised to equal or surpass the renowned Italian Carrara marble, Charles made a contract with a Boston mining firm and invested all his available capital.[41] The timing seemed propitious, given an $80,000 shared windfall recently realized by the sale of some of the Ascot Township mines.[42]

By 1869, however, it had become apparent that the Vermont mine contained very little of the much-vaunted marble.[43] Debts accumulated, land was further mortgaged or sold, until suddenly, in August 1871, Charles's inability to pay an overdue promissory note for US$1,000, with interest, catapulted him into insolvency.[44] In early November 1871 two sales of livestock and implements yielded $1,152, an amount that was less than the debt and the legal fees. Under the terms of the 1869 Insolvency Act, any suit against a debtor who was unable to meet his commitments compelled all other creditors to come forward as opposants to protect their claims. Ten days later, twenty-four claimants entered into legal proceedings, and in January 1872 Charles and his family moved into a frame house on their property next door to the stone house that he and Hattie had entered with such anticipation as newlyweds. Since there was no limited liability, all household goods and chattels were subsequently seized and auctioned. All of the Stanstead land – consisting of the family homestead, the 832-acre farm left by Moses, and several small parcels of land – was sold.[45] By June the proceeds of $8,191.45, which represented only a portion of the $54,809 owed, had been proportionately disbursed among the litigants.[46]

William's trajectory followed a similar route, aggravated by the impact of the alcoholism that had already cost him the farm willed to him by his father. In 1871, in the midst of his own economic woes, Charles received an abject note, written by William at the insistence of his wife Melvina, informing him that he had "fallen again" and could no longer avoid calling together his creditors.[47] This disaster was staved off, and William's pattern of mortgaging land and being financially rescued by his mother continued until 1874, when he finally declared bankruptcy and was forced into the penurious livelihood of an insurance salesman.[48]

The loss of the family estate, which Moses Colby had so feared at the time of construction of the family home in 1857, had become a reality fifteen years later. The 1860s and early 1870s were indeed a time of much economic speculation in the Eastern Townships as men gambled recklessly in mining, oil, and land. And Moses' sons had been in the thick of it. Moses had not been alone in voicing his concerns, for his views echoed those of many clergy and educators of his generation, who uttered severe denunciations of financial speculation during the antebellum period in the United States. Historians such as Karen Halttunen have interpreted such pronouncements as part of an expression of anxiety on the part of those who saw traditional authority slipping in a society driven by the prospect of fast wealth and upward social mobility.[49] Other scholars have noted the influence of common-sense thought in shaping moral attitudes.[50] In the view of the evangelical clergy of that period, for whom the individualistic doctrines of personal sin, trial, and judgment had real implications in the economic realm, financial speculation implied not merely economic irresponsibility but, more seriously, philosophic doubt and atheism. Thus, in worrying from the pulpit about the impact of the new economic climate, clergy were expressing a deep concern for the souls of businessmen.[51]

It should not come as a surprise, therefore, that the only recorded criticism of Charles Colby's insolvency came not from his fellow businessmen or social acquaintances but from an elderly Methodist minister who had "located," or retired, in Stanstead. It was his outspoken view that Colby was no worse off after his insolvency than before, since "he had *always* speculated upon borrowed capital and had never had any property of his own." Thanks to the quick defence offered by the town's Roman Catholic grocer, who said that he knew of at least one transaction whereby Colby had made a $40,000 profit, the clerical critic was silenced.[52] His criticism, however, reflected the distinction made by evangelicals of his generation, including those of Charles's religious denomination, between "visionary" and "real" wealth. Reflecting a constituency of small manufacturers and tradesmen, the Methodist rules governing a member who had failed in business contained the stern injunction, "Let two or three judicious members of our Church inspect the accounts of the supposed delinquent; and if he has behaved dishonestly, or borrowed money without a probability of paying, let him be expelled."[53] This had also been the view of Methodism's founder, John Wesley, a century earlier. His biographer, Henry Rack, has concluded that Wesley's well-known pronouncement, "Gain all you can; save all you can, give all you can," was not intended to encourage "the ruthless, competitive entrepreneur but rather the small manufacturer and tradesman with limited horizons and rather old-fashioned ways."[54] The economic thought of mid-nineteenth-century British evangelicals such as the Presbyterian Thomas Chalmers followed a similar course. In Chalmers's no-nonsense terms, "bankruptcies were not 'mysterious visitations, inscrutable as potato-rot or rinder pest, but were the logical outcome of sin.'"[55]

By the time of the insolvency, Charles and Hattie Colby had been active and prominent members of Stanstead's Methodist church for five years. The well-to-do regional entrepreneurs with whom Colby had entered into mining and railway partnerships in the 1860s and early 1870s – Wilder and Carlos Pierce, Albert Knight, A.P. Ball, Ozro Morrill, Benjamin Pomroy, and W.S. Hunter – though not all members or adherents, were all Methodist pew holders.[56] A number were personally affected by Charles's insolvency, yet it occasioned none of the censure laid down by John Wesley. Nor did Charles's creditors appear to share Thomas Chalmers's view that bankruptcies were the logical outcome of personal sin. Rather, the evidence points to considerable sympathy for the plight of a respected fellow businessman. Discreet offers of financial help came from sources as disparate as a Vermont farmer and family friend, and the local Roman Catholic priest, Father Macaulay, who over the years had become the source of the household's various Irish "serving girls."[57] The insolvency did not have any adverse effect on the family's social relations; their place in the community continued to provide a source of stability. Despite the move to the humbler frame house and the strained state of their finances, they continued to receive friends and acquaintances as before.

Although the majority of creditors had been personal friends or business partners and took a substantial financial beating, it was clear that they made every effort to accommodate the Colbys as far as the terms of the insolvency law permitted, a number of them withdrawing their claims.[58] The bailiff's inventory of the goods and chattels seized in the stone house itemized a goodly supply of middle-class comforts. (The first line alone of a thirteen-line summary of these goods listed ten carpets, thirty-six chairs, ten clocks, and six sofas.) All of these netted the surprisingly low sum of $91.05 (from which had to be deducted $33.16 in bailiff's fees) and thus appear to have been sold only "pro forma" within a sympathetic community. Much of the now excess furniture remained in storage in the back rooms of the stone house, which was sold to a local widow for more than $3,000 above its value on the unwritten understanding that on the widow's death the house could be repurchased by Charles Colby if his fortunes improved.

In the months and years following his insolvency, Charles continued to seek out potential backers for new financial ventures, especially after his election as the member of parliament for Stanstead County in 1867, for he desperately needed to supplement his modest stipend with additional revenue.[59] Hitting the road the minute the parliamentary session closed, he spent his summers travelling to Ontario and the western United States in an effort to raise shares for a McCormack harvester. This was followed by the pursuit of various mining and ranching ventures in the American and Canadian West, all with little success and usually involving long stretches of time away from his family. In these difficult years, Hattie was at least able to make a helpful contribution when, after the sudden death of her father in the summer of 1872, she signed over to her husband as a Christmas gift her portion of the family inheritance. This consisted of "the Mountain House and homestead farm," which realized $6,000.[60] Charles was able to repay her eight years later when it was invested in her youngest brother's merino sheep farm.⁶¹ Although by then, thanks to the sale of the remainder of the Ascot Township mine, Charles could estimate his assets at $40,000, there were several occasions in the 1880s and 1890s when the Eastern Townships Bank had to warn him that his credit was stretched to the limit.⁶²

Nevertheless, the family's condition did begin to recover slowly as Stanstead's economic interests gradually shifted from the earlier Boston axis to Montreal and, later, also to the West and then to Britain.⁶³ In 1887 the Colbys were able to buy back their family home, though it was somewhat the worse for wear. As the result of a major fire shortly after the bankruptcy sale, caused by overheated pipes (and anxiously observed from their new home next door), it required extensive renovation.⁶⁴ Now proudly named Carrollcroft, the house finally received the attention and furnishings previously denied as the family began to travel to Europe and make judicious purchases.⁶⁵

FAMILY, INSOLVENCY, AND RELIGION

The insolvency and its economic aftermath had not undermined the family's sense of identity. The tug between a father's responsibility to be away in order to provide for his family and his desire to be home with wife and children continued to surface in Charles's letters to his children. "My dear Jessie ... It seems very wrong for a husband and a father to be away from his family so much," he wrote to his younger daughter from Ottawa.⁶⁶ Letters, often written on a daily basis, became an indispensable component of family life. They reassured an absent father of the children's well-being at a time when fragile health was a gnawing concern, and they also provided him with an ongoing commentary on the activities and accomplishments of his children. As Jessie and her sister Abby grew older and began to take on the responsibilities of letter writing, correspondence shaped a web of family connectedness, a reflection of the ideal of a family unit in which the bonds of intimacy acted as a buffer against material hardship. The year after their forced move, Hattie had reminded her husband of Jessie's admiration for him: "You know she thinks you are perfection just as you are." Meanwhile, she reread and wept over the letters she and Charles had exchanged during their courtship.⁶⁷

At no point did the correspondence contain any mutual incrimination, and there is much evidence that emotional ties remained as strong as before. In filling the breach occasioned by material loss, religion was of major importance. The habit early in their marriage of closing the day with family prayers had been extended to the children, who were taught from infancy to pray at bedtime and especially to remember their father when he was absent.⁶⁸ In such ways, religion

Hattie Colby and Harriet Alice, c 1870, shortly
before the insolvency and the baby's death (CCM)

and family worked together to mitigate the periods of parental absence. In the spring of 1871, when financial collapse appeared imminent and their youngest daughter, Alice, a sickly baby from birth, was weakening further, Charles sought to encourage his wife and himself with the reminder, "We are in the hands of One who controls all things – for the best."[69] The following year, when they lost not only the child but also their house and land, religion and family again offered strength for the present and hope for the future. As Charles noted to his wife, "In such trials philosophy and religion should aid by reminding us that as all the good things of this life must inevitably slip away from us it is not of the greatest consequence whether they are parted with all at once or one by one, and that far better things are in store for us if we rightly seek them."[70]

The mottos "time, faith, energy" and "faith, hope, charity" which the couple had selected during the trials of the early 1870s were, therefore, not only complementary but were also capable of readjustment and reinterpretation. Just as Hattie interpreted hers in terms appropriate to her experience, so did Charles, but his interpretation of the connection between the marketplace and religion was quite different from that of Stanstead's retired Methodist minister who had bruited his criticism at the time of the insolvency. This did not mean that Charles's business practices were always free from criticism, including self-criticism. "It required neither skill nor experience to get rich in those days," he later reflected on the heady U.S.-Canadian economic climate of the 1861–72 period. "One had only to buy today and sell tomorrow ... Speculation was rife. Every conceivable scheme prospered."[71] In the years when he was an MP, he was accused of conflict of interest on several occasions, as were many of his colleagues.[72] Many of his investments, both before and after his entry into politics, did not pan out and the risks were high. Nevertheless, the hope remained that eventually he would succeed and the family's fortune would be assured, as did finally begin to happen in the 1890s with his interest in the Imperial Writing Machine Company. Throughout all this, in ways unexplored in the advice literature – and at times in contradiction to the official tenets of evangelicalism – Charles Colby crafted a life that somehow tried to hold in dynamic tension the disparate demands of gender, religion, politics, and business. In the process, reality at times did diverge from the ideal, but at his death in 1907 it was the trope of the "Christian businessman" that shaped his eulogy as "a devout Christian, regular in his attendance upon the services of the church, deeply concerned in her prosperity, and expressing his religion in his daily life."[73]

To dismiss such a eulogy simply as a conventional tribute, without substance and fact, overlooks an important reality about religion as a lived phenomenon. "Religion comes into being in an ongoing, dynamic relationship with the realities of daily life," historian Robert Orsi argues.[74] This means that it must find ways to help decrease the tensions and smooth out the contradictions that erupt within the social and economic structures of a given place and time. Charles Colby was not the first to face these tensions. As we have seen, his father Moses had been deeply troubled by the impact of social and economic change on his sons. Once the moral wisdom of an earlier generation no longer provided real direction to the economic lives of their children, it was not surprising that middle-class men and women would begin to rewrite religion so that it meshed with their own experience and understanding of ultimate concerns.

Here, Charles Colby's troubled path to establishing his family on a sound material base is part of the larger story of Christian economic thought and practice in the nineteenth century, which is only just beginning to be understood.[75] The financial crisis of 1857–58 and the subsequent wide-scale revivals in major urban centres in Canada and the United States have been seen as a turning point towards a more positive linkage between business and religion. In retrospect, these revivals – whose intent was to bring into the churches the husbands of devout wives – were instrumental in effecting changes in evangelical religion that were unforeseen by revivalists and ministers. Preaching God's love rather than divine judgment, ministers had presented businessmen with a new religious emphasis but with little practical direction concerning the actual incarnation of this emphasis into their everyday lives. Indeed, in an effort to ascertain the attitude of evangelical leaders to business practices, a detailed examination of evangelical writing has concluded that "Protestants regularly, consistently, and without sense of contradiction both enunciated traditional Christian exhortations about financial stewardship and simply took for granted the workings of an expanding commercial society."[76]

Family history, however, rather than theology nuances such an observation. The Christian exhortations directed at businessmen, whether in the economic thought of the moral philosophers, the writings of evangelicals such as Thomas Chalmers, or from local ministers, largely reflected the values of an agrarian society. This was not the competitive world of an emerging industrial capitalism with its business cycles, technological innovation, exploitation of mineral resources, and private corporations – the real world in which Charles Colby and others endeavoured to make a living for their families.[77] Ministerial exhortations were often contradictory. The same ministers who railed against speculation and visionary wealth were also the catalysts and fundraisers of the new church buildings made possible by economic boom. Indeed, a good number, including the ministers selected for Stanstead by the Stationing Committee of the Methodist Church, were themselves known for their entrepreneurial activity.[78] By sharing the world of the businessmen seated in the pews, such ministers could in fact play a vital role in helping them overcome the scruples that often prevented them from seeking full church membership.[79]

As Charles Colby's letters and activities indicate, a religiously minded businessman found his source of inspiration not in clerical economic thought but in his love and concern for his wife and family. A family for whom one had to care, but who also offered much love in return, was the greatest gift a man could have. Writing to Hattie in the thick of the mining speculation of the mid-1860s and comparing her to "other men's wives (& pretty good ones too whom I meet here & there)," Charles made what amounted to a religious confession: "My judgment tells me that I am the most favored of mortals and does not my heart say Amen & Amen. Yes my dearest: when I go upon my knees to thank the Giver of every good gift for all he has done for me, I thank him more fervently and devoutly for *you* than for any and *all* other gifts to me – This is the burden of my silent thanksgiving – and knowing this if you love me, and I were worse than an infidel to doubt it."[80] The next day, writing in a hopeful mood to attract investment for his marble mine, he solicited her good wishes and prayers for success.[81]

On another occasion, on business in New York City and finding a scheduled meeting postponed, Charles decided to use the free time to attend a lecture by Henry Ward Beecher. Entitled "Beauty and the Beast," its message could not have resonated more with the self-understanding that Charles had carefully crafted and practically implemented in both his married and his professional life. Beecher, calling on his male audience to integrate rather than compartmentalize their religious, family, and business concerns, held up the following ideal: "And the way to come to one's whole self is through a true Christian experience. A man who knows how to be a better husband, a better father, a better friend and a better neighbor, is happier for it. A man who is called to the Christian life, and responds to the call, does business easier and more naturally."[82]

Although Beecher was one of the main preachers in the 1857–58 revivals, he has not fared well in the history of theological thought. Indeed, he has been dismissed as subsequently devoting his time "toward helping his parishioners adapt, guilt-free, to the affluence that urban living offered the successful."[83] That affluence necessarily evokes guilt is by no means proven. Moreover, it may well be that many in Beecher's audience found themselves in a position not unlike that of Charles Colby, simply scrambling to provide for their families. An earlier generation of ministers had been able to do little more than offer businessmen warnings about the dangers of the economic world in which they daily worked. But Beecher (whose own son had been caught up in the Canadian economic boom) helped his audience overcome the compartmentalization of religion and economic activity necessitated by the earlier ministerial critique of capitalist activity.[84] His conclusion to "Beauty and the Beast" offered the integrating principle which allowed religion, family, and the competitive entrepreneurial business world to be interconnected in the Late Victorian period. As Beecher presented it, divine love had become immanent in a man's love of and efforts on behalf of his family. No guilt need be felt, for the Christian person was now the natural person, the Christian life the natural life. Beecher's model of the Christian businessman was in essence an amalgam of the mottos that Charles and Hattie Colby had adopted early in their marriage. Her more static "faith, hope, charity" was in part a way to temper the potentially aggressive individualism of his "time, faith, energy." The bonds of family and the closely related understanding of God as the source of all love were, therefore, the glue uniting these two mutually dependent tropes.

This shift in religious emphasis, exemplified by Charles and Hattie Colby's experience, was not limited to American writers such as Beecher. It could be discerned even earlier in Britain, where Boyd Hilton and other historians have suggested that the evangelical or retributive view of economic activity had lost ground by the 1850s to a more optimistic expansionist, industrializing, and cosmopolitan vision. A theology centred on the substitutionary nature of the atonement, with its call for repentance of sin before a holy God, began to give way to an emphasis on the incarnation, drawing greater attention to God's love and immanence in the world.[85]

From the time of Charles Colby's conversion in 1858, religion had been incarnate in his everyday life, but only slowly did it begin to express itself in public terms. In the United States and in larger urban centres in British North America, the businessmen's revivals were already taking place in an established ecclesiastical context, but another decade passed before churches in regions such as Stanstead began to experience the impact of economic and religious change. During the intervening period, the major denominations in British North America began to consolidate, paying more attention to matters that were of importance to middle-class churchgoers, such as ministerial training, the construction of new and more ornate churches, and intellectual and cultural refinement generally. In short, the same volatile economic climate of the 1860s and 1870s that placed its imprint on the fortunes of the Colby family also laid the foundations on which the main Protestant denominations strengthened their presence and redefined the faith. It was during these years that Stanstead's Wesleyans joined forces to build a new church and that Charles and Hattie Colby made the decisive step of formally joining the Methodist denomination (developments that will be elaborated in chapter 6). As the critics feared, the second half of the nineteenth century in both Canada and the United States continued to be an economically volatile period. Worth noting, however, is that notwithstanding the concerns of Moses Colby and his contemporaries, the men who wheeled and dealed in the marketplace became the financial mainstays of the evangelical denominations precisely during this period. While neither Moses nor his grandson was remembered for active church involvement, this was not true for the middle generation: Charles Colby and his wife.[86]

In order for this to happen, religion as expressed in everyday life did become redefined. By not taking an antagonistic form, it mirrored culture in reassuring ways that gave meaning and purpose to life. Instead of censoring a fellow Methodist who had become insolvent, one admired his moral concern in seeking to provide for his family. Instead of a theology of the atonement that focused on personal sin and confession, a new emphasis on Christ's incarnation drew attention to God's great love, a love which was seen to pervade the culture and which made the family, not the cross, the symbol of redemption.[87] As a result, religion for Charles Colby and his family, as for many middle-class Victorians, was not something experienced in isolation. It was intimately interwoven with economic, social, and political concerns, which in turn bound families to larger networks of kinship and community. In fact, Protestant Christianity had become entirely natural.

CHAPTER FIVE

Nurture and Education: The Christian Home

In March 1871, when despite her husband's frantic mining efforts the fear of bankruptcy began to loom, Hattie reminded him, "The quiet way we live now brings us all very near to each other, and I have great comfort in mother & Charley and our good little girls. It never can be just home without you but it is a duty to make it and feel it as pleasant as we can."[1] Much has been written about the ways in which the Victorian home, presided over by the mother as the ministering angel of light, increasingly became a haven for businessmen caught up in the loneliness and frenetic activity of the commercial "outside world."[2] In this way, historians have seen it taking on a religious function, replacing the institutional church in a secularizing society by being a private site of Christian socialization and moral formation. As one historian has succinctly summarized the development, "The outer world had become destitute, but the home was still endowed with the old, positive values; it had not relinquished tested standards and Christian morals; it was the place of the old order; it was the sanctuary of traditional principles. It was separated from the outside world and better for it."[3]

On the surface, Hattie's comments to her husband fit well into this typology, as does his frequently reiterated desire to spend more time with his family. But the candour that surfaces at times in her letters, when referring to her shortness of temper and the long hours spent in housework, suggests that the lives of real mothers often failed to live up to the prescriptive literature. Similarly, the prototype of the hard-pressed businessman exiled to the amoral marketplace has come under significant revision as gender historians such as John Tosh have drawn attention to the value that middle-class Victorians placed on paternal domesticity.[4] As the old patriarchy of Moses Colby's day began to crumble and as the burden of providing a family livelihood shifted from land to the marketplace, fathers found that spending time with their children could be emotionally gratifying as well as giving them "the satisfaction of fulfilling a critical role of adult masculinity – the ability to feed, clothe and shelter children."[5] For Charles Colby, this found expression in a wide range of activities, from carrying out requests of his wife and daughters for purchases in the various urban centres to which his work took him, to assuring his children frequently by letter of his constant love, and, as they grew older, by taking them along when his travels allowed visits to distant relatives.[6]

For men as well as women, this domesticity was rooted in a livelihood derived from the marketplace. The form of patriarchy that Moses Colby had tried to ensure in his will by basing his family's security on land no longer worked for his sons. Having lost the land, they had to find other means to achieve economic security for their families. "Do not think I had no feeling at parting with our old home the walls of which I had reared under great difficulties and around and through which cluster so many associations of happiness and sorrow," Charles wrote to Hattie two days after the sale of the stone house. Valuable as a house might be to a middle-class family's self-worth, other less tangible but more enduring forms of security had to be found in a world in which fortunes could be lost as quickly as they were acquired. As Charles elaborated, "All the means which we are likely to have over and above the bare cost of living are needed to educate and fit out the children – and as they grow older they need more of our personal care."[7]

At the time, the children consisted of Abby age twelve, Jessie age ten, and Charles William who had just turned five. As Charles intimated in his letter, education and self-formation had taken on new importance in the family's straitened circumstances, calling for careful distribution of their financial resources. This held true not only for his sons (John would be born the following year) but also for his daughters, whose only dowry would be their family name and reputation, their physical attributes, and their ability to excel in the graces of a developing middle-class society. As it turned out, Abby did not marry until the age of twenty-eight and Jessie remained single. The two sons spent considerable time in postgraduate studies as preparation for careers in, respectively, university teaching and medicine. Paternal provision was therefore a lengthy process and fell entirely on the male head of the household – unlike the case with their parents and William's two daughters, all of whom worked briefly as schoolteachers to help with family finances.

Although practical in their purpose, education and formation were also, according to Victorian domesticity, to be shaped by love and order, two qualities that were notably absent in the unpredictable marketplace. Here religion, especially the domesticated heart religion of evangelical Protestantism, had much to offer, and historians have drawn attention to the close fit between evangelical family religion and the home as its most perfect location.[8] How this fit took place, however, is less well understood. Did religion turn the home into a "haven in a heartless world," into a surrogate church, as was argued above? Or – following the lead of research that has questioned the explanatory value of such dualisms as sacred and secular, material and spiritual, male and female, private and public – did religion in the home help the middle-class family adapt to the socio-economic order, and if so, what was its relationship to the institutional church?[9]

As this chapter will explore more fully, the Colbys, like many other Victorian families, did place very high expectations on the home. And as a businessman who in 1858 had experienced a "new birth," which led him to exchange his understanding of a righteous, awe-inspiring God for a loving Father, Charles Colby tried to work out its implications for domestic life, just as he did for the marketplace. Meanwhile Hattie, drawing on her childhood formation, her training as a teacher, and her literary tastes, found her own ways of making religion a meaningful element in the nurture of their children. And though at times – as when the family's material fortunes plummeted – she wrote appreciatively of their quiet home life, the home emerges in many of the family letters not as a retreat but as the place of integration, from which gender, school, church, community, and nation ultimately assumed their significance. This was also the intention of evangelical ministers and educators. But as laypeople, the Colbys found their own ways of integration, which were sometimes at variance with the official tenets of religion. Through such means, their story enters into a much larger narrative of social and religious change in which the symbolic universe of religion begins to merge with the family as a source of ultimate meaning.

Since the seventeenth century, when the first Colbys and Childs emigrated to the New World, Puritan teaching had underscored the importance of the home as a "nursery of virtue" in preparing children to take up their adult responsibilities in church and state. By law, the heads of the Colby and Child households in the Massachusetts Bay colony had been required to catechize their children and servants at least weekly and to instruct them in the Scriptures.[10] The subsequent separation of church and state and the shift to revivalism had the potential to undermine this tradition, and ministers unrelentingly continued to emphasize the importance of family religious instruction by the head of the household.[11] Rather than seeing the eternal safety of their offspring depending on the experience of a "new birth," or conversion, many clergy as well as laypeople such as Moses and Lemira Colby had chosen to uphold the old tradition of religious instruction in the home. This had been supported by the increasing prevalence of the Sunday school.[12] Even such revivalist denominations as Canada's Wesleyan Methodists, though equivocating on the need for the conversion of children raised in the faith, were beginning by the 1860s to emphasize the importance of childhood religious instruction.[13]

Roman Catholic priests in Quebec were equally zealous in pointing out to parents their duty to begin instructing their children in the truths of the Christian faith the moment the children's intelligence "awakened." Where Protestants relied on the Scriptures and a flood of tracts and moral publications, Roman Catholic parents had the *petit catéchisme*. About 15 per cent of this was devoted to the sacrament of penance, which was the chosen vehicle for training the child's conscience by seeking God's forgiveness through repentance and monthly confession of sin.[14] In their theological stance on infant depravity, Roman Catholics, despite their many differences from Protestantism, held to a view of the human condition that was significantly closer to the Puritan understanding than the view beginning to hold sway among many middle-class Protestants. The liberalizing shift in Protestant theology from an emphasis on the atonement to the incarnation affected not only a businessman's self-understanding but also had profound implications for the religious nurture which parents provided for their children.

Officially, in their baptismal liturgies, mainline Protestant denominations continued to uphold the view that every infant entered the world tainted with the sin of Adam and was thus in need of regeneration. In the Wesleyan Methodist liturgy, for example, which was followed when baptizing Charles and Hattie's children and which faithfully reflected its Anglican predecessor (derived in turn from the Roman Catholic form), the minister, while sprinkling water on the newborn infant, solemnly intoned, "All men are conceived and born in sin" and "None can enter into the kingdom of God, except he be regenerate and born anew of water and of the Holy Ghost."[15] How this rebirth was to take place, however, became a matter of theological controversy. Was it through the breaking of a child's will in order to experience a conversion by accepting God's forgiveness through the atonement, as the revivalists preached? Or could such a rebirth occur naturally and slowly, within the confines of a Christian home? In his highly influential book *Christian Nurture*, published in 1847, Horace Bushnell, Congregationalist minister in Hartford, Connecticut, argued that evangelical conversion, with its emphasis on sin, provided a negative model for the religious formation of the child and had every chance of turning the child away from religion as an adult. Instead, the child should be surrounded by loving parental influences from the time of its birth, enabling it to experience religion as part of the normal process of growth. Bushnell did not reject the belief in original sin, but his remedy placed a new emphasis on the role of parents to become positive agents of grace in the lives of their children.[16] Although its impact among mainline evangelicals was slow initially, in retrospect *Christian Nurture* has been seen as a critical turning point – away from revivalism and towards religious socialization. "In its entirety," historian Margaret Bendroth has succinctly summarized, "Bushnell's theology brought God closer to human reach, an emphasis that places him at the forefront of an emerging liberal strain within Protestant Christianity, emphasizing divine immanence in human reality."[17]

This theological shift did not occur in isolation. Stressing the "organic bonds" that linked families together spiritually, and extolling childhood as a time of intrinsic value, Bushnell's thought meshed well with the more romantic mood of the latter half of the nineteenth century. And at a time when the preoccupation of faculty psychology with the discipline of the mind (which Charles Colby had encountered at Dartmouth) had begun to give way to a more hopeful understanding whereby youthful minds were considered to be malleable as clay, it fitted equally well with the reforming efforts of American educators such as Horace Mann. Theology, the arts, and educational theory all worked together, therefore, to enhance the importance of environment, which included not only the family but also the school classroom and the surrounding community. If children were exposed to positive, benevolent influences, their characters were expected to flourish accordingly.[18]

These intellectual changes were congruent with the experience of educated middle-class families such as the Colbys, who found ways of accommodating the new with the old in everyday life.[19] In January 1858, for example (and thus predating his engagement and his conversion), Charles Colby, as an aspiring civic leader addressing the recently established Stanstead County Teachers' Association, approvingly noted that moral training was primarily inculcated by a disciplined conscience – a position that had been taken by his parents and his college educators.[20] At the same time, he left little doubt that the possibilities for moral training had greatly improved in his day as a result of new understandings of childhood: "Kindness, gentleness, persuasion operate among young minds in rendering them fitting receptacles of truth like the genial influences of vernal suns and showers and winds upon the face of nature." Thus, rather than resorting to anger, teachers were to rely on kindness in helping children move from their natural state of "instinct" to an openness to "moral and scientific truth."[21]

Hattie held similar views, as a result of the religious nurture given her by her father, her interest in romantic poetry, and no doubt some of her reading as a teacher. Improvements in communication through train travel, mail service, and increased choice in periodicals and newspapers ensured that even in such villages as Stanstead, people were kept abreast of developments in social and religious thought. Although there exists no record of Hattie reading Bushnell's *Christian Nurture*, there were many other like-minded treatises. One that she did read enthusiastically described marriage and family as the earthly foretaste of the bliss of heaven. Since "God we are told is love," the author asserted, "it is but reasonable to suppose that he would establish between his children a relation designed to inspire universal and eternal love."[22]

In the course of the couple's economic woes, Hattie reassured her husband that their love for one another constituted the one certainty in life.[23] Implicitly endowing the family with an absolute value formerly reserved only for religion, she reflected the belief of Bushnell, Beecher, and other liberal Protestant writers that the love of family members for one another was truly the nursery of religion. The love that Charles and Hattie expressed for their children was indeed unconditional, total, and exuberant. "Papa sends Charley three kisses – one on his two lips, each of his red cheeks and a Scotch kiss beside," wrote Charles to his daughter Jessie after she and Charley had been sent to Weybridge during the fatal illness of their baby sister, Alice.[24] Cleaning up after a birthday party for one of the children, Hattie commented to her husband, "Certainly nothing is wasted that tends to make home happy for children."[25]

Although Bushnell had argued the importance of environment as a redemptive force and thus had cleared the ground for romantic views of childhood innocence, he had not rejected the Calvinist view of total depravity. Where his peers were critical of such theological inconsistency, laypeople were less troubled. Among Hattie's papers, for instance, can be found a poem, written by a friend but preserved in her own handwriting, entitled "Little Hattie."[26] Intended as comfort for a mother who is about to lose an infant daughter (and thus possibly written in 1871 during Alice's terminal illness), the lines place the new emphasis on childhood innocence side by side with an older belief in the inscrutable ways of God described in the hymn that Lemira had sung at the funeral of her daughter Emily. The updated poem was a humanized (and feminized) confession, in which a loving Saviour welcomes the "gem ... borrowed from Paradise":

> Yea! thy cherished babe will slumber there
> On the holy Saviour's breast
> Perchance long years of woe mother
> May be spared thy little one
> For our Father sees *not* as we *see*,
> *His* will not *ours* be done.

Although in Methodist circles the theological debate about infant depravity continued to rage for another twenty years, long before that, middle-class women such as Hattie had already rewritten official doctrine in ways that reflected their own experience.[27]

On those occasions when experience pointed otherwise, however, and when childhood behaviour did not reflect a natural innocence, the old theological doctrine remained persuasive, even though the means of addressing its effects might change. When Jessie wrote home from Weybridge complaining about the behaviour of her five-year-old brother, their mother retorted, "I am quite aware of Charley's good and bad points and *because* we were not succeeding in eradicating his selfishness we wished to change the treatment, knowing the dangerous if not fatal disease inherited from Adam."[28] The disease might continue to be fatal, but in a world where love was God's essential attribute, punitive measures were no longer appropriate. Instead of breaking a child's will through physical punishment, the new views on the religious nurture of children promoted subtler forms of pedagogy, by which loving parents appealed to internal rather than external control.[29] Thus, rather than pointing out her children's faults, Hattie tried to shape their behaviour through what became known as "positive reinforcement." An 1865 printed sermon entitled *God's Covenant with Believing Mothers*, written by the well-known Congregationalist minister Edward Kirk, has been saved among her papers, and its conclusion epitomizes her own approach: "Teach by precept; teach from the Bible; teach by example. Let your words and your life say, 'Come my child, this is the way to God and heaven.' Seriously but cheerfully lead it to Jesus, and onward toward heaven. Beware of gloomy piety."[30]

Middle-class evangelical families had at their disposal a number of ways in which "gloomy piety" could be replaced by a religious nurture that was more in tune with the optimistic spirit of the age. Although the religious press continued to stress the role of the father when reminding readers of the importance of family devotions, the shift in responsibility for leadership from the father to the mother was part of a wide and well-documented pattern.[31] In the Colby household, since the father was often away and since Hattie had been a teacher as a young woman, it was the mother who took on the task of religious instruction. Early in her marriage, to mark Charles's infrequent periods at home, and reflecting the new interest in quality "family time," Hattie had instituted a special Sunday domestic ritual after the usual church and Sunday school attendance.[32] Known as "dressing and combing father's whiskers," the practice (and its much-regretted absence when he was away) surfaced regularly in family correspondence in the 1860s.[33] Juxtaposed with this family ritual, rich in its potential for physical intimacy, was an hour each Sunday afternoon when the children systematically read aloud to their mother a chapter of Scripture and committed to memory selected verses for Sunday school. Changed into "prayers and psalms" once the children had ceased attending Sunday school, the practice continued well into the 1890s, with their father becoming a more frequent participant after his retirement from political life.[34]

Sunday Bible reading in the home was a long-established Puritan tradition in children's lives, but in the nineteenth century the growing trade in inexpensively published books and Bibles offered a new context.[35] Gifts for the Colby children drew on the growing religious consumerism that by the nineteenth century was fuelling both Protestant and Roman Catholic piety.[36] To prudent parents, the educational purpose of religiously inspired children's gifts justified the monetary outlay.[37] When money was at its scarcest during the year of the bankruptcy, Hattie was able to justify the one-dollar purchase of a Noah's Ark, which delighted Charley during a visit to her friends, the Cowles. Birthday gifts for Jessie, who from an early age showed an interest in religion, included a gilt little Wesleyan hymnal from her uncle William, followed some years later by the gift of the Bible that had once belonged to her grandfather Moses.[38] Whether handed down or newly purchased, Bibles became coveted children's gifts in the religiously charged culture of the period; their contents were considered essential to furnishing a child's mind with a wealth of imagery, which later would inform an understanding of literature and poetry. Charles William, the eldest son, precociously already reading at age three, was given an illustrated copy of *Pilgrim's Progress* by his grandmother and a Bible by his mother on his sixth birthday. "He is pleased as can be with each gift, but regards the Bible, all his own, as most too good to be true," Hattie proudly informed her husband. "He returns to it again and again: reading now in the Old Testament and now in the New: finding alone the places he is familiar with."[39] Thanks to such encouragement, a child's mind became richly furnished with biblical imagery, some of which could be put to remarkable use. When, for example, his careless playing with matches set the barn on fire and he was faced with a rare paternal use of the switch, young Charley was able to deflect his well-deserved corporal punishment by pointedly comparing his situation to the New Testament martyr Stephen, thereby seeing his solicitous and largely female audience dissolve into laughter.[40]

The fact that none of the children required encouragement in reading can in large part be attributed to their mother's example. A favourite family pastime, reading aloud to one another was begun by the couple in the first months of their marriage, and it was transmitted to the children, the two eldest daughters taking it upon themselves to read to their brothers, and all four later taking turns to read to their grandmother in her final years. Since their father had ready access to the parliamentary library in Ottawa after his election in 1867, requests for books surfaced regularly in the family letters. These included a request from Hattie for *Moods* by Louisa May Alcott, *Robinson Crusoe* for Charley, and a biography of the evangelical hymn writer Frances Havergal, which in 1883 was read aloud to Lemira and other household members, including Rosalie, the Roman Catholic servant. By his own account Charles Williams was "a boyish bookworm." At seven he was deeply enamoured of Richard the Lionheart and soon developed an admiration for the novels of Sir Walter Scott. By the age of twelve he had completed the extensive *Commonplace Book of Shakespeare*, and extending beyond the Anglo-Saxon corpus he read the Koran to his grandmother.[41] Thanks to this steady fare of books, literary and biblical images fuelled the children's imagination, as well as providing subject matter for games such as charades and their own theatrical productions.

Poetry and song, like reading aloud, especially when presented from a mother's lips, were seen by educators as ideal ways of inculcating early childhood religious influences. Hearth, home, and song figured prominently in the nostalgia of the later Victorians, and among Hattie Colby's happiest experiences was an evening of singing around the piano when her brother Jack made an unexpected visit with his young son.[42] Jessie and Abby were both given piano lessons, and their mother took every opportunity to have them display their musical talent before admiring house guests. Such accomplishments, in tandem with the family's exposure to literature, refined the taste of both adults and children.

In a society that placed a high value on self-formation, these also became an essential component to religious nurture. Here, too, historians have pointed to the influence of Horace Bushnell who, in addition to his interest in child nurture, expressed strong views about the difference between what he called "fashion" and "taste." While fashion marked the values of an effete aristocracy, taste was a God-given quality through which people participated in God's creative work of beautifying the universe. Thus, the moral for middle-class evangelical Americans was, as historian Richard Bushman has pointed out, "to cultivate taste and avoid fashion."[43] Others have gone further, seeing in this "refinement" of religion a new secular understanding of the process of sanctification, a practical updated expression of Christian perfection – the "second blessing" (as Charles Colby called his 1858 experience of divine love). Given the social value placed on self-improvement, moral formation came to be seen as a religious duty, no longer the preserve of a small number of male intellectuals, as it had been in the eighteenth century, but a popular ideal available to all. Since the literary culture of the period was polite, evangelicalism began to take on accents of this broader culture, aided by the availability of inexpensive printed material and its own emphasis on individual transformation. The true Christian was not only someone whose sins were forgiven but was also a person who was refined, balanced, and had benefited from the increasingly available opportunities for self-development.[44]

The marriage between good taste and religion inevitably challenged some forms of evangelical expression, and in the Colby household not all of the didactic material available to a juvenile audience received approval. A travelling panorama of *Pilgrim's Progress*, for example, performed at the Stanstead town hall, to which Hattie took the children, left her profoundly disappointed. Its pictures seemed "fearful daubs," the angels' wings reminded her of "half-worn store wings from the goose," and "the pearly gates anything but what a fine faith sees."[45] In like manner, the moralistic children's literature that flooded the evangelical book market and was highly favoured by adults as gifts did not escape the criticism of the Colby children (and, no doubt, other juvenile readers). "Charley's book is beautifully illustrated," Hattie wrote in a letter to Abby, "but he doesn't care much about the story. It is written in the 'goody-goody' style. Jess began reading it aloud to me, but would say every other sentence 'now it's going to moralize.'"[46] This literary form of self-development, redolent of an earlier generation and still solemnly extolled in children's literature, resonated little with the lives of well-read middle-class youth.[47]

An aversion to moralization did not mean that children should not be exposed to moral influences. In fact, such influences were seen to lie at the heart of the new understanding of religion, whereby children were socialized into the faith rather than being brought to conversion as had been the practice a generation earlier. Since refinement was no longer a capitulation to fashion but was seen as a desirable characteristic, it was to be cultivated like other virtues, such as courage and kindness. And it was the task of the mother, as the central figure in family religious nurture, to impart to the next generation the importance of good manners and good taste. Manners and morals went together. "Charley waits upon me elegantly everywhere I go, and he did last night," Hattie informed her daughters when describing a recent Methodist social, whose "first rate" entertainment had included several duets, a violin solo, and sundry readings and declamations by Stanstead youth.[48]

This refinement assumed that religion was not simply a spiritual concern but also had an important material dimension. Nineteenth-century evangelical religion was a religion of the heart and could endure only if it remained sensitive to the changing material culture of its adherents.[49] "All this material scene is but the homestead, the play-ground, the workshop and schoolhouse, of human nature," one contemporary writer reminded his readers as he impressed upon them the value of childhood religious nurture.[50] In a Christianity that stressed the incarnation of God's love, high-toned poetry, literature, and tastefully manufactured religious commodities all became part of "the material scene" of family religion. Since religious beliefs are in large part transmitted through image and language, refinement may well have been more instrumental than the well-publicized theological disputes of the period in bringing about the shift in evangelical Protestantism from an emphasis on the atonement to the incarnation.[51]

Studies of the Victorian middle-class home, with a few notable exceptions, have focused on the nuclear family – a claustrophobic unit comprising father, mother, and children – and they have devoted little attention to the wider context of kinship and community.[52] However, as social workers and psychologists emphasize, these networks play an indispensable role in child formation.[53] Victorian educators were no less assiduous in reminding parents of the importance of surrounding children and youths with sound moral influences. "The family is not a unit, cast alone into space," Mrs Julia McNair Wright, author of *The Complete Home*, told her readers. "It is one of many which make up the grand sum-total of the race; in every department of life we touch on our fellows: we were born social animals, and we will exercise our social instincts."[54] Not every family had a resident grandmother and an assortment of cousins and family friends living with them for extended periods, as was the case with the Colbys. But nineteenth-century children, like their parents, were part of larger communal networks. Hattie and Charles Colby were therefore no less assiduous than Mrs Wright in ensuring that their children's social instincts were well shaped.

In their youth, the burden of moral formation had rested on the immediate family, on the church, and on whatever rudiments of a public/private system of education happened to be in place in the area. By the 1860s and 1870s, their children were able to benefit from a greatly widened circle, thanks to the large output of the religious presses, a host of material refinements, and an increase in voluntary societies such as Sunday schools and Bands of Hope directed at the young. As a result, decisions concerning formal education, the selection of marriage partners, and a career now took place in an environment permeated by religious and moral influences. Like the older custom of seeking patrons, the new emphasis on refining influences meant that young people needed to be part of a wide network of social interaction. Although not always borne out in practice, ministerial families were considered specially endowed to extend such refinement. "It is good to get a little out of the commonplace talk of weather, health and servants which makes up the staple of our talk usually, and hear governments and aristocracy and literature," Hattie appreciatively commented, with her daughters in mind, after a visit by the recently appointed Methodist minister and his wife.[55]

Leisure activities of a communal nature provided the children with opportunities for self-development unavailable a generation earlier. In a village such as Stanstead with a population of 575, rural and urbanized life frequently intersected, but for its children aged fourteen and under (who, notwithstanding a declining birthrate, in the 1871 census accounted for 56 per cent of the population), activities associated with rural life predominated.[56] The letters of the Colby children abound with such traditional events as sugaring and taffy pulling, buggy rides in the area, and bathing in the region's large cool lakes. As well, there were family and community picnics, fishing and hunting for the boys, visits to the homes of local residents, and a steady stream of children's parties. Depending on the age and gender of the guests, such gatherings included long-established games such as blind-man's buff, hide and go seek, and charades, but the children also had the opportunity to learn dancing and card playing, whist being a favourite.[57]

Lemira, Charles, and Hattie had grown up in the shadow of a middle-class society whose evangelical ministers had frowned on moral "dissipations" such as dancing and cards (though this had not prevented Hattie from enjoying a game of whist). By the 1870s, Stanstead claimed a number of prominent Universalists, and while Hattie tended to decline invitations from members of this more "worldly" religious denomination, the children mixed freely and attended one another's parties. For children, dancing consisted largely of hopping in step with the music, but by the time the two Colby daughters had reached their

Family picnics became a favourite way to reunite the Colbys and their American cousins, the Childs. Photo taken in 1910, during a visit by Sheridan Child, Hattie's nephew (CCM)

early teens and were ready to learn more formal dancing, they encountered no parental opposition to what had become a general peer practice in Stanstead.[58] Nor, as long as one was not a church member, was there much ministerial opposition.[59] In 1886, implicitly acknowledging the prevalence of dancing, the Methodist denomination prohibited members from taking part not only in the "buying, using, or selling" of liquor, but also in "the dance, gambling games, the theatre, the circus, and the race course."[60] Long before this effort to regulate the behaviour of the laity in an increasingly worldly society, Stanstead's ministers, like some of their colleagues elsewhere, had already quietly accepted for adherents such "refined" activities as dancing in homes and attending the theatre.[61] This was facilitated by the fact that Stanstead's Methodists, by then the most influential Protestant denomination in the region, usually managed to ensure that only ministers who shared their values were sent to them by the denominational stationing committee. There were evangelical families who resisted dancing, but in the eyes of the Colby children this made the socials they put on rather dull affairs.[62]

While there was some disagreement on the matter of dancing, this was not the case with "dry socials," which were the prevalent form of entertainment among all the region's Protestants, young as well as old.

Within the evangelical framework of individual moral responsibility, intemperance represented the greatest threat to family harmony and unity; but also, happily, it offered the greatest opportunity for social reform. The cold winters of the Eastern Townships and the availability of beer and rye whiskey (as the cheapest way of marketing hops and wheat in the early days) continued to be a formidable challenge to the temperance movement.[63] By the 1870s and 1880s, when the Colby children were reaching adolescence, support for Prohibition had become strong and widespread, especially among women, children, and civic leaders. Few families seemed to be immune from the ravages of alcohol – including, at one point, Stanstead's Anglican rector, whose wife's black eye and children's neglected state did not go unnoticed.[64] Closer to home, where the Colby children's own beloved Uncle William sometimes went on an extended spree, it was his wife Melvina who took forceful charge of the village's juvenile temperance organization, which was known as the Band of Hope. Whether they liked it or not, children were often harnessed into the good causes promoted by their parents. When, on her niece Mary's birthday, she had been requested to bring bread and butter to a parlour meeting which Melvina was holding to talk up the Band of Hope to the young guests, Hattie noted, tongue in cheek, "I hope Mary will like that form of celebration."[65] In Hattie's approach to nurture, this was putting Prohibition ahead of the children's need to enjoy themselves.

A major reason for juvenile involvement in Protestant voluntary societies was their role in character building and nation building.[66] In a world where evangelicals presented public duties as part of convivial pleasures and where a father's role in civic life was a way of impressing his children of his importance in the wider world, even the political picnics of the 1870s, with their endless speech making, were of interest.[67] "It was a treat," fifteen-year-old Jessie enthusiastically told her sister when describing twelve successive speeches (including two by her father, who "spoke *splendidly*") delivered one fine July day in 1877 when Sir John A. Macdonald and his entourage visited Stanstead.[68] No less political, but more tuned to juvenile participation, was the temperance movement. During a temperance picnic held at Derby, a visiting niece (also called Hattie) decided to join the Temperance Lodge, and as the older Hattie confided to Jessie, joining the lodge in this small American border community would enable young Hattie to enter into contact with "all the best portions" of its population.[69]

Membership in a voluntary society was only one way in which children could receive useful training and make helpful connections for later life. In a community where church-related activity was the dominant pastime, young people found many opportunities for volunteering. Charley, for example, collected money for foreign missions and, followed by his younger brother, pumped the church organ for Jessie.[70] The latter, after taking on the salaried position of church organist in 1881, two years later was able to emulate the adult practice of patronage and present a pulpit Bible to Stanstead's new Wesleyan Methodist Centenary Church upon its rebuilding after destruction by fire.[71] As her mother's health deteriorated and she became the manageress of the Colby household, Jessie took it upon herself to cook and deliver food to sick village friends, as well as leading her church's Sunday school class, the children's meetings, and the youth choir. In all these activities, the young people were simply following the example of lay service that pervaded adult society, encouraged by their mother's dictum on the importance of "being useful."

Sunday church services formed the focal point of this network of volunteer activity, as Sunday after Sunday the children sat in the family pew with their mother, and with their father when he was home.[72] Church services were a forum for a range of experiences, from representing the family on days when neither parent could attend, to seeing who was back after a prolonged absence or vacation, to being addressed as an adult in the Sunday sermon. Letters exchanged between the Colby children, like those of their elders, invariably made reference to the Sunday service and the sermon. "My dear sister, ... we all (but grandma) went to Church this morning. Mr. Hansford preached a splendid sermon," thirteen-year-old Abby solemnly informed her younger sister, who was taking part in a family exchange in Weybridge, Vermont.[73] That same Sunday evening, Abby and her cousin Hattie planned to attend the Episcopal church to witness the christening of the rector's baby. Such "promiscuous" church hopping was not unusual among village residents during the evening services, which were usually less of a family affair. Ministerial farewell sermons were generally preached at the evening service and always drew a flock of interested youngsters.[74]

The impact of sustained exposure to church services, on average two a Sunday, should not be minimized. In a lifespan of seventy-five years, an ardent churchgoer – whose critical faculties would have been sufficiently developed at age five to acquire some understanding of sermonic discourse – could count on hearing roughly seven thousand hour-length sermons.[75] Although much of what was said may have wafted past the listeners, in families where the Sunday sermon was regularly discussed, children could be among the most critical auditors. Such was the case in the Colby family. Reproving Jessie, who was visiting Weybridge, for openly criticizing the minister's preaching in front of her aunt and uncle, Hattie drew attention to "his forcible simplicity of style" and noted that his annoying habit of repeating himself arose simply "because he doesn't just preach for bright people, but for all."[76]

Although the Methodist ministers selected for Stanstead generally did "preach for bright people," there were a few exceptions. One of these, the Reverend S. Bond (who also happened to be the one minister who disapproved of the prevailing Methodist lifestyle) became the catalyst that eventually sent Abby into the Episcopal fold. One Sunday evening in 1884 she became so offended at "the Rev. Bond being all mixed up in his announcements" that she declared to her family that henceforth she would attend the Anglican service on Sunday evenings.[77] This was followed by the decision six months later to be confirmed in the Anglican Church.[78]

While her parents, upon assuring themselves of the sincerity of her decision, offered no objections, Abby was breaking with an earlier pattern in exercising individual choice in the matter of church membership. Her father had indeed changed his own church affiliation and moved from the Congregational faith of his parents to that of the Methodist faith of his wife, but only after a revival in 1867. By contrast, for Abby, denominational membership had become a matter of individual preference.[79] The decision was not an easy one and was accompanied by an assurance not to "make any violent break any time." Concern for family unity and the plight of a Methodist church recently destroyed by fire delayed her decision. When she finally made it, she softened it by announcing that she would reserve a seat in the Anglican church only for the evening services and would continue to play the piano for the Methodist Sunday school, in which both her mother and her sister were active.

In making a break with family custom even in a limited way, Abby reflected the growing propensity to seek a fit between the aesthetic dimension in religion and the needs of a prospering and educated middle class. For most Methodist young people, this need could be met by remaining within the denomination and playing a role in its gradual "refinement."[80] This was the position adopted by her siblings, at least for the time being (as an adult, her brother Charles followed her example). Since early childhood, Sunday school and choral singing, especially after they fell under Hattie's cultivating influence, formed part of the Colby children's weekly round of activity. While Sunday school and, on occasion, ministerial preaching might lose some of their lustre in the eyes of maturing young people, the latter were still encouraged to seek church membership. Denominational discourse continued to make reference to revivals, but by the 1870s reports of revivals were also underscoring with pride the youthfulness of the converts. Although the Colby children attended camp meetings during their summer visits in Weybridge, these were no longer seen as a means to bring respectable middle-class people into the church.[81] Nevertheless, joining a Methodist class and undertaking the responsibilities of membership remained an important ritual, and large numbers of Methodist young people, nurtured and socialized in the faith, routinely made the decision to enter the church in the company of their peers. "Jessie and Dexter and a lot of new ones are going to join the Church next Sunday, which is Communion," Hattie informed Abby in 1879.[82]

By the mid-1880s, the major Protestant denominations had become more concerned with attending to the social needs of young women and men by forming young people's societies.[83] Stanstead's Methodist Young People's Association, established in 1884, like many others, reflected the tastes and skills of its membership by offering such entertainment as piano duets, recitations, and related fundraising for church-related causes. These societies with their expected etiquette, like the ritualized entry of denominational youth into full church membership, were indicative of a pattern of carefully planned stages in religious socialization informed by commitment to family and community. In turn, young people who had been socialized into religion took it upon themselves, through church groups, to transmit to the next generation some of the influences that had shaped their own outlook.[84] Nineteen-year-old Jessie's efforts through study and activities at "children's meetings" evoked from her mother the approving comment: "Grown people are what they are and cannot (generally) be materially changed – but youth is plastic and can be moulded to good purpose."[85] In a variety of ways, therefore, the new ideals of Christian nurture were extended beyond the home to a younger generation and a wider community.

A central institution in this process of socialization was the school, and here parental influence also was strong. By 1865 the population of the area around Stanstead Plain had grown to 2,250, while that of the county had increased by 40 per cent in a single decade. A third generation of children was entering the school system which their grandparents had established sixty years earlier. The booming economy after the American Civil War that had fuelled the investment activity of Charles Colby and his peers offered the prospect of replacing the existing Stanstead Seminary with an entirely new building, which would allow boarding students and would extend the program to encompass a complete collegiate education. The self-interest of the second generation, whose children would benefit from the new school, ensured that a number of the more prominent citizens, including Charles Colby, were willing to take on the onerous and time-consuming task of board membership. Their children were approaching the end of their elementary schooling and now faced either the termination of their formal education or the prospect of leaving the Eastern Townships for further studies.

Conceived in 1865, but temporarily abandoned because of the economic reversal that followed, a plan to address this dilemma was resurrected in the winter of 1871–72. At the initiative of a number of Wesleyan ministers meeting in Sherbrooke, the decision was taken to establish a college in the Eastern Townships for the sake of "the moral progress of the country."[86] Charles Colby had been involved in the seminary since 1860, at first as a visitor and after 1862 as a trustee, a task he shared with an older generation of civic leaders.[87] As parents who placed a high value on education, he and his wife quickly became among the most enthusiastic supporters in persuading the Wesleyans to choose Stanstead as the site. In January 1874, fully furnished, thanks to the ladies of Stanstead and Derby Line's success at raising $800, Stanstead Wesleyan College was able to open its doors.

The two oldest Colby children, who had begun their schooling in the seminary, were among its first pupils, joining the non-boarding students, who formed the majority of the enrolment. Thanks to their home environment and family expectations, all four Colby children excelled at schoolwork. Some thought was given to turning the institution into a ladies' college, but it remained co-educational, offering a varied program in keeping with provincial standards: the common English course, the academic course, the teachers' preparatory course, the college preparatory course, the commercial course, the ladies' collegiate course, and fine arts.[88] In actual fact, because of financial constraints and staffing difficulties in the early years, there was much makeshift cobbling together of the courses, to the chagrin of the Colby girls at times.[89] More advanced students often found themselves at a disadvantage as they waited for the others to catch up. At age seventeen, just before graduation, Abby, whose patience was often short, was happy to drop out of school when given the enticing offer of travelling to Britain with friends and possibly even being presented at Buckingham Palace.[90] Jessie, who was the more scholarly of the two, availed herself of her superior skills in Latin to teach a class of younger students, thereby earning either a small stipend or the right to have her tuition waived. These were years when family finances were stretched, and even though tuition was only ten dollars per term, Jessie's decision to work for her tuition, along with the stipend she received for playing the church organ, helped her parents financially.[91]

Abby Lemira, Charles William, Jessie Maud, and John Child Colby, children of Charles and Hattie Colby, c 1885, a time of expanding opportunities for the three oldest (CCM)

In 1879, on graduating with an MLA (Mistress of Liberal Arts), as well as having completed the requirements of the Eastern Townships Conservatory of Music, Jessie ended her formal education. This decision was made partly because of the family's economic circumstances but also, it seems, by her own wishes.[92]

With her brothers there was no question that, as in their grandfather's and father's day, financial sacrifices would have to be made in order to further their education. The boys' upbringing and family tradition naturally inclined them towards the professions, and Charles William eventually selected a career as a historian and university professor while John, like his grandfather, chose to become a medical doctor in Stanstead. For each, though not without its challenges, the educational experience was markedly smoother than that of their male forebears, and it was significantly less frustrating than their sisters' experience at Stanstead College. As Charles William approached the end of his collegiate studies in 1884, the choice of a university became a frequent topic of family discussion. While the college by this time was able to offer the first two years of the BA at a cost far below that of the nearest Canadian university, McGill in Montreal, neither he nor his brother availed himself of the opportunity. One low-cost possibility was the military program available at Kingston College, which their father checked out for Charles William while on a visit to Kingston with his daughters. Proclaiming himself highly impressed in a letter home to his wife, he made explicit reference to the type of moral and religious environment he and Hattie were seeking for their son: "As to religious influence and instruction no institution unless a theological or Roman Catholic makes any provision for that – but religion is held in respect and inculcated. It is not subverted as is the case in many of the colleges which are in other respects among the best."[93]

By this date the best-known and oldest American colleges, including Charles's alma mater, Dartmouth, had departed significantly from their origins as church-founded institutions.[94] This was not the case yet in Canada, and in the end the Colbys selected Principal William Dawson's McGill University in Montreal as acceptable in every way for their elder son, a decision aided by the offer of several major scholarships. As in the past, family networks were important in meeting expenses, for by exchanging tutoring skills, Charles was able to make mutually advantageous boarding arrangements with a number of family friends, including a son of the French Protestant Amaron family, at whose pension in Berthier he and the female family members had stayed in the late 1870s. Family networks again proved their value in 1889, when after graduation from McGill, Charles William enrolled at Harvard for an MA and PH D. In his first year he was able to board at the home of Rufus Wendell, the same family with whom his mother had stayed during her last two years of schooling thirty-five years earlier. By 1892 when John, the youngest Colby, enrolled at McGill, the family's fortunes had begun to improve, but the earlier connections of family and friends (including now his brother Charles) again provided him with a congenial and hospitable university experience.[95]

In the 1880s the prospects of the two Colby daughters had been a subject of equal if not greater scrutiny and interest. In its calendar, Stanstead Wesleyan College placed an emphasis on decorum in the instruction of its female students, describing in some detail a course of conversational lectures intended "to make easy all the graces and proprieties of refined and accomplished womanhood."[96] The college's uneven early years had largely deprived Abby and Jessie of this element of the curriculum, but the deficiency had been addressed by their mother's refining influences. By 1879, when Jessie graduated from college, Hattie Colby felt reasonably assured that her two daughters could be trusted to make judicious choices in matters as disparate as selecting an appropriate piano piece for public performance and the ultimate choice – selecting their life's partners. The early 1880s were therefore a period of "coming out" for the two Colby daughters, a time when, despite cramped finances, they were able to travel and to see and be seen, though always within the safety of a family environment.

Abby's fragile health made her the first to embark on what became a female family tradition of travel in search of improved well-being. Accompanying her father on one of his western business trips in the spring of 1875, she spent some time with a great aunt's family in Chicago (where her mother, with an eye on the future, sent her a strong encouragement to "get a taste of dancing").[97] After a brief visit with her mother's brother Jack and his family in St Louis, Missouri, Abby stayed for over a year at the Apache, a large ranch in Colorado, where another uncle, Dan, and his wife Neva had taken up sheep farming.[98] Hattie, who joined Abby in January 1880, found herself two months later faced with the delicate task of having to deal with the first of three western suitors for her daughter's hand. Regretting profoundly her husband's absence when his advice was so needed, she confided in a letter home, "The fact is as you and I know, that Abby is qualified to adorn *any* position, the higher the better, and it would seem a sad waste, for her to accept anything or anybody who was second rate. With her good head and good heart and her very rare social qualities she is fairly entitled to the best."[99] Although Hattie noted the family background of the suitors, including denominational affiliation, for her husband's information, she did not have to make a decision. Abby, who agreed with her mother's assessment of her attributes, decided that "the best" was to be pursued not in the West but in the nation's capital, through the connections of her politician father. By the spring of 1881, therefore, she began to spend time in Ottawa, boarding with her father at the Russell Hotel, and after 1883 Jessie often accompanied her.[100] Marriage did not appear to be a priority for Jessie, but spending increasing amounts of time in Ottawa allowed her to perfect her musical training, and her letters home gave detailed accounts of the fun available in the national capital for two attractive young women of marriageable age.[101]

Their mother, at home in Stanstead, accompanied them vicariously, unable to restrain either her enthusiasm or her inclination to offer advice: "Isn't papa lovely and elegant at the parties tho? I knew you w'd find it out. I think he w'd have been willing to see you dance a few times (I would just –) after supper and not disappoint the partners on your list."[102] Abby, who as the more attractive and coquettish seems to have been especially receptive to her mother's coaching, received several proposals. Two of these were refused, one resulted in a brief but brilliant engagement to a Winnipeg business partner of her father, and a fourth, at first refused, ultimately led to marriage.[103] Concerned that her daughter's tempestuous road to engagement might have led to gossip in Ottawa and elsewhere, Hattie sought to reassure herself while giving her daughter a subtle reminder of the standard of true womanly behaviour: "I am thankful to know that in every instance, where you have declined 'the highest compliment,' it has been through no fault of yours that it was offered – on the contrary that it has been [offered] notwithstanding very guarded conduct on your part."[104]

The final choice, Somerset Aikins, was everything a mother could desire in a son-in-law. He was the second son of James Cox Aikins, a Conservative MP from Winnipeg, who had recently been appointed lieutenant governor of Manitoba and was an active Methodist.[105] Initially refused by Abby, the suitor had briefly transferred his affections to Jessie, but by the spring of 1887, upon the termination of Abby's earlier engagement, he was encouraged to make a second proposal. It was a time of major change in the lives of the Colby family. That May, thanks to improved material circumstances and the death of the previous owner of the stone house, Charles was able to buy back the family home, henceforth to be called Carrollcroft. In addition, his son Charles William graduated from McGill with first-class honours and the Shakespeare gold medal in English. The final thread was tied down when Somerset Aikins arrived in Stanstead, stayed nine days, proposed to Abby, and in the words of Jessie's journal, "went away happy."[106] The next few months, in anticipation of Abby's wedding on 13 October, saw furious activity around the stone house before the family reentered it in August. Since the bride was "not strong" and her mother was "very poorly," the decision was made to have a private wedding. As evidence of the extent to which a private family was also part of a larger public network, eight hundred invitations were sent out, but fortunately only two hundred guests were able to attend. Conducted in Stanstead's small Anglican church, it was followed by a reception at Carrollcroft, which reflected in every way that taste and refinement had become well-entrenched evangelical values.[107]

As evidenced by this highly acclaimed wedding, the expanding marketplace of the 1880s and Charles Colby's growing success therein had indeed brought a remarkable change in the opportunities for self-definition available to at least some young people, when compared with those of their parents and grandparents. To the earlier emphasis on self-control, self-development had been added as an important way for members of the middle class to advance in a commercial society shaped by expanding economic opportunity. In this process, polite culture which, as a number of historians have observed, had earlier begun to shape the values of "the middling sort" in Britain, had also begun to permeate the domestic life of middle-class evangelicals in North America.[108] Having proudly informed his mother that his costs in his first year at McGill had been significantly lower than those of his housemates, Charles William promptly received a stinging rebuke: "Never sponge in any way – but take your share in paying for treats. To be prudent is one thing and to be 'mean and small' is quite another. The family tradition & practice will warrant you in spending all you need to *spend*, and in doing it frankly like a man."[109] Although Charles and John Colby's financial circumstances as students remained cramped, the concept of character had undergone a sea change since the days when their father as a student at Dartmouth had carefully noted his expenses in order to assure his parents that he was making every possible economy.

By the 1880s, frugality, which had once been seen as a commendable character trait in the middle class, had come to be equated with unmanly behaviour. Liberality in spending was no longer a trait that evangelicals associated with a wasteful upper class; it had become the noblesse oblige of upper-middle-class Methodists. Thus, the wedding of the older Colby daughter, her elaborate trousseau, and her lifestyle as a newlywed member of a prominent Winnipeg Methodist family were far removed from the experience of her mother. The latter's wedding had been noteworthy only in its soberness, and as a young bride she had had to defer material purchases and remind her husband that "costliness is not happiness." Abby, through her marriage, and Jessie, in her single life as a companion to her parents, had entered a way of life reminiscent of that of late-eighteenth-century English gentlewomen, so well described by Amanda Vickery and others.[110]

By the latter part of the nineteenth century, Canadian Methodists as a group had become solidly middle class, respectable, and in many cases, "refined." Their world, including that of the Colbys in the 1880s, was not, however, the genteel world of Georgian England, of which Methodism's founder John Wesley had been critical. What separated the two were the economic and technological changes of the North American commercial and industrial marketplace, a widening democracy (for white males), and an educational process that affirmed the place of morality in character formation. Integrally connected, the three converged with evangelical religion in the Victorian period to form a distinctive Christian domesticity. In a world in which God was seen to be immanent, the Christian family became the site where self-improvement and religious nurture worked together to prepare a child for this life as well as for eternity. From the time of the Puritans to that of Moses Colby's generation, the family had been seen as "a little church" in which the child was taught the eternal truths of salvation. Evangelicals took a distinctive turn when they went further and added to their concern for salvation "the conviction that the particular arrangements of family life could have eternal consequences," to cite historian Margaret Bendroth.[111] It is not surprising, therefore, that some have seen the Victorian fascination with domestic religion as an important step in the gradual disenchantment of Western society"[112]

For late-nineteenth-century evangelicals, however, the equation was precisely the reverse: instead of the family replacing religion, religion sacralized the family. As Hattie Colby had reminded her husband during the nadir of their economic fortunes, in the unpredictable world of industrializing North America, family was the one constant that promised stability and security. Taken together, family and religious moral formation provided security, order, and practical assistance, and it is not surprising that both were seen to be of divine origin and universal. The well-documented academic fascination with philosophical idealism in the latter decades of the nineteenth century needs, therefore, to be understood as part of a much wider blurring of transcendence and immanence, which was already evident in the Victorian concept of the Christian family. Such a process turned particulars into universals and thus promised continuity to cherished institutions.[113] In the words of an 1865 publication, "As the family is a divine institution and a type of the church and of heaven it cannot be understood in its isolation from Christianity; it must involve Christian principles, duties and interests; and embrace in its educational functions, a preparation not only for the State, but also for the church."[114]

Universals, by their nature, can have a persuasive hold and explanatory power only if there are no competing alternatives. Victorian domestic religion was, therefore, not free-standing but was integrally dependent on the community and, by the end of the century, on the state. And while patriarchal authority may have given way to parental domesticity in the home, power and religion took on their own form outside its four walls, a matter to which we now turn.

CHAPTER SIX

Family, Community, and Religion

"It is 1 p.m. of the Corner Stone day, and a more unpropitious state of the elements is scarcely imaginable," Hattie Colby had informed her husband on 30 October 1866, the long-awaited day of the cornerstone laying for Stanstead's new Wesleyan Methodist Centenary Church. Four months pregnant, and having decided that her throat simply could not withstand the damp weather, Hattie had yielded to the "lack of strength" she had endured all morning and was staying at home, sending in her place the family carriage with the two little Colby girls, her younger brother Dan, and her recently widowed brother-in-law William White. While the family waited for the guest speaker, the Reverend John Carroll, to come downstairs, Hattie, in the warmth of her parlour, wrote to her husband describing the scene of Stanstead's inhabitants valiantly braving the pouring rain and heavy eastern winds as they passed her window on their way to the nearby site of the proposed church. Regretting that she would be unable to join the assembled female contingent, she confided to her husband, "You see we feel uncommonly patriotic about this ceremony because *Mrs.* Carlos has the honor of 'laying' the corner stone and it would be a pity if she were the only lady under the shed they have erected over the spot."[1] Equally regrettable was the inclement weather; the building committee, including Charles Colby, had gone to great pains to make this an unforgettable occasion. There had even been the thoughtful refining touch of bringing evergreens and shrubbery to the site "to give the place a rural appearance." As well, in view of this being the sesquicentenary of Methodism in the United States, and given Stanstead's historic ties with its neighbouring state, an invitation had been extended to the governor of Vermont.[2]

The carefully crafted ceremony, the invitation to Carroll (an elderly chronicler of "the heroic age of Methodism"), and the presence of the Colby children as representatives of the area's fourth generation were all signs that by 1866 religious and community life in Stanstead, as elsewhere in central Canada, had entered a new phase. The choice of Mary Ann Mills to lay the cornerstone and the presence of her husband, Carlos Pierce, and the Reverend W.R. Parker, the two other principal speakers, drew attention to another demographic shift – the increased education and wealth of many of the laity. Pierce, a member of one of the oldest families, was the principal benefactor of the new church and was one of a growing number of Methodists whose financial generosity was markedly enhancing the denomination's material presence. One expression of this accompanying shift to middle-class status was the increasing number of college-educated ministers – men such as Parker, Stanstead's recently appointed Wesleyan minister, who had been one of the first graduates of the denominational Victoria College. There, in the early 1850s, along with several other up-and-coming Methodist leaders, he had taken part in a large-scale college revival, whose sober, earnest style was becoming increasingly the norm in urban Methodism.[3]

At the same time, the decision to invite Carroll, a prolific writer on the denomination's early-nineteenth-century exuberant camp meetings and revivals, reflected the desire to remember the past even as the congregation moved into the visible improvements of the present. These ambiguities of the relationship between past and present, the denominational and the local, were further captured by the vast assortment of local, denominational, and patriotic memorabilia that filled the huge tin box to be inserted under the cornerstone. Most of its contents – ranging from a Bible, sundry denominational newspapers and histories, and a copy of the church deed, to photographs of board members and village notables – were of a suitably religious and civic nature, but the inclusion of an American and a Canadian five-cent coin was a reminder of the wealth which in the 1860s was driving new church construction and was visibly altering the townscape.[4]

Such changes in people's experience of space and time, brought on during this period by the burgeoning commercial and industrializing economy of the early 1860s, did not only affect the personal piety and family relationships discussed in the previous chapters. They also had a profound impact on communal relations. In his path-breaking work *Imagined Communities,* Benedict Anderson has offered insight into the ways in which, in the West, communities, which were once integrated by the sacred language of Latin and its ecclesiastical interpreters, were gradually fragmented, pluralized, and territorialized.[5] Other historians, focusing on the Victorian period, have described this fragmentation in terms of the loss of "temporal convoys" – those groups whose shared sense of cosmic time once enabled the individual and the family to see themselves as part of something larger and continuous.[6] Still others, speaking for nineteenth-century English-speaking Canada, have drawn attention to the hegemonic influence of Protestantism during this period.[7] "Imagined communities," "temporal convoys," and "cultural hegemony" are three ways of approaching the concern that informs this chapter – namely, how religious concepts, symbols, and practices helped reshape not only the identity of a family but also that of the local community by providing a shared sense of time and place that transcended individual differences. A growing number of studies using a variety of methodologies have explored both Protestantism and Roman Catholicism as a cultural force at the local level in nineteenth-century Canada; but for our purposes, the point of entry will again be the Colby family, focusing this time on their communal context in the 1860s and 1870s, and in particular on Stanstead's Methodist congregation, which Charles and Hattie formally joined in 1867.[8]

In the course of his visit to Stanstead, Carroll availed himself of the opportunity to make what he called a "flying visit" through the area, detailed in three instalments in the denominational paper, the *Christian Guardian*.[9] Although he was deeply impressed by the prosperity of the homes and farmland he had encountered and was pleased at the generous financial contributions that were pouring into denominational coffers, he was concerned that on some circuits Methodism had lost its earlier vitality, and he sadly concluded that "a revival is much needed throughout that region."[10] Nostalgic reminiscences of old-time Methodism and calls for revival were especially frequent that year because of the sesquicentenary of the Methodist Episcopal Church in the United States. In British North America as well, Methodists had begun, through the prolific pen of John Carroll and a number of other aging clerical writers, to craft their own memories of a fading past.[11]

In such accounts, nowhere had the sound of salvation rung more joyfully than in the camp and revival meetings of the early nineteenth century. Here, as people gathered together for several days in the open air under the silent trees or in rough meeting houses to participate in preaching, prayer, and song, faith had taken on a new dimension, and the participants had been able to return "spiritually refreshed" to their homes and places of work.[12] Historian Leigh Eric Schmidt reminds us that such gatherings formed part of a wider experience, whereby North Atlantic evangelicals were knit together into "communities with a shared, even universal, sense of time and eternity."[13] Held in many places in British North America, these lengthy revivals, like the autumn camp meetings, offered participants a different sense of time, as the profane took on a sacred dimension and as the daily demands of back-breaking toil and the loneliness of immigration were for a brief time transformed into a sense of community in which all were one in the spirit.

Outdoor camp meetings and exuberant revivals had not been part of the Eastern Townships experience, as they had in the Upper Canadian and Maritime heartlands of British North American Methodism. In Stanstead, where Methodists had settled from New England as early as 1804, ministers had initially been sent by the parent Methodist Episcopal Church, but with little continuity in funding and oversight. It was not until the early 1820s, when they came under the purview of Wesleyan ministers who were more adequately subsidized and supervised by their missionary society in Britain, that congregations here too began to experience a time of revival and see their numbers slowly begin to increase. The first revival, in 1826, brought in such a large number of converts that a new building was subsequently erected. A second, occurring in 1835 in the recently completed brick church, was remembered for its length and intensity as "the forty-days meeting," as night after night new believers and those renewing their commitment met to sing together, give witness to their joy of salvation, and profess their desire to live transformed lives.[14]

Where contemporary historians such as Carroll drew attention to the transformative impact of these early-nineteenth-century revivals, more recent studies have underscored the divisiveness, which often preceded as well as followed periods of revival. In the case of Stanstead's Methodists, Jack Little has observed that in the period 1821–52, friction between the more conservative Wesleyan ministers and their independently minded congregants of American birth surfaced regularly to undermine the benefits of revival.[15] Another and often related source of disunity, relegated largely to church minute books and memory but well known to Carroll's mid-nineteenth-century Methodist middle-class audience, was the cost of maintaining and extending the denomination's material fabric. Revivals such as that in Stanstead in 1826 did increase membership, thereby creating the need for a more commodious place of worship, but building projects could not be sustained by spiritual zeal only, and they made heavy demands on the skills and financial resources of lay members. Nor did the resulting boost in membership usually last or translate itself into the kind of steady funding required to make a congregation financially secure.

The work on the above-mentioned brick church, for example, which was begun in 1829 when the membership stood at two hundred, was undertaken with great enthusiasm and many promises of labour and payment, but it foundered as crops failed, and in its dragged-out completion it became a threat to congregational unity. Only the timely financial assistance of the area's two wealthy Methodists, Wilder Pierce and Ichabod Smith, saved the situation. With the building finally completed and a system of pew rents firmly in place, the achieved material security led to the 1835 revival, which in turn increased membership from 260 to 336.[16] Methodism, in Stanstead as elsewhere, relied heavily on its wealthy members to bail it out during times of financial crisis, as well as to offer their expertise in the planning of capital projects and the execution of normal church administration.[17]

Historians, then and now, have often overlooked the presence of these early capitalists, focusing instead on the denomination's eighteenth-century origins as a movement of the poor and dispossessed. To Charles Sellers, for example, in an important study of the market revolution in Jacksonian America, early-nineteenth-century Methodists figure as the defenders of a traditional, rural, democratic order of subsistence farming against a competitive and individualistic market economy. While not disputing that Methodism began as an egalitarian counter-culture in eighteenth-century England, extensive new research on the economic practices and political allegiances of Methodists in the antebellum United States has led to a more complex picture.[18] Rather than depicting Methodists first as anti-market and then having to explain the denomination's well-documented middle-class membership by mid-century, Richard Carwardine's revisionist reading has concluded, "The truth is that American Methodism experienced no searing conflicts over its churches' embourgeoisement because, although the early Methodists were poor, they were far from hostile to enterprise and the capitalist ethic."[19]

The same can be said of British North America, where already in the 1820s in Halifax, Nova Scotia, the denomination included a number of socially prominent and economically successful members.[20] Stanstead's Ichabod Smith and Wilder Pierce also saw no tension between their Methodist faith and the opportunities provided by commercial agriculture in the 1840s and 1850s. A native of New Hampshire, Smith had come to Stanstead Plain via Vermont in 1810, and having set up a lucrative store he invested his profits in mortgages, trying unsuccessfully with a number of other successful entrepreneurs to obtain a bank charter in 1831, and again in 1853. A man of considerable civic prominence, in addition to supporting the Wesleyan Methodist church, he was a local magistrate, a founder of the Stanstead Seminary, and for many years president of the Stanstead County Bible Society.[21] Wilder Pierce, also a native of New Hampshire and a Vermont resident, arrived around the same time, and after working briefly with Smith he set up his own store, and by 1837, at the age of forty-nine, he was able to retire as a "gentleman farmer." He devoted the remaining thirty years of his life to large-scale commercial farming in beef and grain and to a range of civic activities: as a magistrate, briefly as a Mason, as a board member of the Stanstead Seminary, and as a generous supporter and trustee of the Wesleyan Methodist church. According to a descendant, his tireless work in the church was motivated not so much by theology as by a practical understanding that saw "the church primarily as a social institution, a means for the betterment of society."[22]

Although they were the most affluent, Pierce and Smith were not alone, and the happy combination of a number of well-to-do members and adherents and a practical approach to religion ensured that by the end of the 1850s the Wesleyan Methodists had become the region's most self-confident and wealthy Protestant denomination.[23] Forty-day revivals had become events of a distant and hallowed past and were now the preserve of more radical evangelical groups such as the Free Will Baptists, the Millerites, and their successors the Evangelical, Christian, and Seventh-Day Adventists, with some of the latter group gathering annually in camp meetings until well into the twentieth century.[24] In the 1870s the four Colby children, as their parents and grandparents had done years earlier, listened with amusement to accounts of the group's extravagant behaviour, even though camp meetings of a more staid type were still part of their summer culture when they visited their mother's Methodist Episcopal family in rural Vermont.[25]

Nevertheless, early in 1867 revival did break out again among Stanstead's Methodists – in fact, soon after the laying of the cornerstone – but it was in an environment quite different from that remembered in the heroic literature. It brought not only their parents and a number of their social peers into active church membership, but it also inaugurated a period of stability and unity that stood in sharp contrast to the denomination's early-nineteenth-century history of divisiveness. By this time, the early Methodist benefactors had gone, Wilder Pierce having died in 1866 and Ichabod Smith the following year, but it was their example of putting material affluence to service in congregational and community life that defined the Methodism of the latter part of the century.

The roots of this religious change lay in the economic opportunities and increased travel made possible in the 1840s and 1850s by the canals and railroads and by the unification of Upper and Lower Canada. In the course of the 1850s the number of municipalities throughout the Canadas greatly increased: Stanstead Plain was incorporated in 1855, and by the end of the decade a system of municipal government was in place that would endure for a century. Through their control of roads, security, and public health and through the regulation of the retail trade, including the traffic of liquor, municipal governments had a much more immediate impact on daily life than colonial governments and, after 1867, the federal government.[26] For many people, especially children and women, communal life continued to be intensely local, involving the same people day in and day out. This was not the case, however, for families and single people, for whom the cost of farmland had become prohibitive and who moved west in search of a better livelihood.[27] Nor was it true for the sons of the area's substantial farmers, who in the course of the 1860s began to invest the profits of the earlier phase of commercial agriculture into mining, railways, and manufacturing.[28] First investing primarily regionally, by the 1880s they were extending their interests to the American and Canadian West and to Britain and Europe.[29] And while during these years there were times of financial hardship for individual families as well as on a communal scale, there were also many public signs of new prosperity in the form of church and civic buildings and flourishing voluntary societies.

The 1861 census offers a helpful entry into the community on the eve of socio-economic and religious change. In 1861 Stanstead Township, which included the three villages of Stanstead Plain, Rock Island, and Beebe, had a population of 4,847, making it the most populous seat of the county.[30] It was largely English speaking, and one-fifth of its population was still American-born and continued to comprise the area's wealthiest farmers and businessmen. Sherbrooke was by now the largest town in the Eastern Townships, but as Jean-Pierre Kesteman has noted generally of this period, what counted was not so much the size of a town's population as the services it offered the surrounding area.[31] With a population of 574 and approximately 100 dwellings, the village of Stanstead Plain in 1861 contained a surprising number of public buildings and businesses: a town hall, an academy and a schoolhouse, four churches, two hotels, four stores, two groceries, a druggist, a tailor, a silversmith, three blacksmiths, a carriage shop, two harness shops, a tin shop, a shoemaker, a bank agent, four physicians, six advocates, a registry office, a post office, a telegraph office, a custom house, and a masonic hall.[32] Occupying an area of three square miles, the village was stretched out along a single road, which was cut by a few short alleys. The road ran south through the smaller and more industrial Rock Island to the Vermont border town of Derby, the entry point for the early American settlers.[33]

Although by 1861 British immigration had eroded American numerical ascendancy, the early American presence could still be detected in the types of religious denominations. The Methodists, now consisting of Wesleyans and a very small group of New Connexion Methodists, were by far the largest denomination, constituting 34.6 per cent of the population, followed by the Roman Catholics at 14.3 per cent (of whom 82.5 per cent were anglophone), the Anglicans (usually referred to as Episcopals) at 8 per cent, the Congregationalists and Baptists, each at 12 per cent, the Millerites or Adventists at 9 per cent, and the Universalists at 6 per cent.[34] By this date, the meeting houses of the Baptists, Universalists, and Adventists were all located outside Stanstead Plain, but the four remaining denominations had built their churches within the village. As attested by the Colby correspondence, interaction in church attendance and fundraising was frequent among the various Protestant denominations.[35]

The favourable economic environment resulting from the American Civil War which had briefly improved the economic prospects of Charles Colby and others had also helped to enhance the public presence of the four main denominations. Already in 1850 the Roman Catholics had replaced their small church with a magnificent edifice in the centre of the village.[36] Six years later the Congregationalists, who in 1854 had experienced a schism, regrouped and commenced to renovate their building, and the following year the Episcopals laid the cornerstone for an attractive, modestly sized stone church.[37] The most visible signs of new affluence, however, issued from the Methodists, who in 1860 had built a commodious new parsonage, and four years later, concluding that their numbers had become too large for the brick chapel, began to build the large new church whose cornerstone ceremony was described at the beginning of this chapter.[38]

From the start, it became clear that the Methodist church project would be heavily dependent for its success on the newly invested wealth and American connections that were driving the economic development of the period. This time, it was not Wilder Pierce but two of his sons, first Carlos and later Charles, who became the major benefactors and rescued the project from financial disaster. In 1863, at the age of thirty-four, Carlos Pierce had retired from a short but lucrative career as a Boston merchant and had settled in Stanstead, purchasing one of the area's oldest and most prosperous farms.[39] Known for his financial generosity and public-spiritedness (which in 1864 led him to donate a giant white ox to Abraham Lincoln as his contribution to the North's war chest), he quickly became a major benefactor. Purchasing and offering the former racecourse to the agricultural society as a place for its annual fair, he also gave the district the state-of-the-art Crystal Lake Cemetery where, in the increasingly popular style of the period, mourners were able to remember the deceased in the tranquillity of a manicured rural setting.[40]

One of the greatest beneficiaries of his wealth was Stanstead's Wesleyan congregation. It was widely known that as a young man working in Boston, Carlos had, against all odds, been rescued when in 1848 the granite store in which he was employed had collapsed and buried him beneath its rubble – a perceived miracle, which continued to motivate him to works of charity.[41] In Boston, and after his return to Stanstead, his business concerns were frequently linked to those of Charles Colby, and even though Colby was still nominally Congregationalist, both men became heavily committed to fundraising for the new Wesleyan church. At the first meeting held to discuss the project, Carlos made a "firm offer" of US$5,000, which was followed at a respectable distance by Charles Colby's substantial pledge of $1,000 as the second-highest offer.[42] To be modelled on Boston's Tremont Methodist Church, which the Pierce family attended during their frequent residence in that city, the new Wesleyan Methodist Centenary Church, like its American counterpart, was intended to reflect the middle-class refinement of urban church life.[43]

In a community such as Stanstead where the well-to-do were scattered among several major denominations, this project could have been divisive if church fundraising had not been considered a civic as well as a denominational matter. As had earlier been the case with the Union Meeting House and the Wesleyan brick chapel, well-to-do donors were of a variety of denominational backgrounds but had shared business connections. Indeed, so little distinction was made between civic and ecclesiastical fundraising during this time of community euphoria that, one anxious evening in 1866, the fundraising campaign for the new church briefly faced the threat of derailment because of a spontaneous frenzy of subscriptions for a hotel in tandem with a proposed international fair. This was led by Carlos Pierce and Ozro Morrill, who as two of Charles Colby's business associates had taken the liberty in his absence of proposing a $500 subscription on his behalf. But to the great relief of the Wesleyan minister, the affair did not proceed any further.[44]

Communal enthusiasm, especially when based on economic aspiration rather than achievement, could easily reverse itself into strife when conditions deteriorated. With the failure in 1866 of oil companies whose prospects for quick profits had driven much of the speculation, it became imperative to find other means of funding the Methodist church project. The problem was made worse by the death of the denomination's two longtime benefactors and community patriarchs, Wilder Pierce and Ichabod Smith. Plans for the building were seriously beginning to founder when Carlos stepped in again. On top of his earlier contribution (which he had since supplemented with the donation of a building site adjacent to his farm and the offer of granite from the family quarry, at a reduced rate), he now promised an extra $2,500, on condition that church members and adherents collectively match his gifts. Ten days before the laying of the cornerstone, when the congregation held a special centenary collection for the new church, he further offered a bell tower in memory of his father, and his sister Martha presented an organ as a memorial to a recently deceased brother, George Pierce. When one considers that the special collection gathered only $29.37, it is clear that no church could have been built without the largesse of one or more wealthy donors. This may explain why – after a sermon on 1 Samuel 7:12 on the Sunday before the cornerstone was laid – the trustees hastily inscribed on the stone the biblical name Ebenezer. Summarizing the text "Thus far the Lord has helped us," the name was meant to be a sign of the congregation's faith that, somehow, a building which by then far outstripped their resources would be completed.[45]

The skills as well as the financial resources of businessmen were of direct benefit to church communities, especially at this time of escalating costs and financial reverses. The Toronto Methodist businessman John Macdonald, writing in the *Christian Guardian* in January 1867 on the matter of "Church Edifices," astutely noted the dangers involved in financing costly church buildings through pledges "at distant dates from parties who may become bankrupt or in some other way fail to pay their subscriptions."[46] To save "the rising generation" from such a legacy, Stanstead's Carlos Pierce put forward a more conservative approach. In keeping with the view of his father's generation, he expressly stipulated that the church was not to be occupied until it was debt-free.[47] This in no way dampened the escalating costs, however. "Why is it that we Architects have so much trouble in collecting our commissions on church work?" read the anguished letter accompanying a fourth notice of the $500 which the project's trustees owed his Boston firm.[48] When by December 1867 the debt had risen to $25,000, "notwithstanding the strictest economy," Carlos increased his donation yet again. Given the fact that many of the donors were business associates with varied denominational affiliation, this timely intervention managed to forestall any rupture in existing community relations. Charles Colby was not only a donor, but in December 1866 the subscribers to the new church elected him to the building committee; so now, along with his own financial worries, he found himself devoting increasing amounts of time to fundraising and planning.[49] It was not unusual for male adherents to involve themselves in church building projects, but his selection also reflected confidence on the part of the subscribers that he would be able to provide effective leadership.

It was in the midst of these financial worries and increased church involvement that in February 1867 revival again broke out among the Wesleyan Methodists. The first contingent of converts, though small (two men and eight women), brought in Charles Colby. Of this religious experience he left no written record as he had done in 1858. But that experience had been personal and spiritual, recentring his sense of God, self, and family, whereas this conversion was an expression of commitment to community and church. For the remainder of his life, as a politician and businessman he was closely identified with the Methodist cause in Stanstead. Thus, although the 1857–58 businessmen's revivals have been described as pivotal in making businessmen the mainstay of public Protestantism, it was not until the economic and building boom of the 1860s that Charles Colby began to take on a major public role in church life.[50]

Earlier revivals were remembered for their spiritual intensity and length, but the 1867 revival left no record other than the names of new members "on trial," which were recorded in the preacher's circuit membership register.[51] It is impossible, therefore, to know anything of its inner story, other than the fact that on 2 May eleven more men and forty-eight women were added to the membership roll. Among these was Hattie Colby, who in March had given birth to a son and for that reason may have delayed her entry until May. Included in this second group of converts were her friend Mary Pierce (Carlos's sister) and Benjamin Pomroy, one of her husband's business associates. The latter had been a member previously, but it was not uncommon for men to re-enter after a time of "backsliding."[52]

The mid-1860s were a time of extensive revival in the larger Wesleyan Methodist denomination.[53] Accounts, including a brief submission by Stanstead's minister, all underscored the important role played by consistent preaching and reliance on the "means of grace," which for Methodists consisted of love feasts and class meetings, as well as the usual Sunday church attendance and participation in the sacraments.[54] All sixty-nine converts were immediately enrolled in one of the congregation's five class meetings, Hattie and Charles being placed in the group that met on a Sunday evening in the minister's study. A traditional structure since the time of Wesley, the class meetings were intended to offer mutual spiritual counsel in a small group setting; but increasingly, in response to lay criticism, they had changed in urban centres into large classes devoted to Bible study. In Stanstead, where the class meeting had fallen into neglect, it was resurrected and now met on a quarterly basis in preparation for the love feast that preceded the communion service and was open only to members.[55]

Unlike Hattie and Charles, few of the area's well-to-do middle class had become Methodist members. Of the nineteen men and forty-nine women who accompanied the Colbys into membership, only Mary Pierce and Benjamin Pomroy belonged to Stanstead's social elite, and both had long-standing family ties with Methodism. In a pattern discernible elsewhere in an economically fragile society where male transiency was necessarily high, records show that the majority of the male converts soon moved away, leaving only six to be caught in the 1871 census. From a high of a hundred and fifty members during the 1867 revival, a year later church membership again stood at a hundred – only nine more than in the year preceding the revival and considerably less than during the revival years in the earlier part of the century.[56]

While evangelical ministers and their denominational leadership considered church membership to be the pulse of an active church, for lay people attendance and affiliation were much more significant in determining church expansion projects.[57] Stanstead's Congregationalists, for example – who, unlike the Methodists, kept a count of adherents as well as members – reported two hundred adherents and forty members in 1866. Although in 1868 the number of adherents briefly swelled to three hundred, membership stood at forty-five; and while each group included some individuals of substance, there was not enough collective wealth to emulate the Methodists in church building and civic display.[58]

In a society where church activities provided a major source of entertainment, a congregation's ability to mount impressive public events was a powerful statement. As a form of communal entertainment, the 1866 Wesleyan cornerstone ceremony paled beside the actual dedication of the church, which took place on Sunday, 26 September 1869. Notwithstanding a repeat of the inclement weather, and the fact that it would be another two years before the building was free of debt, some fifteen hundred people crowded into the pews, the aisles, and the adjoining lecture hall to hear the guest preacher, the Reverend Morley Punshon, president of the British Wesleyan Conference; and, in the evening, to hear the Reverend J.A.C. Chapman of Boston. Their eloquent sermons, each of which focused on the redemptive work of Christ, and the musical contributions of the choir led by a visiting Montreal organist, were but part of a larger extravaganza. Before the week was over, an exhausted population had heard Punshon's well-travelled lecture on Macaulay on Monday and, the following evening, a concert featuring the town's finest musicians. Then, on Wednesday, they received an unexpected lecture on "The Relations of Science, Art, and Literature to the Bible," since Punshon, through a change in travel plans, had an extra day at his disposal.[59]

Because of Stanstead's location as a border town on a major transportation artery, public lectures on inspirational and instructive topics were a regular feature, but few speakers could rival Morley Punshon. Unofficially in Canada on a family matter (namely, to circumvent the prohibition in his native country against marrying a deceased wife's sister), he became a sensation as a speaker at church dedications and fundraising events during his three-year stay in Canada as president of the Wesleyan Conference. With such lecture titles as "The Siege of Londonderry" and "Wilberforce," topics that highlighted English historical and social themes, he riveted the attention of Canadian Methodists and helped draw them into the British cultural orbit. His lectures, like the site of their delivery (the dedication of new church building in the gothic style), became important markers of Wesleyan Methodism's Canadian trajectory into middle-class refinement.[60]

As illustrated by Stanstead's Wesleyan church-building project and its attendant ceremonies, religion for lay people in the nineteenth century was shaped more by the dictates of voluntarism than by theological pronouncements from pulpits and college lecterns. This may be one reason why accounts of revivals in the later period focused not on the spiritual heat of preachers and converts but on more mundane matters such as the middle-class respectability of converts and on the preparatory role of disciplined church practice. Voluntarism called for unending lay involvement in both time and money, and thus socio-economic change affected religious institutions and practices more than had been the case when churches received state financial support. Along with the initial cost and planning of the imposing romanesque and gothic-style churches which began to proliferate in Canadian towns and villages in the 1860s and 1870s, there was the ongoing need to maintain their fabric and to pay a minister worthy to preside over Sunday services. All of this inevitably resulted in more socio-economic differentiation within a local congregation.[61]

One of the major agents of change in this direction was the system of pew rentals, which began to appear in the 1830s. Strongly resisted by the Congregationalists, who wished to maintain an egalitarian church community, they had become a standard source of revenue in the majority of Protestant denominations by the mid-1850s.[62] Initially, as in Stanstead's old Union Meeting House, pews had been sold outright, but like Henry VIII's sale of monastic lands in the sixteenth century, a one-time sale of church property removed all potential for further revenue. Once the trustees opted for pew rentals, they found themselves having to buy back pews from owners who were often loath to part with their property.[63] Since the Union Meeting House had been under Congregational authority, this problem had not plagued the Methodists when they began to build their first church in 1829. At that time it had been Marcus Child, a Reform member of the legislative assembly, who had drawn up the rules governing pew rental. Making allowance for payment in "wood, hay, grain or meat," the regulations ranked pews at from four to seven dollars annually, according to the value of their location, leaving four of the fifty pews "free."[64] Over the years, the annual rental fees had remained unchanged, even as the headache of collecting them increased.

The system of pew rentals put in place for the new Wesleyan Methodist Centenary Church in 1869 breathed the spirit of sound business sense, recognizing that the old method had been woefully inadequate in meeting the church's financial needs.[65] It also reflected the socio-economic changes of the intervening three decades. Quickly following the excitement of the Sunday opening of the new church came the allocation of pews the next day. At precisely 9 AM, in order to forestall any misunderstanding, Charles Colby, on behalf of the trustees, read (twice over) the carefully drawn-up regulations to the large crowd that had gathered. This time there were no free pews offered, except to the minister and to the principal donor, Carlos Pierce (who, as might be expected, graciously declined the honour). Of the ninety-eight pews, approximately half were rented at an annual rate of twenty dollars and the remainder at ten, with a few let at fifteen and five dollars. The fact that the more costly pews were clustered together in the centre, like the best seats in a theatre, sent a clear signal that social class had taken on added importance within the walls of the Methodist church – not unlike that in the Church of England, from which Methodists had strongly differentiated themselves only a half-century earlier. Added to this change was the introduction of a voluntary premium, which in the case of Carlos Pierce, "with his usual liberality," consisted of one hundred dollars, and this was followed by substantial sums from other prominent pew holders and local businessmen. At a time when pew rents still failed to cover the cost of running a church, the addition of premiums was intended to send an unequivocal appeal of noblesse oblige to the well-to-do to give financial support in keeping with their means.[66] In actual fact, expenses continued to exceed income, and thus congregations remained dependent on the generosity of their wealthier members and adherents. In the case of Stanstead's Methodists, the contributions of Carlos Pierce and, after his untimely death in 1870, that of his estate proved indispensable, for regular income consistently fell well below expenses. In 1874, with the retirement of the debt on the parsonage (which had been imposed to pay off the church mortgage more speedily), the trustees decided to supplement pew rents with the increasingly

Methodist Centenary Church, Stanstead, rebuilt after the 1883 fire (J.J. Parker Collection, CCM)

popular "envelope" system, but unpaid pew rents and subscriptions to the building fund remained on the books.[67]

In challenging economic times, insurance premiums, to which astute church trustees were beginning to direct scarce dollars, were an expression of pragmatic business sense that often paid great dividends. Given the nature of a wood heating system, accidents were bound to happen (for a while a person was even appointed to sleep in the new Methodist church because of fear of fire).[68] When in 1883 the long-dreaded disaster did occur and the church was totally gutted by fire, the trustees' foresight to take out an insurance policy paid off richly. While the new building did not, therefore, call for the same frenzied fundraising as its predecessor, its considerably grander scale meant that it did need a benefactor. Thus, after Carlos Pierce's death, his younger brother Charles Wilder Pierce, a man of equal piety, business acumen, and generosity, donned the mantle of benefactor – a task which in no way undermined his ongoing bequests to evangelical enterprises in his home city of Boston.[69]

The intrusion of male capitalist endeavour into religious life has been deplored by such historians as A. Gregory Schneider and Curtis Johnson, the latter making the derivative argument that the true source of a congregation's vitality lay not in its material fabric but in the piety of its female members.[70] More in keeping with the present study is the view advanced by David Hempton, that successive phases in congregational fundraising involved not only different approaches to Methodist operations (as illustrated here in the 1829 and 1867 pew rental systems) but also a different social experience of religion for those giving and receiving the money. In Stanstead, the latter can be seen both in the differences in the experience and reporting of revivals over a forty-year period and in the middle-class expectations that guided the building of the Wesleyan Methodist Centenary Church. "In religious organizations," Hempton insightfully concludes, "money is not simply a necessary and neutral commodity for getting things done but rather carries with it a symbolic revelation of the values for which it was collected."[71]

Charles Colby, for example, at a time when his financial resources were stretched to the tightest, offered a magnificent pledge of $1,000 to the building program of the local Methodist congregation with which his wife and children were affiliated.[72] Although it was never fully paid because of his subsequent insolvency, the pledge symbolized an amalgam of values. These included concern to provide fittingly for the religious socialization of a young family, the civic boosterism of the period, and its closely related heady economic climate as the local bourgeoisie shifted its resources from farming to mining and railway development. Thanks as well to the voluntary nature of church life, no building program could succeed without the investment of significant amounts of time, arguably a businessman's most valuable commodity. From the moment he was appointed to the church's building committee in 1866, and later as a trustee, Charles continued to wedge into his busy schedule formal and informal church-related meetings, often in his own home or the homes of fellow church officers, a number of whom were business associates and family friends. In such ways, the values guiding a layman's business dealings became inextricably connected to his family concerns.[73]

These values were not simply related to church life. They also found expression in educational enterprises such as the new Stanstead Wesleyan College. Charles was unable to offer much in the way of personal funds to this enterprise, but as a trustee he became heavily involved in writing its charter, setting up a curriculum committee, and indefatigably fundraising among his business associates.[74] When, during the depression of the mid-1870s, the initial plan to follow a corporate model and raise funds by selling shares foundered, the college and its debts were transferred, in 1876, to the control of the Methodist Church of Canada. The latter had recently been formed by the union of the Wesleyans with a number of smaller Methodist groups, a move that had forced the denomination to become more open to formal lay participation at the regional and national level. It was now actively promoting theological and higher education among its increasingly middle-class constituency, as well as safeguarding the next generation from religious skepticism and intellectual doubt.[75] The increased size and power heightened denominational identity. This was also the case in Stanstead, where the board of the college had originally included businessmen and professionals of non-Methodist affiliation, such as the local physician C.P. Cowles, who was a Congregationalist and a close friend of the Colby family, but under the new arrangement all laymen had to be Methodists. While this brought in several prominent laymen from outside, such as Edwin Chown of Kingston and Dougall Graham of Montreal, the majority remained linked to the economic network that was actively seeking to develop the resources of the St Francis district (and also played a part in Colby's successful election to the first dominion parliament).[76]

Aside from its educational offerings, the college opened up for Stanstead's female elite more genteel opportunities for participation in church life than the annual cleaning of the church and parsonage. As the wife of a college trustee, Hattie had been actively involved in the furnishing of the college, and when it was decided in 1887 to board only female students (though remaining co-ed), she became class leader to a group of female students, regularly inviting them to her home for tea and noting their physical and spiritual welfare in her family correspondence, including giving accounts of college revivals.[77] In a way very different from that of the male world of church and college finances, the social dimension of religion offered women a culture where the private and public intersected in a manner that strengthened their sense of self within a wider middle-class identity. As local businessmen increasingly found themselves on extended trips away from home, women took on a more prominent public function. As Hattie's letters illustrate, it was the women who ensured that the family was represented in the family pew, that collections for the minister's salary netted the requisite amount, and that messages concerning church meetings were relayed to their husbands. In this way, their activities were part of the restructuring of sacred time brought about by changes in the male business world.[78] For dignitaries travelling to Stanstead on official church business the Colby home became a regular billeting place. With her husband frequently away in Ottawa or on business ventures, Hattie was expected to provide hospitality on her own. Informing her daughter Jessie of the Methodist district meeting to be held in Stanstead in September 1872, she noted that the Ladies' Aid was to give a social at the vestry and that in all probability "we shall ... have clergy billeted here as usual."[79] Her comments, written soon after the family insolvency, the move to a smaller house, and the death of her infant daughter, offer insight into how voluntary activity had its own communal rhythms. These at times had to override private family concerns, because without such female contributions as billeting, cleaning, and fundraising, local and regional church structures could not be maintained. In 1867, when the $25,000 in debts incurred by the building committee threatened to lead to divisiveness, the Ladies' Sewing Circle raised $200 for the new Methodist church – a contribution that may seem modest, but by joining forces regardless of class, Stanstead's women kept together the community's social fabric.[80]

Although, during the week, Hattie's round of visiting revolved largely around members of her own social class, a more socially diverse group gathered together in church. The Colbys' practice during the first eight years of their marriage of attending the Methodist service each Sunday morning, the Congregationalist church in the afternoon, and, from time to time, an Anglican service in the late afternoon allowed them to interact with 75 per cent of Stanstead's population on a weekly basis. Thereafter, communal contact was maintained by attendance (especially by the Colby children) at such special Sunday events as an Anglican confirmation service, the Congregational preacher's farewell sermon, and even, on occasion, Roman Catholic vespers. Thus, church attendance and related Sunday activities functioned to maintain the community in the same way that Sunday rituals were intended to strengthen family identity in the home. The nondenominational nature of many religious social events, as well as the fluidity of church membership and attendance – a reality shared by a good number of the village's inhabitants – further ensured that, as in the home, there was very little separation between one's weekly "secular" activities and the "sacred" Sabbath.[81]

Within the community, as the state's census takers insisted, the family was the primary expression of identity. Church attendance reinforced one's identity as part of a family or drew attention to one's single status. People did not scatter themselves within the church sanctuary by age groups or friendships, but unfailingly were found in the same rented family pew. Empty spaces in a family pew stood out, and Sunday church was the time when Hattie Colby, sitting all too often alone with the children, invariably missed her husband.[82] The absence and reappearance of community members were a matter of general interest during the Sunday service – sufficiently noteworthy to receive commentary in Hattie's letters, with criticism that was always politely veiled. "Mr. and Mrs. Lawyer Johnson made their appearance in Church yesterday," she informed her husband in 1868, "and the gossips say her velvet sacque is quite beyond Mrs. Terrill's, which was beyond everything else."[83] Such observations did not only reflect a middle-class lifestyle; it was in the communal setting of church that a woman compared herself with her peers and felt most keenly any experience of inequality.[84]

Church attendance was supplemented by participation in voluntary societies, and even in a relatively small community there were many possibilities for a woman. There had been the Singing School in Hattie's early years in Stanstead, then the choir, the Ladies' Aid, the Ladies' Sewing Circle, the mid-week evening prayer meeting, Sunday school teaching, donation parties for ministers and their families, and temperance meetings. Most of these were church related, with fundraising activities in the form of a "moose supper" or an "oyster supper," which marked the seasons of the year as well as heightening the social occasion.[85] Where in earlier revivals women were depicted as experiencing a new, liberating self-confidence through conversion, in the middle-class world of church and voluntary associations, religion offered a more discreet form of valorization. Prayer meetings, circulating weekly in the homes of participants, were part of this changed social dimension of religion. "The Tuesday P.M. prayer meeting was here today and Mrs. Frost is now visiting mother. We had the doors open so she could hear the hymns," Hattie observed in 1883 as part of her ongoing report to Charles of the condition of his ailing mother.[86] As her last comment suggests, such meetings of laypeople, most of whom were women, offered meaningful and less formal opportunities than the Sunday sermon to strengthen one's own personal faith. For Hattie, who tended to look to her husband to help her in times of spiritual difficulty, such self-reliance was an important step in strengthening emotional independence. Comments such as "good prayer meeting" were frequent in her letters and were often linked specifically to the people who happened to be present at the time and whose comments and insights spoke to her own situation.[87]

Feminist historians have noted that women's involvement in voluntary activity did not only strengthen personal identity but also offered some a public forum through which they were able to exert a limited influence.[88] In Hattie's case, an interest in music frequently led to efforts to influence the choral music presented at the Sunday service. It was she who persuaded the choir director to select for Easter Sunday the "famous old Easter anthem (from Young's Night Thoughts)" in 1870.[89] Similarly, Sunday school teaching offered an opportunity to be "useful" and also to influence the taste of the younger generation, for instance, by asking her Sunday school class of college girls to her home for tea on Easter Monday.

"Polite culture and evangelical religion had much in common," Daniel Walker Howe has observed. "Together, politeness and evangelical moral reform helped reshape the world into a place where violent behaviour was discouraged and commercial relations between strangers would be facilitated."[90] It is little wonder, therefore, that both often appealed to the same people – those who aspired to middle-class identity but also those for whom this identity was a given, people like Hattie and Charles Colby and their peers, who worked to ensure that its values would be visibly present in the environment of their children. This included not only the classroom and the church sanctuary but also the material world which surrounded them as they walked to and from school, visited their friends, and decided how they would spend their free time.

In the course of such efforts, the construction of the community had gradually taken on a very different form from the pre-1860 days. The new church site, next to the parsonage, had been chosen expressly by Carlos Pierce, against the wishes of those opting for the location of the old brick church in the northern and older part of town. As a result, the social and cultural centre of the village began to shift. The college, the new church, and the parsonage, along with the Colby house and the homes of other prominent families such as the Pierces and their in-laws the Butters, were in the newer, southern section of the village.[91] The timely but unlawful influence of prominent Methodist laymen such as Charles Colby on the annual stationing committee ensured that ministerial appointments to Stanstead increasingly shared the interests of the congregation's leading lay families. Visits back and forth between ministers, their families, and laity occurred regularly and, in the case of the men, sometimes also included meetings in urban business centres such as Boston and Montreal.[92]

Intimacy can also, of course, "breed contempt," and a price paid by ministerial families for growing lay influence, longer settlement periods, and higher salaries was to have their lives laid open to the daily scrutiny of their congregation, in particular its female contingent. Problems within a minister's home, as well as conflicts within a congregation, invariably offered a threat to community unity in a world where people, regardless of denominational affiliation, "minded one

The village of Stanstead Plain, c 1905. View of Methodist Centenary Church, showing the village centre's shift to the south (J.J. Parker Collection, CCM)

another's business." When, for example, the "sisterhood" of the Methodist congregation concluded that their minister was spending insufficient time with his ailing wife, they began to withdraw the care they had up to that point unstintingly provided to the family.[93]

In short, strife continued to lurk beneath the surface of community life, but in this more genteel, polite middle-class world, its fangs had been clipped. As in the past, it was the growing power of the laity – now expressed in a form of religious consumerism – that endangered communal harmony. In 1878 the recently appointed minister at the Methodist Centenary Church,[94] the Reverend William Scott (father of future poet Duncan Campbell Scott), who was also chairman of the college board, sent an anguished letter to Charles Colby in Ottawa, stating that he was being asked to leave at the end of the church year in July as a result of complaints about his weak voice and his alleged neglect of pastoral work. Although Charles was indignant that "a fine honest old man" should receive such treatment, he was unable to have the decision reversed. But having great sympathy with Scott's concern that his wife, for the first time in her life, would have to live in a "poor parsonage," he did what he could to shore up the old man's self-esteem.

Just when this congregational rift was beginning to heal, however, a new crisis surfaced. That summer, when Charles was alone in Stanstead while his wife and daughters were in Berthier, he learned that at the instigation of the aggrieved Scott a few of his friends, including the Oddfellow Lodge, were planning a farewell party in the Methodist church. Rather than allowing the Oddfellows, who traditionally had little use for the culturally powerful Methodists, "to take possession of the Methodist church to abuse the Methodists in, while those who ought to be foremost would be conspicuous by their absence," Charles quickly worked to forestall another congregational rift. A well-tried blueprint was put into effect, and by the end of the next day, after contacting several of his fellow church trustees as well as a few of the minister's more militant antagonists, he had arranged for a proper social gathering under a "Committee of Entertainment" consisting of the congregation's leading women. A counterpart "Committee of Gentlemen" was to look after raising money for a gift and finding suitable testimonial speakers. Confiding to his wife that there had been "a peculiar lack of common sense on both sides of the question," Charles said he hoped that by arranging a proper farewell under the direction of the congregation's leading men and women he would, as he colourfully put it, "drag in by the tails the cats of both sides hoping to make harmony out of the caterwauling." The slighted Scott was prevailed upon to cooperate; the testimonials, which were intended "to please all parties and offend none," paid tribute to his temperance and college work and the esteem in which he was held; Charles arranged for ice cream and cake, and thanks to the generosity of the planners, "a respectable purse" was duly given to the departing couple.[95]

All of this took considerable time and effort by a man who, besides his regular business duties, was facing another federal election at the end of the summer. Electoral victories did not rest on the achievement of congregational unity, but such unity was nevertheless important. As the Scott incident illustrates, men such as Charles Colby who immersed themselves in church life had at their disposal a ready-made script for a familiar social event, which, if carefully followed, could leave intact a departing minister's self-esteem even as it covered over a congregation's divisive and hurtful behaviour. Community, as Colby had tried to show in the Scott affair, was not a matter of having one's needs as a religious consumer met but was a matter of shared moral behaviour. Courtesy and evangelical religion were close partners, each offering a vision of a world where people of different backgrounds and tastes found a common meeting ground. Even John Carroll, representative of an earlier, heroic era of Methodism, would have agreed. Describing in the *Christian Guardian* his 1866 visit to Stanstead, where he had been billeted at the Colby "mansion," he had taken care to shower praise on his "princely quarters" and his "American" hostess whom, he noted, with just a hint of preacherly condescension, "like most American ladies, I found able to converse on all general and public matters with any *gentleman* in the world."[96]

In an earlier era, itinerant preachers would have spoken glowingly of the piety of the "Mothers of Israel" who offered them lodging; but in the changed world of 1866, middle-class gentility had become the bridge between an aged circuit rider and his young hostess. Shared values are the basis of "imagined communities," Benedict Anderson reminds us. Moral values such as courtesy, financial generosity, and hard work – all of which were visibly put into practice by Stanstead's Wesleyan Methodists in the 1860s and 1870s – identify a group. There is a direct connection between morality and collective identity, sociologist Sonya Rose points out; a group defines what is moral by what we do and what we don't do.[97] The power to define moral behaviour is the result of a process of institutionalization, and thus, as illustrated in the symbolism of the church cornerstone ceremony, the moral message becomes part of a group heritage.

In their many-sided participation in church and voluntary societies, the Colby family, both young and old, was in its way reflecting a moral understanding of community, which implicitly was informed by the potentially divisive impact of industrializing capitalism. As the Congregationalists understood when they built the Old Union Meeting House in the early days of settlement, unity had a sacred dimension because it ensured the well-being and continuity of a community which otherwise might fragment through warring factions and private disputes. When social divisions deepened under the impact of economic change, and when religious voluntarism encouraged denominational diversity, new ways of reasserting unity had to be found. Sunday church attendance, participation in voluntary societies, the ceremonies connected with the laying of a church cornerstone and the dedication of a new church, teas and other social fundraising events can all be seen as forms of ritualized behaviour directed to this purpose. In the accompanying official rhetoric, the emphasis was on faith, on God's blessings, on hope for the future, and on shared values and hopes.[98] In such ways, people of different temperaments and social backgrounds asserted to themselves and to the outside world that they were part of something greater, part of an apparently seamless web of family, religion, and community.

However, as Charles Colby discovered as a politician in Ottawa, translating evangelical ideals of moral community and moral leadership from the local sphere to the national was a formidable challenge. Here, religious divisions were not a matter of taste or preference, as they were among Protestants, but involved profound differences in theology and practice, which in turn reflected a very different ordering of time and space. Nevertheless, as will be illustrated in the next chapter, which details Colby's experience as a federal politician, social harmony and moral order were not simply ideals for family and community life. Their influence, though often contested, placed a strong imprint on the newly formed Canadian federation.

CHAPTER SEVEN

Protestants, Social Harmony, and Moral Order

"I must confess that not the least among the motives which involved me to seek the present position was a desire that your friends should not feel that you had thrown yourself away. If the position is well-sustained we may view whatever sacrifice it involves as so much done for our children," Colby confided to his wife in the fall of 1867, shortly after his successful election to the first dominion parliament.[1] At a time when his economic fortunes had taken a nosedive, political office offered an opportunity to move in a new direction, one that built on the brief political career of his father, on his own popularity as a native son and articulate lawyer in Stanstead County, and on his extensive business contacts. Remuneration for a member of the first federal parliament at six hundred dollars per session and a travel allowance of ten cents a mile offered no great financial inducement, but the position, if "well sustained," was prestigious and thus would add to the educational patrimony which the couple hoped to pass on to their children.[2] Prevailed upon regularly since 1858 to seek election, Charles had finally agreed and in the summer of 1867 had let his name stand as an Independent.

Concern for his family's material well-being was inextricably connected to restoring the prosperity of the Stanstead region. As he and the county's electorate well knew, in the economically hard times following the cessation of the American Civil War, the region's economic fate was bound up less with New England than with the new Canadian confederation, western expansion, and Great Britain. Therefore it had been imperative to send to Ottawa a well-informed and articulate spokesman who was capable of seizing and encouraging the economic opportunities opened up by Confederation, including the prospect of western expansion. This Charles Colby did diligently until his defeat in 1891, even though he was often distracted by his own business concerns.

Economic concerns had been his primary motivation in seeking political office, but at an early date he was confronted with the practical impossibility of separating these from moral and religious concerns. While evangelical ideals of economic development, moral order, and social harmony might shape a local community such as Stanstead, to translate these to the new Canadian nation represented a formidable challenge. The economic and communication changes brought about by the new political arrangement inevitably affected social relations. Religious denominations – which now had a national presence that had been strengthened for the Methodists and Presbyterians by a series of internal unions – began to call for new forms of regulation through government legislation.[3] The difficulty of setting aside the Sabbath as a day of universal rest, for example, became an obvious concern as the demands of the new transportation system of canals and railways increased. Similarly, the continuing high incidence of intemperance led to calls for collective measures rather than reliance on individual voluntary abstinence.[4] Divorce bills, now transferred to the federal legislature, were another area where the moral dimension of family life became a matter of political scrutiny and debate.

Parliamentary debate took place in a religiously divided country in which evangelical Protestants and ultramontane Roman Catholics were increasingly militant. As Michael Ignatieff has noted, one of the novel features of the nineteenth-century Canadian federation was its validation of group minority rights within a liberal economic and political framework.[5] These minority rights, specifically in the area of education, were expressed not in linguistic but in religious terms of "Protestant" and "Roman Catholic." Religiopolitical issues, whether of moral reform, divorce, or minority rights, were therefore fraught with tensions and ambiguities for parliamentarians. Elected primarily to advance the economic interests of their constituents, the MPs were generally on their own, with little theological and spiritual guidance, to negotiate the minefields that lay in waiting in the religiously charged culture of post-Confederation Canada.[6] What they learned was the practical impossibility of compartmentalizing religion from politics and economics.

All of this Charles Colby experienced first-hand. Continually representing his riding from 1867 until his defeat in 1891, he had an unusually lengthy parliamentary career, and in his many letters home and public addresses he expressed his views on most of the issues that confronted Canada's legislators during the nation's first three decades. In the name of brevity, however, and to keep a tight focus on the major themes of this study, I propose to focus on just three issues in his political career: economic policy, moral reform, and minority rights. Although ostensibly different, each illustrates how family, economic matters, and moral concerns remained interwoven and helped shape a vision of social harmony, which, as a politician, he assiduously promoted but which also created tensions that ultimately led to his defeat. Economic growth, a desire for social harmony, and a propensity towards moral reform do not constitute the total evangelical agenda or creed. But taken together, they are central to understanding the ways in which religion, politics, and economics intersected in public life in Ottawa in the years 1867–91 to shape the specifically Anglo-Protestant perceptions of space and time that have been outlined in the preceding chapters.

PARTY SPIRIT, ECONOMIC POLICY, AND SOCIAL HARMONY

Evangelical leaders differed in their beliefs and in their political views, but the one matter on which they expressed complete agreement was their abhorrence of any form of "sectarianism" or "factionalism." Denunciations of "party spirit" and the corruption of patronage were a staple of evangelical discourse in the public sphere, in Canada as well as in the United States. There was good reason for this: in politics, principle did not always translate into practice.[7] Patronage and its attendant social divisiveness had surfaced regularly in Stanstead's elections in the pre-Confederation period, causing the county's electorate to shift its support back and forth between Reform and Tory, often turning members within a religious congregation against one another.

A member of a younger and, in his eyes, more enlightened generation, Charles Colby had seen how the promotion of party and denominational loyalties had undermined social harmony in his father's time and later.[8] Presenting himself in 1867 as at heart a liberal-conservative, he emphasized that he was running as an Independent candidate on the principle that a member of parliament represented all constituents, regardless of political affiliation, race, or religion.[9] Unfortunately, his assertion soon flew in the face of reality, and the 1867 election campaign in Stanstead County, which had promised to be an uncontested event, suddenly turned into a heated battle.[10] Not only did Colby find himself unexpectedly opposed by the candidacy of a fellow businessman, Albert Knight, but factionalism reared its head within the very congregation which he and Hattie had only recently formally

Charles Carroll Colby, 1867, about to begin his career as an MP (CCM)

joined and on whose church-building program he was spending considerable time. The opposition was led by three elderly Methodist ministers and supported by the congregation's benefactor, Carlos Pierce, who attempted to convince constituents that under the new arrangement of Confederation, it was Knight who would best safeguard the interests of the region's Anglo-Protestants.[11] But Colby was staunchly supported by the *Stanstead Journal*, and forcefully directing his appeal to the "independent and unpurchasable yeomanry of the County," he responded with moral indignation at the resurgence of electoral "corruption" and "party spirit." Emphasizing the region's promising economic future under Confederation, he won the ensuing election by a slim majority of 198.

Thanks to the survival of Stanstead County's 1867 federal poll lists and with the help of census records, it is possible to discover how precisely the pre-election factionalism among Stanstead's Methodists actually translated itself into votes. Only 64 per cent of the voters could be located in the 1871 census, but of these, 62 per cent of those listed as Wesleyan Methodist cast their votes for Colby, which leads one to conclude that most voted not out of religious affiliation but out of economic concern.[12] When in his electoral campaign Colby had appealed to the "independent and unpurchaseable yeomanry," he had done more than proclaim his desire to clean up electoral politics. He had in fact targeted that segment of the population whose roots were longest and most firmly planted in the riding. As Colby knew first-hand from his own legal and business contacts, by the 1860s a good number of Stanstead's farmers had become substantial entrepreneurs involved in major economic diversification that included mining, railway, and industrial investment. In the 1867 election, those who listed their occupation as "farmer" formed the largest single occupational sector of the voting population (384 of 792), and the majority (62 per cent) voted for Colby.[13]

Elected to represent the economic interests of his region, Charles Colby, even when he joined the Conservative banner in 1872, continued to emphasize that in his view a member of parliament represented all constituents, regardless of political affiliation, race, or religion. His resistance to party spirit and factionalism agreed with the official pronouncements of evangelical clergy (regardless of their actual activity), but more probably, in Colby's case, it reflected the stance of his political mentor, the American Whig leader Daniel Webster. Like Webster, who had had such an influence on him years earlier when he was a student at Dartmouth (and whose portrait continued to be prominently displayed in his home office), Colby saw himself as both economically progressive and socially conservative.[14] Thus, overlooking the inherent tension in Whig thought that had been so starkly exposed by the sectional divisions over slavery and by the American Civil War, Colby insisted in 1867 that traditional communal moral values were to be the bedrock of the new country. At the same time, he promised to advance his riding's economic interests, and he maintained these two tenets throughout his lengthy tenure in office. That he was acclaimed as the county's candidate in the 1872 and 1874 elections, and won by sizable majorities in the others (764 in 1878, 295 in 1882, and 434 in 1887) would lead one to assume that his values and economic policies were generally shared by his constituents.[15] Concerned to restore social harmony, he quickly mended relations with the local Methodist opposition, and thereafter, as one of a small group of denominational politicians in Ottawa, he was occasionally able to advance the cause of his co-religionists, despite his aversion to patronage.[16]

Elected to represent the material interests of his region, he preferred to direct his efforts to economic policy and legislation, and on these he became an acknowledged expert. Hesitant to take the floor at first, and critical of members who spoke often and at length with little preparation, he in time won for himself the reputation of being a careful, distinct, and thoughtful speaker, one whose views were worth listening to.[17] His first address to the House of Commons, in 1868, dealt with a matter of particular concern to his constituent farmers – a request for a five-cents-a-pound duty on American hops, which were undercutting Canadian prices. A little later, in 1872, fuelled by his own experience of insolvency but also by the effect which the early 1870s economic depression was having on many small businessmen and farmers, he devoted much energy to shepherding through the Commons an insolvency bill, which was intended to terminate the generally unsatisfactory insolvency legislation of 1869.[18] In March 1876, during the debate on the Liberal government's supply bill, he spoke forcefully on the need for more comprehensive tariff protection. In the course of this well-researched address, he alluded specifically to a proposal advanced by Daniel Webster and the American Whigs, advocating a policy of protection for manufacturers, agricultural products, woollen fabrics, and wool, and he approvingly noted the way in which the subsequent Morrill tariff had benefited the New England economy.[19] Two years later, in 1878, he was one of the foremost speakers in favour of John A Macdonald's proposed amendment to the Liberal budget calling for a "re-adjustment of the Dominion Tariff" in order to protect Canadian mining, agricultural, and manufacturing interests.[20] The amendment failed, but in the election held that summer, Stanstead's voters returned Colby with a large majority; and the following year, with the Conservatives firmly back in power, the tariff changes, known as the National Policy, were successfully passed.

Colby's concern to protect Canadian businesses and markets reflected the changes taking place in the Eastern Townships as its trade began to move away from its earlier southern axis of Boston and New York City towards Montreal, the West, and Britain.[21] Although his support was motivated by the desire to advance his region's economic interests, he saw tariff protection as a means of encouraging a harmonious society. This conviction he underscored with an allusion to Daniel Webster and a nostalgic reconstruction of a New England economy of integrated town and country markets, small businesses, and close employer-employee relationships. Like Webster and the American Whigs generally, he welcomed economic change while at the same time seeking to curb the attendant social changes by appealing to traditional moral values.²² Thus, on 1 July 1876, in an address with the evocative title "Canada Our Home," Colby emphasized to his constituents the moral ideals that had formed a steady refrain since the time of his first election campaign. Having explained how the postwar American recovery and high tariffs had led to the region's current economic malaise, and how too many men had been caught up in the rush to become rich quickly during the booming Civil War years, he exhorted his audience to find contentment in building a permanent home on Canadian soil: "Let us be content with the goodly places in which Providence has cast our lives and so improve them that our children shall not desire to stray from the homes of their fathers." In his view, the proposed change in Canadian economic policy was ultimately a matter of moral nationalism.²³

Colby was not alone in trying to wed tariff protection to social stability. As one Canadian economic historian has concluded, in its efforts to construct a nationality that would avoid the social conflicts wracking industrial Great Britain, the National Policy can be seen from an ideological perspective as an "intellectual bridge to the large-scale industrialization and integrated markets of an emerging mass society."²⁴ Here, economics and religion found a point of contact. When it came to free trade or protection, historian Richard Carwardine has noted that in the United States there was often no clear congruence between the theological outlook of evangelicals and their attitude to economic matters. Where Colby favoured protection, the Liberal leader Alexander Mackenzie considered tariffs to be a means to build up the fortunes "of a few manufacturers, and in the course of a few years, [ruin] ... even those manufacturers, after they have accomplished the ruin of the working classes."²⁵ What evangelicals did have in common, as Carwardine points out, was that "in practice their economic attitudes were not freestanding: they were sustained by a moral vision whose sharp focus was derived from religious belief."²⁶ Thus, where Colby's motivating concern in tariff protection was the country's ability to create wealth in ways that protected a wide range of interest groups, Mackenzie's support of free trade emphasized the importance of the equitable distribution of wealth. What both visions shared was the desire to maintain an organic society, protected from the divisiveness of an unfettered individualistic capitalism. In a wider sense, this same concern also informed evangelical criticism of the evils of sectarianism, factionalism, and party spirit. In 1878, as Colby expressed his strong support for Macdonald's "amendment to the tariff," he had argued that this was not an issue that should be decided through partisan politics, for "we have at last a great question, an economical question, a question upon the solution of which will largely depend the future of the Dominion."[27] In the evangelical vision, social harmony and "the economical question" were inseparable.

EVANGELICALS AND MORAL REFORM

Free trade and the National Policy, with their promise to stimulate economic growth (though presented as part of a larger moral vision) carried with them the erosion of long-standing communal ways and moral standards. National transportation systems of canals and railways, for example, moved people and goods more quickly and efficiently, but at the cost of being in operation seven days a week, thereby undermining the hallowed evangelical Sabbath. Similarly, efforts to control intemperance were difficult for a population on the move, when individuals could escape church and community surveillance in the anonymity of urban centres or the unsettled West. Marriage ties also became more vulnerable in a mobile society in which people kept less of a close eye on one another's family arrangements.

Earlier chapters have drawn attention to the ways in which religion was part of a larger pattern, in which middle-class evangelicals like Colby sought to support economic growth and at the same time tried to control its social impact on family and community life. Parliamentary debates on marriage, Sabbatarianism, and Prohibition, their discussion in Charles Colby's correspondence with his family, and his own practice as a member of parliament all underscore that in the new federal government legislators continued to link socio-economic change with moral reform. Profiting from economic growth, the evangelical middle class has often been depicted as obsessed with social control in its support of moral reform. Such an interpretation, according to American historian Daniel Walker Howe, is only partly persuasive. Control was not an end in itself, he points out, but was part of a broader attitude, informed by the capitalist rationality of the marketplace and expressed in self-help, discipline, and a voluntary pursuit of order, dignity, and decency: "The evangelical emphasis on conscious, voluntary decision and action represents a conjunction of Christianity with modernity. The new personal identity the evangelical attained was both follower of Christ *and* rational, autonomous individual – paradoxical as that may seem to historians today."[28] What Howe has concluded for antebellum Americans may help us understand the attitudes to moral and social issues taken by evangelical legislators in the early decades of post-Confederation Canada. There was, however, one significant difference from the American experience. In Canada, modernity encountered not one but two forms of Christianity. Both expressions, Roman Catholic and Protestant, shared a concern to shape the new nation in terms of Christian belief and practice; but it was their differences in approach that stood out most clearly to contemporaries. In a society where identity was in the first place familial, nowhere was this difference more apparent than in the matter of marital breakup and divorce.

MARRIAGE AND DIVORCE: THE 1872 MARTIN CASE

With Confederation, legislative control of divorce passed to the federal parliament, with the proviso that divorce laws in individual provinces should stand. Of the four newly created provinces, only Nova Scotia and New Brunswick had such laws at the time of Confederation. Thus, in Quebec and Ontario the sole recourse for their inhabitants was to petition Parliament for an act to dissolve the marriage, and this was available only on the grounds of proven adultery by the wife – or, if by a husband (in a manifestly double standard), proven adultery and one additional ground: desertion, bigamy, rape, sodomy, or bestiality. Since religion was no longer established but was voluntary, it was now the state, not the churches, that ultimately regulated such family matters as divorce, but this did not by any means eliminate religious perspectives. Canada – the only significant member country in the British Empire not to give its population access to judicial divorce in the nineteenth century – reflected the strong influence of the Roman Catholic hierarchy as well as an evangelical moralistic concern that Canadian couples not follow the U.S. example of "easy divorce," facilitated by a welter of state divorce laws. Thanks to a cumbersome and highly public legal process, divorce in Canada was expensive and largely available only to the well-to-do, for all costs were born by the petitioner. Divorce bills, accordingly, were few in number, with only sixty-nine bills passed between 1867 and 1900.[29] Among the first of these bills, none was more revealing of the impact of a changing social order on conjugal relations than the notorious case of John Robert and Sophia Martin.

As spring began to move into summer in 1872, and as Colby, awaiting the end of a packed session, fretted over the delay in attending to his own urgent business interests, there appeared before the House of Commons a petition for divorce which catapulted Canada's parliamentarians into the steaming, sensuous drama of middle-class infidelity enacted in two Ontario towns. The case involved the petitioner John Robert Martin, a Hamilton barrister; his allegedly unfaithful wife Sophia, née Stinson, with whom he had been wed since 1855 (who also happened to be the sister-in-law of the MP for Haldimand); and her lover, the Barrie barrister William Lount, a former Ontario MPP. Following the established procedure for divorce petitions, testimony was examined by a Select Senate Committee, and after passing three readings in the Senate, a bill and the necessary evidence were submitted to the House of Commons for its concurrence.[30] Known pejoratively by Colby and other MPs as "the old ladies," the Senate (whose appointments reflected a stronger evangelical presence than the Commons) had been zealous in gathering evidence, which in its moralistic mode of questioning was heavily slanted in favour of the petitioner.[31] Redolent of an older oral culture of village gossip, the Senate committee's earnest research unearthed such sensationalist details as artful disguises and subterfuge by Mrs Martin as she spent time with Lount in his home in Barrie, and a snooping maid servant's graphic account of a compromising and intimate encounter between the couple observed through the crack of a door.

Unaccustomed to this world of sexual intrigue, Charles Colby, appointed on 3 June as one of eight members of a Select House of Commons Committee to examine the evidence further and summon witnesses if needed, turned to seek the opinion of his wife. Mailing her for private perusal "the scandalous record," he noted with evident frustration, "Such cases should be tried by a mixed tribunal of men and women."[32] His closest friends, the members of the committee, and "the straight Protestants" (those not having many Roman Catholic electors) were all solidly in favour of granting the divorce, all the more so since Martin had already successfully sued Lount for adultery in the Ontario Court of Common Pleas. Hattie Colby, however, dissented. Not even her husband's testimony that as a committee member he had seen many letters written by Sophia Martin's "paramour and signed Honeybird which were full of sweetness" (strong reasons for Charles's sympathy with Martin) made the slightest dent in Hattie's position. Her response to her husband was sent by return mail, and he proudly shared it with several parliamentarians, including "Sir John," who, evidently much pleased, sent his thanks, accompanied by the wish that he might soon have the pleasure of making her acquaintance.[33] Hattie's "excellent" letter fully persuaded her husband (though not Macdonald) to change his position, as it did that of a colleague who had also been privy to the letter. Colby had briefly contemplated hiding out in the smoking room when the vote was taken, but in the end, as a compromise, he paired his negative vote with that of a colleague, who was for the divorce but who also wanted to show sensitivity to the situation of his Haldimand colleague, the brother-in-law of the accused.[34] Through such casuistry, with one vote cancelling another as members balanced expediency with integrity, the decision on the Martin divorce bill was deferred for three months by an adverse majority of six, and thereby it died on the books, at least temporarily.³⁵ While this represented a victory for the Roman Catholic position – for whom, in Colby's words, divorce was simply "legalized adultery" – in practical terms, the bill was probably defeated because fewer members in the elected Commons than in the appointed Senate could afford to be "straight Protestants," despite their sympathy for Martin.

Looking back on the details of the divorce case, what is striking is not so much their sensationalism as the way they pointed to the potential impact of social change on married life. Although constructed in the traditional style of village gossip, this was a story that, with the help of good railway and mail systems, spanned several cities and two countries. Thanks to this new mobility and quick communication, and assisted by obliging relatives, Sophia Martin and her lover had managed to arrange their various encounters and had even, to the great frustration of the members of the Senate committee, remained out of reach when called to give evidence. On the surface, this was an escapade where the female partner was able to take considerably more liberty than was generally her lot in a middle-class marriage. As may be expected, therefore, the men appointed and elected to safeguard the country's family values – members of the Senate and Commons committees – drew heavily on conventional Victorian notions of womanhood as they reconstructed the evidence. Although they were careful to refrain from moralistic commentary, the result was shaped by a built-in bias which assumed that women, whether Sophia Martin or the female servants who testified against her, were by nature led by sexual needs and not by reasoned action. Nor was there any effort to separate gossip from fact or to pursue conflicting testimony concerning Mrs Martin's character.³⁶

In this they received ample help from John Robert Martin, the aggrieved partner. When telling Hattie of Martin's great disappointment at the failure of his petition, Charles Colby observed with some sympathy that while Mrs Martin (who since 1872 had been living with relatives in New York State) could get a divorce and remarry if she so chose, her husband "will not be liberated here."³⁷ Dependent for liberation on the costly Canadian judicial process, Martin had pulled out all the stops to attain his goal. This was not his first application to Parliament, nor would it be his last. He had begun to instigate proceedings in 1870, only to see his petition fail in the Senate; armed with much more testimony, he had reapplied in 1872. Then, in 1873 he applied a third time, and as Colby wearily told Hattie, on this occasion Martin's persistence was rewarded.³⁸

Martin's was one of only three successful petitions between 1871 and 1875. Although the number of decrees granted inched up thereafter until divorce legislation was finally overhauled in 1968, the low incidence of divorce in the intervening century is noteworthy and has in large part been attributed to the Roman Catholic Church's strong presence in state and society.[39] Worth noting, however, is that its position was shared by Hattie Colby, whose much-acclaimed letter on the matter unfortunately became lost in its circulation among her husband's colleagues, but whose argument against divorce can be gleaned from her husband's response, as well as from her own situation as a married woman.[40]

Martin's carefully crafted account of his wife's infidelity had been calculated to arouse a predictable response of moral outrage from male evangelical parliamentarians, one that was sufficiently high in temperature to sanction the dissolution of the marriage bond. Hattie Colby, on the other hand, though she would have shared such outrage, did not see it as sufficient cause for supporting divorce. This was a case, it should be noted, where proceedings for divorce had been instigated by the husband, not the wife, and from Hattie's perspective, as long as women remained financially dependent, any curb on a man's ability to seek a divorce was ultimately to a woman's benefit.[41] In an age when women were socially, economically, and politically vulnerable, marriage ensured them a secure position in the middle class. When a husband divorced his wife, he robbed her of respectability and assigned her to a fragile existence on the margins of society, where, like Sophia Martin, she might have to resort to the use of disguises or to hide with family and move to the United States. Since the rules of evidence in divorce cases were unclear, MPs could more easily be swayed by Protestant or Roman Catholic moral positions than by judicious, impartial assessment.[42] The whole idea of fault in deciding divorce cases was, therefore, highly problematic and was stacked against women, who, it should be remembered, had to base their own requests for divorce on more than the husband's adultery.

Although her reasons differed, Hattie's position on divorce was not that dissimilar from the Roman Catholic stance, for whom marriage was a sacrament, a term she herself had used years earlier when advising her sister-in-law on the trials of childbearing. In the eyes of the church, marriage and family formation were sacred matters leading to eternal salvation or damnation, and therefore men and women who shirked their family duties were not to be cast off but were to be called to repentance and reclaimed to resume their vocation as parents and marriage partners. Where Protestant men were willing to petition Parliament for a bill of divorce which ended an existing marriage and opened the way for another, the Roman Catholic Church modelled a more ancient way of dealing with marital infidelity: repentance, confession, and absolution.

It may be that Sophia Martin was operating out of such a mindset when, according to the written testimony taken down by a hostile barrister (and her husband's brother), she had stated, "I do not deny my guilt, but that it is never too late for repentance: I have lived a perfectly correct life ever since, and intend to continue to do so."[43] Situated in the midst of a litany of damning evidence, the confession, which is also the only time we hear her own voice, seems curiously out of place, and it appeared to carry no weight in the Senate committee's investigation. However, the words would have been meaningful to Hattie Colby's evangelical frame of reference, one that privately her husband shared. Repentance and forgiveness were premised on the belief that what had been broken could be restored. Theologically, this approach to individual change was based on the doctrine of the atonement, whereby vicariously through the priest, as in the Roman Catholic Church, or privately before God, as in evangelical revivalism, a sinner repented, confessed, and was forgiven. In evangelical circles, as was noted previously, the theology of atonement was slowly being replaced by a theology of incarnation, a shift that placed less emphasis on repentance and God's forgiveness and more on moral action and on reshaping an individual's environment.

Congruent with these theological changes, and also emerging out of broad socio-economic shifts, the Martin divorce case points to another development, the gradual replacement of covenant by contract. Feared a generation earlier by Moses Colby in a different context of family relations, this shift, when applied to marriage, was seen in the loss of coverture discussed in chapter 3, fracturing the unified property regime of marriage in order to free real estate from traditional encumbrances. In giving legislatures the power to alter marriage and property traditions, society was in fact saying that ultimately marriage was "political rather than simply natural or God-given."[44] It is little wonder, therefore, that clergymen in the United States wrung their hands over the growing rate of divorce, that Canada's federal government did its utmost to restrict divorce accessibility, and that the hapless John Martin had to go to such lengths to convince Protestant legislators of the righteousness of his cause. Where in Roman Catholic terms, marriage was a sacrament and thus was entirely in the hands of God (who did not play fast and loose with sacraments), in a contractual arrangement the default of one partner (which in Martin's case necessarily had to be couched in the language of moral outrage at unconventional female behaviour) ended the obligations of the other and became a justification for divorce.⁴⁵ Yet both the Roman Catholic hierarchy and Protestant middle-class women such as Hattie Colby viewed state-sanctioned divorce as a threat to the social fabric. For Hattie, living in a voluntary society and financially dependent on male family members, divorce was an enterprise entirely in male hands, which invariably left the female partner, and ultimately the family, at risk. Although the potentially revolutionary implications of leaving divorce in the hands of the state did receive some attention in the evangelical press, this was largely in terms of caution against the American example of "easy" divorce.⁴⁶

THE SABBATARIAN AND TEMPERANCE MOVEMENTS

Much less complex than issues of marriage and divorce for evangelicals were the matters of Sunday observance and temperance, the two main ways by which they sought to control and regulate the potentially destructive impact of industrialization upon social and family life. The Roman Catholic Church had its own ways of inducing individual and community conformity and did not feel compelled to jump on either the temperance or the Sabbatarian bandwagon.⁴⁷ As a parliamentary debater pointed out, while Protestants "had a most tender regard to the observance of the Sabbath Day, believing that it was a divine institution which no man had a right to wrest from the meanest subject in the Queen's Dominion," this sentiment was not shared by Roman Catholics.⁴⁸ Instead of the sacred one day out of seven, the Roman Catholic Church retained numerous feast days, which to Protestant eyes reflected a cavalier attitude to the work ethic.

With Confederation and the consolidation of mainline evangelical denominations such as the Methodists and the Presbyterians, the stakes in the Prohibition and Sabbatarian movements increased dramatically. Expressed in the religious language of the moral millennium, the goal became the Christian nation, God's Dominion, that ideal society that Canada would become as long as men and women continued to work together for the moral reform of the nation.⁴⁹ Put forward most enthusiastically by the Liberal Party, Sabbatarianism and temperance flourished during its years as the federal government, from 1873 to 1878. But it also became evident to parliamentarians, if not to their constituencies, that although these issues were hotly debated, they invariably foundered at the federal level on the rocks of political expediency and practical logic. Evangelical reform, unlike the much more consistent nineteenth-century Roman Catholic clerical stance of resistance to change, was a decidedly ambiguous process.

Despite the rhetoric of moral progress, it involved the simultaneous embrace and rejection of change. Reformer George Brown, for example, who in the 1850s had campaigned vigorously for temperance and against Sabbath desecration, had also enthusiastically promoted the further development of railroads and the canal system, both of which potentially undermined the sobriety and Sabbath observance he so ardently promoted.[50] His successor at the federal level, Alexander Mackenzie, a total abstainer and a convinced Sabbatarian, saw during his term as prime minister how the logic of economic and technological progress undermined the earnest efforts of his supporters to legislate evangelical morality for the nation.[51]

The matter of Sabbath observance was thoroughly aired on 27 March 1876 when Adam Gordon, Liberal member for North Ontario, proposed a resolution calling for the total cessation of Sunday activity by all federal agencies, such as survey crews, post offices, canals, and railways. This was an issue of long-standing concern to evangelicals and in the 1850s had been unsuccessfully pursued by the Reform Party in the legislature of the United Canadas. More recently, in 1873, the General Assembly of Gordon's own Presbyterian denomination had passed a solemn memorial, endorsed by nine evangelical denominations and sent to the Ontario heads of all the major railways, pointing out "the large number of congregations in which the public worship is painfully disturbed by the noise and commotion of passing trains Sabbath after Sabbath ... in violation of both the law of God and the public law of the Dominion."[52]

If this was to be a matter of legislative action, however, more objective arguments than the irritation of church congregations were needed to ensure that on one day out of seven, all economic and technological progress in Canada ground to a reverent halt. Accordingly, the scientific data Gordon marshalled in evidence ranged widely, from observations showing how Sabbatarianism had become a subject of enlightened popular concern, to a survey of railway companies, testimonials from clergy on the deleterious effects of Sabbath desecration on employees, and quotations from public men on the inestimable national benefits of Sunday observance. In the discussion that followed, Gordon's Protestant colleagues professed, to a man, their strong conviction on "the advisability of observing the Lord's Day as a day of rest and worship."[53] Unfortunately, they also raised some perplexing questions, which pitted one tenet of evangelical reform against another. None excelled in this more than Prime Minister Mackenzie, who asked the customary question, whether this was a federal or a provincial matter, and proceeded with unrelenting logic to outline the implications of Gordon's motion. What would happen, for example, when a steamer en route from

Montreal to Chicago happened to reach the Welland Canal at 11:30 PM on a Saturday? Might not the crew and less piously inclined passengers become a disorderly nuisance and take to the grog shops as they sat through the stopover until Monday, whereupon, after a day of dissipation, might not the captain have to take most of the day getting the steamer in operation again? These and similar arguments, such as the unavailability of places of worship along railway and canal routes, coupled with assurances from Mackenzie that the government would countenance no unnecessary Sabbath work in federal agencies, finally led Gordon to withdraw his motion, at least for the time being.

The issue of Sabbath observance, though inconclusive in its results, does offer a glimpse into how traditional ways were being challenged by the social impact of technology and by growing continental trade and industry. Unlike evangelical rhetoric in the pulpit and pew, parliamentary debates on moral issues, in which MPs exposed the contradictions between economic growth and social conservatism, were a laboratory for the complex society that was emerging. There was, for example, a reaction of horror at the mischievous suggestion by one MP that, to be consistent with Gordon's motion to shut down all federal services, the parliamentary library and club also should be closed on Sundays. Upon investigating the Sabbath observance of his colleagues, this MP had been shocked to find a good number busily working on their correspondence at a time when they should have been in church. Besides stoutly denying his observation, many MPs were aghast and lost no time countering one expression of evangelical morality with another. If the library were closed, wailed one, "Where would the members spend their Sabbath afternoons? Would the hon. gentleman have them loafing about hotels and in their bedrooms when they could obtain books with which to improve their minds? It would be intolerable to live in a city of this kind during Session if they were shut out from the Library on Sabbath."[54] The question of how men away from their families on Sundays were to spend their time then shifted to a more theoretical and safer discussion of the services provided by organizations such as the Young Men's Christian Association for men working on the canals.

Evangelical efforts in urban centres to ensure Sunday observance and offer substitutes for "the family circle" to single men (and by the 1880s also to women) were indeed extensive.[55] Unfortunately, we know more about the well-intentioned organizers of such services than about the responses of the recipients. The moral resources offered by the YMCA would have had little appeal, for example, to Ottawa's federal politicians or, for that matter, to the growing number of businessmen spending time away from home. Charles Colby, as representative as any, tried to spend his Sundays in Stanstead as much as possible and, failing that, made the best of the opportunities available for traditional Sunday activities in Ottawa. This usually included attendance at the city's Wesleyan Methodist church in the morning and, frequently, because he appreciated the preaching ability of its Presbyterian ministers, "the Scotch church" for the evening service.[56] After dinner in the 1870s, now spending more time in Ottawa after his insolvency, he often accompanied his friend and colleague Tom White, the member for Cardwell, to his brother David's home, known as "the cottage."[57] David and Marianne White, who were relatives of William White, Emily Colby's widower, offered a hospitable Sunday retreat for quite a number of their Ottawa friends who were interested in the five-mile return stroll. Back in his lodgings in the evening, Colby would describe the Sabbath's events to his family in the correspondence that daily flowed between Ottawa and Stanstead. By the mid-1880s, now one of the old-timers and often accompanied by his daughters, he enjoyed an increasing number of invitations to social events. More than once, a late Saturday evening event caused father and daughters to miss morning church. Hattie Colby and her mother-in-law might frown on the Ottawa habit of Saturday and Sunday evening dinner parties, but it was impossible for the capital's social life to replicate the agrarian routine of villages such as Stanstead.[58] Increased mobility, more affluence, larger urban centres, and especially the impact of imperial influence through successive high-ranking governor general appointments were all catalysts to a more sophisticated social life that undermined evangelical middle-class morality.[59]

More than evangelical expectations of Sabbath observance were being challenged in the emerging social life of the nation's capital. Intemperance, despite all the efforts at its eradication as the deadliest of evangelical sins, was as prevalent there as elsewhere. No one could accuse the prime minister, Sir John A. Macdonald, of pronounced evangelical principles, at least not before his dramatic but enigmatic "conversion" in 1889 at an Ottawa revival led by the well-known Methodist evangelistic team, Crossley and Hunter.[60] Serious Protestants could therefore dismiss his penchant for the bottle as a regrettable residue of his former Church of Scotland affiliation. With a history as an established church, the Kirk retained a much less negative position on worldly behaviour than that of the Free Church, whose members included George Brown and the Ontario premier Oliver Mowat.[61] Macdonald's intemperance, however, was only the best-known example in a wider culture, which Peter Waite has aptly described as "lively, raucous, and occasionally brutal" and decidedly "un-Victorian."[62] Lively and raucous, parliamentary debates certainly often were, as was

Ottawa's social culture, which has been masterfully described in Sandra Gwyn's *The Private Capital*.[63]

Although Charles Colby offered his family few epistolary remarks on the impact of alcohol in fostering such an atmosphere, his wife Hattie, visiting Ottawa in 1884 to listen to parliamentary debate on the issue, in her capacity as a parliamentary wife and active Woman's Christian Temperance Union (WCTU) worker, felt much less restraint. Intemperance was rarely a theoretical matter, regardless of the "scientific objectivity" with which parliamentary advocates of Prohibition were increasingly debating the issue. Hattie's visit followed immediately on the sad and shocking death of her brother-in-law William Colby after one of his drinking binges, and her trip to Ottawa had been partly motivated by the need to remove herself from Stanstead's melancholy surroundings. As she confided to her daughters by letter from the reassuring and familiar setting of Ottawa's Russell Hotel, only when its searing immediacy began to wane were she and Charles able to speak to one another about the death. The capital city and the Russell Hotel were a suitably distracting place, and many parliamentary wives could be found there, especially for the 1884 debate on Prohibition. While in Ottawa, Hattie paid several visits to Roberta Tilton, the director of the Protestant Orphans' Home. Mrs Tilton was also a leading member of the Canadian WCTU, and she had befriended the Colby daughters on one of their visits.[64] Like a number of other prominent Ottawa women, Mrs Tilton had her own special "At Home" day each week, and Hattie Colby, aware of the WCTU's new approach to alcoholism, was eager "to see her methods" in order to be able to share them with her friend and fellow temperance worker in Stanstead, Emma Cowles.[65]

Hattie's comments on the new professional approach to temperance were spiced with much Ottawa gossip of a more personal nature, most of it centring around her own observation of the ravages of alcohol among Canada's parliamentary leaders. John Henry Pope, the Eastern Townships' representative in the cabinet, who reputedly was in ill health, actually had a severe drinking problem (which, Hattie's informant intimated, might lead him to resign and open the way for Charles Colby as his successor). Then there was the MP who, according to Charles's forewarning, habitually "keeps himself so full of whiskey" as to make him incoherent, though when Hattie met him he showed no visible signs of intemperance, despite a strong smell of alcohol. Even more interesting and probably an exception (but not to be mentioned in Stanstead gossip) was the country's leading Baptist layman, Senator William McMaster who, carefully holding his hat between himself and his conversation partner, was obviously "primed" on the night he was to address the Senate.[66]

The highlight, however, of Hattie's foray into Ottawa's theatre of demon rum was the splendid speech by George Foster, famed temperance advocate and source of the most up-to-date scientific data on the ruinous effects of alcohol. But while requesting her daughters to share with the WCTU forces at home the astounding statistic that "84% or nearly nine tenths of all crime came directly or indirectly from drink!," Hattie failed to mention that the speech made hardly a dent on Ottawa's parliamentarians. Foster's valiant motion calling for immediate Prohibition was soundly defeated by a non-party vote in favour of an amendment that the House adopt Prohibition "as soon as public opinion was ripe for its enforcement."[67] The religious gender divide between ardent local female temperance workers and male political realists had become all too obvious in the course of the debate, when even such evangelical diehards as Sir Leonard Tilley spoke against immediate Prohibition by pointing out his own party's ill-fated efforts in 1855 to push the measure through in the New Brunswick legislature.[68]

The defeat of Foster's Prohibition motion put the matter squarely back into the hands of local workers, whose only recourse was to try to implement the one piece of temperance legislation that Parliament had managed to pass – the Liberal government's Canada Temperance Act of 1878, which allowed for a local Prohibition option if the male voting population so desired. This, the seasoned parliamentary sages were convinced, was all that public opinion was ready for at that time. Consequently, during the summer of 1884, Hattie Colby, her recently widowed sister-in-law Melvina, and their friend Emma Cowles (who was driven around the county by the Colbys' untiring horse, Old Ed "the Temperance Worker") again immersed themselves in the temperance crusade in Stanstead County, which only the previous winter had been visited by the Canadian WCTU president, Letitia Youmans.[69]

In early October, women, children, and men gathered one last time for a long weekend of temperance activity, which included an earnest address by a Boston WCTU speaker, a Sunday afternoon prayer meeting in the Baptist church, and two evening temperance meetings at Ayer's Flat and Coaticook. At the latter, they listened attentively while Charles Colby, MP, presented a brief history of the temperance movement, describing the great positive changes of the past four decades in the public's attitude to alcohol consumption. The next day, after being reassured by their member of parliament that Prohibition would not put at risk the area's unfermented cider industry, the people of Stanstead County, which only three years earlier had defeated Prohibition by 250 votes, adopted the measure by a majority of 252.[70] In an exultant letter to one of her daughters, Hattie attributed the change primarily to the "good hard steady work done in every neighborhood." Theirs was a victory, she enthused, in defiance of $10,000 in cash pumped into the county by the Sherbrooke and Montreal wholesale liquor dealers. (Her information about this sum came directly from the local Irish Roman Catholic rector and Colby family friend, Father Macaulay.)

Although there was Roman Catholic support, Stanstead's battle for Prohibition was primarily a Protestant evangelical movement, mounted with the spiritual excitement of an earlier era's religious revivalism. As described by Hattie, the Quebec WCTU, which had assembled in Stanstead's Methodist church for its first annual meeting, ceased discussion as the results were made known; the church bell pealed, and men and women with radiant faces broke spontaneously into song, prayer, and the venerable revival practice of "testimonies."[71] As in religion, the danger of backsliding was ever prevalent, and a few days later readers of the *Stanstead Journal* were sternly warned by one of the local Methodist ministers that "the best organization and most constant vigilance will be necessary to enforce the law, for some of those who have predicted that the law will be a failure, will do all they can to fulfill their predictions."[72]

Charles Colby's presence in Stanstead during these weeks deprives us of any record of his reaction to the acceptance of the Canada Temperance Act in his riding; nor, despite his long-standing work in temperance at the local level as a member of the International Temple, does he appear to have taken an active part in the major House of Commons debates on Prohibition in 1873, 1876, 1877, and 1884.[73] Notwithstanding the fact that Parliament had voted to shut down its in-house bar some years earlier and had prohibited the "entertainment" of electors by political candidates, alcohol continued to flow freely during elections and also – as Hattie Colby's letters illustrate – within parliamentary circles.[74]

Although intemperance had a deleterious effect in his own family circle, Colby's pronouncements on the issue, since the time of his first election campaign in 1867, had focused on the more public aspects, drawing attention to the corrupting influence of drink on electoral politics. What it did, in his view, was undermine the ideal of communal solidarity that had initially motivated him to run for Parliament and champion the economic interests of his constituency. This same ideal also informed the millennial optimism that historians have seen as so characteristic of the earlier temperance movement. While the WCTU and temperance speakers such as George Foster were increasingly using the more "objective" statistical approach of the developing social sciences, Colby's own temperance rhetoric, laced with Christian symbols and ideals, depicted the temperance movement as a brotherhood and sisterhood where, in divinely gendered ways, both worked together to rescue the fallen and help them lead a new and productive life. Although the language differed from that in his speeches on economic policy, the socially conservative goal presented in his temperance addresses was the same. In each case, his protective approach reflected the conviction that, to use his own succinct phrase, "the State is the guardian of public morals."[75] However, as most of his colleagues in Parliament were aware, the public did not always live up to the millennial hope of temperance speeches and crusades. Thus, in a democracy, the guardians of morals were wise not to outrun their constituents if they wished to be re-elected, as Sir Leonard Tilley had so poignantly reminded them in the 1884 debate on Prohibition.

MINORITY RIGHTS AND SOCIAL HARMONY

In a country divided not only between those who imbibed and those determined to rescue them, but also between vocal evangelical Protestant denominations and a well-entrenched Roman Catholic Church, tensions were bound to erupt when the two religious moral orders diverged. As every student of Canadian history knows – and as Charles Colby, who prided himself on his talents as a peacemaker, would learn to his great cost – when issues arose involving both race and religion, elected representatives were advised to equivocate and seek not to offend anyone. This was manifestly impossible, given the personal dimension of race and religion for every constituent, male as well as non-voting female; but it did not prevent elected representatives from at least trying.

As a member representing a minority group in a francophone Roman Catholic province, Colby showed himself to be particularly sensitive to the need to balance the country's two religious interests and avoid offending either. One of his treasured moments, hallowed in family memory and documented with a short note in John A. Macdonald's own handwriting, occurred in 1872. At that time he helped extricate the government from the constitutional dilemma caused by the decision of the New Brunswick legislature to rescind funding for religious schools – an act that especially affected the province's minority Roman Catholics, whose educational system, unlike that in Ontario and Quebec, had not been safeguarded in the British North America Act.[76] A sensitive issue on which religious feelings ran high, the request for disallowance by the aggrieved Roman Catholics came before Parliament in May that year, just when a federal election appeared in the offing, causing MPs to have to face the possible ire of their constituents. On one side were evangelical Protestants, who had no use for "religious schools" and wanted no tampering with what was a provincial issue; on the other side were Roman Catholics, who sought the only redress available under the new confederation – namely, disallowance of the provincial law by the federal government or appeal to the imperial government to change the constitution.

As Colby modestly told his wife when describing his role in coming up with a compromise to this complex issue, "It became my 'happy lot,' as Sir George Cartier has it, to solve the New Brunswick School difficulty."[77] After consultation with Macdonald, the Roman Catholic MPs, and the Protestant New Brunswick MPs, whose numerical support was crucial, Colby presented a motion expressing, first, the regret of the House that the new provincial School Act was unsatisfactory to a large number of New Brunswick inhabitants (in other words, its Roman Catholic population) and, secondly, the hope that the provincial legislature would itself redress the grievance. A Liberal amendment asking for disallowance had been defeated, but to forestall a second amendment by another Liberal, A.A. Dorion, which would be equally divisive to Protestants, it was imperative that Colby be the first to catch the attention of the Speaker. Warned by a note from Macdonald, "Look out for the Speaker's eye. Be smart as a steel trap," Colby leapt to his feet and was the first to be heard and acknowledged by the Speaker. With the opposition looking "blank and discomfited," he proceeded to read his amendment – and saw it carried by 117 to 42.[78] Although this action won him much approval from his colleagues, such pragmatic politics were less likely to impress his constituents. Only two days later, he found himself wearily having to explain to Protestant critics the subtle reasoning behind his motion: it was *not* a push for "religious supervision of schools"; it was merely a profession "of respect for the opinions and feelings of those who entertained such views."[79]

This conundrum of trying to convince both Protestants and Roman Catholics that Confederation worked in their best interests, yet never succeeding in satisfying either party entirely, resurfaced regularly during Colby's parliamentary career, and it eventually became one of the contributing reasons for his defeat in 1891. In the course of his years as a federal politician, he saw a steady increase in his riding's Roman Catholic population (both English and French), as well as in the Eastern Townships generally. This shift was caused by a decline in the Protestant birth rate in the older counties and by Roman Catholic in-migration along with a higher Catholic birth rate, and by the 1880s it had left the English-speaking Protestant population in a minority position in the Eastern Townships.[80] At the same time, a number of political events, most notably the execution of the Métis leader Louis Riel, were exacerbating ethnic and religious differences and fuelling francophone nationalist sentiment. In 1886, when Quebec's provincial election was won by Honoré Mercier and his Parti national (as the new nationalist movement was called), the close cooperation that had been in place since 1867 between Quebec's provincial and federal Conservative politicians came to an end.[81] No longer could Quebec politics be expected to follow the federal Conservative lead. In the federal election of 1887, which was an unusually bitter affair in Stanstead County, Colby's ideal of harmony and clean voting behaviour in the riding received its greatest challenge to date.[82] Shortly thereafter, religion was added to the divisive mix when in 1888 the Quebec legislature passed the Jesuits' Estates Act in an attempt to settle once and for all the vexing question of compensating the Roman Catholic Church for lands taken away from the Society of Jesus in the late eighteenth century.

Although both houses of the legislature passed the act unanimously and there was very little Protestant reaction in Quebec, it provoked an outcry from Ontario's Protestants, especially from the Orange Order. Because Rome was asked to be the final arbiter on the allocation of funds, the Protestant press and Protestant pulpits launched angry charges of Catholic aggression, accompanied by litanies recounting Roman and Jesuit machinations since the days of the Reformation.[83] By March 1889, the House of Commons was embroiled in a debate over whether or not to nullify the act by the power of disallowance. Charles Colby, who was one of the relatively small number of debaters on the Jesuits' Estates Act, was quick to point out the parallel with the 1872 request for disallowance of the New Brunswick schools legislation, except that this time the shoe was on the other foot. As a Protestant anglophone member from Quebec, he sought to reassure his counterparts in Ontario that, contrary to their allegations, there was no strong groundswell against the legislation by his Quebec co-religionists. Indeed, as he ironically observed, far from feeling threatened, "the Protestants of Quebec and the Catholics of the Province of Quebec, so far as I know their relations, live together happily upon mutually respecting terms, each respecting the other's rights, each respecting even the other's sensibilities and prejudices, and cooperating together, working together, for what they believe to be for the common interest."[84]

With the exception of the supporting votes of a "noble thirteen" of Protestant stalwarts, the request for disallowance was soundly defeated. But, for Colby, the debate had only just begun. Although he had privately consulted representatives of Montreal's Methodists before his address, his portrayal of Canadian religious relations led to a furious denial by the evangelical *Montreal Witness* and the Protestant Ministerial Association of Montreal. The latter went so far as to have its letter of protest read into the minutes of the House of Commons. Not only did Colby's idyllic picture in no way represent the feelings of the Protestants of Quebec, the association firmly asserted, but the Protestant minority in the province did have real and numerous grievances.[85] Given its position, it is little wonder that the primary theme of Colby's address – Roman Catholicism's contribution to Canada's distinctive nature as a stable society – received no comment. Speaking from a socio-political perspective rather than the usual theological stance, he had forcefully emphasized his conviction:

> I am a Protestant. The Roman Catholic Church – I will not speak of it as a religious body – I look upon to-day, speaking from a political standpoint, and a political standpoint only – as one of the strongest if not the strongest bulwark we have in our country against what I conceive to be the most dangerous element abroad in the world today. The Roman Catholic Church recognizes the supremacy of authority; it teaches observance to law; it teaches respect for the good order and constituted authorities of society. It does that and there is need of such teaching; for the most dangerous enemy abroad today in this land and on this continent is a spirit of anarchy, which has no respect for any institution, human or divine ...
>
> I think the time is near at hand [he concluded] when it will be recognized by the two great religions of this country, the Protestant and the Roman Catholic, that the time for bickering has passed, that they have a common interest, and that for the promotion of that common interest they should stand shoulder to shoulder, work confidingly and in a friendly way together for the preservation of a common Christianity and all that is more dear and sacred to both, and thus, I conceive, will the best interest of this Dominion, and the best interest of civilisation on this continent, be promoted.[86]

Colby's words are worth quoting at some length, for they reflect a view that was relatively rare at the time, though it was shared by a handful of other Protestant politicians, including Oliver Mowat and Colby's federal colleague and friend, the late Tom White, minister of the interior.[87] A similar ecumenism, focusing on political rather than religious unity, had also informed the national vision of his American Whig mentor, Daniel Webster. Colby's Canadian adaptation of Webster's view, reflecting the ideal of a unified society, was similar to that held by many other evangelicals as they fulminated against sectarianism and party spirit. In the United States, any possibility of unity had foundered on the issue of slavery; and in Canada, despite a few dissenting voices such as his own, evangelicals and Roman Catholics were crusades in collision, emphasizing one another's differences rather than commonalities.

Even those who responded favourably to Colby's address ignored his comments on the social value of Roman Catholicism. Yet in his eyes, this was the best speech he had made since his tariff address of 1878 ushering in the National Policy. As he observed to Hattie, Sir John had slapped him on the shoulders and said, "That was the speech of a statesman." It was not surprising, therefore, that (given the death of John Henry Pope, the Eastern Townships' member of the cabinet) Colby concluded, "Whatever that may mean, I think it has settled the question of the succession."[88] It was something for which he had waited a very long time. As an elected representative who considered the state to be the guardian of morals and who, in relationship to his constituents, cast himself *in loco parentis*, Colby took his office extremely seriously.[89] Regular reports from his wife reassured him that his constituents were highly satisfied, and the relatively rare negative comments about him in the newspapers were easily dismissed. Nevertheless, preferment had remained elusive, despite several tantalizing hints from Macdonald, including a fatherly note when Colby had considered resigning his seat at the time of his insolvency.[90] Having entered political life with a good deal of healthy ambition, considerable talent, and significant financial need, Colby had soon realized that as a member for one of the federal ridings in the English Townships, these qualities could only take him so far.[91] It was not until 1887 that he was offered the Deputy Speaker's chair. Although this was below his aspirations and would require "hard work and close confinement," he could not refuse, especially as its annual salary of $2,000 offered the welcome prospect of a steady income at a time when his business ventures were still unrewarding. Besides, as he confided to Hattie, "It is understood that an ET [Eastern Townships] man cannot have either the speakership or the Lieutenant Governorship of Quebec. From the necessity of our position we must be content with second-rate appointments – but this shouldn't interfere with higher positions if these were to appear."[92]

There was really only one of these "higher positions," the cabinet position and patronage allocated to the Conservative Party spokesman for the Eastern Townships. Before Pope, it had been held by Alexander Galt. Yet on Pope's death, Sir John prevaricated for months, leading Secretary of State Joseph Chapleau, who had his own unfulfilled ambitions, to write to Colby in June telling him, "Il faut battre le fer tandis qu'il est chaud," and to advance his own cause.[93] Meanwhile, Stanstead County's minister-in-waiting was attending to that other part of his life, his elusive but ever-promising economic prospects. These currently centred primarily around a Quebec phosphate mining enterprise, whose shares he tried to promote in England in the fall of 1889. He returned in late November, and as he disembarked in New York he received a telegram from Macdonald, telling him to proceed immediately to

Charles Carroll Colby, 1890, attired in his new outfit as president of the Privy Council (CCM)

Ottawa for a consultation on filling the vacancy left by Pope. Six days later, Charles Colby was sworn in as president of the Privy Council. As he proudly told his wife, who was visiting their recently married daughter in Winnipeg, his appointment was the most popular one made in a long time and the cause for much congratulation by "several leading men from Ontario."[94] Furnished with a tailor-made privy councillor suit, a private secretary, and a telephone, he was showered with letters of congratulation during the following weeks. The congratulators

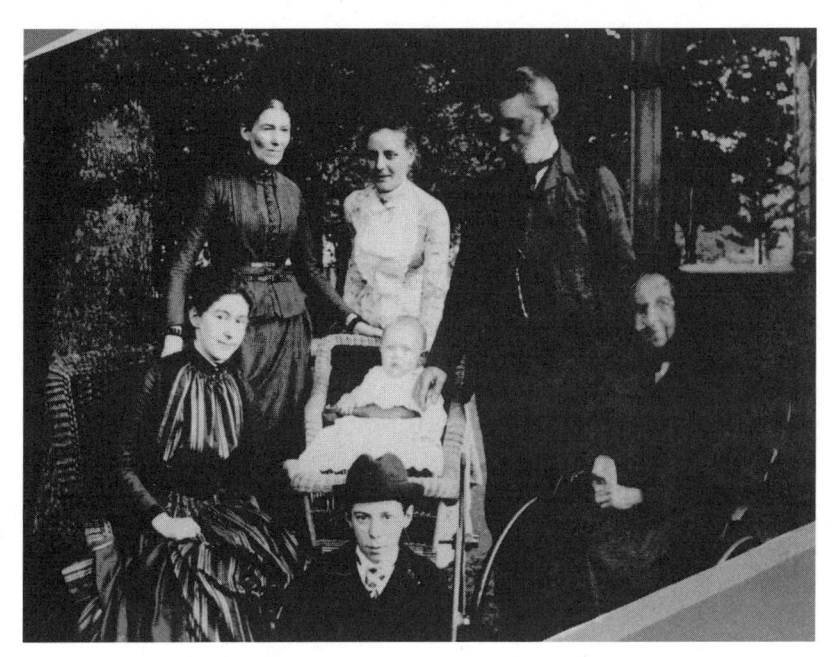

Clockwise from top left: Hattie, Jessie, Charles, Lemira, John, Abby and her infant son Carroll Aikins, 1890, in the garden of Carrollcroft during one of Charles's increasingly brief times away from Ottawa (CCM)

included his elderly friend, the Reverend William Scott, and a French Canadian Roman Catholic correspondent, both of whom took the opportunity to voice their appreciation for his highly publicized stand on the Jesuits' Estates Act.[95]

Although very pleasing, Colby's appointment to the cabinet exacted a heavy toll in time and energy. The cabinet met on Saturdays, and far too often to his liking, pressing business kept him from returning to Stanstead by train for a Sunday family gathering. Even before the appointment, he had begun to consider retiring from politics in order to attend fully to his business interests.[96] Thus, in his concern to provide a proper livelihood for his family, Colby, the ambitious politician, was a man divided. From the letter book he instituted after his appointment as chair of the Privy Council, there is little doubt that despite his heavy cabinet duties, personal business matters were making ever greater demands on his time and attention.[97]

In addition, federal elections in Stanstead County had become increasingly divisive as the Mercier government swung its support behind federal Liberal candidates. In 1882 and 1887 the federal Liberals had contested Stanstead County by choosing as their candidate

Banquet honouring Charles Carroll Colby on his appointment as president of the Privy Council, 1889. His re-election, by acclamation, was celebrated on this occasion in the village of Coaticook, but in 1891 its electors turned against him and he went down to defeat (CCM)

H.M. Rider, a well-known Fitch Bay storekeeper and landowner. Although Rider, a fellow Methodist, had taken pains to maintain his cordial relations with Colby, the latter remained publicly aloof and privately voiced his disapproval of the opposition's election tactics, while ignoring the heavy-handedness of his own side.[98] His appointment to the cabinet in 1889 called for a federal by-election, which, despite the public outcry in some Protestant circles about his speech on the Jesuits' Estates, he won by acclamation.

EPILOGUE: MORAL ORDER AND SOCIAL HARMONY IN COLLISION

Upon Colby's victory in 1889, the intricate web of providing for his family, meeting the patronage requests of anxious constituents, and maintaining community unity and Conservative control of the riding all became stretched to the point of rupture. First, there was the matter of patronage and the incessant volley of letters requesting preferment that followed his appointment to the Privy Council; these requests ranged from a raise for the local postmistress to a post in the army.[99] In March 1890, when the position of collector of customs at Coaticook suddenly became open due to the death of the incumbent,

Melvina Wallingford Colby, William's widow, with daughters Martha Stoddard (left) and Mary French (right) after their move to Winnipeg in 1890 (CCM)

Colby believed he had nipped in the bud the flood of applications (including one accompanied by the offer of a $1,000 bribe) by moving swiftly to appoint a local man whom he considered well suited for the position and whose loyalty to the party was proven.[100] The latter was simply assumed to be a *sine qua non* for preferment, a point totally at variance with the ideals Colby had had when first elected to Parliament. But far from achieving the desired peace, over the next six months the appointment produced an avalanche of letters from disgruntled aspirants or their patrons and in fact turned out to be extremely unpopular.[101] With the prospect of an imminent federal general election, Colby could not ignore the possible reverberations, and finally, through a technicality, he was able to nullify his decision, having obtained the agreement of the appointee. The next person he appointed to the position was John Daly, a well-known Stanstead storekeeper who was a personal friend and political supporter of Colby. This placated the Conservatives in Stanstead, but it threatened to divide the party and lose its support in the Coaticook area.[102]

The fact that Daly was an Irish Catholic did not endear Colby to those Protestant members of his riding whom he had earlier alienated by his stand on the Jesuits' Estates question. The latter included his sister-in-law Melvina, who in 1890 had moved with her two daughters to Winnipeg. From there, now caught in the early rumblings of yet another ethnic-religious conflict, the Manitoba Schools Question, she strongly censured her brother-in-law's behaviour in that "priest-ridden" province she had been so happy to leave.[103] Had she been able to read his correspondence, she would have been even more vexed to know that he consulted his friend and "father confessor," Father Macaulay of Coaticook, to ensure that his patronage appointments balanced the interests not only of Protestants but also of the French and Irish Roman Catholics in his riding.[104]

In the midst of all this was the constant nagging of business matters, especially his desperate need to travel personally to England.[105] Besides the fact that his business concerns were absorbing far more time than his political duties allowed, he now found himself in dissent as a cabinet minister with his government's policy calling for the remission of export duties on sawlogs, a policy that he saw as harmful to his riding's economic interests. At Macdonald's request he had temporarily withdrawn a proffered letter of resignation, but, mindful of the latter's concern that he not embarrass the cabinet when an election was imminent, he intended to resubmit it upon his return from England, though giving personal rather than political reasons.[106] But this was not to be. Upon his return to Canada in mid-February he found "the country in the thick of elections" and saw no choice but to run again.[107] Things did not look good. As Macdonald warned him, "The Grits are fighting us all over the Dominion." Since it was clear that the Liberals intended to contest every Conservative seat in the Eastern Townships, Macdonald further informed him, "Arrangements have to be made for counter [word illegible] funds to carry on the war &c &c that someone must attend to this and that it is your duty as representing the Townships in the Cabinet to do so."[108] And so, a political career that had begun on the high moral platform of eradicating electoral corruption and party patronage came to an end in entanglement with these same forces. For the first time in twenty years, Charles Colby was not re-elected.[109] Defeated by a small majority, he proceeded unsuccessfully to contest the result, and on 23 April 1891 he submitted his letter of resignation to Macdonald, who accepted it with kind but few words.[110]

Macdonald's desperate letter calling for electoral bribery is one detail that is missing from the reconstruction by press and family of what transpired in the 1891 election in Stanstead. From Melvina Colby's vantage point in Winnipeg, the reasons for her brother-in-law's defeat were clear: his misguided stance on the Jesuits' Estates Act, his catering to such Roman Catholic "sycophants" as John Daly, and his unwillingness to curb corruption within party ranks at election time.[111] To Hattie Colby, the reasons were no less moral, though cast in a radically different light: her husband's refusal to engage in unsavoury electoral practices and the Liberal Party's wide-scale use of liquor and bribes. And far from attributing his defeat to Protestant objections to his support of Roman Catholic minority rights, Hattie noted that her husband had won the support of the majority of Protestants, except in one polling station, North Hatley, whose Baptists went solidly Liberal.[112]

The press added yet another moral dimension to the narrative, emphasizing the role played by the patronage appointment of a Stanstead man as Coaticook's collector of customs, an observation supported by the fact that Colby encountered the greatest loss of electoral support in Coaticook.[113] Although letters of regret at his defeat poured in (including an apology from the editor of the *Coaticook Observer*) and although at the next federal election Stanstead County moved back into the Conservative camp, Colby resisted all requests in subsequent years to re-enter politics.[114] For the remainder of his life he devoted himself to what had been his major concern from the start – to place his family on a sound and comfortable financial base.

In this preoccupation it is evident that religion, politics, economics, and family concerns could never be entirely separated. Elected to enact the economic promises of Confederation, parliamentarians were confronted with their impact in restructuring the rhythms of everyday life. Their response, as Canadian economic historians have noted, was to counter the competitiveness inherent in an individualistic, free-market economy with restrictive legislation, from the National Policy at the federal level to regulating the hours of business at the provincial and municipal levels.[115] Religion played a vital role in shaping this conservative, collectivist response. In a population divided between Roman Catholics and Protestants, its place was often contested and was at best ambiguous, as many of Ottawa's parliamentarians had quickly learned. Although a few Protestants, like Charles Colby, valued the contribution of Roman Catholicism to social protectionism, many regarded the denomination's resistance to evangelical moral crusades as part of the problem rather than the solution to a collective Canadian identity. From the few instances, however, where evangelically informed legislation was actually passed, as in New Brunswick's brief flirtation with Prohibition in the 1850s, it had become evident that in fact the population at large, whether Protestant or Roman Catholic, showed a cavalier disregard for legislated morality. Even when, under the Canada Temperance Act, a region opted for Prohibition, no amount of accompanying religious fervour could ensure a permanent victory. Only four years after the astounding success of Prohibition in Stanstead County, Hattie Colby and her hard-working cohorts found themselves taking on the newly invigorated "liquor interests" in a new vote, the results of which allowed drink to flow freely again.[116]

Where legislative action and plebiscites failed, evangelicals fell back on self-discipline. Far from being an individualistic tool, this was a collective weapon, the very core of their religion and the reason why their legislative efforts and moralistic crusades have often been misunderstood as efforts at social control.[117] Writing about the social purity movement in Canada during these years, Mariana Valverde has rightly pointed out that despite its obviously repressive efforts to control vice, its aims and methods should more accurately be seen as "regulation" rather than coercion.[118] The ideal was self-regulation, and it lay at the heart of the nineteenth-century evangelical assertion of the freedom of the will. "In the evangelical tradition," Daniel Walker Howe has succinctly summarized, "conversion, that is, commitment to Christ, initiates a long process on the part of the convert to lead a better life, to remake himself or herself. It is a process that typically demands sustained self-discipline."[119] One has only to recall the evidence presented in the Martin divorce proceedings to be reminded of the high moral stakes in such a religious system. Roman Catholics could leave matters of sin and forgiveness safely in the hands of an institutional church and priesthood, but evangelicals placed the burden of moral decision-making squarely on the shoulders of the individual. The awe of a righteous God, which had shaped Puritan moral discourse and whose echoes could still be discerned in the life of Moses Colby, had lost theological sway by the 1870s. In its place, once religious revival had given way to moral education, there was self-discipline, the same self-discipline that defined the middle-class family and business world of Charles Colby and the lawyers and entrepreneurs who sat in Canada's new parliament.

This emphasis on self-discipline left little space for the older theological concepts of sin, grace, and forgiveness. As a result, the moral decibel was often very high, and such economic realities as patronage and preferment always had to be presented within a collectively acceptable framework. This Charles Colby had ignored, to his grief, when expediency led him to make a quick appointment for the vacant customs collectorship in Coaticook. The outrage he encountered at the time was only one extreme expression of a moral order based not on coercion but on self-discipline, where individual concerns had to be presented in the language of collective well-being and where there was little room for dissent. In many ways, as previous chapters have elaborated, this was also Charles Colby's personal world and that of his wife, children, and community. How these various spheres interlocked with religion to shape a distinct late-nineteenth-century social culture will be discussed briefly in the conclusion that follows.

Conclusion

Charles Colby's 1891 election defeat brought to an end a period which, despite affording personal satisfaction, had left him little time to devote to his scattered business interests. Although Colby was plagued by deteriorating health in the final sixteen years of his life, growing returns from the Imperial Writing Machine Company brought him the stability and prosperity that until then had eluded him.[1] Travel overseas for the entire family, long dreamed about, had begun in 1890 when he took his older son, Charles William, on a business trip to England; as a recently minted Harvard PH D, Charles William wished to do postgraduate work at Oxford and Freiburg.[2] Once free of politics, and anxious to develop his emerging interest in the Imperial Writing Machine Company, Colby took his wife and daughter Jessie to Europe in September 1891, staying until October 1893. There, they were joined at various intervals by the younger son, John, as well as by Abby, her husband Somerset Aikins, and their infant son Carroll.

Finances remained a concern during the first European visit, and with more time than money available, Hattie and Jessie availed themselves of the many opportunities for religious consumerism that were offered by British and European church life. Nothing could match an unforgettable Easter "field day" in Montreal a few years earlier, when Hattie had managed to attend six different church services in a single day, but London offered its own highlights, such as first-class religious concerts, and sermons by the famed American preacher Phillips Brooks at Westminster Abbey.[3] For Jessie, Sunday afternoons in London

Hattie and Charles Colby, retired at Carrollcroft and back from their extensive visit to Europe, 1895 (CCM)

provided the chance to help in various missions, including the West Central Mission established by the Methodist social reformer Hugh Price Hughes.[4] Maintaining for the remainder of her long life a lively interest in the religious literature on social issues, she was, however, more an observer of the new religious responses to urban and industrial problems than a participant. While travel abroad allowed the two women to revel in sightseeing and some consumerism, it did not effect any marked change in outlook and values. Even in Europe's cultural centres, it was possible to maintain such familiar evangelical rhythms as Sunday visiting and church attendance, often in the presence of fellow Canadian travellers, among whom were a surprising number of Stanstead neighbours.[5]

Once they were home, it took little effort to slip back into a familiar village culture, now enhanced by the increased travel and social sophistication of Stanstead's well-to-do. Accounts of prayer meetings, congregational gossip, church socials, and revivals of the more subdued style among the student body at Stanstead College continued to surface on a regular basis in the writings of mother and daughter.[6] As

Tea at Carrollcroft in 1910 for a new family configuration: Jessie, Hattie (now widowed), Dr John Child Colby, and his wife Mary (May) Williams Colby (CCM)

her mother's health deteriorated, it was the public-spirited and religiously minded Jessie who, first as secretary to her father and after his death in 1907 as *de facto* household head, provided continuity with old-established patterns of family life. Until her death in 1958 at the age of ninety-seven, she followed her parents' example of benevolence and church participation from her base at Carrollcroft. The owner of a temperance hotel from 1917 until its closing in 1934, and a trustee and generous benefactor of both Stanstead College and Centenary United Church (so named after church union in 1925), she was also active in such secular organizations as the Imperial Order Daughters of the Empire.[7]

Despite this loyalty to her parents' ways and despite her own self-designation after church union as "the last leaf on the Methodist tree," there were signs of change. While church and community life in Stanstead remained outwardly stable, the region's economic activity, and hence the interests and the presence of male leaders, had continued the shift to the West that had begun in the 1870s and towards Britain a few decades later. Instructive here are the lives of Jessie's two brothers. In choice of career, each continued in the family tradition, but this did not include the religious leadership that marked their father's and sister's community involvement. John, the younger, who followed his grandfather Moses into the medical profession, established a practice in Stanstead in 1904. Although often detained by his busy practice, he attended Methodist Centenary Church when time permitted, but civic leadership found expression in other community concerns, such as sitting as a trustee of Stanstead College, being involved in the county's agricultural events, as well as serving as a village councillor and in 1923 as mayor. With his young wife Mary (May) Spafford Williams of Knowlton and their two children, he lived at Carrollcroft, where in 1921 May suddenly succumbed to typhoid fever. Tragedy struck again in 1926, when only a few days after having agreed to let his name stand as the Conservative candidate for Stanstead County, he died of a heart attack, leaving his young children in the care of their uncle Charles William.[8]

Change in the old patterns was also evident in the life of Charles William. He, too, married locally, selecting in 1897, to the delight of his family, a Bostonian of Stanstead extraction, Emma Cobb (known as Kitty), granddaughter of Wilder Pierce, Stanstead's Methodist benefactor of an earlier era.[9] In 1894 Charles William was appointed to the chair of Canadian history at McGill University, and thus he and Emma continued to be within easy travelling distance of Stanstead. In time, they followed Abby into the Anglican Church, but for many years Emma, along with the other Colby women, remained a pew holder and a contributor to Stanstead's Methodist Centenary Church. However, her husband's civic duties did not include the same degree of religious participation that had marked his father's active years. Church suppers, for example, which had provided an earlier generation with a space for matchmaking, had been replaced by such leisure activities as the theatre, dancing, and tennis. It may have been this type of social change that had prompted Charles William lightheartedly to inform his bride to be, "I love THEE exceedingly but don't ask me to sing for the missionaries. I don't think I *could*. Nor even for the temperance people as I recollect it is."[10]

Although Charles William's site of identity was no longer Stanstead but Montreal (and later, with his increased business commitments, became New York), one element did remain unchanged – the moral responsibility to provide for one's family. In 1905 this had entailed heeding his aging father's request to remain in Canada to look after the family; thus he turned down an appointment to the chair of colonial history at Oxford University, a chair recently established by Cecil Rhodes.[11] Two years after his father's death, he shifted his time commitments into the family's business interests and in 1920 resigned from McGill. While material conditions had considerably improved in the past decade, his father's investments still called for active and aggressive management if the lifestyle of his widowed mother and his sister were to be maintained.[12] His efforts met with growing success, to the benefit not only of Hattie and Jessie but also his older sister Abby, who, widowed in 1911 and in financially straitened circumstances, intermittently stayed at Carrollcroft until her death in 1943.[13] During these years, life at Carrollcroft continued its steady refinement as its female occupants involved themselves in church and community affairs, supported literature and the arts, and travelled extensively, keeping in contact through ceaseless correspondence with their extended and increasingly dispersed family.[14] To embark on that story would move us into a very different space and time from the period 1830–90 that has provided the main focus of this study. Instead, a review of its findings and a brief analysis of the wider implications of the connections between family, religion, and community life during these years are in order.

"In religious belief and practice a group's ethos is rendered intellectually reasonable by being shown to present a way of life ideally adapted to the actual state of affairs," cultural anthropologist Clifford Geertz has noted in an oft-quoted sentence.[15] His words are a helpful reminder of the interpenetration of the religious and the social, the sacred and the secular, the private and public when, as in this study, the family becomes the primary site of belief and practice. The implications of this for our understanding of the specific form taken by evangelical religion in nineteenth-century Canada need now to be briefly laid out.

Even to imply that evangelical religion took on one single form contradicts its nature as a lived phenomenon. Along with Geertz's ideal type, in any society there are also individuals and groups who may experience a dissonance with the prevailing religious idiom. Instructive here are the religious beliefs and practices of the first generation of this study, Moses and Lemira Colby. Devout Christians, well-educated members of the middle class, they failed to be drawn to the religious revivalism which in most of the historical literature has been presented as *the* progressive religious movement of the early nineteenth century. Although neither Moses nor Lemira could speak of having undergone an evangelical conversion, this did not undermine his assiduous Bible reading or her concern to transmit to her children a biblical understanding of salvation. Both, moreover, faithfully attended their local Congregational church and thus participated in a denominational evangelical identity. For their children, evangelical religion took on a different form. For Charles and Hattie, this was most comfortably expressed in the Methodist Church and in the idiom of a liberal evangelical theology. Stressing divine love rather than God's righteousness, this thought blended easily with other prevailing idioms, such as common-sense philosophy and romantic literature, and had been popularized through the writings of Henry Ward Beecher and middle-class periodical literature such as *Scribner's* and the Methodist *Ladies' Repository*. Their sister-in-law Melvina, on the other hand, experienced evangelical religion in a less irenic form. For her, as indeed for a number of Charles Colby's political critics, its moral dimension was more black and white, as reflected in the evangelical weekly the *Montreal Witness*, whose editor fought a continual battle against Roman Catholic influence in his province and country. Melvina's few extant pieces of correspondence reflect a similar besieged mentality and, unlike Hattie's letters, are laced with traditional devotional language.[16] That evangelical religion found expression in more than one idiom, even among members of the same generation, should come as no surprise. Examining the writings of Methodist ministers in early republican America, historian Russell Richey has uncovered at least four "languages" of Methodism.[17] His insights underscore that at any given time, even within a single family, there might coexist several "varieties of religious experience," a term coined a century later by William James, whose own faith defied any simplistic categorization.[18]

This simple conclusion leads us to a second, more complex, observation. Implicit in Geertz's comment is the assumption that, to be meaningful, religious idioms do more than reflect a world. They also make it, and they do so within the social and economic structures of a given time and place. The defining influence of these structures on family life needs to be recalled. Think, for example, of Moses' careful land purchases and medical research, of his elder son's untiring business and political activity, and of the often financially cramped efforts of Hattie and Lemira to run a household and educate their children. Such activity was directed to one end, providing for the needs of the family. Theirs was a socio-economic world in the process of rapid transformation, a world where fortunes could be quickly made but where carefully accumulated land could easily be lost. These were decades when economic interests were redefining long-standing social relations through such means as provincial education systems, a Quebec Civil Code, and, as was illustrated by the John Martin case, through new marriage and divorce legislation. It was within this changed context that family took on its meaning. Providing for its welfare became the single goal of otherwise incoherent business efforts for entrepreneurs such as Charles Colby. The love its members extended to one another

The tombstones of Charles and Hattie Colby, with carefully selected Bible texts, part of the family burial plot in the Crystal Lake Cemetery, established in 1861 by Stanstead entrepreneur and philanthropist Carlos Pierce (CCM)

became the one reliable source of security in a competitive marketplace, where formerly familiar signposts of time and space no longer held meaning. All of this has been much discussed by family historians and is richly illustrated in the correspondence that flowed so steadily between Charles and Hattie Colby and their children.

Less studied than the world they were making is the religious belief and practice through which they interpreted it. Religious symbols, beliefs, and practices were part of the world they helped shape. When some of these lost their salience, as happened with Moses and Lemira, their children turned for meaning to new forms, congruent with their changing middle-class experience. I am not speaking here of "accommodation" or "adaptation," terms frequently – and usually negatively – used in conjunction with the period's emerging forms of liberal Protestantism; I mean religion as lived experience. As lived experience, religion by its nature adopts a cultural form. Foremost among these were the sober businessmen's urban revivals of 1857–58, a theology that stressed God's love and immanence within the family, and such shared rituals as family prayers and Sabbath observance, which united loved ones separated by distance. Equally important as cultural forms, but operating more at the communal level, were voluntary societies, church-building projects, the temperance movement, travelling lecturers, and a burgeoning industry in religious products, from family Bibles to children's books and toys. The pews in Stanstead's Wesleyan Methodist Centenary Church, its wall plaques commemorating benefactors, the new Crystal Lake Cemetery with its family plots and biblically inscribed gravestones were only the local expression of a material religious idiom that was pervasive.

Taken together, these helped shape everyday life. They offered a sense of stability and continuity in a society whose order was threatened by transiency, fragmentation, and competitiveness. They did so by recasting forms of order and community in new ways. Where earlier generations of Protestants had reshaped the older identity of Christendom by sacralizing the group – whether in terms of an elect nation, a "godly community," or "a city on a hill" – in the dramatically changed world of the latter nineteenth century, sacralization devolved upon the family. In Stanstead's pioneer days it had been the Congregationalists who had tried to carry on the old New England ideal of an integrated ecclesiastical and secular community. When this had fragmented under the impact of competing religious denominations, revivalism, and growing economic disparity, community was reconfigured in ways congruent with changing experience. Voluntary societies, church-building projects, new pew-rental systems, and a new educational institution for higher learning all ensured the continuity of the community by making its base the needs and aspirations of the middle-class family. People joined a church as members of a family; they sat together in a family pew; men and women in gendered ways devoted valuable time to the maintenance of the church fabric; and their children gathered in Sunday schools and young people's societies and were introduced into youth branches of the temperance movement. By such means, religion continued to be an integral part of community identity even as it reinforced family identity.

The fit between this lived religion and the social structures of the time did not, however, come without strains and tensions, ranging from internal congregational strife to the Roman Catholic and Protestant differences that laid a minefield for politicians in the new Canadian state. As in the newly minted name, the Dominion of Canada, religious language and ideals served to proclaim that, all appearances to the contrary, life remained organically connected. Whether through philosophical idealism taught in university classrooms, policies of economic protectionism, patriotic references to a mother country, or through the emerging social gospel's slogan "the fatherhood of God and the brotherhood of man," unity was not simply a family ideal. It was to be seen to be applicable to all of public life. As was noted earlier in references to American Whig thought, Protestants in Canada were not alone in proclaiming ideals of social harmony. They were, however, spared the wrenching experience of a civil war; and only after the period examined in this study did they begin to realize the enormity of the urban problems arising from large-scale urbanization and immigration. Even then, as illustrated by the experience of Hattie and Jessie Colby in the post-1890 years, material affluence and a base in small-town Canada could effectively remind one that, at its root, life remained unchanged.

This was not the case for everyone – for some, the old ways were growing thin – as I have hinted in the brief description of the changing world of the Colby men. It was their world, as I have come to see at the end of this family study, that ultimately holds the answer to the question raised in the introduction. How indeed could it happen that the same period that saw the sacralization of the family also contributed to its secularization? Here we need to return briefly to the concept of "lived religion" as it has been developed in the preceding pages. The close fit observed between the socio-economic structures, the family, and Protestant religion in this period entailed that for Victorian domestic religion to endure, society had to remain static. It was, in short, dependent on a unique set of socio-economic, religious, and cultural forces not only for its origins but also for its continuance. As these forces changed, so did the family and so did religion. This does not mean that religion disappeared, but it did change its form. As Moses and Lemira Colby knew all too well, the world that parents bequeath to their children is not the one the children inherit.

Notes

ABBREVIATIONS

ALCA   Abby Lemira Colby Aikins
ANQM   Archives nationales du Québec à Montréal
ANQS   Archives nationales du Québec à Sherbrooke
CCC   Charles Carroll Colby
CWC   Charles William Colby
ESC   Emily Strong Colby
FC   Fonds Colby, Stanstead Historical Society
HCC   Harriet (Hattie) Child Colby
JMC   Jessie Maud Colby
LAC   Library and Archives Canada
LSC   Lemira Strong Colby
MFC   Moses French Colby
WBC   William Benton Colby

INTRODUCTION

1 B.F. Hubbard, *Forests and Clearings: The History of Stanstead County* (Montreal: Lovell 1874), 114–15.
2 Reginald Bibby, *Restless Gods: The Renaissance of Religion in Canada* (Toronto: Stoddart 2002), 210. For old patterns and new trends, see also Nancy Tatom Ammerman and Wade Clark Roof, eds., *Work, Family, and Religion in Contemporary Society* (London: Routledge 1995).

3 John Gillis, *A World of Their Own Making: Myth, Ritual, and the Quest for Family Values* (New York: Basic Books 1996), 18. See especially his ch. 1, "Myths of Family Past."

4 Bettina Bradbury, "The Fragmented Family: Family Strategies in the Face of Death, Illness, and Poverty, Montreal, 1860–1893," in *Childhood and Family in Canadian History*, ed. Joy Parr (Toronto: McClelland & Stewart 1982), 109–28. See also her *Working Families: Ages, Gender, and Daily Survival in Industrializing Montreal* (Toronto: Oxford University Press 1993), and Peter Gossage, *Families in Transition: Industry and Population in Nineteenth-Century Saint-Hyacinthe* (Montreal/Kingston: McGill-Queen's University Press 1999).

5 As a sampling, see Frances Gies and Joseph Gies, *Marriage and Family in the Middle Ages* (New York: Harper & Row c1987); Natalie Davis, *The Return of Martin Guerre* (Cambridge, Mass.: Harvard University Press 1983); Stephen Ozment, *When Fathers Ruled: Family Life in Reformation Europe* (Cambridge, Mass.: Harvard University Press 1983); Rosemary O'Day, *The Family and Family Relationships, 1500–1900: England, France, and the United States of America* (New York: St Martin's Press 1994); John Demos, *A Little Commonwealth: Family Life in Plymouth Colony* (New York: Oxford University Press 1970), and Gerald Moran and Maris Vinovskis, *Religion, Family, and the Life Course* (Ann Arbor: University of Michigan Press 1992).

6 See, for example, Stephen Mintz and Susan Kellog, *Domestic Revolutions: A Social History of American Family Life* (New York: Free Press 1988); Gillis, *A World of Their Own Making*; Mary P. Ryan, *Cradle of the Middle Class: The Family in Oneida County, New York, 1790–1865* (Cambridge, Mass.: Cambridge University Press 1981); and Leonore Davidoff et al., *The Family Story: Blood, Contract, and Intimacy, 1830–1960* (London: Longman 1999). A study that takes a more static approach but offers helpful insight into family life in early Victorian Canada is Françoise Noël's *Family Life and Sociability in Upper and Lower Canada, 1780–1870: A View from Diaries and Family Correspondence* (Montreal/Kingston: McGill-Queen's University Press 2003).

7 This is discussed in some detail in two fine studies that do focus on religion and the Victorian family and have been very helpful in the present study: Colleen McDannell, *The Christian Home in Victorian America, 1840–1900* (Bloomington: Indiana University Press 1986), and Margaret Lamberts Bendroth, *Growing Up Protestant: Parents, Children, and the Mainline Churches* (New Brunswick, NJ: Rutgers University Press 2002). For studies that look negatively on the impact on religion, see, for example, A. Gregory Schneider, *The Way of the Cross Leads Home: The Domestication of American Methodism* (Bloomington: Indiana University Press 1993), and Janet Fishburn, *Confronting the Idolatry of Family: A New Vision for the Family of God* (Nashville: Abingdon Press

1991). An excellent introduction to the American historiography on the more general subject of gender and religion is David G. Hackett, "Gender and Religion in American Culture, 1870–1930," *Religion and American Culture* 5 (Summer 1995): 127–57.
8 Bendroth, *Growing Up Protestant*, 13, 36.
9 Davidoff et al., *The Family Story*, 81.
10 Gillis, *A World of Their Own Making*, 72.
11 Mark A. Noll, *A History of Christianity in the United States and Canada* (Grand Rapids: Eerdmans 1992), 545–50.
12 For a succinct description of ultramontanism in its Canadian application, see John W. Grant, *The Church in the Canadian Era*, new edn. (Burlington: Welch 1988), 69–73. For an analysis of the institutional role of Rome, see Roberto Perin, *Rome in Canada: The Vatican and the Canadian Affairs in the Late Victorian Age* (Toronto: University of Toronto Press 1990). The implementation in Victorian Toronto is masterfully examined in Mark McGowan, *The Waning of the Green: Catholics, the Irish, and Identity in Toronto, 1887–1922* (Montreal/Kingston: McGill-Queen's University Press 1999), and in Quebec by Roberto Perin, "Elaborating a Public Culture: The Catholic Church in Nineteenth-Century Quebec," in *Religion and Public Life in Canada: Historical and Comparative Perspectives*, ed. Marguerite Van Die (Toronto: University of Toronto Press 2001), 87–108. McDannell, *The Christian Home in Victorian America*, compares Protestant to Roman Catholic domestic piety. Two studies that draw attention to the familial dimensions of ultramontanism are Ann Taves, *The Household of Faith: Roman Catholic Devotions in Mid-Nineteenth-Century America* (South Bend, Ind.: University of Notre Dame Press 1986), and Brian P. Clarke, *Piety and Nationalism: Lay Voluntary Associations and the Creation of an Irish-Catholic Community in Toronto, 1850–1895* (Montreal/Kingston: McGill-Queen's University Press 1993).
13 The denominational varieties of evangelicalism in Canada are explored in *Aspects of the Canadian Evangelical Experience*, ed. George A. Rawlyk (Montreal/Kingston: McGill-Queen's University Press 1997). See also Neil Semple, *The Lord's Dominion: The History of Canadian Methodism* (Montreal/Kingston: McGill-Queen's University Press 1996), and Richard W. Vaudry, *The Free Church in Victorian Canada, 1844–1861* (Waterloo: Wilfrid Laurier University Press 1989). A good introduction to evangelicalism as a movement is Leonard I. Sweet, "Nineteenth-Century Evangelicalism," in *Encyclopedia of the American Religious Experience*, 3 vols., ed. Peter Williams and Charles Lippy (New York: Charles Scribner's Sons 1988), 2:875–900.
14 These widely used categories originated in David Bebbington, *Evangelicalism in Modern Britain: A History from the 1730s to the 1980s* (Winchester, Mass.: Allen & Unwin 1988).

15 Sweet, "Nineteenth-Century Evangelicalism." As an example of the conflation of evangelicalism with revivalism, see George A. Rawlyk, *The Canada Fire: Radical Evangelicalism in British North America 1775–1812* (Montreal/Kingston: McGill-Queen's University Press 1994), especially the conclusion.

16 For analyses of the impact of disestablishment, see R.D. Gidney and W.P.J. Millar, *Professional Gentlemen: The Professions in Nineteenth-Century Ontario* (Toronto: University of Toronto Press 1994), 106–24; William Westfall, *Two Worlds: The Protestant Culture of Nineteenth-Century Ontario* (Montreal/Kingston: McGill-Queen's University Press 1989), and Marguerite Van Die, "'The Double Vision': Evangelical Piety as Derivative and Indigenous in Victorian English Canada," in *Evangelicalism: Comparative Studies of Popular Protestantism in North America, the British Isles, and Beyond, 1700–1900*, ed. Mark Noll et al. (Oxford: Oxford University Press 1994), 253–72.

17 For the American experience, see Mark A. Noll, ed., *God and Mammon: Protestants, Money, and the Market, 1760–1860* (Oxford: Oxford University Press 2002). For Britain, see especially Leonore Davidoff and Catherine Hall, *Family Fortunes: Men and Women of the English Middle Class, 1780–1850* (London: Hutchinson 1987), 71–192. For Canada, research is more limited but suggestive. See, for example, J.I. Little, *The Child Letters: Public and Private Life in a Canadian Merchant-Politician's Family, 1841–1845* (Montreal/Kingston: McGill-Queen's University Press 1995), and Marguerite Van Die, "The Marks of a Genuine Revival: Religion, Social Change, Gender, and Community in Mid-Victorian Brantford, Ontario," *Canadian Historical Review* 79, no. 3 (1998): 524–63. Gordon Darroch and Lee Soltow, drawing on a detailed examination of the relationship between religious affiliation and home ownership in the 1871 census in Ontario, note that "the groups with the strongest Protestant sectarian roots were most likely to foster middle-class standards of family life, social responsibility, and self-discipline"; see their *Property and Inequality in Victorian Ontario: Structural Patterns and Cultural Communities in the 1871 Census* (Toronto: University of Toronto Press 1994), 97. See also David G. Burley, *A Particular Condition in Life: Self-Employment and Social Mobility in Mid-Victorian Brantford* (Montreal/Kingston: McGill-Queen's University Press, 1994), 76–8; and T.W. Acheson, "The Problem of Methodist Identity," in *The Methodist Contribution to Atlantic Canada*, ed. Charles Scobie and J.W. Grant (Montreal/Kingston: McGill-Queen's University Press 1992), 122, note 32.

18 See Lynne Marks, *Revivals and Roller Rinks: Religion, Leisure, and Identity in Late-Nineteenth-Century Small Town Ontario* (Toronto: University of Toronto Press 1996); Albert Schrauwers, *Awaiting the Millennium: The*

Children of Peace and the Village of Hope (Toronto: University of Toronto Press 1993); Royden Lœuwen, *Family, Church, and Market: A Mennonite Community in the Old and New Worlds, 1850–1930* (Urbana: University of Chicago Press 1993); Nancy Christie, ed., *Households of Faith: Family, Community and Gender in Canada, 1760–1969* (Montreal/Kingston: McGill-Queen's University Press 2001); Hannah M. Lane, "'Wife, Mother, Sister, Friend': Methodist Women in St. Stephen, New Brunswick, 1861–1881," in *Separate Spheres: Women's Worlds in the Nineteenth-Century Maritimes*, ed. Janet Guildford and Suzanne Morton (Fredericton: Acadiensis Press 1994), 93–117; and Van Die, "The Marks of A Genuine Revival."

19 Ramsay Cook, *The Regenerators: Social Criticism in Late Victorian English Canada* (Toronto: University of Toronto Press 1985); David Marshall, *Secularizing the Faith: Canadian Protestant Clergy and the Crisis of Belief, 1850–1940* (Toronto: University of Toronto Press 1992); A.B. McKillop, *A Disciplined Intelligence: Critical Inquiry and Canadian Thought in the Victorian Era* (Montreal/Kingston: McGill-Queen's University Press 1979); and Westfall, *Two Worlds.*

20 I have briefly made this point in *An Evangelical Mind: Nathanael Burwash and the Methodist Tradition in Canada* (Montreal/Kingston: McGill-Queen's University Press 1989), ch. 4.

21 For a thoughtful critique, see Michael Gauvreau, "Beyond the Half-Way House: Evangelicalism and the Shaping of English Canadian Culture," *Acadiensis* 20, no. 2 (1990): 158–72. The liberal and reform-minded thrust of evangelicalism in Canada during this period and beyond is discussed in Richard Allen, "The Background of the Social Gospel in Canada," in *The Social Gospel in Canada: Papers on the Interdisciplinary Conference on the Social Gospel in Canada,* ed. Allen (Ottawa: National Museums of Canada 1975), 2–36. Michael Gauvreau, *The Evangelical Century: College and Creed in English Canada from the Great Revival to the Great Depression* (Kingston/Montreal: McGill-Queen's University Press 1991); Phyllis Airhart, *Serving the Present Age: Revivalism, Progressivism, and the Methodist Tradition in Canada* (Montreal/Kingston: McGill-Queen's University Press 1992); Nancy Christie and Michael Gauvreau, *A Full-Orbed Christianity: The Protestant Churches and Social Welfare in Canada, 1900–1945* (Montreal/Kingston: McGill-Queen's University Press 1996).

22 Gary Dorrien, *The Making of American Liberal Theology: Imagining Progressive Religion, 1805–1900* (Louisville: Westminster John Knox Press 2001), xxiii. An introduction to liberal Protestantism in the United States (and a work helpful in charting its links to late-nineteenth-century evangelicalism) is William R. Hutchison, *The Modernist Impulse in American Protestantism* (Oxford: Oxford University

Press 1976). The fracturing of nineteenth-century evangelicalism into fundamentalist and "liberal" forms is detailed in George Marsden, *Fundamentalism and American Culture: The Shaping of Twentieth-Century Evangelicalism, 1870–1925* (Oxford: Oxford University Press, 1980).

23 I have used the problematic but commonly employed term "mainline" to designate the larger Protestant denominations in Canada that held cultural authority in the nineteenth and early twentieth centuries, as distinct from numerically smaller groups. I have also used it to distinguish them from evangelicals such as the Free Methodists and members of the Christian and Missionary Alliance, who had taken a more conservative stance on cultural change by the turn of the century. For a helpful discussion on the use of the term in the contemporary U.S. context, see Robert Wuthnow, *The Restructuring of American Religion* (Princeton, NJ: Princeton University Press 1988).

24 Ian McKay, "CHR Forum: The Liberal Order Framework: A Prospectus for a Reconnaissance of Canadian History," *Canadian Historical Review* 81, no. 4 (2000): 925, note 16. I have not, however, followed the advice of my valued colleague to move the "secularization" discourse into a debate about "liberalization." In my view, rather than subsuming it into either agenda, domestic religion in the nineteenth century needs first to be understood on its own terms.

25 Gerald Friesen has rightly pointed out that the historical study of religion in Canada has been handicapped by a reliance on ecclesiastical and, more recently, functionalist definitions of religion; see Gerald Friesen, *Citizens and Nation: An Essay on History, Communication, and Canada* (Toronto: University of Toronto Press 2000), 272, note 21. Both of these definitions have informed the historiography on secularization. For a definition emphasizing the substantive nature of religion as "an attempt to order individual and societal life in terms of culturally received ultimate priorities," see "Religion" in *The Encyclopedia of Religion*, 282–92.

26 Exemplary studies include the trilogy by Serge Gagnon, *Mourir: hier et aujourd'hui* (Sainte-Foy: Presses de l'Université Laval 1987), *Plaisir d'amour et crainte de Dieu: sexualité et confession au Bas-Canada* (Sainte-Foy: Presses de l'Université Laval 1990), and *Mariage et famille au temps de Papineau* (Sainte-Foy: Presses de l'Université Laval 1993); and Christine Hudon, *Prêtres et fidèles dans le diocèse de Saint-Hyacinthe 1820–1875* (Sillery: Septentrion 1996).

27 For the concept "lived religion" as developed by Emmanuel LeRoy Ladurie, Carlo Ginzberg, and others, and introduced to an English-speaking audience, see David D. Hall, ed., *Lived Religion in America: Toward a History of Practice* (Princeton: Princeton University Press 1997).

28 In addition to the preceding citation, see Philip R. Vandermeer and Robert P. Swierenga, eds., *Belief and Behavior: Essays in the New Religious History* (New Brunswick, NJ: Rutgers, 1991); Thomas A. Tweed, ed., *Retelling U.S. Religious History* (Berkeley: University of California Press 1997); Harry S. Stout and D.G. Hart, eds., *New Directions in American Religious History* (Oxford: Oxford University Press 1997); and Jon Butler and Harry S. Stout, *Religion in American History: A Reader* (Oxford: Oxford University Press 1998).

29 Exemplary works are Colleen McDannell, *Material Christianity: Religion and Popular Culture in America* (New Haven: Yale University Press 1995); Robert Orsi, *The Madonna of 115th Street: Faith and Community in Italian Harlem, 1880–1950* (New Haven: Yale University Press 1985) and *Thank You, St. Jude: Women's Devotion to the Patrion Saint of Hopeless Causes* (New Haven: Yale University Press 1996); Richard Bushman, *The Refinement of America: Persons, Houses, Cities* (New York: Vantage Books 1993); and David Morgan, *Visual Piety: A History and Theory of Popular Religious Images* (Berkeley: University of California Press 1998).

30 Anne S. Brown and David D. Hall, "Family Strategies and Religious Practice: Baptism and the Lord's Supper in Early New England, in *Lived Religion*, ed. Hall, 41–68.

31 Robert Orsi, "Everyday Miracles: The Study of Lived Religion," in *Lived Religion*, ed. Hall, 10.

32 Ibid., 7.

33 Noll, ed., *God and Mammon*; Larry Eskridge and Mark A. Noll, eds., *More Money, More Ministry: Money and Evangelicals in Recent North American History* (Grand Rapids: Eerdmans 2000); Leigh Eric Schmidt, *Consumer Rites: The Buying and Selling of American Holidays* (Princeton: Princeton University Press 1995); and R. Laurence Moore, *Selling God: American Religion in the Marketplace of Culture* (Oxford: Oxford University Press 1994). For Britain, see, for example, David J. Jeremy, ed., *Religion, Business, and Wealth in Modern Britain* (London: Routledge 1998), and Boyd Hilton, *The Age of Atonement: The Influence of Evangelicalism on Social and Economic Thought, 1795–1865* (Oxford: Clarendon Press 1988).

34 See, for example, Noll, ed., *God and Mammon*, 54–120, and the approach to religion and class in Davidoff and Hall, *Family Fortunes*, esp. 71–192. A careful Canadian study is Allen B. Robertson, *John Wesley's Nova Scotia Businessmen: Halifax Methodist Merchants, 1815–1855* (New York: Peter Lang 2000), esp. ch. 3.

35 For an insightful and suggestive analysis, viewed through the thought of Antonio Gramsci, see T. Jackson Lears, "The Concept of Cultural Hegemony: Problems and Possibilities," *American Historical Review* 90 (1985): 567–93. I am especially indebted, in my understanding of the

form taken by evangelicalism in nineteenth-century Canada, to his observation (p. 571) that while the economic base does not determine specific forms of consciousness, it does determine which forms are possible. A comprehensive study of evangelical cultural hegemony in the United States is Richard J. Carwardine, *Evangelicals and Politics in Antebellum America* (Knoxville: University of Tennessee Press 1993). For an outstanding study that evaluates the extent of Protestant hegemony in three Ontario communities, see Marks, *Revivals and Roller Rinks*.

36 Mark Noll, *America's God: From Jonathan Edwards to Abraham Lincoln* (Oxford: Oxford University Press 2002), esp. 93–113, and Daniel Walker Howe, *Making the American Self: Jonathan Edwards to Abraham Lincoln* (Cambridge, Mass.: Harvard University Press 1997), 50–77. A helpful survey of the historiography can be found in Daniel Walker Howe, "Protestantism, Voluntarism, and Personal Identity in Antebellum America, in *New Directions in American Religious History*, ed. Stout and Hart, 206–38.

37 Daniel Walker Howe, *The Political Culture of the American Whigs* (Chicago: University of Chicago Press 1979); Carwardine, *Evangelicals and Politics in Antebellum America*. See also the essays by Carwardine, Howe, Robert Swierenga, and John F. Wilson, in *Religion and American Politics from the Colonial Period to the 1980s*, ed. Mark. A. Noll (Oxford: Oxford University Press 1990); and George M. Thomas, *Revivalism and Cultural Change: Christianity, Nation Building, and the Market in the Nineteenth-Century United States* (Chicago: University of Chicago Press 1989), which makes a less convincing argument for evangelical support of the Republican Party later in the century. Still of interest for its examination of evangelical support for Anglo-American liberal parties, but predating the research into evangelical support for the Whigs, is Robert Kelley, *Transatlantic Persuasion: The Liberal-Democratic Mind in the Age of Gladstone* (New York: Knopf 1969). For Canada, see Robertson, *John Wesley's Nova Scotia Businessmen*, ch. 5, and T.W. Acheson, "Evangelicals and Public Life in Southern New Brunswick, 1830–1880," in *Religion and Public Life in Canada: Historical and Comparative Perspectives*, ed. Marguerite Van Die (Toronto: University of Toronto Press 2001), 50–68.

38 For the prevalence of common-sense thought in nineteenth-century Canadian higher education, see McKillop, *A Disciplined Intelligence*, Gauvreau, *The Evangelical Century*, and Van Die, *An Evangelical Mind*.

39 John W. Grant, "Canadian Confederation and the Protestant Churches," *Church History* 38 (1969): 1–11.

40 Scholarship on evangelical participation in political life in nineteenth-century Canada is limited, but Methodist attitudes to politics pre-1850 have been examined in Goldwin French, *Parsons and Politics: The Role of the Wesleyan Methodists in Upper Canada and the Maritimes from 1850 to*

1855 (Toronto: Ryerson 1962). A correlation between denominational affiliation and voting patterns has been discerned in Toronto in the 1836 election, with Canadian Methodists (whose ties were originally with the U.S. parent church) favouring Reform, while the Wesleyan Methodists (whose institutional ties were British) favoured the Tories; see Paul Romney, "On the Eve of the Rebellion: Nationality, Religion, and Class in the Toronto Election of 1836," in *Old Ontario: Essays in Honour of J.M.S. Careless,* ed. David Keane and Colin Read (Toronto: Dundurn Press 1990), 192–216. Some local Methodist support for Reform is also noted in Little, *The Child Letters,* 10–30. T.W. Acheson has made an important comparison between American Whig and New Brunswick Reform support for moral reform legislation; Acheson, "Evangelicals and Public Life in Southern New Brunswick, 1830–1880," 50–68. Evangelical opposition to Roman Catholicism in public life in the last quarter of the nineteenth century is masterfully analysed in J.R. Miller, *Equal Rights: The Jesuits' Estates Act Controversy* (Montreal/Kingston: McGill-Queen's University Press 1979).

41 For wide-ranging study of the discrepancy between the real and ideal British home in the nineteenth and twentieth centuries, see Tony Chapman and Jenny Hockey, eds., *Ideal Homes? Social Change and Domestic Life* (London: Routledge 1999), esp. 1–29.

42 Here I am following the path of my esteemed colleague, the late George Rawlyk, who used the term as an initial entry into amorphous and largely overlooked areas of investigation.

43 This study could not have been written without the excellent recent research on social and political life in the Eastern Townships by Jean-Pierre Kesteman and J.I. Little, especially in Jean-Pierre Kesteman, Peter Southam, and Diane Saint-Pierre, *Histoire des cantons de l'Est* (Sainte-Foy: Presses de l'Université Laval 1998), and J.I. Little, *State and Society in Transition: The Politics of Institutional Reform in the Eastern Townships, 1838–1852* (Montreal/Kingston: McGill-Queen's University Press 1997). Invaluable for understanding the role of the various Protestant religions in the Eastern Townships in the first half of the nineteenth century is Little's *Borderland Religion: The Emergence of an English-Canadian Identity, 1792–1852* (Toronto: University of Toronto Press 2004).

44 The reasons for Moses' decision to support the Conservative rather than the Patriote or republican cause are briefly described on page 32. Charles Carroll of Carrollton (1737–1832) was a member of the failed mission in 1776 to persuade French Canadians to relinquish their allegiance to the crown of England, and represented his native Maryland at the Continental Congress, becoming the only Roman Catholic to sign the Declaration of Independence;

http://www.colonialhall/com/carroll. I thank John Colby for sharing his uncle Charles William's recollection of the origins of the name Charles Carroll.

45 Interest in one's family roots has been seen as a significant step in the larger Victorian project of reconstructing the family as a separate entity with its own distinct past; see Gillis, *A World of Their Own Making*, 75. Epistolary conventions and the role of letters in maintaining family ties are examined in Jane E. Harrison, *Adieu pour cette année: la correspondance au Canada, 1640–1830* (Ottawa: Musée canadien des civilisations 1997); Lorraine Gadoury, *La famille dans son intimité: échanges épistolaires de l'élite canadienne au XVIIIe siècle* (Montreal: Hurtubise 1998), and in Noël, *Family Life and Sociability*, 3–15.

46 I have examined aspects of Charles Colby's career as an evangelical businessman in "A Christian Businessman in the Eastern Townships: The Convergence of Precept and Practice in Nineteenth-Century Evangelical Gender Construction," *Journal of the Canadian Historical Association*, New Series, 10 (1999): 103–27.

CHAPTER ONE

1 Telegram, 8 January 1884, RMS *Germanic*, Charles Carroll Colby (CCC) Papers, Series 4:A, Box 4:5, Fonds Colby (FC), Stanstead Historical Society.

2 Moses French Colby (MFC) Papers, Series 2, Box 1:1, Biographical Material (unsigned, but written in Charles Colby's hand), FC.

3 Robert Orsi, *Thank You, St. Jude: Women's Devotion to the Patron Saint of Hopeless Causes* (New Haven: Yale University Press 1996), 200.

4 For a brief description, see Harry Stout, *The New England Soul: Preaching and Religious Culture in Colonial New England* (Oxford: Oxford University Press 1986), 13–31, and Charles Hambrick-Stowe, *The Practice of Piety: Puritan Devotional Disciplines in Seventeenth-Century New England* (Chapel Hill: University of North Carolina Press 1982), 130–4, 246–77.

5 This process is succinctly described in Anne S. Brown and David D. Hall, "Family Strategies and Religious Practice: Baptism and the Lord's Supper in Early New England," in *Lived Religion in America: Toward a History of Practice*, ed. David. D. Hall (Princeton: Princeton University Press 1997), 41–68.

6 Helpful summaries consulted include William L. Barney, *The Passage of the Republic: An Interdisciplinary History of Nineteenth-Century America* (Toronto: D.C. Heath 1987), 1–155, and Jean-Pierre Kesteman, Peter Southam, and Diane Saint-Pierre, *Histoire des cantons de l'Est* (Sainte-Foy: Presses de l'Université Laval 1998), 1–217.

7 Especially helpful as an introduction into the impact of the American Revolution on gender relations is Nancy Cott, *Public Vows: A History of Marriage and the Nation* (Cambridge, Mass.: Harvard University Press 2000), 9–23. See also Susan Juster, "Patriarchy Reborn: The Gendering of Authority in the Evangelical Church in Revolutionary New England," *Gender and History* 6 (Winter 1994): 58–81, and Linda Kerber et al., "Beyond Roles, Beyond Spheres: Thinking about Gender in the Early Republic," *William and Mary Quarterly*, 3rd ser., 46 (July 1989): 565–85.

8 For early-nineteenth-century radical religion in British North America, see George Rawlyk, *The Canada Fire: Radical Evangelicalism in British North America, 1775–1812* (Montreal/Kingston: McGill-Queen's University Press 1994). The combined influence of economic and political change in bringing about church disestablishment in Ontario is briefly examined in William Westfall, *Two Worlds: The Protestant Culture of Nineteenth-Century Ontario* (Montreal/Kingston: McGill-Queen's University Press 1989). For the Eastern Townships, see Françoise Noël, *Competing for Souls: Missionary Activity and Settlement in the Eastern Townships, 1784–1851* (Sherbrooke: Département d'histoire, Université de Sherbrooke 1988); J.I. Little, "The Methodistical Way: Revivalism and Popular Resistance to the Wesleyan Church Discipline in the Stanstead Circuit, Lower Canada, 1821–1852," *Studies in Religion/Sciences Religieuses* 31, no. 2 (2002): 171–94, and his *Borderland Religion: The Emergence of an English-Canadian Identity, 1792–1852* (Toronto: University of Toronto Press 2004).

9 Kesteman et al., *Histoire des cantons de l'Est*, 108–16, and J.I. Little, *Ethno-Cultural Transition and Regional Identity in the Eastern Townships of Quebec* (Ottawa: Canadian Historical Association Historical Booklet 1989).

10 In the course of a business trip to Paris in 1910, Moses Colby's grandson, Charles William, happened to stumble across another American Colby, who informed him of his family's English roots. A professional historian by training, Charles William pursued the information, and he spoke of the family history in two manuscripts and some notes, which are the source of my brief summary. See "Address on Charles Carroll Colby I," Charles William Colby (CWC) Papers, Series 1:C, Box 11:1, FC; "Garrulities of an Octogenarian" (typescript), 1–9, Series 1:C, Box 11:2, 3, FC; and Colby Genealogy Notes: CWC Papers, Series 1:C, Box 11:4, FC. For the context of the immigration, see David Grayson Allen, *In English Ways: The Movement of Societies and Transferral of English Local Law and Custom to Massachusetts Bay, 1600–1690* (Chapel Hill: University of North Carolina Press 1981). A reference to "Arthur [Anthony?] Colebye" of Fressingfield, Suffolk, is given on

p. 277, listing the settlers of Ipswich, Mass., prior to 1640. The Suffolk origins of this Anthony Colby, accepted by his Canadian descendants, have since been convincingly disputed and redirected to Horbling, Lincolnshire; see "Anthony Colby" in Robert Charles Anderson, *The Great Migration Begins: Immigrants to New England 1620–1633*, vol. 1 (Boston: New England Historical Genealogical Society 1995), 413–16.

11 John Stoddard, a Welshman, was a proprietor in Hingham, Mass., but moved early to Taunton in the Plymouth colony, and later to the Connecticut Valley. One of his descendants was Josiah Strong, well-known supporter of the missionary movement at the end of the nineteenth century. There is a brief genealogy in Lemira's notebook, in MFC Papers, Series 2, Box 1:13, FC. See also Cedric B. Cowing, *The Saving Remnant: Religion and the Settlement of New England* (Urbana: University of Illinois Press 1995), 54–6. For a brief, insightful analysis of the influence of Edwards and Stoddard upon American theology, see Mark A. Noll, *America's God: From Jonathan Edwards to Abraham Lincoln* (New York: Oxford University Press 2002), 37–50.

12 For the earliest migrations as part of the spread of evangelism, see Cowing, *Saving Remnant*, 208–42. For examples of the economic and family dimensions of migration, see Philip J. Greven Jr., *Four Generations: Population, Land, and Family in Colonial Andover, Massachusetts* (Ithaca: Cornell University Press 1970), and John J. Waters, "Family, Inheritance, and Migration in Colonial New England: The Evidence from Guilford, Connecticut," *William and Mary Quarterly*, 3rd ser., no. 29 (1982): 78–85. On settlement patterns in northern Vermont in the late eighteenth century, see P. Jeffrey Potash, *Vermont's Burned-Over District: Patterns of Community Development and Religious Activity, 1761–1850* (Brooklyn, NY: Carlson 1991), 3–60.

13 The first U.S. census of 1790 for Thornton Township lists Samuel Colby, as household head of three white males under 16 years, and one white female; see *Heads of Families at the first census of the United States taken in the year 1790. New Hampshire* (Sparanburg, SC: Reprint Company 1983), 38.

14 Kesteman et al., *Histoire des cantons de l'Est*, 83–111; B.F. Hubbard, *Forests and Clearings: The History of Stanstead County* (Montreal: Lovell 1874), 1–6.

15 Dr Luther Newcombe of Derby. Medical apprenticeships were also the only means of education in early-nineteenth-century Quebec; see Jacques Bernier, *La médecine au Québec: naissance d'une profession* (Quebec: Presses de l'Université Laval 1989), 32–6.

16 Mary P. Ryan had demonstrated this for the corporate household in Oneida County, New York, 1790–1820, in *Cradle of the Middle Class:*

The Family in Oneida County, New York, 1790–1865 (Cambridge: Cambridge University Press 1981), 18–31.

17 All references are from MFC Papers, Series 3, Box 1:1, Manuscript Diary of trip from Derby, Vt, to Yale (1817), FC.

18 On the internalization of time, see Beldon C. Lane, *Landscapes of the Sacred: Geography and Narrative in American Spirituality* (New York: Paulist Press 1988), 28–31, and Eviatar Zerubavel, *The Seven Day Circle: The History and Meaning of the Week* (New York: Free Press 1985), 130–41. For the rhythms of a pre-industrial society, see Serge Gagnon, *Plaisir d'amour et crainte de Dieu: sexualité et confession au Bas-Canada* (Sainte-Foy: Presses de l'Université Laval 1990), 72–8, and Boyd Hilton, *The Age of Atonement: The Influence of Evangelicalism on Social and Economic Thought, 1795–1865* (Oxford: Clarendon Press 1988), 33–5.

19 For a thoughtful analysis of the historical construct of the market revolution, see Richard Bushman, "Markets and Composite Farms in Early America," *William and Mary Quarterly*, 3rd ser., 55, no. 3 (1998): 351–74.

20 John R. Gillis, *A World of Their Own Making: Myth, Ritual, and the Quest for Family Values* (New York: Basic Books 1996), 20–40. By 1817 such itinerant hospitality was no longer followed by the well-to-do; see Joy Day Buel and Richard Buel, Jr., *The Way of Duty: A Woman and Her Family in Revolutionary America* (New York: W.W. Norton 1984), 277–9.

21 For the historical expression of self-construction I am especially indebted to Daniel Walker Howe, *Making the American Self: Jonathan Edwards to Abraham Lincoln* (Cambridge, Mass.: Harvard University Press 1997), influenced by Charles Taylor's authoritative *Sources of the Self: The Making of Modern Identity* (Cambridge, Mass.: Harvard University Press 1989).

22 David D. Hall, *Worlds of Wonder, Days of Judgment: Popular Religious Belief in Early New England* (Cambridge, Mass.: Harvard University Press 1989), 71–116, 239–45.

23 On the stereotyping of Native people, see, for example, Joel W. Martin, "Indians, Contact, and Colonialism in the Deep South: Themes for a Postcolonial History of American Religion," in *Retelling U.S. Religious History*, ed. Thomas A. Tweed (Berkeley: University of California Press 1997), 149–80.

24 Classic studies that are still the essential entries into the topic are Whitney Cross, *The Burned-Over District: The Social and Intellectual History of Enthusiastic Religion in Western New York, 1800–1850* (Ithaca: Cornell University Press 1950), and, on New England, Stephen Marini, *Radical Sects of Revolutionary New England* (Cambridge, Mass.: Harvard University Press 1982). For Vermont, see Randolph Roth, *The*

Democratic Dilemma: Religion, Reform, and the Social Order in the Connecticut River Valley of Vermont, 1791–1850 (Cambridge: Cambridge University Press 1987), and Potash, *Vermont's Burned-Over District.* Revivals in Vermont were many during this period, and neither study makes specific mention of 1817.

25 The early-nineteenth-century liberal critique of revivalism as excessively emotional is examined in Gary Dorrien, *The Making of American Liberal Theology: Imagining Progressive Religion, 1805–1900* (Louisville: Westminster John Knox Press 2001), 1–57. Noll, *America's God,* 183–4, argues that by the 1830s there was in place a pervasive shift from evangelical enthusiasm to steady state religion.

26 For the difference between evangelical and rationalistic preaching styles, see Stout, *The New England Soul,* 218–32.

27 Hambrick-Stowe, *The Practice of Piety,* 54–90; Jerald C. Brauer, "Conversion: From Puritanism to Revivalism," *Journal of Religion* 58 (1978): 227–43.

28 This information is taken from CCC's notes on his father, in Biographical Material [unsigned address on Moses], MFC Papers, Series 2, Box 1:1, FC. See also MFC, cards of admission to medical lectures at Yale, Dartmouth, and Harvard (1817–28), MFC Papers, Series 3, Box 1:2, FC.

29 "Fisk, Wilbur (1792–1839)," *Encyclopedia of World Methodism,* vol. 1 (Nashville: United Methodist Publishing House 1974), 847–8.

30 The difficulties for men are analysed in Susan Juster, "'In a Different Voice': Male and Female Narratives of Religious Conversion in Post-Revolutionary America," *American Quarterly* 41 (March 1989): 34–62.

31 For common-sense thought and its impact in the early nineteenth century, see Henry May, *The Enlightenment in America* (New York. Oxford University Press 1976), and Noll, *America's God,* 93–113.

32 The impact of common-sense thought in Canada has been examined in A.B. McKillop, *A Disciplined Intelligence: Critical Inquiry and Canadian Thought in the Victorian Era* (Montreal/Kingston: McGill-Queen's University Press 1979). For its impact on theology, see Michael Gauvreau, *The Evangelical Century: College and Creed in English Canada from the Great Revival to the Great Depression* (Montreal/Kingston: McGill-Queen's University Press 1991). The ideals of American educators are analysed in Donald H. Meyer, *The Instructed Conscience: The Shaping of the American National Ethic* (Philadelphia: University of Pennsylvania Press 1972).

33 Baconian thought as presented at Yale and elsewhere in higher education is examined in T.D. Bozeman, *Protestants in an Age of Science: The Baconian Ideal and Antebellum American Religious Thought* (Chapel Hill: University of North Carolina Press 1977). Moses preserved his

cards of admission to medical lectures at Yale as well as at Dartmouth and Harvard; MFC Papers, Series 3, Box 1:2, FC.
34 Nathan Hatch, *The Democratization of American Christianity* (New Haven: Yale University Press 1989), 49.
35 Noll, *America's God*, 138–43, 209–24, 332–41. Noll defines Arminianism theologically in terms of Methodist doctrine, especially that of God's "prevenient grace" given to all people, allowing them freely to come to God, to seek forgiveness, and be reconciled (p. 563). Unlike Calvinism, which stresses God's sovereignty, Arminian theology emphasizes human responsibility to respond to God's free offer of forgiveness.
36 Louise L. Stevenson, "Between the Old Time College and the Modern University: Noah Porter and the New Haven Scholars," *History of Higher Education Annual* 3 (1983): 39–55.
37 This is the main argument in Hall and Brown, "Family Strategies and Religious Practice," 50–68.
38 MFC Papers, Series 2, Box 1:10, FC.
39 A point of entry into the literature on "woman's sphere," including her alleged spiritual superiority, is Leonore Davidoff et al., *The Family Story: Blood, Contract, and Intimacy, 1830–1960* (New York: Addison Wesley Longman 1999), 25–31. The classic critique is Amanda Vickery, "Golden Age to Separate Spheres: A Review of the Categories and Chronology of English Women's History," *Historical Journal* 36, no. 2 (1993): 383–414.
40 Amanda Vickery, *The Gentleman's Daughter: Women's Lives in Georgian England* (New Haven: Yale University Press 1998), ch. 2; Leonore Davidoff and Catherine Hall, *Family Fortunes: Men and Women of the English Middle-Class, 1780–1850* (London: Hutchinson 1987), 180–92. For Canada, see especially Peter Ward, *Courtship, Love, and Marriage in Nineteenth-Century English Canada* (Montreal/Kingston: McGill-Queen's University Press 1989), 64–89; Françoise Noël, *Family Life and Sociability in Upper and Lower Canada, 1780–1870: A View from Diaries and Family Correspondence* (Montreal/Kingston: McGill-Queen's University Press 2003), 19–59. For a discussion of the more complexly regulated relations in French Canada, see Serge Gagnon, *Mariage et famille au temps de Papineau* (Sainte-Foy: Presses de l'Université Laval 1993), esp. 89–146.
41 Mrs Timothy Hinman, "Address on CCC1," CWC Papers, Series 1:C, Box 11:1, FC.
42 Biographical Material [unsigned address on Moses by his eldest son], MFC Papers, Series 2, Box 1:1, FC. This would have offered him medical training superior to what was available in Quebec, where he practiced shortly thereafter. In 1831 Quebec instituted an elected board of

medical examiners. Between 1831 and 1837 it admitted 69 physicians, of whom 42 were native Canadian and 21 were American and other nationalities; see Bernier, *La médecine au Québec,* 43–70.

43 Moses to Lemira, 24 November 1828 (typescript), MFC Papers, Series 1, Box 1:1, FC.

44 This congruence is forcefully argued by W.G. McLoughlin, *Revivals, Awakenings, and Reform: An Essay on Religion and Social Change in America, 1607–1977* (Chicago: University of Chicago Press 1978), chs. 3 and 4.

45 Here I am following Brown and Hall, "Family Strategies and Religious Practice," 41–50.

46 George M. Marsden. *Jonathan Edwards: A Life* (New Haven: Yale University Press 2003), esp. chs. 2 and 7. A good summary of the problems faced by the second generation can be found in Hambrick-Stowe, *The Practice of Piety,* 242–77. For the role of the sacraments, see 123–32. See also the informative literature review given by Allen C. Guelzo, "God's Designs: The Literature of the Colonial Revivals of Religion, 1735–1760, " in *New Directions in American Religious History,* ed. Harry S. Stout and D.G. Hart (Oxford: Oxford University Press 1997), 141–72.

47 The preceding is based on a letter Lemira received on her eightieth birthday from her sister, Flora, living in Chicago, 9 May 1886; MFC Papers, Series 1, Box 1:15, FC. The difficulties experienced by other women of her generation have been analysed in Juster, "In a Different Voice"; Virginia Lieson Brereton, *From Sin to Salvation: Stories of Women's Conversions, 1800 to the Present* (Bloomington: Indiana University Press 1991); and Kathryn Kish Sklar, *Catharine Beecher: A Study in American Domesticity* (New Haven: Yale University Press 1973), 31–8.

48 For Vermont, see Roth, *The Democratic Dilemma,* 117–41. Analysing the demographic changes of the fourth generation in eighteenth-century Andover, Philip Greven has noted a real decline in family size as the result of an increase in infant deaths, a declining birth rate, and longer intervals between births; *Four Generations,* 200. A similar decline has been noted in the second generation of middle-class families in younger communities such as Utica, New York, where it appears that native-born couples had begun "to rationalize the process of reproduction" by the 1830s; Ryan, *Cradle of the Middle Class,* 155.

49 By the 1830s methods of contraception used in the United States, other than withdrawal, were douching, the vaginal sponge, condoms, and the rhythm method; Marilyn Yalom, *A History of the Wife* (New York: HarperCollins 2001), 298–301.

50 Kesteman et al., *Histoire des cantons de l'Est,* 100, notes the comparative land value.

51 A partnership establishing a business of physicians and accoucheurs was formed by Colby and Joseph Barnard for a term of ten years, as of 27 January 1834; files of William Ritchie, no. 2417, 9 September 1834, Archives nationales du Québec, Sherbrooke (ANQS).
52 The preceding is based on Kesteman et al., *Histoire des cantons de l'Est*, 162–8, *passim*, and J.I. Little, *State and Society in Transition: The Politics of Institutional Reforms in the Eastern Townships, 1838–1852* (Montreal/Kingston: McGill-Queen's University Press 1997), esp. chs. 4 and 5 describing the establishment of municipal government. Among the most prominent of the early men of substance were Ichabod Smith, Wilder Pierce, Erastus Lee, and Wright Chamberlin.
53 Hubbard, *Forests and Clearings*, 8.
54 Ibid., 92.
55 Karl P. Stofko, "Old Union Meeting House at Stanstead, Quebec, Canada," *Stanstead Historical Society Journal* 13 (1989): 9–11.
56 For a brief account, see Dennis Fortin, "'The World Turned Upside Down': Millerism in the Eastern Townships, 1834–1845," *Journal of Eastern Townships Studies* 11 (Fall 1997): 39–56; Hubbard, *Forests and Clearings*, 99–102. For a more detailed description of religious denominationalism during this period, see Little, *Borderland Religion*, and Noël, *Competing for Souls*.
57 For the Millerites in the Eastern Townships and their Adventist successors, see J.I. Little, "Millennial Invasion: Millerism in the Eastern Townships of Lower Canada," in *Anglo-American Millennialism, from Milton to the Millerites*, ed. Richard Connors and Andrew Colin Gow (Leiden: Brill 2004), 177–204.
58 See the detailed discussion on community regulation through voluntary societies in Little, *State and Society*, 83–118. Helpful analysis of the urban experience can be found in Stuart Blumin, *The Emergence of the Middle Class: Social Experience in the American City, 1760–1900* (Cambridge: Cambridge University Press 1989), 192–230.
59 Little, *State and Society*, 83–8. The prevalence of alcoholism in Lower Canada is developed by Jan Noel in "Dry Patriotism: The Chiniquy Crusade," *Canadian Historical Review* 71, no. 2 (1990): 189–207, and *Canada Dry: Temperance Crusades before Confederation* (Toronto: University of Toronto Press 1995), 55–88.
60 Most notably Alexander Kilborn, Timothy Rose, Daniel Mansur, Ichabod Smith, and Marcus Child; see Kesteman et al., *Histoire des cantons de l'Est*, 136, 188, 393–4. On Stanstead's masonic lodge, see Hubbard, *Forests and Clearings*, 108–13, and Arthur Henry Moore, *History of the Golden Rule Lodge no. 5, Q.R., A.F. and A.M., Stanstead Quebec, 1802–1903* (Toronto: William Briggs 1905).

61 For a brief history of the movement, see J.I. Little, "'Such Incalculable Power': The Temperance Movement in the Eastern Townships, 1830–52," *Journal of Eastern Townships Studies* 11 (Fall 1997): 3–39. The role of voluntary societies in shaping a public voice in pre-Confederation Ontario is examined in Jeffrey McNairn, *The Capacity to Judge: Public Opinion and Deliberative Democracy in Upper Canada, 1791–1854* (Toronto: University of Toronto Press 2000), 63–115.

62 His interest in independent Bible reading is noted by his eldest son, who commented that "for days & weeks & months he would read his bible constantly"; Biographical Material [unsigned address on Moses], MFC Papers, Series 2, Box 1:1, FC, and in the eulogy, "Moses French Colby," *Stanstead Journal*, 7 May 1863.

63 In December 1834 he was $15 in arrears on his promised donation of $30. All information is taken from the Minute Book, vol. 1, 1833–61, Wesleyan Methodist Church, Stanstead, United Church of Canada, Montreal Conference Archives, Archives nationales du Québec, Montréal (ANQM).

64 On 5 May 1849 the Methodist quarterly meeting passed unanimously a resolution of thanks: "Having heard from the Rev. Mr. Borland that drs. Colby and Cowles have declined to take any fee for their attendance upon his family during the year, this meeting would record its sense of their kindness and liberality." On 29 October 1849 mention was made of the need to assess Methodist Society members because of the great deficiency in raising money for the minister's salary. Interestingly, Colby, though offering his services without charge, had forcefully criticized in public what he considered to be the minister's overly aggressive temperance tactics; Little, "A Moral Engine," 3–39.

65 Biographical Material [unsigned address on Moses by his eldest son], MFC Papers, Series 2, Box 1:1, FC.

66 This point will be elaborated in chapter 6.

67 This is based on the following land transactions: files of William Ritchie, no. 2106, 24 January 1833, and no. 2906, 8 April 1837; C.A. Richardson, no. 772, 18 April 1834, no. 1093, 22 July 1836, and no. 1154, 1 December 1836; all in ANQS.

68 Shirley Whipple and Amphion Pelley, "The Agricultural Society for the County of Stanstead, 1845–1900," *Stanstead Historical Society Journal* 10 (1983): 38–58. Moses' hotel became one of the sites for the fall and winter shows held between 1845 and 1866.

69 For the background and context, see Allan Greer, *The Patriots and the People: The Rebellion of 1837 in Lower Canada* (Toronto: University of Toronto Press 1993), 120–52.

70 "Garrulities," 18, CWC Papers, Series 1:C, Box 1:3, FC.

71 He outlined his reservations about the Lower Canadian reform position on land tenure in a lengthy account, dated 23 August 1857, and intended for publication; "Case of Alleged Malpractice Suit," "MFC Malpractice Suit (1839–1857)," MFC Papers, Series 3, Box 1:1, FC.
72 The election and its issues are discussed in J.I. Little, *The Child Letters: Public and Private Life in a Canadian Merchant-Politician's Family, 1841– 1845* (Montreal/Kingston: McGill-Queen's University Press 1995), 10–30, and in Little, *State and Society*, 31–6.
73 "Electors of Stanstead," Political Tracts 1836–1851, MFC Papers, Series 3, Box 1:5, FC.
74 Ironically, on the land issue he and Robert Nelson were in agreement; see Greer, *The Patriots and the People*, 339–41. Entreaties to the government for some patronage that would help him with his legal expenses were unsuccessful. After much pleading, he did receive a favourable response in 1841 from Lord Sydenham, but the governor's sudden death shortly thereafter brought the promise to naught. The correspondence and Colby's own account of the event are in "MFC Malpractice Suit (1839–1857)," MFC Papers, Series 3, Box 1:1, FC. A detailed account of the medical aspects of the case, "Fracture of the Thigh Bone – The Late Suit against Dr. Colby," submitted by Stoddard Colby, was published in the *Boston Medical and Surgical Journal* 33, no. 26 (1844): 509–14. An agreement in 1841 with the retiring customs collector, Robert Hoyle, to take his vacant post fell to naught when thwarted by the new political incumbent and Colby's rival, Reformer Marcus Child; files of William Ritchie, no. 3491, 7 July 1841, ANQS. Little, *State and Society*, 104.
75 MFC Malpractice Suit (1839–1857), MFC Papers, Series 3, Box 1:1, FC. On Stoddard Colby, see T.P. Redford, "Stoddard Benham Colby," *Vermont Historical Gazetteer* (Montpellier, Vt.: Vermont Watchman and State Journal Press 1882), 468–9.
76 "Case of Alleged Malpractice Suit," "MFC Malpractice Suit (1839– 1857)," MFC Papers, Series 3, Box 1:1, FC.
77 Files of William Ritchie, no. 1983, 28 December 1844, ANQS. The reference to Lemira and Moses picking hops is in a letter Charles wrote while studying at Dartmouth; CCC to parents, 15 September 1845, CCC Papers, Series 4:A, Box 1:2, FC. The conflict between Moses and the local Methodist minister on the issue of temperance is described in Little, "A Moral Engine," 3–39.
78 Trained in divinity at the University of Edinburgh, Elder, who like so many other Scottish theologues was unable to find a call under the then prevalent system of lay patronage, had emigrated to Canada on his graduation in 1822 and had taken up school teaching. After

spending some time in Ottawa and Montreal, he moved his family to Stanstead, where he became a lifelong friend of the Colby family and, like Moses, was actively involved in temperance work, as well as taking a leadership role shaping the township's educational facilities; see Hubbard, *Forests and Clearings*, 230, and Kathleen Brown, *Schooling in the Clearings: Stanstead 1800–1850* (Stanstead: Stanstead Historical Society 2001), 161.

79 CCC to MFC, 29 August 1845, CCC Papers, Series 4:A, Box 1:2, FC. Mining speculation in the area at this time is noted in Kesteman et al., *Histoire des cantons de l'Est*, 152.

80 Files of William Ritchie, no. 4537, 3 August 1847, Articles of Clerkship, Agreement between M.F. Colby and John S. Sanborn, ANQS.

81 I have been unable to ascertain the actual financial loss occasioned by the malpractice suit. There is, in Moses' handwriting, an undated rough sketch outlining the extent of his property and claiming a total property of 1,350 acres of largely wooded land; "Diagram of M.F.C. Farm and mill – Burrough's Falls, MFC Papers, Series 2, Box 1:4, FC. In 1855, however, when he made a will, he gave the total acreage as a little over 800; files of C.A. Richardson, no. 5747, 2 August 1855, Last Will and Testament, Moses F. Colby, ANQS. A letter to his son William several years later still refers to his mill; MFC to William [1858?], MFC Papers, Series 1, Box 1:12, FC.

82 Register of Marriages, Baptisms and Burials of the Congregational Society in the Township of Stanstead 1838, n.d. (photocopy), Stanstead Historical Society. Moses' entry, which has no witnesses, is for 22 July 1855.

83 His request to participate in the Lord's Supper is in "Moses French Colby," *Stanstead Journal*, 14 May 1863.

84 Files of C.A. Richardson, no. 5747, 2 August 1855, Last Will and Testament, Moses F. Colby. ANQS.

85 A good analysis of Calvinist attitudes can be found in Richard W. Pointer, "Philadelphia Presbyterians, Capitalism, and the Morality of Economic Success," in *God and Mammon: Protestants, Money, and the Market, 1790–1860*, ed. Mark A. Noll (Oxford: Oxford University Press 2001), 171–91. See also Karen Halttunen, *Confidence Men and Painted Women: A Study of Middle-Class Culture in America, 1830–1870* (New Haven: Yale University Press 1982), 1–32. For "narrow social views" in Protestant thought in pre-Confederation Canada, see William H. Elgee, *The Social Teachings of the Canadian Churches: Protestant. The Early Period, before 1850* (Toronto: Ryerson Press 1964), 92–9.

86 That this shows only a 260-acre increase since 1837 may be the result of the impact of the 1839 lawsuit.

87 This was in keeping with New England and Vermont customs on coverture and dowries as described in Jane C. Nylander, *Images of the New England Home, 1760–1860* (New Haven: Yale University Press 1993), 62–5, and Yalom, *A History of the Wife*, 185–91.
88 Bettina Bradbury, "Debating Dower: Patriarchy, Capitalism, and Widows' Rights in Lower Canada," in *Power, Place, and Identity: Historical Studies of Social and Legal Regulation in Quebec*, ed. Tamara Myers et al. (Montreal: Montreal History Group 1998), 56. Bradbury notes that where, under the Coutume, a widow's right of dower had been attached to all of a man's land – which he had acquired before as well as after his marriage – under the new legislation, dower was limited to such property held by the husband at time of death. Secondly, where previously dower had been an inalienable right attached to a piece of land – even after it was sold by the husband – now, in order to make the alienation of land as easy as possible, a woman could release her dower rights on any property her husband wished to sell during their marriage.
89 Files of C.A. Richardson, no. 5752, 15 August 1855, ANQS.
90 The details of what led Moses to do this lie buried, but several land transactions, registered with C.A. Richardson, who also notarized both wills, may provide a clue. In the course of registering the first will, Moses may have become aware of two recent land transactions by his son registered with the same notary. The first, in 1853 (shortly after Charles had completed his legal apprenticeship and while he was spending a year teaching), was the purchase of a 100-acre tract of land, to be paid for in instalments over four years; the second, only a year later, indicates that in the interim the land had been sold at less than a quarter of its original price; files of C.A. Richardson [no. unknown], 12 March 1853, nos. 5569 and 5570, 6 September 1854, ANQS. Whether or not this sale had been made to cover debts, one can only surmise, but whatever the reason, it is clear that Moses saw a need to severely restrict his son's financial independence.
91 Little, *State and Society*, 45. But in the end, Stanstead was bypassed in favour of Coaticook, and a railway link was not built until 1870; see Kesteman et al., *Histoire des cantons de l'Est*, 230.
92 Moses' anxieties are detailed in a long letter to his youngest son William; MFC to William [1858?], MFC Papers, Series 1, Box 1:12, FC.
93 Jean-Pierre Kesteman, "Une bourgeoisie et son espace: industrialisation et développement du capitalisme dans le district de Saint-François (Québec), 1823–1879," (PH D thesis, Université du Québec à Montréal, 1985).
94 Cited without a source in "Garrulities of an Octogenarian" (typescript), 3, CWC Papers, Series 1:C, Box 11:2, FC.

95 Gregory Schneider, examining the relations between men in the early and later nineteenth-century Methodist cultures in the United States, has interpreted this shift from an agrarian to a marketplace-driven economy as marking the transition from a culture defined by honour, self-abnegating virtue, and patriarchy to one characterized by moral individualism, a breakdown of deference, and an increased emphasis on affection and self-interest as the basis for family relations; see A. Gregory Schneider, *The Way of the Cross Leads Home: The Domestication of American Methodism* (Bloomington: Indiana University Press 1991), 1–27.

96 I have been unable to locate documents indicating whether or not he finally won his malpractice suit, but it seems that in 1857 the State of Vermont relented and gave him some compensation for the losses he had encountered almost twenty years earlier. If so, this may have enabled the building of the new house. Comments by his grandson indicate that he, too, was unaware of the source of funds for the house; "Garrulities of an Octogenarian" (typescript), 14–15, CWC Papers, Series 1:C, Box 11:2, FC.

97 Land transactions by the two brothers show in 1858 a one-acre purchase for $600 and a $1,500 mortgage obligation for 10%; and in 1859 a $1,000 mortgage obligation at 6% and a $500 mortgage obligation at 6%; files of Richardson, no. 6509, 7 May 1858, no. 6510, 20 November 1858, and no. 6666, 20 May 1859, ANQS; and 6 September 1859, unnotarized mortgage obligation for $500, register B, vol. 8, p. 477, no. 446, Stanstead registry office.

98 William is listed as a "tavern, hotel and boarding house keeper" in the *Quebec Directory for 1851* (London: Genealogical Research Library 1984), 120. The sale of the hotel is recorded in files of C.A. Richardson, no. 5369, 5 November 1853, ANQS.

99 Some of the blame, as Moses himself knew, could be placed at his own doorstep. For the purpose of letting his eldest son qualify as an elector, he had placed part of his land in Charles's name – land that was now being sold to meet building costs. J.I. Little notes that in 1829 it was tacitly agreed that the following could be included in the electoral process: "persons settled in the County from twenty to thirty years, and in possession of Lands without having their Title Deeds ... and their sons being of age and cultivating Lands originally occupied by their fathers, but now set off as theirs"; Little, *State and Society*, 10.

100 MFC to Willam [1858?], MFC Papers, Series 1, Box 1:12, FC.

101 Hilton, *The Age of Atonement*, esp. ch. 4.

102 For a brief analysis of this emphasis on moral probation and its relationship to "the penal-satisfaction" view of Christ's atonement in American thought, see Dorrien, *The Making of American Liberal Theology*, 114–18, and Noll, *America's God*, 269–81.

103 Hattie Child Colby (HCC) to Jessie Colby, 8 September 1872, HCC Papers, Series 1, Box 2:7, FC.
104 In Lemira's "in" correspondence, n.d., 1863–87, MFC Papers, Series 1, Box 1:15, FC.
105 This is well brought out in Gary Laderman, "Locating the Dead: A Cultural History of Death in the Antebellum, Anglo-Protestant Communities of the Northeast," *Journal of the American Academy of Religion* 68 (Spring 1995): 27–52.
106 "The Burial of the Dead," *The Liturgy or Formulary of Services in Use in the Wesleyan-Methodist Church in Canada* (Toronto: S. Rose 1867), 78–81. An unsigned eulogy, printed in the local paper notes that Moses was buried from the Wesleyan church. Census returns for 1861 indicate his Congregationalist status, but the Wesleyan church may have been chosen because of its larger size, its connections with his son and daughter-in-law, and the fact that its minister regularly visited him in his final years; see Manuscript Census, Village of Stanstead Plain, Stanstead County/Township, 1861 and 1871, C-1323, C-10089, Library and Archives Canada (LAC). "Dr. Colby – wandering in mind. Rev. M. McD had been in & was with us when we thought him dying"; Diary, 19 February 1861, HCC Papers, Series 2, Box 1, FC.
107 "Moses French Colby," *Stanstead Journal*, 14 May 1863. This is also the source of Moses' final words, mentioned above.
108 See the account of Mrs Abigail Cass, published in 1835 in the *Boston Medical and Surgical Journal* by Colby and his medical partner, S. Barnard, and copied in Hubbard, *Forests and Clearings*, 345–7.
109 Leigh Eric Schmidt, "From Demon Possession to Magic Show: Ventriloquism, Religion, and the Enlightenment," *Church History* 67 (June 1998): 302.
110 Ann Taves, *Fits, Trances, and Visions: Experiencing Religion and Explaining Experience from Wesley to James* (Princeton: Princeton University Press 1999), 207–12, and Jane Shaw, "Religious Experience and the Formation of the Early Enlightenment Self," in *Rewriting the Self: Histories from the Renaissance to the Present*, ed. Roy Porter (London: Routledge 1997), 61–71.
111 Timothy Dwight, *Travels in New England and New-York*, 4 vols. (1821–22), 1:468. Cited in Thomas Bender, *Community and Social Change in America* (New Brunswick, NJ: Rutgers University Press 1978), 86.
112 Bender, *Community and Social Change*, 78–150.
113 M.F. Colby, *Abstract of the New Physiological and Pathological Views as set forth in a work entitled "New Views of the Digestive Tube," &c (now preparing for the press)* (Stanstead: L.R. Robinson 1860), 5.
114 Helpful for understanding the religious beliefs of Moses' generation is Herbert Hovenkamp, *Science and Religion in America, 1800–1860* (Philadelphia: University of Pennsylvania Press 1978).

CHAPTER TWO

1 John R. Gillis, *A World of Their Own Making: Myth, Ritual, and the Quest for Family Values* (New York: Basic Books 1996), 61.
2 Mark A. Noll, *America's God: From Jonathan Edwards to Abraham Lincoln* (New York: Oxford University Press 2002), 330, 341, 345. See also his discussion of the moderate "Americanized" Calvinism that emerged in the 1830s until 1860, ibid., 293–329. The numerical growth of Methodism is tabled in ibid., 169. For a forceful (and controversial) argument showing the numerical explosion of the Methodists and Free Will Baptists – the two main Arminian groups in the antebellum United States – see Rodney Stark and Roger Finke, *The Churching of America: Winners and Losers in Our Religious Economy* (New Brunswick, NJ: Rutgers University Press 1992).
3 Here I am following Daniel Walker Howe, *Making the American Self: Jonathan Edwards to Abraham Lincoln* (Cambridge, Mass.: Harvard University Press 1997), 110.
4 Charles Carroll Colby (CCC) to parents, 22 March 1845 and 24 April 1846, CCC Papers, Series 4:A, Box 1:2, Fonds Colby (FC), Stanstead Historical Society. For Brooks's political career and family, see Charlotte Thibault, *Samuel Brooks, entrepreneur et homme politique de Sherbrooke, 1793–1849* ([Sherbrooke]: Département d'histoire de l'Université de Sherbrooke 1985).
5 See Daniel Walker Howe, *The Political Culture of the American Whigs* (Chicago: University of Chicago Press 1979), esp. ch. 9, for a succinct analysis of Webster's views. Charles William Colby (CWC) speaks of Webster's influence on his father in "Garrulities of an Octogenerian" (typescript), 12–19, CWC Papers, Series 1:C, Box 1:3, FC.
6 The description of chapel is in CCC to parents, 12 March 1844, CCC Papers, Series 4:A, Box 1:2, FC.
7 For a brief analysis of its influence in the United States, see Mark Noll, "Christian Thinking and the Rise of the American University," *Christian Scholar's Review* 9 (1979): 3–16, and Noll, *America's God*, 93–113. For Canada, see A.B. McKillop, *A Disciplined Intelligence: Critical Inquiry and Canadian Thought in the Victorian Era* (Montreal/Kingston: McGill-Queen's University Press 1979), and Michael Gauvreau, *The Evangelical Century: College and Creed in English Canada from the Great Revival to the Great Depression* (Montreal/Kingston: McGill-Queen's University Press 1991), 13–56.
8 The *Catalogue of the Officers and Students of Dartmouth College for the Academical Year, 1844–5* (Hanover: September 1844), 22, lists Wayland's *Moral Philosophy* [sic] in the spring term of the final year. This presumably is his *Elements of Moral Science* (1836). Other common-sense staples

studied were Paley's *Natural Theology*, Whately's *Logic* (both in the junior year), Stewart's *Elements of the Mind* and Butler's *Analogy* (both in the senior year).

9 "Moral Philosophy proceeds upon the supposition that there exists in the action of men a moral quality, and that there are certain sequences connected by our Creator with the exhibition of that quality"; Francis Wayland, *Elements of Moral Science*, rev. edn. (Boston: Garland and Lincoln 1870), 26.
10 For the role played by the moral philosophy in redefining evangelical Protestantism, see Donald H. Meyer, *The Instructed Conscience: The Shaping of the American National Ethic* (Philadelphia: University of Philadelphia Press 1972).
11 Expressing his satisfaction at being able to make some contribution to the family income, he successfully applied for the position, only to find his teaching abruptly terminated in December as a result of the school's destruction by fire; see CCC to parents [Winter 1847], CCC Papers, Series 4:A, Box 1:2, FC. The fire is noted in Kathleen H. Brown, *Schooling in the Clearings: Stanstead 1800–1850* (Stanstead: Stanstead Historical Society 2001), 168.
12 CCC to Lemira Strong Colby (LSC), 29 October 1846, CCC Papers, Series 4:A, Box 1:2, FC.
13 Wayland, *Elements of Moral Science*, 308–9.
14 Ibid., 45–83. For the Roman Catholic view, see Serge Gagnon, *Plaisir d'amour et crainte de Dieu: sexualité et confession au Bas-Canada* (Sainte-Foy: Presses de l'Université Laval 1990), 78–84.
15 CCC to parents, 1 April 1846, CCC Papers, Series 4:A, Box 1:2, FC.
16 Republican and evangelical concern about the "tyranny" of the passions is insightfully analysed in Howe, *Making the American Self*, 1–15, 108–14.
17 Noll, *America's God*, 229, notes the parallel use of revivalist and common-sense language in antebellum American theology and public discourse.
18 Terrill was part of the same economic and political network which a decade earlier had launched Charles's father to run as a conservative candidate representing the emerging economic and political concerns of Stanstead's middle class. A promising young lawyer of American background and trained in Quebec City and Sherbrooke, Terrill began his practice in Stanstead in 1836. Strongly critical of the government's decision to have the railway bypass Stanstead, and of a number of its educational and colonization projects, he ran successfully as an independent MLA for Stanstead County in the 1851 election against the aging Marcus Child, Moses Colby's old political foe. On Terrill's death, his seat had gone without opposition to his younger brother, Timothy

Lee Terrill, also a lawyer, who had settled in Stanstead Plain in 1844. Re-elected in 1854, 1856, and 1858, Timothy Terrill was appointed provincial secretary in the Taché-Macdonald government from 1856 to 1857, when he resigned for health reasons. A well-to-do farmer, Terrill was a powerful patron of Charles Colby, and by the time of his political retirement in 1857 he had begun to groom Charles as his successor. See B.F. Hubbard, *Forests and Clearings: The History of Stanstead County* (Montreal: Lovell 1874), 139–41; J.I. Little, *State and Society in Transition: The Politics of Institutional Reform in the Eastern Townships, 1838–1852* (Montreal/Kingston: McGill-Queen's University Press 1997), 43–6; J.I. Little, *The Child Letters: Public and Private Life in a Canadian Merchant-Politician's Family, 1841–1845* (Montreal/Kingston: McGill-Queen's University Press 1995), 25; and Jean-Pierre Kesteman, Peter Southam, and Diane Saint-Pierre, *Histoire des cantons de l'Est* (Sainte-Foy: Presses de l'Université Laval 1998), 424–9. CWC, Address on CCC1, 36–7, and CWC Papers, Series 1:C, Box 11:1, FC, gives biographical detail and speaks of his father's admiration for Daniel Webster and H.B. Terrill.

19 CWC, Address on CCC1, 36–7, and CWC Papers, Series 1:C, Box 11:1, FC. There exists no correspondence for the period 1847 to 1859.

20 *Stanstead Journal*, 24 January 1856, and Minute Book, vol. 1, 1833–61, Wesleyan Methodist Church, Stanstead, United Church of Canada, Montreal Conference Archives, Archives nationales du Québec, Montréal (ANQM). His was one of the donations to the minister's salary made by non-members in 1856; that December he also started to rent a pew in the Methodist chapel.

21 Brown, *Schooling in the Clearings*, 276, cites from the 1857 Board Minutes: "Miss Child, a graduate of a distinguished literary institution in the United States, brought testimonials of character, qualifications etc. of the very best order." Like many local schools established by Protestants in Canada East, Stanstead Seminary (the name held no religious significance) was non-denominational and was attended by children of all ages and social backgrounds; see Robert MacLeod and Mary Anne Poutanen, *A Meeting of the People: School Boards and Protestant Communities in Quebec, 1801–1998* (Montreal/Kingston: McGill-Queen's University Press 2004), 168.

22 Hattie Child Colby (HCC) to parents, 10 October 1857 and 10 April 1858, HCC Papers, Series 1, Box 3:6, FC.

23 Françoise Noël, *Family Life and Sociability in Upper and Lower Canada, 1780–1870: A View from Diaries and Family Correspondence* (Montreal/Kingston: McGill-Queen's University Press 2003), 226–8, which briefly describes such activities but overlooks voluntary religious societies.

24 HCC to parents and brothers, 10 April 1858, HCC Papers, Series 1, Box 3:6, FC.
25 HCC to CCC, 26 May 1867, HCC Papers, Series 1, Box 1:1, FC.
26 Glenna Matthews, *The Rise of Public Woman: Woman's Power and Woman's Place in the United States, 1630–1970* (New York: Oxford University Press 1992), 34.
27 The 1850 Vermont census for Weybridge, Addison County, lists John Child, age 53, his wife Mahala, age 33, and five children: John (21), Andrew (16), Harriet (12), Daniel (10), and Samuel (1 month), as well as one male and two female servants. The 1850 assessment roll lists John Child owning real estate valued at $15,000, which by 1860 had increased to $20,000, with the value of his personal estate listed at $3,000. In 1826 John Child married Abigail Wright, who bore eight children, of whom four reached adulthood: John Quincy Adams, Andrew Jackson, Harriet, and Daniel. After Abigail's death in childbirth in 1843, he married Mahala Pratt (née Briggs) in 1849. Of their three children, only George Edward survived infancy. See Child Genealogy, Child Family Papers, Box 1:1, FC.
28 CWC, "Garrulities of an Octogenerian" (typescript) 15–18, CWC Papers, Series 1:C, Box 1:3, FC.
29 Ibid. Writing to her parents shortly after her engagement, she expressed her regret that her education had been truncated: "Did I not have but two years and one term out of a four year course at school when I should have staid the other year and 2/3 to acquire the ornamentals & music & more languages"; HCC to Mahala Child, 15 May 1858, HCC Papers, Series 1, Box 3:6, FC.
30 Abby Maria Hemenway, *Poets and Poetry of Vermont* (Rutland: Tuttle 1858). See also "Poetry and Other Writings," HCC Papers, Series 2, Box 2, FC.
31 Letter of appointment, 15 August 1858, HCC Papers, Series 1, Box 3:5, FC. The friend was Anna Tomkins.
32 W. Peter Ward, *Courtship, Love, and Marriage in Nineteenth-Century English Canada* (Montreal/Kingston: McGill-Queen's University Press 1990), 149–56, and Noël, *Family Life and Sociability*, 19–20, 102–4.
33 Wayland, *Elements of Moral Science*, 313.
34 In addition to Ward and Noël, see Nancy Cott, *Public Vows: A History of Marriage and the Nation* (Cambridge, Mass.: Harvard University Press 2000), 19. A more complex, socially diversified reading is given in John R. Gillis, *For Better, For Worse: British Marriages, 1600 to the Present* (New York: Oxford University Press 1985).
35 "Of Marriage," *The Doctrines and Discipline of the Methodist Episcopal Church in Canada* (Hamilton, CW: Christian Advocate Office 1861), 19. Preferable to marriage, however, in Wesley's view, was celibacy. For

Wesley's peculiar views on sexuality, see Henry Abelove, *The Evangelist of Desire: John Wesley and the Methodists* (Stanford: Stanford University Press 1990), 49–73.

36 HCC to parents and brothers, 10 April 1858, HCC Papers, Series 1, Box 3:6, FC.

37 Richard Carwardine, *Evangelicals and Politics in Antebellum America* (Knoxville: University of Tennessee Press 1997), 120, has drawn attention to the strong support for Andrew Jackson among Methodists. It is reflected in the naming of Hattie's brother, Andrew Jackson Child. Stoddard Colby, on the other hand, as a Democrat, represented the Derby area, known for its strong support of the Whigs; *Vermont Historical Gazetteer*, 468.

38 Howe, *Making the American Self*, 122. A similar argument is made for middle-class English males in John Tosh, *A Man's Place: Masculinity and the Middle-Class Home in Victorian England* (New Haven: Yale University Press 1999), 138.

39 CCC to John Child, 10 April and 10 May 1858, CCC Papers, Series 4:A, Box 1:3, FC.

40 HCC to Mahala Child, 15 May 1858, HCC Papers, Series 1, Box 3:6, FC.

41 Ward, *Courtship, Love, and Marriage*, 42, and Noël, *Family Life and Sociability*, 62, which note that in both Upper and Lower Canada parents helped establish their sons on land as they reached an age to marry, while they provided their daughters with movable goods. Ward does, however, state that, based on his limited evidence in these two provinces, marriage did not seem to depend on the transmission of wealth from parents to children in the way it often did in early modern Europe and New England.

42 CCC to John Child, 28 June 1858, CCC Papers, Series 4:A, Box 1:3, FC. Charles William notes that "her father deprecated the expenditure involved but her brothers rallied around and enabled her to learn what french sounded like when spoken by the native born"; CWC, "Garrulities of an Octogenerian" (typescript) 18, and CWC Papers, Series 1:C, Box 1:3, FC. Earlier, in a letter to her parents on 11 April 1858, Hattie had already mentioned her desire to spend six months in "the French Country" rather than going directly from the seminary to her "new station."

43 In her lively defence of her plan to spend half a year in a francophone family, she had observed to her parents, "The family I expect to live with both parler and comprendre french [sic] – and when Charles is in Parliament (like his father before him …)" a bilingual, cultured wife would be a necessary asset; see HCC to Mahala Child, 15 May 1858, HCC Papers, Series 1, Box 3:6, FC.

44 Ward, *Courtship, Love, and Marriage*, 88–106, and Amanda Vickery, *The Gentleman's Daughter: Women's Life in Georgian England* (New Haven: Yale University Press 1998), ch. 2.
45 I have explored this in "'A Woman's Awakening': Evangelical Belief and Female Spirituality in Mid-Nineteenth-Century Canada," in *Canadian Women: A Reader*, ed. Wendy Mitchinson et al. (Toronto: Harcourt Brace 1996), 49–68.
46 "To my Father on his Birthday Anniversary Dec. 8 1857," HCC Papers, Series 2, Box 2, FC.
47 "He used to recite to *us children*, scripture stories in verse by *Rufus* [?] *Weeks*, a Quaker Poet, and also verses by another Quaker, an Englishman, *Bernard Barton*" [emphasis hers], HCC to CCC2 (grandson), 3 December 1909, HCC Papers, Series 1, Box 3:6, FC.
48 Philip Greven, *The Protestant Temperament: Patterns of Child-Rearing, Religious Experience, and the Self in Early America* (New York: Alfred A. Knopf 1977), 265–81.
49 Matthews, *The Rise of Public Woman*, 63, and Howe, *Making the American Self*, 121.
50 Leonore Davidoff, *The Family Story: Blood, Contract, and Intimacy, 1860–1960* (New York: Addison Wesley Longman 1999), 65. The contrasting structure of female conversion accounts is analysed in Virginia Lieson Brereton, *From Sin to Salvation: Stories of Women's Conversions, 1800 to the Present* (Bloomington: Indiana University Press 1991).
51 "Contemplating Ruins," presented at the Public Exercises of the Fort Edward Institute, 21 November 1855, HCC Papers, Series 2, Box 2, FC.
52 Ann Braude, "Women's History *Is* American Religious History," in *Retelling U.S. History*, ed. Thomas Tweed (Berkeley: University of California Press 1997), 87–107.
53 For this shift, depicted as an expression of religious declension, see, for example, A. Gregory Schneider, *The Way of the Cross Leads Home: The Domestication of American Methodism* (Bloomington: Indiana University Press 1993), esp. ch. 12.
54 Marguerite Van Die, *An Evangelical Mind: Nathanael Burwash and the Methodist Tradition in Canada, 1839–1918* (Montreal/Kingston, McGill-Queen's University Press 1989), ch. 1, and Susan Juster, "'In a Different Voice': Male and Female Narratives of Religious Conversion in Post-Revolutionary America," *American Quarterly* 41 (March 1989): 34–62. Male resistance to conversion well predated the revivals of the nineteenth century, as demonstrated in Gerald F. Moran, "'Sinners Are Turned into Saints in Numbers': Puritanism and Revivalism in Colonial Connecticut," in *Belief and Behavior: Essays in the New Religious History*, ed. Philip Vandermeer and Robert Swierenga (New Brunswick, NJ: Rutgers University Press 1991), 56–7, and Terry Bilhartz, "Sex and

55 Emily Strong Colby (ESC) to HCC, 28 May [1862], ESC Papers, Box 1:1, FC. Richard Carwardine, on the other hand, notes that Caughey's quiet manner and thoughtful approach distanced him from some of his more fiery American colleagues and increased his attraction for Canadian and British Wesleyan Methodists; Carwardine, *Trans-atlantic Revivalism: Popular Evangelicalism in Britain and America, 1790–1865* (Westport, Conn.: Greenwood 1978), 23–40. A favourable Canadian response to Caughey a decade earlier than Emily's can be found in W. H. Pearson, *Recollections and Records of Toronto of Old* (Toronto: William Briggs 1914), 304–5.

56 CCC to Mahala Child, 20 October 1858, CCC Papers, Series 4:A, Box 1:3, FC.

57 Rather than asserting agency, he expressed a concern that his prospective mother-in-law might think him "egotistical" for saying so much about himself. Only because he believed it would give her the greatest pleasure could he even justify writing her of his religious change. For comparison to the traditional "breaking of the will," see Juster, "In a Different Voice," 34–62.

58 "The Methodists & Congregationalists of the Plain, together with the church at the Line are holding a series of union prayer meetings with a view to awaken a revival, should their efforts be prospered like those in other places, which all seem devoutly to wish. The 4th one is Tues. Eve. at M.E. Chapel. The attendance has been large at all the preceding meetings, and increases at each"; HCC to "Home-ies," 11 April [1858], HCC Papers, Series 1, Box 3:6, FC.

59 Kathryn Teresa Long, *The Revival of 1857–58: Interpreting an American Religious Awakening* (New York: Oxford University Press 1998), 80.

60 For Palmer and her influence in Canada, see Peter George Bush, "James Caughey, Phoebe and Walter Palmer and the Methodist Revival Experience in Canada West, 1850–1858," MA thesis, Queen's University, 1985.

61 For a discussion of Palmer's perfectionist theology in its wider context, see John L. Peters, *Christian Perfection and American Methodism* (Nashville: Abingdon 1956), and Melvin Dieter, *The Holiness Revival of the Nineteenth Century* (Meteuchen, NJ: Scarecrow 1980).

62 A short introduction to the impact of the businessmen's revival and Palmer's influence on Methodism in Canada can be found in Marguerite Van Die, "A March of Triumph in Praise of the 'Beauty of Holiness': Laity and the Evangelical Impulse in Canadian Methodism, 1800–1884," in *Aspects of the Canadian Evangelical Experience*, ed. G.A. Rawlyk (Montreal/Kingston: McGill-Queen's University Press 1996), 79–89.

63 *Stanstead Journal*, 25 March and 15 April 1858.
64 Joan D. Hedrick, *Harriet Beecher Stowe: A Life* (Oxford: Oxford University Press 1994), 149–50. This was Harriet's second conversion. For the prevalence of perfectionist thought in the antebellum period, see especially Timothy L. Smith, *Revivalism and Social Reform: American Protestantism on the Eve of the Civil War*, rev. edn. (Baltimore: Johns Hopkins University Press 1980), 103–13, 135–62. For CCC's attendance at Plymouth Congregational, see CCC to HCC, 25 January 1863, CCC Papers, Series 4:A, Box 2:2, FC.
65 For Beecher's liberal theology, see Gary Dorrien, *The Making of American Liberal Theology: Imagining Progressive Religion, 1805–1900* (Louiseville: Westminster John Knox Press 2001), 181–224.
66 Henry Ward Beecher, *New Star Papers; or Views and Experiences of Religious Subjects* (New York: Derby & Jackson 1859), 309.
67 Ibid., 308.
68 In 1871 CCC wanted to ask Beecher to speak in Stanstead, but he changed his mind when he heard of Beecher's reluctance to take on more commitments (not to mention his rate of $200 per lecture); HCC to CCC, 8 March 1871, HCC Papers, Series 1, Box 1:2, FC. For the scandal, see Richard Wightman Fox, *Trials of Intimacy: Love and Loss in the Beecher-Tilton Scandal* (Chicago: University of Chicago Press 1999).
69 Diary, 18 September 1859, HCC Papers, Series 2, Box 1, FC.
70 Andrew Jackson Child to HCC, 11 April 1861, Child Family Papers, Box 1:5, FC.
71 Pencilled note, n.d., CCC Papers, Series 4:B, Box 5:3, FC.
72 I have developed this further in "A March of Triumph in Praise of the 'Beauty of Holiness.'"
73 Its proposed sobriety aroused the ire of HCC's brother, Andrew Jackson Child; see his letter to HCC, 6 December 1858, Child Family Papers, Box 1:5, FC.
74 The latter was obviously unaccustomed to writing his signature; Marriage Certificate, 1858, CCC Papers, Series 4:B, Box 5:2, FC.
75 By 1858, the time of the couple's marriage, the Methodist Episcopal Church, probably more out of considerations of economy of time than gender, had cut Wesley's original form to its bare bones, excising the three reasons for marriage: procreation, a remedy against sin, and a source of mutual comfort. See "Form of Solemnization of Marriage," *The Doctrines and Disciplines of the Methodist Episcopal Church in Canada* (Hamilton, CW: The "Christian Advocate" Office 1861), 92–5. The form used in Weybridge, Vt, in 1858 would have been identical.
76 Cott, *Public Vows*, 54–5.

77 George S. Weaver, *The Christian Household: Embracing the Christian Home, Husband, Wife, Father, Mother, Child, Brother, and Sister* (Boston: Tompkins and Musey 1856), 35.

CHAPTER THREE

1 Hattie Child Colby (HCC) to Charles Carroll Colby (CCC), 31 March 1873, HCC Papers, Series 1, Box 1:2, Fonds Colby (FC), Stanstead Historical Society.
2 CCC to Mahala Child, 30 December 1858, CCC Papers, Series 4:A, Box 1:3, FC.
3 Suzanne Lebsock, *The Free Women of Petersburg: Status and Culture in a Southern Town, 1784–1860* (New York: W.W. Norton 1984), 30.
4 Elizabeth Jane Errington, *Wives and Mothers, Schoolmistresses and Scullery Maids: Working Women in Upper Canada, 1790–1840* (Montreal/Kingston: McGill-Queen's University Press 1995); Barbara Welter, "The Cult of True Womanhood, 1820–1860," *American Quarterly* 18 (1966): 151–74; Mary P. Ryan, *Cradle of the Middle Class: The Family in Oneida County, New York, 1790–1865* (New York: Cambridge University Press 1981), and E. Anthony Rotundo, "Boy Culture: Middle-Class Boyhood in Nineteenth-Century America," in *Meanings for Modern Manhood: Constructions of Masculinity in Victorian America*, ed. M. Carnes and C. Griffen (Chicago: University of Chicago Press 1990), 27–35.
5 Jane Flax, "Postmodernism and Gender Relations in Feminist Theory," *Signs: Journal of Women in Culture and Society* 12 (1987): 621–44; Denise Riley, *"Am I That Name?" Feminism and the Category of "Women" in History* (London: Macmillan 1988); and Amanda Vickery, "Golden Age to Separate Spheres? A Review of the Categories and Chronology of English Women's History," *Historical Journal* 36 (1993): 383–414.
6 Ann Braude, "Women's History *Is* American Religious History," in *Retelling U.S. Religious History*, ed. Thomas A. Tweed (Berkeley: University of California Press, 1997), 107. Glenna Matthews argues that by valorizing female subjectivity, religion in the first half of the nineteenth century helped secular woman's rise to public prominence after 1850; *The Rise of the Public Woman: Woman's Power and Woman's Place in the United States, 1630–1970* (New York: Oxford University Press 1992). The following works explore in greater detail the role of religion in shaping a space for women: Ryan, *Cradle of the Middle Class*; Catherine Hall and Leonore Davidoff, *Family Fortunes: Men and Women of the English Middle Class, 1780–1850* (London: Hutchinson 1987); and Hannah M. Lane, "Wife, Mother, Sister, Friend: Methodist Women in St. Stephen New Brunswick, 1861–1881," in *Separate Spheres: Women's Worlds in the Nineteenth-Century Maritimes*, ed. Janet Guildford and

Suzanne Morton (Fredericton: Acadiensis Press 1994), 93–117. The constraints experienced by women in public life are perceptively analysed in Carmen Nielson Varty, "A 'Laudable Undertaking': Women, Charity, and the Public Sphere in Mid-Nineteenth-Century Hamilton, Canada West" (PH D dissertation, Queen's University, Kingston, 2004).

7 CCC to Mahala Child, 30 December 1858, CCC Papers, Series 4:A, 1:3, FC.

8 Bettina Bradbury, "Debating Dower," in *Power, Place, and Identity: Historical Studies of Social and Legal Regulation in Quebec*, ed. Tamara Myers et al. (Montreal: Montreal History Group 1998), 73–8.

9 Brian Young, *The Politics of Codification: The Lower Canadian Civil Code of 1866* (Montreal/Kingston: Osgoode Society for Canadian Legal History and McGill-Queen's University Press 1994).

10 Here I am following Young, *Codification*, 144–74.

11 Quoted in Karen Halttunen, *Confidence Men and Painted Women: A Study of Middle-Class Culture in America, 1830–1870* (New Haven: Yale University Press 1982), 29.

12 For a succinct and insightful analysis of the connection between domesticity and evangelical religion, see John Tosh, *A Man's Place: Masculinity and the Middle-Class Home in Victorian England* (New Haven: Yale University Press 1999), 34–9.

13 Diary, 10 March 1861, HCC Papers, Series 2, Box 1, FC.

14 Diary, 1 January 1859, HCC Papers, Series 2, Box 1, FC.

15 On transiency, see John R. Gillis, *A World of Their Own Making: Myth, Ritual, and the Quest for Family Values* (New York: Basic Books 1996), 20–40.

16 In his will, Moses specified that Lemira would continue to have home and board with her eldest son and his family. Having an elderly relative share a house was a usual arrangement in the period, and in the case of the Colbys, Hattie's mother, widowed in 1872, also spent extended periods of time in Stanstead until her death in 1887; see Jessie Maud Colby (JMC) Diary, 31 January 1888, JMC Papers, Series 2, Box 1, FC.

17 Jack's year in military service is documented in Child Papers, Box 1:6, FC.

18 On Rosalie's hiring, see HCC to Charles William Colby (CWC), 7 August 1882, HCC Papers, Series 1, Box 1:6, FC. Even in retirement, having moved to the U.S., she remained in contact; see Rosalie Valley to JMC and HCC, JMC Papers, Series 1, Box 9:5, FC.

19 Often overlapping with this concept of the family was the use of the term "friends." Defined by Alison Prentice as "an all-encompassing term to designate parents, guardians, and relatives, as well as dependent members of households," the term "friends" recurred

frequently in the Colby family correspondence; Alison Prentice, "Education and the Metaphor of the Family: The Upper Canadian Example," in *Education and Social Change*, ed. Michael B. Katz and Paul Mattingly (New York: New York University Press 1975), 110–32.

20 For the role of friendship in shaping female networks, see Nancy Grey Osterud, *Bonds of Community: The Lives of Farm Women in Nineteenth-Century New York* (Ithaca: Cornell University Press 1991). For contrasts between male and female networks of friends, see Joan Cashin, *A Family Venture: Men and Women on the Southern Frontier* (New York: Oxford University Press 1991), 99, 120.

21 This process is the subject of A. Gregory Schneider's *The Way of the Cross Leads Home: The Domestication of American Methodism* (Bloomington: Indiana University Press 1993).

22 For the role of family prayers in Puritan piety, see Charles Hambrick-Stowe, *The Practice of Piety: Puritan Devotional Disciplines in Seventeenth-Century New England* (Chapel Hill: University of North Carolina Press 1982), 143–50. For the evangelical family, see Ian C. Bradley, *The Call to Seriousness: The Evangelical Impact upon the Victorians* (New York: Macmillan 1969), 178–93. Examples of clerical anxiety about the perceived decline of family devotions can be found in "Family Religion," *Canadian Baptist*, 26 April 1866; "Family Worship," *Canadian Baptist*, 21 May 1868; and "Children in Church," *Christian Guardian*, 25 August 1875.

23 Diary, 4 January 1859, HCC Papers, Series 2, Box 1, FC.

24 Diary, 5 June 1859, HCC Papers, Series 2, Box 1, FC.

25 Manuscript census, Village of Stanstead Plain, Stanstead County/Township, 1861 and 1871, C-1323, C-10089, Library and Archives Canada (LAC).

26 Tosh, *A Man's Place*, 59.

27 Diary, 13 February 1859, HCC Papers, Series 2, Box 1, FC.

28 See, for example, Diary, 4 and 5 January, 28 and 29 April 1859, HCC Papers, Series 2, Box 1, FC. There is a reference to the conception – "What Hope was born this day five months? Only you know, dear Husband" – in HCC to CCC, 15 June 1859, HCC Papers, Series 1, Box 1:1, FC. Intimacy between newlyweds is further examined in Serge Gagnon, *Mariage et famille au temps de Papineau* (Sainte-Foy: Presses de l'Université Laval 1993), 205–64.

29 Diary, 20 September 1859, HCC Papers, Series 2, Box 1, FC: "Was sick in the night and our Dr Colby pricked my arm for a pint of blood to flow out. Took morphia and went to sleep." 22 September: "Had a wretched night but dear Mama and my own, own husband rendered it endurable. Was cupped and injected. Took morphia tincture etc. ... Had a severe headache and a good cry." By 1800 morphine was being

used by some doctors; see Sylvia D. Hoffert, *Private Matters: American Attitudes toward Childbearing and Infant Nurture in the Urban North* (Urbana: University of Illinois Press 1989), 81–2. "Before the advent of anaesthesia doctors could only offer their patients alcohol, opiates, or in some cases resort to mesmerism as a palliative to the pain of surgery"; Wendy Mitchinson, *The Nature of Their Bodies: Women and Their Doctors in Victorian Canada* (Toronto: University of Toronto Press 1991), 175. For turn-of-the-century obstetrical practices, including bloodletting, see Laurel Thatcher Ulrich, *A Midwife's Tale: The Life of Martha Ballard, Based on Her Diary, 1785–1812* (New York: Vintage Books 1991), 56–8, 259.

30 CCC to Mahala Child, 1 October [1859], CCC Papers, Series 4:A, Box 1:3, FC. A succinct summary of older concepts of mothering is in Gillis, *A World of Their Own Making*, 155–8.

31 This is the time it took Hattie and her brother Jack to travel from Stanstead to Weybridge in June 1859, not counting stops along the way; Diary 6–9 June 1859, HCC Papers, Series 2, Box 1, FC. Although they were much pined for and missed after their departure a week later, it is clear that the visit had not been an unmitigated success, since living conditions in the new house were still unsettled; see HCC to parents, 4 November 1859, HCC Papers, Series 1, Box 3:6, FC

32 Diary, 4 December 1859, HCC Papers, Series 2, Box 1, FC.

33 Mitchinson, *The Nature of Their Bodies*, 128, notes that by 1871 a decline in family size was particularly evident in the urban centres and among the middle classes.

34 HCC to CCC, 9 December 1859, HCC Papers, Series 1, Box 1:1, FC.

35 Tosh, *A Man's Place*, 79–80.

36 HCC to Emily Strong Colby (ESC), 22 November 1861, ESC Papers, Box 1:1, FC.

37 "Churching of Women," *Oxford Dictionary of the Christian Church*, ed. F.L. Cross and E.A. Livingstone, 2nd edn. (Oxford: Oxford University Press 1983), 293. The ceremony was replaced in the Roman Catholic Church by a blessing of the mother following the rite of baptism. On Anglican churching of women in the seventeenth century, see David Cressy, "Thanksgiving and the Churching of Women in Post-Reformation England," *Past and Present* 141 (November 1993): 115–32.

38 Diary, 6 February 1859, HCC Papers, Series 2, Box 1, FC. On her interest in Eliot, see, for example, HCC to CCC, 20 March 1873, HCC Papers, Series 1, Box 1:3, FC.

39 Among her books is a copy of Farrar's, *Life of Christ*, 2nd U.S. edn. (Albany, NY: Rufus Wendell 1876), presented to her by the publisher, with whom she had boarded as a college student. The book was later (in 1883) given to her daughter Jessie as a Christmas present. For

Farrar's place in the liberalization of Protestant thought, see Boyd Hilton, *The Age of Atonement: The Influence of Evangelism on Social and Economical Thought, 1795–1865* (Oxford: Clarendon Press 1988), 275. On her reading of the Swing trial, see HCC to CCC, 26 July 1874, HCC Papers, Series 1, Box 1:4, FC. Swing's "poetic evangelicalism" and his heresy trial are described in William Hutchison, *The Modernist Impulse in American Protestantism* (Durham: Duke University Press 1992), 48–58.

40 Gillis, *A World of Their Own Making*, 170, notes that by mid-century in Britain, the sickly child no longer was hastened to be given the magical protection of baptism (and naming) but was immediately placed under a doctor's care.

41 Emily Colby, Last Will and Testament, ESC Papers, Box 1:1, FC. In Canada in 1851, female life expectancy was 41.4 years, and the infant mortality rate measured 184.1 per 1,000 population; Roderic P. Beaujot and Kevin McQuillan, "The Social Effects of Demographic Change: Canada 1851–1981," *Journal of Canadian Studies* 21, no. 1 (1986): 59.

42 John Child's death is described in CCC to Lemira Strong Colby (LSC), 29 March 1872, CCC Papers, Series A, Box 1:4, FC. The multivalent importance of the Victorian family Bible is examined in Colleen McDannell, *Material Christianity: Religion and Popular Culture in America* (New Haven: Yale University Press 1995), 67–102.

43 Insightful studies of nineteenth-century consumerism include Anne C. Rose, *Voices of the Marketplace: American Thought and Culture, 1830–1860* (Toronto: Maxwell Macmillan Canada 1995), and the more narrowly focused study of religious and family holidays, Leigh Eric Schmidt, *Consumer Rites. The Buying and Selling of American Holidays* (Princeton: Princeton University Press 1995).

44 One such entry was that noted three weeks into the marriage when, returning in the evening from a drive with her husband, Hattie exclaimed: "Nothing to Wear (to the Winn Party). Had a great cry and my love was very kind. I wept plentifully in his dear arms and he sweetly comforted his pet wife." The next day, brother William successfully located a dressmaker for her; Diary, 18 January 1859, HCC Papers, Series 2, Box 1, FC.

45 See, for example, HCC to CCC, 30 March 1868 and 19 March 1871, HCC Papers, Series 1, Box 1:2, FC.

46 See, for example, HCC to CCC, 30 March 1871, HCC Papers, Series 1, Box 1:2, FC, which speaks of two servants, Maria Kelly and Adeline. See also HCC to CCC, 23 December 1864, HCC Papers, Series 1, Box 1:1, FC, which notes: "Alex is on a spree this week while he ought to be doing the Christmas butchering."

47 HCC to CCC, 10 March 1873, HCC Papers, Series 1, Box 1:3, FC. Joan Hedrick, *Harriet Beecher Stowe: The Life of a Literary Woman* (New York: Oxford University Press 1994), ch. 12, offers many parallel examples of women's domestic culture.
48 While she was visiting in Weybridge, for example, a disgruntled Lemira chastised her on the outgrown clothing with which she was expected to dress the infant grandson who had been left in her care; LSC to HCC, 2 December 1867, Moses French Colby (MFC) Papers, Series 1, Box 1:14, FC.
49 27 January 1859: "Charles walked with me all up the street. Got chenille at Dr. Cowles and velvet at Daley's and a new apron at K & Morrill at Paterson, with slipper pattern at Dr's–"; and 6 May 1859: "Husband walked with me to the Line to see the new goods. I received the present of a beautiful parasol purchased at Foster's. Merci, Merci, my very own love"; 1859 Diary, HCC Papers, Series 2, Box 1, FC.
50 1859 Diary, 25 December, HCC Papers, Series 2, Box 1, FC.
51 CCC to HCC, 22 December 1864, CCC Papers, Series 4:A, Box 2:2, FC.
52 HCC to CCC, 22 January 1865, HCC Papers, Series 1, Box 1:1, FC.
53 CCC to HCC, 16 October 1866, CCC Papers, Series 4:A, Box 2:2, FC.
54 HCC to CCC, 26 May 1867, HCC Papers, Series 1, Box 1:1, FC.
55 Andrew Jackson Child to HCC, 5 April 1857, Child Papers, Box 1:5, FC.
56 A reference to her sewing ability is in HCC to CCC, 31 March 1875, HCC Papers, Series 1, Box 1:5, FC. She noted to her eldest daughter the importance for women of "all sorts and conditions" to have a taste for housework; HCC to Abby Lemira Colby Aikins (ALCA), 21 February 1879, HCC Papers, Series 1, Box 2:5, FC.
57 "I feel awfully profane about William ... am angry for mother to think what I should do at her age if my boys serve me so"; HCC to CCC, 23 February 1873, HCC Papers, Series 1, Box 1:3, FC. See also HCC to CCC, 27 December 1864, 25 February and 6 July 1875, HCC Papers, Series 1, Box 1:1, 5, FC.
58 HCC to CCC, 1 November 1869, HCC Papers, Series 1, Box 1:2, FC.
59 HCC to CCC, 5 April 1875, HCC Papers, Series 1, Box 1:5, FC.
60 Bradbury, "Debating Dower," 73–8.
61 C.A. Richardson, no. 7814, 23 May 1862, Archives nationales du Québec, Sherbrooke (ANQS).
62 Ibid., no. 8135, 23 May 1863, ANQS.
63 Ibid., no. 9506, 26 May 1868; D. Thomas, no. 179, 30 July 1869, and no. 502, 2 December 1871, ANQS.
64 C.A. Richardson, no. 8136, 23 May 1863, ANQS, records her acceptance of the disposition of Moses' will.
65 Notebook of LSC, 3 January 1872, MFC Papers, Series 2, Box 1:13, FC.

66 C.A. Richardson, no. 8463, 18 April 1864; no. 8466, 20 April 1864 [Last Will of LSC]; and no. 8467, 20 April 1864; D. Thomas, no. 624, 29 August 1872; no. 767, 30 September 1873; no. 825, 9 April 1874, and no. 830, 10 April, 1874, ANQS.

67 For her views on Hattie, see Melvina to mother [Mrs David Wallingfford], n.d. 1870, and Melvina to Mary, 14 January 1890, William Benton Colby (WBC) Papers, Box 1:1, FC. A more idealized portrait is given by her younger daughter in reminiscences written near the end of her life; see Martha Stoddard Colby, *Above the Post Office: Memories, Sketches, and Stories* (Vancouver 1953), 4–24 *passim*, in WBC Papers, Box 1:3, FC.

68 Charles William speaks of Mrs Bailey and of his mother's deteriorating physical condition in "Garrulities of an Octogenarian" (typescript), 30, CWC Papers, Series 1:C, Box 11:3, FC.

69 HCC to CCC, 4 September 1874 and 27 April 1877, HCC Papers, Series 1, Box 1:4, 6, FC.

70 This is not only a female stance. See Françoise Noël, *Family Life and Sociability in Upper and Lower Canada, 1780–1870: A View from Diaries and Family Correspondence* (Montreal/Kingston: McGill-Queen's University Press 2003), 270.

71 Eldest daughter Abby, whose health as a child was especially fragile, was sent off for rest and renewal to family in Chicago, where she was retrieved at the end of the summer of 1875 by her father returning home from his binder sales; HCC to ALCA, 30 April 1875, HCC Papers, Series 1, Box 2:4, FC.

72 HCC to CCC, 28 March 1894, HCC Papers, Series 1, Box 1:7, FC.

73 Amaron's missionary parents had arrived from Canton Vaud, Switzerland, in 1840. His mother, Mme Daniel Amaron, founded the French Protestant co-educational school at Pointe-aux-Trembles, while he was the founder of the French Protestant college at Lowell, Massachusetts, which later moved to Springfield and became the American International College; see Joan MacDonald, *The Stanstead College Story* (Stanstead: Board of Trustees 1977), 23. Charles W. Colby speaks of the daughters, Mme Clement and Mlle Amaron, and notes his later friendship with Mme Clement's son Benjamin when both of them were students at McGill; "Garrulities," 14, CWC Papers, Series 1:C, Box 11:3, FC. Amaron, who in Quebec worked as a Bible colporteur, was ordained in the Presbyterian Church in 1879; see Douglas Walkington, *Ministers of the Presbyterian Church in Canada, 1875–1925* (privately published 1987), 4–5. A politician who also stayed at the pension was Archibald McLellan, MP for Colchester, Nova Scotia, whose daughter May later married and divorced J.A.M. Aikins, brother of Somerset Aikins, the future husband of Abby Colby.

74 Letters describing life at Berthier are HCC to CCC, 24 June 1874, 1, 26 July and 5 August 1878, HCC Papers, Series 1, Box 1:4, 6, FC; and ALCA to CWC [1874], ALCA Papers, Series 1, Box 3:6, FC.
75 ALCA to CCC, 20 January 1880, and ALCA Papers, Series 1, Box 1:7, FC. This did not, however, prevent Hattie the following December from investing her inheritance in her brother's merino sheep; see "notes" by CCC, December 1880, CCC Papers, Series 4:B, Box 5:3, FC.
76 HCC to CCC, 4 February 1880, HCC Papers, Series 1, Box 1:6, FC.
77 Glenna Matthews, *"Just A Housewife": The Rise and Fall of Domesticity in America* (Oxford: Oxford University Press 1987), looks specifically at the role of didactic literature.
78 Jane Tompkins, "Sentimental Power: Uncle Tom's Cabin and the Politics of Literary History," in *Sensational Designs: The Cultural Work of American Fiction, 1790–1850*, ed. Tompkins (New York: Oxford University Press 1985), 123.
79 Hedrick, *Harriet Beecher Stowe*, esp. chs. 11 and 12.
80 Kathryn Kish Sklar, *Catharine Beecher: A Study in American Domesticity* (New York: W.W. Norton 1976), 204–16.
81 On Beecher's inability to experience conversion in the style of her father Lyman Beecher, see Sklar, *Catharine Beecher*, 28–42. Hedrick examines Stowe's two conversions in *Harriet Beecher Stowe*, 144–5, 155.
82 While initially she had valued his cultured conversation, in time she became highly critical of his expectation that the congregation's women would look after his ailing wife and infant child, and of his treatment of one of the college's female instructors; see HCC to CCC, 22, 25, 27 April 1873 and 19 May 1874, HCC Papers, Series 1, Box 1:3, 4, FC.
83 The revivals were conducted in Derby and Stanstead by a minister and a hotel keeper from St Johnsbury, Vermont; see JMC to CCC, 12 May [1875], JMC Papers, Series 1, Box 1:1, FC.
84 HCC to CCC, 8 May 1875, HCC Papers, Series 1, Box 1:5, FC.
85 On a boat outing with the local minister and his family, where theology was discussed "all the way," she reflected: "I wish you could have been one of the speakers instead of me, and I a listener"; see HCC to CCC, 30 September 1866, HCC Papers, Series 1, Box 1:1, FC. A reference to her husband's help in 1875 "in matters religious" is in HCC to CCC, 25 February 1880, HCC Papers, Series 1, Box 1:6, FC.

CHAPTER FOUR

1 E. Anthony Rotundo, "Boy Culture: Middle-Class Boyhood in Nineteenth-Century America," in *Meanings for Moral Manhood: Constructions of Masculinity in Victorian America*, ed. M. Carnes and C. Griffen (Chicago: University of Chicago Press 1990), 27–35.

2 See in particular Amanda Vickery, "Golden Age to Separate Spheres? A Review of the Categories and Chronology of English Women's History," *Historical Journal* 36 (1993): 383–414, as well as the introduction to Laura McCall and Donald Yacavone, eds., *A Shared Experience: Men, Women, and the History of Gender* (New York: New York University Press 1998), and Leonore Davidoff et al., *The Family Story: Blood, Contract and Intimacy, 1830–1960* (London: Longman 1999).

3 John Tosh, *A Man's Place: Masculinity and the Middle-class Home in Victorian England* (New Haven: Yale University Press 1999); Clyde Griffen, "Reconstructing Masculinity," in *Meanings for Moral Manhood*, ed. Carnes and Griffen, 184–91; Marilyn Lake, "The Politics of Respectability: Identifying the Masculinist Context," *Historical Studies* 22 (1986): 116–31, and Leonore Davidoff and Catherine Hall, *Family Fortunes: Men and Women of the English Middle Class, 1780–1850* (London: Hutchinson 1987), 108–13.

4 See, for example, A.W. Nicolson, *Memories of James Bain Morrow* (Halifax: Methodist Book Room 1881); Nathanael Burwash, *Memorials of the Life of Edward and Lydia Ann Jackson* (Toronto: S. Rose 1876), and Rev. W. Cochrane, ed., *The Canadian Album: Men of Canada or Success by Example*, 5 vols (Brantford: Bradley, Garretson 1891–6).

5 The general substance of this chapter, but within a different analytical framework, has appeared previously in my essay "A 'Christian Businessman' in the Eastern Townships: The Convergence of Precept and Practice in Nineteenth-Century Evangelical Gender Construction," *Journal of the Canadian Historical Association*, New Series, 10 (1999): 103–4. For the popularization of the construct, see Kathryn Long, *The Revival of 1857–58: Interpreting an American Religious Awakening* (New York: Oxford University Press 1998), 86.

6 *Stanstead Journal*, 15 April 1858.

7 For this phrase, as well as an analysis of the congruence in the past between church time and commercial fairs and activities, see Leigh Eric Schmidt, *Consumer Rites: The Buying and Selling of American Holidays* (Princeton: Princeton University Press 1995), esp. ch. 1.

8 Kathryn T. Long, "'Turning ... Piety into Hard Cash': The Marketing of Nineteenth-Century Revivalism," in *God and Mammon: Protestants, Money, and the Market, 1790–1860*, ed. Mark Noll (Oxford: Oxford University Press 2002), 253.

9 Mark Noll, "Protestant Reasoning about Money and the Economy, 1790–1860: A Preliminary Probe," in *God and Mammon*, 272.

10 See, for example, the chapters by Noll and Long mentioned above in Noll, ed., *God and Mammon*. For two perceptive studies of systematic benevolence in nineteenth-century British Methodism, see W.R. Ward, "Methodism and Wealth, 1740–1860," and David J. Jeremy, "Late-

Victorian and Edwardian Methodist Businessmen and Wealth," in *Religion, Business, and Wealth in Modern Britain*, ed. David J. Jeremy (London: Routledge 1998), 63–85. For a Canadian case study, see Allen B. Robertson, *John Wesley's Nova Scotia Businessmen: Halifax Methodist Merchants, 1815–1855* (New York: Peter Lang 2000).

11 Charles Carroll Colby (CCC) to Hattie Child Colby (HCC), 4 July 1860, CCC Papers, Series 4:A, Box 2:2, Fonds Colby (FC), Stanstead Historical Society.

12 Maxine Van De Wetering, "The Popular Concept of "Home" in Nineteenth-Century America," *Journal of American Studies* 18 (1984): 5–28.

13 George S. Weaver, *The Christian Household: Embracing the Christian Home, Husband, Wife, Father, Mother, Brother, and Sister* (Boston: Tompkins and Musey 1856), 15.

14 Literature on the interest of middle-class Victorians in the house as a home, and the naming of homes, is summarized in John R. Gillis, *A World of Their Own Making: Myth, Ritual, and the Quest for Family Values* (New York: Basic Books 1996), ch. 6.

15 Colby gave an update of his own work on the house in CCC to HCC, 23 June 1859, CCC Papers, Series 4:A, Box 2:2, FC.

16 A detailed description of the nature and purpose of rooms in similar houses of the period can be found in Peter Ward, *A History of Domestic Space: Privacy and the Canadian Home* (Vancouver: UBC Press 1999), 8–87. Changing architectural styles in nineteenth-century Stanstead are examined in Susan Bowen, "History of the Architecture of the Three Villages," *Stanstead Historical Society Journal* 7 (1977): 14–29.

17 Circuit Court of Stanstead, Registers 1855–79, Archives nationales du Québec, Sherbrooke (AQNS). In 1861, for example, Colby participated in 43 cases, in 38 of which he represented plaintiffs.

18 Jean-Pierre Kesteman, Peter Southam, and Diane Saint-Pierre, *Histoire des cantons de l'Est* (Sainte-Foy: Presses de l'Université Laval 1998), 233–6.

19 Ibid., 320.

20 Jean-Pierre Kesteman, "Une bourgeoisie et son espace: industrialisation et développement du capitalisme dans le district de Saint-François (Québec), 1823–1879" (PH D thesis, Université du Québec à Montréal, 1985), 601, notes that economic activity in the St Francis District peaked between 1861 and 1865.

21 See, for example, CCC to HCC, 20 June 1860, CCC Papers, Series 4:A, Box 2:2, FC.

22 Kesteman, "Une bourgeoisie," 545, 581, 604–6, 683–4. Colby's business affairs are also amply documented in the regular correspondence with his wife, who maintained an active interest.

23 Kesteman et al., *Histoire des cantons de l'Est*, 321.
24 Ibid., 9.
25 Files of C.A. Richardson, no. 7922, 4 October 1862, ANQS; and CCC to HCC, 24 January 1863, CCC Papers, Series 4:A, Box 2:2, FC.
26 Circuit ledgers show Colby involved in 76 cases in 1862; in 1863 this was reduced to 22, and thereafter to fewer than 5 a year; Stanstead Circuit Court, AQNS.
27 Files of C.A. Richardson, no. 7922; G.H. Napier, no. 2391; unnotarized, 6 November 1863; D. Thomas, nos. 255 and 338; E.P. Felton, nos. 90, 91, 92, and 93; unnotarized, 8 March 1864; D. Thomas, no. 421; J. Lefèbvre, nos. 156, 157; C.A. Richardson, no. 8477; E.P. Felton, no. 24; and unnotarized, 1 April 1865; all in ANQS.
28 Files of C.A. Richardson, no. 8135, 23 May 1863, and no. 8467, 20 April 1864, ANQS.
29 CCC to HCC, 20 April 1868, CCC Papers, Series 4:A, Box 2:3, FC.
30 1861 Journal, 3 February 1861, HCC Papers, Series 2, Box 1, FC.
31 In 1861 Charles Colby, along with his parents and two siblings, is listed as Congregationalist, his wife and daughter as Wesleyan Methodist. In 1871 all Colbys, with the exception of Lemira, are listed as Wesleyan Methodist. See Manuscript census, Village of Stanstead Plain, Stanstead County/Township, 1861 and 1871, C-1323, C-10089, Library and Archives Canada (LAC).
32 1861 Journal, 26 January 1861, CCC Papers, Series 4:B, Box 6:2, FC.
33 "Evangelicalism was at its most effective in revolutionary situations because it communicated enduring political stability in the face of disorder, long-lasting eagerness for discipline, and nearly inexhaustible hope that the dignity of self affirmed by the gospel could be communicated to the larger community"; Noll, "Protestant Reasoning," in *God and Mammon*, 267.
34 Long, *The Revival of 1857–58*, 83–92.
35 CCC to HCC, 26 October 1862, CCC Papers, Series 4:A, Box 2:2, FC. See also his criticism of a Thanksgiving sermon in Middletown, Connecticut, delivered in an artificial and affected manner, CCC to HCC, 18 November 1867, CCC Papers, Series 4:A, Box 2:3, FC.
36 CCC to HCC, 27 January 1864, CCC Papers, Series 4:A, Box 2:2, FC.
37 For the role of evangelical beliefs and values in shaping the nineteenth-century self-made man, see Stuart M. Blumin, *The Emergence of the Middle Class: Social Experience in the American City, 1760–1900* (Cambridge: Harvard University Press 1989), ch. 6.
38 Noll, "Protestant Reasoning," in *God and Mammon*, 274.
39 The Canadian economic context is examined in J.L. Granatstein et al., *Nation: Canada since Confederation*, 3rd. edn. (Toronto: McGraw-Hill

Ryerson 1990), 63–96, and David Burley, *A Particular Condition in Life: Self-Employment and Social Mobility in Mid-Victorian Brantford, Ontario* (Montreal/Kingston: McGill-Queen's University Press 1994). The latter notes the high rate of mortgage indebtedness in 1871 and 1880–81 among those under the age of forty. Kesteman, "Une bourgeoisie," 554, comments on the inflation caused by the end of the Civil War. Besides William, at least one other member of Stanstead's business elite, Charles's mining partner Ozro Morrill, had to face bankruptcy.

40 For the earliest partnership, see CCC to HCC, 20 June and 4 July 1860, CCC Papers, Series 4:A, Box 2:2, FC; Andrew Jackson Child to CCC, 5 March 1866, and Child Letters 1:6, FC.

41 Charles William Colby (CWC), "Garrulities of an Octogenarian" (typescript), 24–5, CWC Papers, Series 1:C, Box 11:3, FC.

42 Unnotarized, 6 February 1866, Sherbrooke Registry Office, Register B, vol. 18, 306, no. 227, ANQS.

43 HCC to CCC, 7 July 1869, HCC Papers, Series 1, Box 1:2, FC.

44 Superior Court Records, St Francis, 1872, register file no. 707, Hannah Howard vs. Charles C. Colby, 1 August 1871, ANQS.

45 The farm was put in the hands of his brother-in-law William White, a lawyer, to ensure that the interests of Lemira and White's late wife Emily would be looked after; CCC to HCC, 30 April 1872, CCC Papers, Series 4:A, Box 2:5, FC.

46 Superior Court Records, St Francis, 1872, file no. 707, Writ of Collation, 20 June 1872, ANQS; and Insolvency Proposal, CCC Papers, Series 4:B, Box 5:5, FC.

47 William Benton Colby (WBC) to CCC, 27 May 1871, WBC Papers, Box 1:1, FC.

48 Insolvency Records, 12 November 1873, file no. 48, ANQS. The records contain no corresponding file for CCC, thus establishing the fact that he, unlike his brother, did not file for bankruptcy. Notice of William's bankruptcy was in the *Quebec Official Gazette*, 2, 9, 16, 23, and 30 May 1874, the *Sherbrooke Gazette*, 1, 8, 15, 22, and 29 May 1874, and the (Sherbrooke) *Pioneer*, 5, 12, 22, and 29 May 1874.

49 Karen Halttunen, *Confidence Men and Painted Women: A Study of Middle-Class Culture in America, 1830–1870* (New Haven: Yale University Press 1982), 1–32.

50 See "Introduction," *God and Mammon*, 14, including notes 46–7.

51 Francis Wayland, *The Elements of Moral Science*, rev. edn. (Boston: Garland and Lincoln 1870), 226–7, saw economic expansion built on speculation as "groundless, hazardous, overcommitted and uncontrolled."

52 HCC to Jessie Maud Colby (JMC), 8 September 1872, HCC Papers, Series 1, Box 2:7, FC.

53 "Reports on the Committee on Discipline. Administration on Discipline, Section 5:9," *Journal of Proceedings of the First United General Conference of the Methodist Church* (Toronto: William Briggs 1883), 274. This repeated the discipline that had been in place at the time of the Colby insolvency.
54 Henry Rack, *Reasonable Enthusiast: John Wesley and the Rise of Methodism* (London: Epworth Press 1992), 367. For an exemplary Canadian expression of Wesley's teachings, see Robertson, *John Wesley's Nova Scotia Businessmen*.
55 Cited in Boyd Hilton, *The Age of Atonement: The Influence of Evangelicalism on Social and Economic Thought, 1795–1865* (Oxford: Clarendon Press 1988), 133.
56 Kesteman, "Une bourgeoisie," 604, and pew list, 1869, Wesleyan Methodist Church, Stanstead, United Church of Canada, Archives nationales du Québec, Montréal (ANQM).
57 See note 53 above and E.W. Judd to CCC, 13 November 1871, CCC Papers, Series 4:B, Box 5:5, FC.
58 Initially, on 17 November 1871, an additional 18 creditors, many of them family friends, had presented amounts owed; see Superior Court Records, St Francis Records, 1872, file no. 707, Respondents' Exhibit, 17 November 1871, ANQS. These people appear to have withdrawn their claims by the time of the writ of collation, 20 June 1872, distributing the assets seized from the defendant.
59 Political preferment had also been slow, despite reassuring and tantalizing hints of advancement by John A. Macdonald: appointment as Deputy Speaker in 1887, and president of the Privy Council in 1889. Convinced that his business affairs required his full attention, CCC commenced actively to consider withdrawing from politics, a decision clinched by his defeat (by a very narrow margin) in the 1891 election. See chapter 7 for more detail.
60 HCC to CCC, 25 December 1872, HCC Papers, Series 1, Box 1:2, FC.
61 Handwritten note, 1880, CCC Personal Finances, 1864–98, CCC Papers, Series 4:B, Box 5:3, FC.
62 See, for example, S. Stevens to CCC, 7 June 1893, CCC Papers, Series 4:B, Box 5:3, FC, in which Stevens, manager of the Eastern Townships Bank, Stanstead, warns that CCC's indebtedness to the bank is $20,000, "a sum beyond which the directors feel we cannot exceed."
63 These are extensively detailed in personal correspondence and business correspondence, CCC Papers, Series 3:A, Box 1–11, FC, and summarized in CWC, "Garrulities of an Octogenarian" (typescript), 67, and CWC Papers, Series 1:C, Box 11:3, FC.
64 "Carrollcroft: Sale and Reposession Details," CCC Papers, Series 4:B, Box 5:5, FC.
65 HCC to CCC, 24 June [1893], HCC Papers, Series 1, Box 1:7, FC.

66 CCC to JMC, 1 March 1874, CCC Papers, Series 4:A, Box 1:5, FC.
67 HCC to CCC, 2 April 1873, HCC Papers, Series 1, Box 1:3, FC.
68 For example, HCC to CCC, 30 January 1863, HCC Papers, Series 1, Box 1:1, FC.
69 CCC to HCC, 19 March 1871, CCC Papers, Series 4:A, Box 2:4, FC.
70 CCC to HCC, 30 April 1872, CCC Papers, Series 4:A, Box 2:2, FC.
71 "Canada Our Home. Address delivered by C.C. Colby, Esq., M.P. at Coaticook, July 1st, 1876," CCC Papers, Series 2:A, Box 1:3, FC. The economic boom in minerals, agriculture, industry, and logging in the Eastern Townships during the period is corroborated in Kesteman et al., *Histoire des cantons de l'Est*, 299–336, passim.
72 A few months after Colby's appointment to the cabinet, the prime minister received a lengthy letter of complaint from the Calgary legal firm of Lougheed, McCarthy, and Beck, which threatened court action, alleging that it had been misled by Colby's participation in a joint stock venture of the Alberta and Athabaska Railway, on the misplaced assumption that this company's route would have government backing. The charge evoked a lengthy and complete denial, in which a morally outraged Colby underscored the indefatigable efforts he had expended to promote national interests at the expense of his own personal welfare; see R. McCarthy to Sir John A. Macdonald, 11 February 1890, Macdonald Papers, 87554, and Charles Colby to Sir John A. Macdonald, 19 February 1890, Macdonald Papers, 87548, LAC. For an earlier controversy, see Macdonald Papers, 87528–35 (9 July 1883), LAC, reporting on Colby's decision to explore timber lands in the Rocky Mountains along the route of the proposed Canadian Pacific Railway.
73 "Death of Hon. C.C. Colby," *Stanstead Journal*, 17 January 1907.
74 Robert Orsi, "Everyday Miracles: The Study of Lived Religion," in *Lived Religion in America: Toward a History of Practice*, ed. David D. Hall (Princeton, NJ: Princeton University Press 1997), 7.
75 Hilton, *The Age of Atonement*; Noll, ed., *God and Mammon*; Jeremy, ed., *Religion, Business and Wealth in Modern Britain*; R. Laurence Moore, *Selling God: American Religion in the Marketplace of Culture* (New York: Oxford University Press 1994); and Larry Eskridge and Mark A. Noll, eds., *More Money: Money and Evangelicals in Recent North American History* (Grand Rapids: William Eerdman's 2000), chs. 1–3, 5.
76 Noll, "Protestant Reasoning," in *God and Mammon*, 271
77 For a brief description, see Ben Forster, *A Conjunction of Interests: Business, Politics, and Tariffs, 1825–1879* (Toronto: University of Toronto Press 1986), esp. chs. 5 and 6.
78 This is developed in chapter 6. Kesteman, "Une bourgeoisie," 389, notes that clergy constituted 11–15% of the investments in financial banks in the St Francis district between 1841 and 1875.

79 For a brief discussion of these scruples, see Marguerite Van Die, "The Marks of a Genuine Revival: Religion, Social Change, Gender, and Community in Mid-Victorian Brantford, Ontario," *Canadian Historical Review* 79, no. 3 (1998): 524–63.
80 CCC to HCC, 21 October 1866, CCC Papers, Series 4:A, Box 2:2, FC.
81 CCC to HCC, 22 October 1866, CCC Papers, Series 4:A, Box 2:2, FC.
82 CCC to HCC, 22 December 1864, CCC Papers, Series 4:A, Box 2:2, FC. Henry Ward Beecher, *The Sermons of Henry Ward Beecher, Preached at Plymouth Church, Brooklyn* (New York: W.B. Ford 1872), 96.
83 Long, "Turning ... Piety into Hard Cash," in *God and Mammon*, ed. Noll, 252. The evidence given is Beecher's novel *Norwood*. For Beecher's theology, see Gary Dorrien, *The Making of American Liberal Theology: Imagining Progressive Religion, 1805–1900* (Louisville: Westminster John Knox Press 2001), 181–224.
84 Colby mentions in a political address in 1876, "William E. Dodge and Henry Ward Beecher had sons in the lumber woods of Ontario. I name these simply as specimen bricks"; see "Canada Our Home," CCC Papers, Series 2:A, Box 1:3, FC.
85 Richard Helmstadter, "The Nonconformist Conscience," in *The Conscience of the Victorial State*, ed. Peter Marsh (Syracuse, NY: Syracuse University Press 1979), 158–62; and Hilton, *The Age of Atonement*, ch. 7. Books such as Frederic W. Farrar's *Life of Christ*, which have been seen as a major contributor to this shift, quickly became an addition to the Colby library. For Farrar's place in this, see Hilton, *The Age of Atonement*, 275.
86 The latter part of the nineteenth century in Canada, as in the United States, witnessed an outburst of literature detailing the exemplary lives of devout businessmen. While some clearly were representatives of an evangelical construct reflecting the agrarian-commercial marketplace of an earlier period, others, like Colby, stood squarely within the economically progressive and socially conservative industrialism of the late nineteenth century. For examples, see note 4 above.
87 For an analysis that sees this shift as religious declension, see A. Gregory Schneider, *The Way of the Cross Leads Home* (Bloomington: Indiana University Press 1993), esp. ch. 13.

CHAPTER FIVE

1 Hattie Child Colby (HCC) to Charles Carroll Colby (CCC), 1 March 1871, HCC Papers, Series 1, Box 1:2, Fonds Colby (FC), Stanstead Historical Society.
2 For an early example, see Anne L. Kuhn, *The Mother's Role in Childhood Education: New England Concepts, 1830–1860* (New Haven: Yale

University Press 1947), and Barbara Welter, "The Cult of True Womanhood, 1820–1860,"*American Quarterly* 18 (1966): 151–74.
3 Maxine Van De Wetering, "The Popular Concept of 'Home' in Nineteenth-Century America," *Journal of American Studies* 28 (1984): 1, 5–28.
4 John Tosh, *A Man's Place: Masculinity and the Middle-Class Home in Victorian England* (New Haven: Yale University Press 1999), 79–86, and Leonore Davidoff, *The Family Story: Blood, Contract, and Intimacy, 1830–1960* (New York: Addison Wesley Longman 1999), 151–7.
5 Tosh, *A Man's Place*, 101.
6 See, for example, his description of purchases in anticipation of a trip to Vermont with his wife and youngest daughter; CCC to HCC, 4 April 1870, CCC Papers, Series 4:A, Box 2:4, FC.
7 CCC to HCC, 30 April 1872, CCC Papers, Series 4:A, Box 2:5, FC.
8 Davidoff, *The Family Story*, 109; Colleen McDannell, *The Christian Home in Victorian America, 1840–1900* (Bloomington: Indiana University Press 1986); and Margaret Bendroth, *Growing Up Protestant: Parents, Children, and Mainline Churches* (New Brunswick, NJ: Rutgers University Press 2002), 1–80. Bendroth (59) notes the readiness of late-nineteenth-century Protestants to collapse home and church into one institution.
9 This has been well argued for Victorian England in Leonore Davidoff and Catherine Hall, *Family Fortunes: Men and Women of the English Middle Class, 1780–1850* (Chicago: University of Chicago Press 1987), 76–148. For the United States, see Mary P. Ryan, *Cradle of the Middle Class: The Family in Oneida County, New York, 1790–1865* (Cambridge: Cambridge University Press 1981). In both, however, the relation to the institutional church has received little attention.
10 Edmund S. Morgan, *The Puritan Family: Religion and Domestic Relations in Seventeenth-Century New England* (New York: Harper and Row 1944), 87–108.
11 J.I. Little, "The Fireside Kingdom: A Mid-Nineteenth-Century Anglican Perspective on Marriage and Parenthood," in *Households of Faith: Family, Gender, and Community in Canada, 1760–1969*, ed. Nancy Christie (Montreal/Kingston: McGill-Queen's University Press 2001), 77–100. For a contemporary publication, see James George, *The Sabbath School of the Fireside; and the Sabbath School of the Congregation as It Should Be* (Kingston: Creighton 1859).
12 The most informative study on the Sunday school movement (for the United States) is Ann Boylan, *The Formation of an American Institution, 1790–1880* (New Haven: Yale University Press 1988). For the Stanstead area, see Kathleen Brown, *Schooling in the Clearings: Stanstead 1800–1850* (Stanstead: Stanstead Historical Society 2001), 38–41; for Methodism in Canada, see Neil Semple, *The Lord's Dominion: The*

History of Canadian Methodism (Montreal/Kingston: McGill-Queen's University Press 1996), ch. 14; and for Upper Canada, see Allan Greer, "The Sunday Schools of Upper Canada," *Ontario History* 67 (September 1975): 169–84.

13 In Canada the official resolution of the theological dispute about whether a child's eternal safety rested on conversion, rather than on baptism and childhood nurture, took significantly longer than in the United States; see Marguerite Van Die, *An Evangelical Mind: Nathanael Burwash and the Methodist Tradition in Canada, 1839–1918* (Montreal/Kingston: McGill-Queen's University Press 1989), 25–37. See also Neil Semple, "'The Nurture and Admonition of the Lord': Nineteenth-Century Canadian Methodism's Response to Childhood," *Histoire Sociale/Social History* 14 (1981): 157–75.

14 Serge Gagnon, *Plaisir d'amour et crainte de Dieu: sexualité et confession au Bas-Canada* (Sainte-Foy: Presses de l'Université Laval 1990), 79.

15 *Liturgy or Formulary of Services in Use in the Wesleyan-Methodist Church in Canada* (Toronto: S. Rose 1867), 7.

16 For a succinct summary of Bushnell's thought, see Gary Dorrien, *The Making of American Liberal Theology: Imagining Progressive Religion, 1805–1900* (Louiseville: Westminster John Knox Press 2001), 111–78. For his views on Christian nurture, see Bendroth, *Growing Up Protestant*, 24–9, and Ann Douglas, *Feminization of American Culture* (New York: Avon Books 1978), 96–159.

17 Bendroth, *Growing Up Protestant*, 25.

18 For moral education in American schools in the nineteenth century, see Lawrence Moore, "What Children Did Not Learn in School: The Intellectual Quickening of Young Americans in the Nineteenth Century," *Church History* 68, no. 1 (1999): 42–61; and David Tyacke, "Onward Christian Soldiers: Religion in the American Common School," in *History and Education: The Educational Uses of the Past*, ed. Paul Nash (New York: Random House 1970), 212–55. Less satisfying is Alison Prentice, *The School Promoters: Education and Social Class in Mid-Nineteenth-Century Upper Canada* (Toronto: McClelland & Stewart 1977), which interprets moral education in Upper Canada through social control theory. See also Alison Prentice and Susan Houston, *Family, School, and Society in Nineteenth-Century Canada* (Toronto: University of Toronto Press 1988), *passim*. Short summaries of moral education in Canadian schools in the nineteenth century can be found in Paul Axelrod, *The Promise of Schooling: Education in Canada, 1800–1914* (Toronto: University of Toronto Press 1997), ch. 3.

19 The legal changes affecting children in the Eastern Townships of Quebec in the 1800s are discussed in Renée Joyal, *Les enfants, la*

Société, et l'État au Québec, 1608–1989: jalons (Montreal: Cahiers du Québec 1999), 17–107.
20 "An Address Delivered before the Teachers' Association at Stanstead, January 1, 1858," *Stanstead Journal*, 14 January 1858.
21 Similar comments, which can be found in religious and educational journals in the 1850s and 1860s, show that even as denominational colleges continued to teach the traditional course in moral psychology, the new emphasis on the importance of childhood nurture in character formation had begun to seep into Canadian Protestant circles. Ideas stressing the malleability of childhood did not immediately drive out earlier views on discipline, which had concentrated on the importance of breaking the will of the child, but in the next few decades they did arouse considerable controversy within theological circles; see Van Die, *An Evangelical Mind*, ch. 1.
22 George S. Weaver, *The Christian Household: Embracing the Christian Home* ... (Boston: Tompkins and Musey 1856), 36. The reference to its reading is in Journal, 10 March 1861, HCC Papers, Series 2, Box 1, FC.
23 HCC to CCC, 1 April 1873, HCC Papers, Series 1, Box 1:3, FC.
24 CCC to Jessie Maud Colby (JMC), 7 July 1872, CCC Papers, Series 4:A, Box 1:5, FC.
25 HCC to CCC, 26 March 1875, HCC Papers, Series 1, Box 1:5, FC.
26 "Little Hattie," HCC Papers, Series 2, Box 2, FC.
27 For the debate on infant depravity in Canadian Methodist circles, including recent historiographical controversy, see Van Die, *An Evangelical Mind*, ch. 1.
28 HCC to JMC, 1 August 1872, HCC Papers, Series 1, Box 2:7, FC.
29 Peter Gregg Slater, *Children in the New England Mind* (Hamden, Conn.: Archon 1977), 101, and Douglas, *Feminization of American Culture*, 96–159.
30 E.N. Kirk, *God's Covenant with Believing Mothers: An Address Delivered at the Anniversary of the Maternal Association of Mount Vernon* (Boston: Rand and Avery 1865), HCC Papers, Series 2, Box 3, FC.
31 McDannell, *The Christian Home*, 108–16, and Bendroth, *Growing Up Protestant*, 14–16.
32 Tosh, *A Man's Place*, 84.
33 See, for example, HCC to CCC, 22 September 1867, HCC Papers, Series 1, Box 1:1, FC.
34 HCC to CCC, 20 and 23 March 1873, HCC Papers, Series 1, Box 1:3, FC; and Diary, 5 April 1903, JMC Papers, Series 2, Box 1, FC.
35 See the fine study on Victorian Bibles as commodities in Colleen McDannell, *Material Christianity: Religion and Popular Culture in America* (New Haven: Yale University Press 1995), 67–102.

36 McDannell, *The Christian Home*, 77–107.
37 Insightful commentary on the moral dimension of consumer choice, though for a later period, is found in Joy Parr, *Domestic Goods: The Material, the Moral, and the Economic in the Postwar Years* (Toronto: University of Toronto Press 1999).
38 HCC to CCC, 12 November 1868, HCC Papers, Series 1, Box 1:1, FC.
39 HCC to CCC, 25 March 1873, HCC Papers, Series 1, Box 1:3, FC.
40 Charles William Colby (CWC), "Garrulities of an Octogenarian" (typescript), 21, CWC Papers, Series 1:C, Box 11:3, FC.
41 Ibid. See also HCC to CCC, 2 March 1883, HCC Papers, Series 1, Box 1:6, FC.
42 HCC to CCC, 31 August 1874, HCC Papers, Series 1, Box 1:4, FC.
43 Richard L. Bushman, *The Refinement of America: Persons, Houses, Cities* (New York: Vintage 1993), 326–31.
44 Daniel Walker Howe, *Making the American Self: Jonathan Edwards to Abraham Lincoln* (Cambridge, Mass.: Harvard University Press 1997), 118–19.
45 HCC to CCC, 27 March 1873, HCC Papers, Series 1, Box 1:3, FC.
46 HCC to Abby Lemira Colby Aikins (ALCA), 11 April 1875, HCC Papers, Series 1, Box 2:4, FC.
47 This did not seem to deter the evangelical press. See David Paul Nord, "Religious Reading and Readers in Antebellum America," *Journal of the Early Republic* 15 (Summer 1995): 241–72.
48 HCC to girls, 23 February 1883, HCC Papers, Series 1, Box 2:1, FC.
49 As argued in William McLoughlin, *Revivals, Awakenings, and Reform: An Essay on Religion and Social Change in America, 1607–1977* (Chicago: University of Chicago Press 1978), which analyses the close fit between nineteenth-century experiential religion and its cultural expression.
50 Weaver, *The Christian Household*, 104.
51 This is also briefly noted in Bushman, *Refinement of America*, 351–2, which draws attention to contradictions between "tasteful religion" and Christian teaching on egalitarianism. For the theological controversies, see William Hutchison, *The Modernist Impulse in American Protestatism* (Oxford: Oxford University Press 1982), 76–110, and Dorrien, *Making of American Liberal Theology*, 179–260.
52 For an example of the former, see Van De Wetering, "The Popular Concept of 'Home' in Nineteenth-Century America." Notable exceptions include Davidoff and Hall, *Family Fortunes*, and Françoise Noël, *Family Life and Sociability in Upper and Lower Canada, 1780–1870: A View from Diaries and Family Correspondence* (Montreal/Kingston: McGill-Queen's University Press 2003).

53 Peter N. Stearns and Timothy Haggerty, "The Role of Fear: Transitions in American Emotional Standards for Children," *American Historical Review* 96, no. 1 (1991): 63–94.
54 Julia McNair Wright, *The Complete Home: An Encyclopedia of Domestic Life and Affairs* (Brantford, Ont.: Bradley, Garretson 1879), 289.
55 HCC to JMC, 28 August 1872, HCC Papers, Series 1, Box 2:7, FC.
56 Census of Canada, 1871, Stanstead (microfilm) C-10089–90, Library and Archives Canada (LAC).
57 A good entry into these varied activities can be found in CWC, "Garrulities of an Octogenarian" (typescript), 22–4, CWC Papers, Series 1:C, Box 11:3, FC.
58 See, for example, HCC to JMC, 5 July 1874, HCC Papers, Series 1, Box 2:7, FC, in which she notes that Abby had been "invited to a little dance on account of Johnny Foster's friends."
59 Hattie told her husband of a female church member's announcement of a Ladies' Aid meeting at the parsonage for the purpose of arranging suitable entertainment "for the young people who are church members want some kind of party that they may go to: and as they are so to speak forbidden to accept the invitations they do receive, they call for something suited to their case." She did not attend. See HCC to CCC, 20 January 1875, HCC Papers, Series 1, Box 1:5, FC.
60 This was done by adding a footnote to paragraph 35 of its official Doctrine and Discipline. For the wider context, see William H. Magney, "The Methodist Church and the National Gospel, 1884–1914," *Bulletin* (Committee on Archives, United Church of Canada), 20 (1968): 3–95.
61 Charles William Colby (who married Emma Cobb, granddaughter of Wilder Pierce, member of another prominent Stanstead Methodist family) recounts that the dancing at his outdoor wedding in 1897 was witnessed by six ministers, who, though they did not participate, did not to object; see Diary, 23 June 1897, CWC Papers, Series 1:C, Box 12, FC.
62 HCC to ALCA, 31 January 1875, HCC Papers, Series 1, Box 2:4, FC.
63 Jean-Pierre Kesteman, Peter Southam, and Diane Saint-Pierre, *Histoire des cantons de l'Est* (Sainte-Foy: Presses de l'Université Laval 1998), 396–8.
64 HCC to CCC, 3 August 1873, HCC Papers, Series 1, Box 1:3, FC.
65 HCC to CCC, 21 October 1884, HCC Papers, Series 1, Box 1:7, FC.
66 Bendroth, *Growing Up Protestant*, 39–50.
67 On the relationship between public duty and paternal domesticity, see Tosh, *A Man's Place*, 124–41.
68 JMC to ALCA, 9 July 1877, JMC Papers, Series 1, Box 7:2, FC.

69 HCC to JMC, 10 and 14 August 1874, HCC Papers, Series 1, Box 2:7, FC.
70 HCC to CCC, 20 March 1875, HCC Papers, Series 1, Box 1:5, FC.
71 Centenary Methodist Church, Stanstead, Minute Book, vol. 2 [1883–1925]. Initially salaried at $15, this was increased to $50 in 1887.
72 For the role of church attendance in the Victorian Sabbath, see, for example, Alexis McCrossen, *Holy Day, Holiday: The American Sabbath* (Ithaca: Cornell University Press 2000), 1–92.
73 ALCA to JMC, 8 September 1872, ALCA Papers, Series 1, Box 3:3, FC.
74 See, for example, HCC to CCC, 31 March 1873, HCC Papers, Series 1, Box 1:3, FC.
75 R.D. Gidney and W.P.J. Millar, *Professional Gentlemen: The Professions in Nineteenth-Century Ontario* (Toronto: University of Toronto Press 1994), 133–4. Examining this from the perspective of the preacher's duties, Gidney and Millar estimate that a devout person, attending three services a week, would be exposed to 156 sermons per year. In Stanstead, the third sermon (that at the weekly prayer service) took the form of a prayer meeting that circulated among various homes.
76 HCC to JMC, 28 July 1872, HCC Papers, Series 1, Box 2:7, FC.
77 HCC to JMC, 15 September 1884, HCC Papers, Series 1, Box 2:8, FC.
78 HCC to JMC, 8 February 1885, HCC Papers, Series 1, Box 2:9, FC.
79 HCC to ALCA, 7 February 1879, HCC Papers, Series 1, Box 2:5, FC, refers to Abby's "Episcopal leanings."
80 This development is described in my "A March of Triumph in Praise of the 'Beauty of Holiness': Laity and the Evangelic Impulse in Canadian Methodism, 1800–1884," in *Aspects of the Canadian Evangelic Experience*, ed. G.A. Rawlyk (Montreal/Kingston: McGill-Queen's University Press 1996), 78–89.
81 On their attendance at camp meetings, see HCC to JMC, 16 July 1872, HCC Papers, Series 1, Box 2:7, FC. For changes in the road to membership and the increased youthfulness of converts in Canadian evangelicalism in the 1870s, see Van Die, "The Marks of a Genuine Revival: Religion, Social Change, Gender, and Community in Mid-Victorian Brantford, Ontario," *Canadian Historical Review* 79, no. 3 (1998): 542–63.
82 HCC to ALCA, 7 February 1879, HCC Papers, Series 1, Box 1:5, FC.
83 For the wider context, see Semple, *The Lord's Dominion*, ch. 14, and Christopher Coble, "The Role of Young People's Societies in the Training of Christian Womanhood (and Manhood), 1880–1910" in *Women and Twentieth-Century Protestantism*, ed. Margaret Lamberts Bendroth and Virginia Lieson Brereton (Urbana: University of Illinois Press 2002), 74–92.
84 Young Canadian Methodists in urban centres applauded the move away from the old barnlike buildings, characteristic of their

denomination's earlier architecture, and displayed their aspirations to taste and gentility in their fundraising and social activities.

85 HCC to JMC [early 1880s], HCC Papers, Series 1, Box 2:7, FC.
86 The founding of Stanstead Wesleyan College is detailed in B.F. Hubbard, *Forests and Clearings: The history of Stanstead County* (Montreal: Lovell 1874), 106–8; Joan MacDonald, *The Stanstead College Story* (Stanstead: Board of Trustees 1977), 1–8; and Minutes 1872–92, Board of Trustees, Stanstead College, Stanstead. For the wider context of Protestant schools in Quebec in these years and their role in socialization, see Roderick MacLeod and Mary Anne Poutanen, *A Meeting of the People: School Boards and Protestant Communities in Quebec, 1801–1998* (Montreal/Kingston: McGill-Queen's University Press 2004), 165–94.
87 These included Ichabod Smith and Wilder Pierce; see Brown, *Schooling in the Clearings*, 277.
88 MacDonald, *Stanstead College Story*, 7.
89 "The ornamental department (except music) is entirely abolished, I should judge"; HCC to CCC, 20 July 1874, HCC Papers, Series 1, Box 1:4, FC.
90 HCC to CCC, 5 January 1880, HCC Papers, Series 1, Box 1:6, FC, refers to Abby's return from England the preceding September and the celebration of her eighteenth birthday.
91 HCC to CCC, 21 February 1879, HCC Papers, Series 1, Box 1:6, FC.
92 "Graduates," *Stanstead Wesleyan College, Session 1878–79*, 9, JMC Papers, Series 3, Box 1:8, FC
93 CCC to family [mid-1880s], CCC Papers, Series 1:C, Box 12:1, FC.
94 George Marsden, *The Soul of the American University: From Protestant Establishment to Established Non-Belief* (Oxford: Oxford University Press 1994), 99–195.
95 The educational preparation of the sons is described in CWC, "Garrulities of an Octogenarian" (typescript), 34–47, CWC Papers, Series 1:C, Box 11:3, FC.
96 The lectures were intended to cover "private personal habits, as to exercise, exposure, eating, sleeping and sitting, walking, dress, and room; domestic manners; table manners; schoolroom manners; hotel and railroad manners; street manners; manners in public assemblies, – as in church, concert, parties and parlors; manners towards kindred and friends; manners in intercourse with other ladies; manners and intercourse with gentlemen"; MacDonald, *The Stanstead College Story*, 7.
97 HCC to ALCA, 30 April 1875, HCC Papers, Series 1, Box 2:4, FC.
98 Letters passing between Colorado and Stanstead hinted at the possibility of her being able to earn a little extra money in sheep herding to pay for her parents' trip a little later; but given her fastidious nature and fragile health, this remained a well-intentioned hope.

99 HCC to CCC, 10 and 25 February 1880, HCC Papers, Series 1, Box 1:6, FC.
100 Although they were very different in temperament, the two daughters were extremely close and, when not together in Ottawa or Stanstead, they shared a lively correspondence. In 1881, for example, it was Jessie's turn to visit the St Louis family. In lengthy letters she described her sampling of the city's musical and theatrical life (the two sisters adopting male names, according to a practice then in vogue, Jessie as Humphrey and Abby as Cornelius); JMC to ALCA, 14 April 1881, JMC Papers, Series 1, Box 7:1, FC. It may have been her attraction to the more interesting male world that led her, at the age of twelve, to announce that she would "never marry any one, because there wouldn't be *another* man *just like papa*"; HCC to CCC, 2 April 1873, HCC Papers, Series 1, Box 1:3, FC.
101 JMC to HCC, and JMC to family, JMC Papers, Series 1, Boxes 1:1,2 and 2:1, FC.
102 HCC to ALCA, 26 February 1881, HCC Papers, Series 1, Box 2:5, FC.
103 By the spring of 1883, with both daughters well established in the Russell Hotel, letters between Ottawa and Stanstead began to make frequent mention of Abby's engagement with a certain K.N. McFee. K.N., as he was generally known, was a Winnipeg entrepreneur who had won the confidence and admiration of her father, as well as the approval of her mother. A frequent visitor in Stanstead, McFee took up a number of business partnerships with Charles Colby in the Northwest.
104 HCC to ALCA, 24 March 1883, HCC Papers, Series 1, Box 2:5, FC.
105 Upon hearing of Abby's engagement to McFee, Aikins had immediately transferred his affections to Jessie, the younger daughter. This led her delighted (and partisan) maternal grandmother to exclaim, "No matter whom he had liked *first,* he would love Jess to death last and always – anyone would who was fortunate enough to get her. Abby was *good enough* for *anybody* – nevertheless Jess was a little better!" See HCC to ALCA and JMC, 26 March 1883, HCC Papers, Series 1, Box 2:1, FC.
106 Diary entries, 11 and 29 May 1887, JMC Papers, Series 2, Box 1, FC.
107 See also description in Diary, 31 January 1881, JMC Papers, Series 2, Box 1, FC. The wedding notice in the *Stanstead Journal* stated that the couple were married on Thursday evening at 7 o'clock, Christ Church, Stanstead, followed by an At Home at 8 o'clock, Mr and Mrs C.C. Colby, Carrollcroft.
108 Amanda Vickery, *The Gentleman's Daughter: Women's Lives in Victorian England* (New Haven: Yale 1998), 161–94, and Marjorie R. Hunt, *The Middling Sort: Commerce, Gender, and the Family in England, 1680–1780* (Berkeley: University of California Press 1996), 193–218. Bushman,

The Refinement of America, 353–401, notes the impact of the urban world such as the one in which the Colby children increasingly moved after the 1880s.

109 HCC to CWC, 23 July 1883, HCC Papers, Series 1, Box 3:1, FC. There were far more respectable young men in receipt of a parental allowance and subject to adult instruction in the 1880s and 1890s than ever before; see Tosh, *A Mans Place*, 150.

110 See note 108 above.

111 Bendroth, *Growing Up Protestant*, 14.

112 "It is the tie between parents and children which has been imbued with ever more poignancy as people's relationship to the transcendental realms of religion, folk belief and magic has gradually disappeared"; Davidoff, *The Family Story*, 81. John R. Gillis, *A World of Their Own Making: Myth, Ritual, and the Quest for Family Values* (New York: Basic Books 1996), esp. ch. 4.

113 For the impact of common-sense thought, see Donald H. Meyer, *The Instructed Conscience: The Shaping of the American National Ethic* (Philadelphia: University of Philadelphia Press 1972), and A.B. McKillop, *A Disciplined Intelligence: Critical Inquiry and Canadian Thought in the Victorian Era* (Montreal/Kingston: McGill-Queen's University Press 1979). Although Schneider does not refer to common-sense thought, the implications of the theological shift upon children's self-understanding is briefly explored in A. Gregory Schneider, *The Way of the Cross Leads Home: The Domestication of American Methodism* (Bloomington: Indiana University Press 1993), 165–8.

114 S. Phillips, *The Christian Home as It Is in the Sphere of Nature and the Church* (New York: Gurdon Mill 1865), 23, donated to the Archives of the Stanstead Historical Society.

CHAPTER SIX

1 Hattie Child Colby (HCC) to Charles Carroll Colby (CCC), 30 October 1866, HCC Papers, Series 1, Box 1:1, Fonds Colby (FC), Stanstead Historical Society.

2 "Centenary Celebration," *Stanstead Journal*, 25 October 1866; and "Organization of the Board of Trustees," Minute Book, Board of Trustees, vol. 1, Wesleyan Methodist Church, Stanstead, Archives nationales du Québec, Montréal (ANQM). William Colby was the secretary, but he disappears from the record soon thereafter.

3 The revival drew in, among others, the future denominational leaders Nathanael Burwash, Albert Carman, and William Kerr. For a brief description of the revival and its impact, see Marguerite Van Die, *An Evangelical Mind: Nathanael Burwash and the Methodist Tradition in*

Canada, 1839–1918 (Montreal/Kingston: McGill-Queen's University Press 1989), 48–64.
4 "The Laying of the Corner Stone of the Wesleyan Methodist Church and the Centenary Meeting, Stanstead Plain," *Stanstead Journal*, 15 November 1866; see also *Christian Guardian*, 21 November 1866.
5 Benedict Anderson, *Imagined Communities: Reflections on the Origin and Spread of Nationalism*, rev. edn. (London: Verso 1991).
6 John R. Gillis, *A World of Their Own Making: Myth, Ritual, and the Quest of Family Values* (New York: Basic Books 1996), 43–4. The term is taken from David Cheal, "Relationships in Time: Ritual, Social Structure, and the Life Course," *Studies in Symbolic Interaction* 9 (1988): 101.
7 See, for example, John Grant, *A Profusion of Spires: Religion in Nineteenth-Century Ontario* (Toronto: University of Toronto Press 1988), which examines the hegemonic role of Protestantism in nineteenth-century Ontario.
8 As local studies of religion in Canada, see, for example, Lynne Marks, *Revivals and Roller Rinks: Religion, Leisure, and Identity in Late-Nineteenth-Century Small Town Ontario* (Toronto: University of Toronto Press 1997); William Westfall, *Two Worlds: The Protestant Culture of Nineteenth-Century Ontario* (Montreal/Kingston: McGill-Queen's University Press 1989); Marguerite Van Die, "The Marks of A Genuine Revival: Religion, Social Change, Gender, and Community in Mid-Victorian Brantford, Ontario," *Canadian Historical Review* 79, no. 3 (1998): 524–63; Brian P. Clarke, *Piety and Nationalism: Lay Voluntary Associations and the Creation of an Irish-Catholic Community in Toronto, 1850–1895* (Montreal/Kingston: McGill-Queen's University Press 1993); and Christine Hudon, *Prêtres et fidèles dans le diocèse de Saint-Hyacinthe, 1820–1875* (Sillery: Septentrion 1996). For the United States, where the literature is much more extensive, a beginning can be made by consulting the following historiographical survey: Jon Butler, "Protestant Success in the New American City, 1870–1920," in *New Directions in American Religious History*, ed. Harry S. Stout and D.G. Hart (Oxford: Oxford University Press 1997), 296–334.
9 The submissions to the *Christian Guardian* were delayed and did not appear until 9 and 16 January and 6 March 1867.
10 *Christian Guardian*, 9 January 1867. Carroll was speaking specifically of the Georgeville area, but in his submission of 6 March he spoke more generally of the "abatement of the fervor and zeal of the early Methodist" which he had perceived on his journey east.
11 Abel Stevens, the designated chronicler of American Methodism during its centenary, noted that "Methodism should feel itself responsible to minister to the public culture by the improvement of its

church architecture"; cited in "Church Edifices," *Christian Guardian*, 23 January 1867.
12 Nancy Christie, "In These Times of Democratic Rage and Delusion," in *The Canadian Protestant Experience*, ed. G. Rawlyk, 9–47, and George Rawlyk, *The Canada Fire: Radical Evangelicalism in British North America 1775–1812* (Montreal/Kingston: McGill-Queen's University Press 1993).
13 Leigh Eric Schmidt, "Time, Celebration, and the Christian Year in Eighteenth-Century Evangelicalism," in *Evangelicalism: Comparative Studies of Popular Protestantism in North America, the British Isles, and Beyond, 1700–1990*, ed. Mark A. Noll et al. (Oxford: Oxford University Press 1994), 104.
14 John Carroll wrote specifically of the revivals in the Stanstead area in *Case and His Contemporaries*, vol. 1 (Toronto: Samuel Rose 1867), 118, 139–40, 191–2, 279, and in vol. 3 (Toronto: Wesleyan Conference Office 1871), 307. See also B.F. Hubbard, *Forests and Clearings: The History of Stanstead County* (Montreal: Lovell 1874), 84–6.
15 J.I Little, "The Methodistical Way: Revivalism and Popular Resistance to the Wesleyan Church Discipline in the Stanstead Circuit, Lower Canada, 1821–52," *Studies in Religion/Sciences Religieuses* 31, no. 2 (2002): 171–94. This and his *Borderland Religion: The Emergence of an English-Canadian Identity, 1792–1852* (Toronto: University of Toronto Press 2004), 149–223, are my sources for the discussion of Methodism in the pre-1850 period.
16 George Cornish, *Cyclopedia of Methodism in Canada*, vol. 1 (Toronto: Methodist Book and Publishing House 1881), 302. The sparse statistics which local Wesleyan Methodist ministers submitted for the Stanstead circuit during this period, beginning in 1804, include only the names of the minister sent each year to the circuit, the annual financial giving to various denominational causes, and the number of members, but they do not include the many adherents who attended church and had not experienced conversion. Françoise Noël, *Competing for Souls: Missionary Activity and Settlement in the Eastern Township, 1784–1851* (Sherbrooke: Département d'histoire, Université de Sherbrooke 1988), 138–42, notes the discrepancy in numbers between the many adherents and the few members, and draws attention to the prevailing indifference to religion at the time.
17 For example, of the $2,354 subscribed for the new chapel, $900 was donated by six individuals, and the remainder by eighty, each making a small donation; Minute Book, Board of Trustees, vol. 1, Wesleyan Methodist Church, Stanstead, ANQM.
18 Charles Sellers, *The Market Revolution: Jacksonian America, 1815–1846* (New York: Oxford University Press 1991), *passim*.

19 Richard Carwardine, "Charles Sellers' 'Antinomians' and 'Arminians': Methodists and the Market Revolution," in *God and Mammon: Protestants, Money, and the Market, 1790–1860*, ed. Mark A. Noll (Oxford: Oxford University Press 2002), 80. See also Daniel Walker Howe, "Charles Sellers, the Market Revolution, and the Shaping of Identity in Whig-Jacksonian America," in *God and Mammon*, ed. Noll, 54–74.

20 Allen B. Robertson, "'Give All You Can': Methodists and Charitable Causes in Nineteenth-Century Nova Scotia," in *The Methodist Contribution to Atlantic Canada*, ed. Charles H.H. Scobie and John Webster Grant (Montreal/Kingston: McGill-Queen's University Press 1992), 92–103.

21 Jean-Pierre Kesteman, Peter Southam, and Diane Saint-Pierre, *Histoire des cantons de l'Est* (Sainte-Foy: Presses de l'Université Laval 1998), 337; and B.F. Hubbard, *Forests and Clearings*, 132.

22 Kesteman et al., *Histoire des cantons de l'Est*, 141, 337; Hubbard, *Forests and Clearings*, 128; John Pierce, *Pierce Pioneers: A History of the Family in Nineteenth-Century Canada* (privately printed 1994), ch. 4.

23 In the 1851 census for Stanstead County, Methodists numbered 1955 (42.8%) in a total population of 4,567; see Françoise Noël, *Competing for Souls*, table D, 239. Other well-to-do Methodists were Erastus Lee (by 1871 an Adventist), George Pomroy, and A.P. Ball (through his daughter). For their wealth, see Jean-Pierre Kesteman, "Une bourgeoisie et son espace: industrialisation et développement du capitalisme dans le district de Saint-François (Québec), 1823–1879," PH D thesis, Université du Québec à Montréal, 577, 580–1.

24 "Beebe Campground" and "Beebe Memories 1975," *Stanstead Historical Society Journal* 12 (1987): 83–5; J.I. Little, "Millennial Invasion: Millerism in the Eastern Townships of Lower Canada," in *Anglo-American Millennialism: From Milton to the Millerites*, ed. Richard Connors and Andrew Colin Gow (Leiden: Brill 2004), 177–204. Little notes that after the failed fulfilment of Millerite millennial expectations, the movement in the Eastern Townships eventually divided into three factions; the Evangelical Adventists supported by the Millerite leaders, the Christian Adventists, and the Seventh-Day Adventists.

25 HCC to Jessie Maud Colby (JMC), 23 August 1874, HCC Papers, Series 1, Box 2:7, FC.

26 This state formation is detailed in J.I. Little, *State and Society in Transition: The Politics of Institutional Reform in the Eastern Townships, 1838–1852* (Montreal/Kingston: McGill-Queen's University Press 1997), and Hubbard, *Forests and Clearings*, 1–59.

27 Kesteman notes that beginning in the 1860s the Eastern Townships experienced a steady emigration, with the 1871 census showing only a population increase of 1.3% (which was less than the natural birth/

death replenishment), compared with 3.7% in 1861; Kesteman et al., *Histoire des cantons de l'Est*, 252, 263.
28 Ibid., 279.
29 Ibid., 299–306. In 1868 Carlos Pierce invested heavily his own and the funds of local men in ranchland in Kansas and also in the Topeka and Santa Fe Railroad; ibid., 335. Regional capital increasingly moved west rather than being reinvested in the area; ibid., 345. J.I. Little, *The Child Letters: Public and Private Life in a Canadian Merchant-Politician's Family, 1841–1845* (Montreal/Kingston: McGill-Queen's University Press 1995), 9, notes that as early as 1836 local people were investing in the Chicago area.
30 Census Report of the Canadas, Lower Canada, County of St Hyacinthe, 1861, 36, LAC. The population of the county was 12,258.
31 Kesteman et al., *Histoire des cantons de l'Est*, 271.
32 Hubbard, *Forests and Clearings*, 30. The list is for 1855.
33 In 1827 a paper mill was in operation in Rock Island, followed in 1845 by the large Morrill Foundry. In 1883 this was integrated into the larger Butterfield Industries; see Kesteman et al., *Histoire des cantons de l'Est*, 371; see also *Illustrated Atlas of the Eastern Townships and Southwestern Quebec* (H. Belden 1881; reprint, Stratford: Cumming Publishers 1980), 13.
34 Census Report of the Canadas, Lower Canada, County of St Hyacinthe, 1861, 116–17, LAC.
35 For example, "The Roman Catholic and Episcopal bishops are both at the confirmation service this evening in Mr. Thornloe's church [Anglican]. Our young people propose attending"; HCC to CCC, 16 June 1875, HCC Papers, Series 1, Box 1:5. FC.
36 For information on Stanstead's Roman Catholics and their numerical comparison to the wider denomination, see Hudon, *Prêtres et fidèles*, 453, 458–9. A confessionally written history, which gives some background but primarily describes the founding of the Ursuline Convent in Stanstead in 1884, is Marie-Emmanuel Chabot, *Elles ont tout donné* (Lac Beauport: Anne Sigier 1983).
37 "Christ Church," *Stanstead Journal*, 8 January 1858; announcement of a Congregationalist Ladies' Soirée to repair the meeting house, *Stanstead Journal*, 24 January 1856; and B.F. Hubbard, "Rise and Progress of the Congregational Church in the Eastern Townships," *Stanstead Journal*, 22 November 1866.
38 Brief history in Minute Book, Board of Trustees, vol. 1, Wesleyan Methodist Church, Stanstead, ANQM.
39 It consisted of 600 acres which, with the improvements he brought about in buildings, involved an expense of $150,000. It had belonged to C.A. Kilborn, one of the founding fathers, and included 55 prize

Durham cows, 250 British pure-bred sheep, and 41 Morgan horses; see Kesteman et al., *Histoire des cantons de l'Est,* 290–1.
40 Pierce, *Pierce Pioneers,* ch. 4 (unpaged).
41 Ibid.
42 Minute Book, Board of Trustees, vol. 1, Wesleyan Methodist Church, Stanstead, ANQM.
43 Ellen Foster, "*Memorial: Charles Wilder Pierce,*" 9, Canadian Institute for Historical Microproductions.
44 HCC to CCC, 6 December 1866, HCC Papers, Series 1, Box 1:1, FC. A donors' list includes paid donations of $100 to $500 by Colby's business partners Pierce, Hunter, Ball, and Pomroy, as well as a good number of unpaid donations. In Colby's case, $400 had been paid, with $600 still owing; CCC Papers, Series 4:B, Box 5:6, FC.
45 Entries for 22 and 25 October 1866, Minute Book, Board of Trustees, vol. 1, Wesleyan Methodist Church, Stanstead, ANQM, and *Stanstead Journal,* 15 November 1866.
46 "Church Edifices," *Christian Guardian,* 23 January 1867.
47 Although much applauded, Pierce's sound financial sense did in the end have to give way to civic pride, for the completed building was dedicated and occupied in 1869, five years before its debts were paid off. The burning of the church mortgage, however, was able to take place because of an additional bequest in 1870 from the estate of Carlos Pierce, who had died that year; entries for 15 November 1870 and 9 September 1874, Minute Book, Board of Trustees, vol. 1, Wesleyan Methodist Church, Stanstead, ANQM. The historical sketch in the minutes gives 1870 as the date of the mortgage redemption, but this is contradicted by the entry of 9 September 1874.
48 S.F.J. Thayer and A.C. Martin to CCC, 1 July 1867, CCC Papers, Series 4:B, Box 5:6, FC. The architects' second request for payment of their fee of $15,000 in gold was met with astonishment that this was the agreed-upon rate; it was far beyond the congregation's capacity.
49 Historical account, and entries for 31 October and 12 November 1866, Minute Book, Board of Trustees, vol. 1, Wesleyan Methodist Church, Stanstead, ANQM.
50 Kathryn Long, *The Revival of 1857–58: Interpreting an American Religious Awakening* (New York: Oxford University Press 1998), 81–92, and Long, "Turning ... Piety into Hard Cash," in *God and Mammon,* ed. Noll, 245–61.
51 Circuit Register, Stanstead Circuit, 1858–94, Stanstead Wesleyan Methodist Church, Stanstead, ANQM. CCC and HCC continued to be listed as members after 1867.
52 For an earlier example, see Van Die, "The Marks of a Genuine Revival: Religion, Social Change, Gender, and Community in Mid-Victorian

Brantford, Ontario," *Canadian Historical Review* 79, no. 3 (1998): 524–63.
53 In 1867 the accounts were especially numerous. See "Revivals," *Christian Guardian*, 20 and 27 March 1867. For the Methodist class meeting, see David Lowes Watson, *The Early Methodist Class Meeting: Its Origins and Significance* (Nashville: Discipleship Resources 1985), and for the Methodist "means of grace" generally, see Neil Semple, *The Lord's Dominion: The History of Canadian Methodism* (Montreal/Kingston: McGill-Queen's University Press 1996), 53–70.
54 Circuit Register, Stanstead Circuit, 1858–94, Stanstead Wesleyan Methodist Church, Stanstead, ANQM.
55 Purchases of cakes for love feasts and wine for communion occur regularly in the Minute Book, Board of Trustees, vol. 2–3, Wesleyan Methodist Church, Stanstead, ANQM.
56 Cornish, *Cyclopedia of Methodism in Canada*, 1:302. A similar pattern of transiency in the early 1860s is described for Brantford, Ontario, in Van Die, "The Marks of a Genuine Revival," 524–30. For a case study that shows male persistence after a revival, see Marks, *Revivals and Roller Rinks*, ch. 8.
57 For an insightful discussion of the numerical relationship between evangelical members and adherents in the antebellum United States see Mark A. Noll, *America's God: From Jonathan Edwards to Abraham Lincoln* (New York: Oxford University Press 2002), 499, n. 17. A conservative estimate for the Congregationalists in the U.S. is 4.5 adherents to 1 member, and for the Methodist Episcopal Church, 3.2 adherents to 1 member; Carwardine, *Evangelicals and Politics in Antebellum America*, 43–4. My guess is that for Stanstead the ratio would be higher, given the fact that the new Wesleyan Methodist Centenary Church, with a membership of 100 in 1868, contained 98 pews, of which only 5 were not rented in 1869. See also ibid., ch. 5, n. 57, which indicates that Methodist rules were consistently applied for members.
58 "Stanstead South," in Douglas Walkington, *The Congregational Churches of Canada: A Statistical and Historical Survey* ([Kirkland, PQ: D. Walkington] 1979), no paging.
59 "Dedication of the New Church" and "Organ Concert," *Stanstead Journal*, 30 September 1869.
60 For Punshon's impact on Canadians, see Frederic W. Macdonald, *The Life of Morley Punshon* (London: Hodder and Stoughton 1887), chs. 11–15.
61 Westfall, *Two Worlds*, 68–73. Westfall (129) notes that in Ontario, Methodism, taking all groups together, became the province's most prolific builder of new churches, increasing their number by a factor of five. For Protestant churches in Montreal, see Louis Rousseau and

Frank W. Remiggi, eds., *Atlas historique des pratiques religieuses: le sud-ouest du Québec au XIXe siècle* (Ottawa: Presses universitaires de l'Université d'Ottawa 1998), 141. The causes and impact of social differentiation within Methodism are insightfully discussed for a somewhat earlier period in Britain by Hempton, "A Tale of Preachers and Beggars," in *God and Mammon*, ed. Noll, 123–46.

62 Pew rents, like church finances generally, remain an underresearched subject, but a good entry is Robin Klay and John Lunn, "Protestants and the American Economy in the Postcolonial Period: An Overview," in *God and Mammon*, ed. Noll, 43–53. Helpful work has been done, however, on social differentiation as shown in American synagogue seating patterns; see Jonathan D. Sarna, "Seating and the American Synagogue," in *Belief and Behavior: Essays in the New Religious History*, ed. Philip R. VanderMeer and Robert P. Swierenga (New Brunswick, NJ: Rutgers University Press 1991), 189–206.

63 See copy of Deed of Pew in Brick Meeting House in Stanstead, Lower Canada, 10 July 1837, in Karl P. Stofko, "Old Union Meeting House," *Stanstead Historical Society Journal* 13 (1989): 11.

64 "An Account of Subscriptions towards Erecting a Wesleyan Chapel on Stanstead Plain," Minute Book, Board of Trustees, vol. 1, Wesleyan Methodist Church, Stanstead, ANQM.

65 "Proceedings of Trustees, 11 and 27 September 1869," Minute Book, Board of Trustees, vol. 1, Wesleyan Methodist Church, Stanstead, ANQM.

66 The final costs of the church reputedly exceeded $60,000, of which $50,000 was contributed by Carlos Pierce and, after his death in 1870, by his estate; Pierce, *Pierce Pioneers*, ch. 4 and intro., Minute Book, Board of Trustees, vol. 1, Wesleyan Methodist Church, Stanstead, ANQM.

67 In 1874, for example, when the congregation adopted the increasingly common practice of envelopes, pew holders were also asked to contribute 25% of their pew rent for expenses occurred in connection with church repairs; entry for 12 October 1874, Minute Book, Board of Trustees, vol. 1, Wesleyan Methodist Church, Stanstead, ANQM. Subscription rates were revised at a later date to show "new subscriptions" and "unpaid." Colby owed $600 at the time of his insolvency in 1872; CCC Papers, Series 4:B, Box 5:6, FC.

68 HCC to CCC, 4 November 1868, HCC Papers, Series 1, Box 1:1, FC. The fire, on 19 May 1883, is described in the introduction to the Minute Book, Board of Trustees, vol. 2, Wesleyan Methodist Church, Stanstead, ANQM.

69 Ellen Foster, *Memorial: Charles Wilder Pierce*. Pierce died in 1889. HCC to CCC, 15 April 1889, HCC Papers, Series 1, Box 1:7, FC, notes that his life was well insured, for he was able to leave over $150,000 in

Notes to pages 140–1

bequests, including $3,000 each to the Centenary Methodist Church and the Crystal Lake Cemetery.

70 Curtis Johnson, *Islands of Holiness: Rural Religion in Upstate New York, 1790–1860* (Ithaca: Cornell University Press 1989), 145–58, and A. Gregory Schneider, *The Way of the Cross Leads Home: The Domestication of American Methodism* (Bloomington: Indiana University Press 1993), 201–7. George M. Thomas, *Revivalism and Cultural Change: Christianity, Nation-Building, and the Market in the Nineteenth-Century United States* (Chicago: University of Chicago Press 1989), forcefully argues the market forces eradicated communal ways in favour of individualist self-interest.

71 Hempton, "A Tale of Preachers and Beggars," 140.

72 See the donors' list-in n. 44 above.

73 Van Die, "A 'Christian Businessman' in the Eastern Townships: The Convergence of Precept and Practice in Gender Construction," *Journal of the Canadian Historical Association*, New Series, 10 (1999): 124–7. Omitting the centrality of family commitments, this is also the argument in Paul Henry Heidebrecht, *Faith and Economic Practice: Protestant Businessmen in Chicago, 1900–1920* (New York: Garland 1989).

74 HCC to CCC, 7 August 1878, HCC Papers, Series 1, Box 1:6, FC, and Minutes 1872–92, Board of Trustees, Stanstead Wesleyan College, Stanstead College, Stanstead. In 28 October 1872, for example, Colby was elected chairman of the charter committee, and in 1877, after the institution's transfer to the Methodist Church, he served on a new charter committee; entry of 25 June 1877.

75 After the transfer, the board was reconstituted to consist of twelve laymen and twelve ministers; Joan MacDonald, *The Stanstead College Story* (Stanstead: Board of Trustees 1977), 63–71. On the role of four generations of Colbys serving as trustees, see ibid., 70–1, 92. For the institutional changes in Methodism and the organization of a denominational Educational Society in 1874, see Semple, *The Lord's Dominion*.

76 Their leadership was further strengthened in 1883 by the decision to appoint a small executive committee of the board, consisting of the trustees of the college who were resident in Stanstead and vicinity. The first executive committee consisted of A.P. Ball, C.C. Colby, H.D. Holmes, S. Foster, Dr Bugbee, the Rev. Tallman Pitcher, the Rev. A. Lee Holmes, headmaster, and, as chairman, the Rev. J.B. Saunders. Until 1909 the chairmen were Methodist ministers, except during 1874–76, when the previous chairman, the Rev. W. Hansford, was embroiled in conflict and the Hon. T. Lee Terrill (MLA and an Anglican) was chair. For a list of chairmen, see MacDonald, *The Stanstead College Story*, 64.

77 Minutes of the Executive Committee, 1883–1900, entry 26 April 1887, Stanstead College, Stanstead. Already in 1883 Hattie had a Sunday

school class of college girls; HCC to CCC, 27 March 1883, HCC Papers, Series 1, Box 1:6, FC. For revivals, see HCC to JMC, 21 June 1894, HCC Papers, Series 1, Box 2:9, FC. An earlier reference is in *Christian Guardian*, 12 February 1880.
78 This congruence between men's business interests and the world of their wives is developed in Lori D. Ginzberg, *Women and the Work of Benevolence: Morality, Politics and Class in the Nineteenth-Century United States* (New Haven: Yale University Press 1990), esp. 36–67. The ambiguities are insightfully analysed in Carmen Nielson Varty, "A 'Laudable Undertaking': Women, Charity, and the Public Sphere in Mid-Nineteenth-Century Hamilton, Canada West" (PH D dissertation, Queen's University, Kingston, 2004).
79 HCC to JMC, 15 September 1872, HCC Papers, Series 1, Box 2:7, FC.
80 The contribution is noted in the history of Centenary in Minute Book, Board of Trustees, vol. 1, Wesleyan Methodist Church, Stanstead, ANQM. Evidence of strains among trustees is in entries for 23 November and 5 December 1868.
81 To cite only one example, on 3 December 1884 the Colby children had the choice of attending a Band of Hope, a church fundraising concert, a dancing class, and two church-related socials; HCC to JMC, 3 December 1884, HCC Papers, Series 1, Box 2:8, FC.
82 "Last Sunday I felt as if you *must* be in the other end of the pew and that it was a good thing the boys were between us or I would have hugged up beside you and held on to your arm"; HCC to CCC, 2 March 1883, HCC Papers, Series 1, Box 1:6, FC.
83 HCC to CCC, 30 March 1868, HCC Papers, Series 1, Box 1:1, FC.
84 Some of the ambiguities between piety and fashion are examined in Leigh Eric Schmidt, "The Easter Parade: Piety, Fashion, and Display," reprinted in *Religion in American History: A Reader*, ed. Jon Butler and Harry S. Stout (Oxford: Oxford University Press 1998), 346–69.
85 The context of sociability and community events is examined in Françoise Noël, *Family Life and Sociability in Upper and Lower Canada, 1780–1870* (Montreal/Kingston: McGill-Queen's University Press 2003), 211–45.
86 HCC to CCC, 8 May 1883, HCC Papers, Series 1, Box 1:6, FC.
87 HCC to JMC, 13 February 1894, HCC Papers, Series 1, Box 2:9, FC.
88 Ginzberg, *Women and the Work of Benevolence*, and Hannah M. Lane, "'Wife, Mother, Sister, Friend': Methodist Women in St. Stephen, New Brunswick, 1861–1881," in *Separate Spheres: Women's Worlds in the Nineteenth-Century Maritimes*, ed. Janet Guildford and Suzanne Morton (Fredericton: Acadiensis Press 1994), 93–117.
89 HCC to CCC, 17 April 1870, HCC Papers, Series 1, Box 1:1, FC.
90 Howe, "Charles Sellers," in *God and Mammon*, ed. Noll, 66.

91 The college site was donated by Charles Wilder Pierce; MacDonald, *The Stanstead College Story*, 63.
92 For example, "The Pierce ladies sent Mrs. Hansford a most superb black silk dress pattern by Mr. Hansford [the Methodist minister] when he was in Boston"; HCC to CCC, 21 March 1873, HCC Papers, Series 1, Box 1:3, FC. Ministers sent to Stanstead included Edward Ryckman (1868–70), BA, MA; and the son-in-law of Morley Punshon, William Galbraith (1875–76), who was subsequently the recipient of an LLB (1881) and a PH D (1891); and Daniel Van Norman Lucas (1872), MA, DD, a fellow of the Royal Colonial Institute of London and an author. Most illustrious of all was Charles Hanson (1878–80) who, on ceasing active ministerial work in 1882, founded an investment banking firm, Hanson Brothers in Montreal, and in 1890 settled permanently in England, where he became a partner of the firm Coates, Son and Co. and, after a number of political appointments, was made Lord Mayor of London in 1917; see William Lamb, "Sir Charles Augustin Hanson, Canadian Circuit Rider, Stock Broker, Lord Mayor of London," *Hay Bay Guardian* 6 (1998): 3–6. Church trustees regularly asked Conference for specific ministers, for example, on 30 May 1880, "asking Conference to return to us the third year our much beloved Pastor Rev. C. Hanson." On 30 May 1881 there was a similar (but unsuccessful) request for the Rev. Hugh Johnson. See Minute Book, Board of Trustees, vol. 2, Wesleyan Methodist Church, Stanstead, ANQM.
93 The minister in question was William Hansford; HCC to CCC, 22, 25, and 27 April 1873, HCC Papers, Series 1, Box 1:3, FC.
94 "Wesleyan" was dropped from the name of Stanstead's Centenary Church in 1874 when the Wesleyan Methodist Church united with the New Connexion Church.
95 CCC to HCC, 6 and 10 April, 14 and 17 July 1878, CCC Papers, Series 4:A, Box 3:6, 7, FC.
96 "A Flying Visit to the East," *Christian Guardian*, 9 January 1867.
97 Sonya Rose, "Cultural Analysis and Moral Discourses: Episodes, Continuities, and Transformations," in *Beyond the Cultural Turn: New Directions in the Study of Society and Culture*, ed. Victoria E. Bonnell and Lynn Hunt (Berkeley: University of California Press 1999), 217–38.
98 Linda Colley gives insightful analysis into the way Protestant identity was similarly formed in early-nineteenth-century Britain, in *Britons: Forging the Nation 1707–1837* (London: Pimlico 1992), 11–54.

CHAPTER SEVEN

1 Charles Carroll Colby (CCC) to Hattie Child Colby (HCC), 29 September 1867, CCC Papers, Series 4:A, Box 2:3, Fonds Colby (FC), Stanstead Historical Society.

2 The financial compensation is given in CCC to HCC, 17 November 1867, CCC Papers, Series 4:A, Box 2:3, FC.
3 Confederation had initially evoked only cautious support from Canada's Protestant churches. However, as voluntary institutions with a strong community base, they quickly extended responsibility for the spiritual and moral welfare from the local level to that of society in general. See John W. Grant, "Canadian Confederation and the Protestant Churches," *Church History* 38 (1969): 1–11.
4 The slow shift to looking to government legislation on the part of the Methodist denomination is described in William H. Magney, "The Methodist Church and the National Gospel," *Bulletin* (Committee on Archives of the United Church of Canada), 20 (1968): 3–95. For the wider Protestant position, see Richard Allen, *The Social Passion: Religion and Reform in Canada, 1914–28* (Toronto: University of Toronto Press 1971), ch. 1.
5 Michael Ignatieff, *The Rights Revolution* (Toronto: Anansi 2000), 113–41.
6 There was also little positive direction for French Canadian Roman Catholic businessmen – only greater clerical interference; see Fernande Roy, *Progrès, harmonie, liberté: le libéralisme des milieux d'affaires francophone de Montréal au tournant du siècle* (Montreal: Boréal 1988), 111–50, 260–8.
7 Richard J. Carwardine, *Evangelicals and Politics in Antebellum America* (Knoxville: University of Tennessee Press 1993), 5–14.
8 J.I. Little, *The Child Letters: Public and Private Life in a Canadian Merchant-Politician's Family, 1841–1845* (Montreal/Kingston: McGill-Queen's University Press 1995), 10–30, gives a summary of the political turmoil and the considerable Methodist support for Moses' rival, Reformer Marcus Child. Although Child defeated Moses in the 1841 election, he was in turn defeated in a bid for re-election in 1843. Having encountered strong opposition from the Methodists, who had turned against him, Child departed to the Anglican Church, but he retained his Methodist pew. See entry for 1 January 1849, Minute Book, Board of Trustees, vol. 1, Wesleyan Methodist Church, Stanstead, ANQM.
9 *Stanstead Journal*, 8 August 1867.
10 Ibid.
11 The ministers had been requested to put their support behind Knight by a prominent Montreal Methodist, James Ferrier, who had been appointed to the new Senate. One of the speakers at Knight's nomination was A.T. Galt, a Presbyterian who had married into the prominent Methodist Torrance family and was a pew holder in Montreal's St James Methodist Church. As the member for Sherbrooke, Galt was

the leading Anglo-Protestant spokesman and patron in the Eastern Townships; see Jean-Pierre Kesteman, "Alexander Tilloch Galt," *Dictionary of Canadian Biography*, 12: 348–56, and Oscar Douglas Skelton, *Life and Times of Sir Alexander Tilloch Galt* (Toronto: McClelland & Stewart 1966). Though the congregation's own minister, W.R. Parker, supported Colby, these three – John Tomkins, J.P. Lee, a local preacher, and Malcolm Macdonald – were an older generation with deep roots in the area. For the integral role of patronage networks in nineteenth-century Ontario, see S.J.R. Noel, *Patrons, Clients, Brokers: Ontario Society and Politics, 1791–1896* (Toronto: University of Toronto Press 1990), esp. 61–78. The details of the religious opposition, the issue of patronage, and Colby's reaction can be gleaned from pre-election accounts in the *Stanstead Journal*, 15, 23, and 29 August 1867 and, more explicitly, from the correspondence between Charles and Hattie: HCC to CCC, 20 and 28 September, HCC Papers, Series 1, Box 1:1, FC, and CCC to HCC, 22 and 30 September, 2 October 1867, CCC Papers, Series 4:A, Box 2:3, FC.

12 "Electoral District of Stanstead. C.C. Colby Esq. M.P. 1871" [incorrectly titled "List of Voters 1871" in the Finding Aid], CCC Papers, Series 2:D, Box 4:4, FC. Census Returns on microfilm, Stanstead 1871, C-10089–90, Library and Archives Canada (LAC). Albert Knight, the opponent, was a Universalist, and the fact that 75% of those in the county of Universalist persuasion chose not to support their fellow brother in the faith would further support the observation that economic rather than religious factors motivated the voters.

13 The one exception was the township of Barford, where over two-thirds of all votes were cast for Knight (which, if factored out of the total, would have left Colby with 70% of the support of the county's farmers). Possibly to hedge their bets, the Agricultural Society for Stanstead County had elected both Knight and Colby to its committee of management in 1867. Five years later, on the death of the former director, Carlos Pierce, the position of director fell to Colby; see Shirley Whipple and Amphion Pelley, "The Agricultural Society for the County of Stanstead: 1845–1900," *Stanstead Historical Society Journal* 10 (1983), 38–58. Pierce, who in 1866 had also donated land for a permanent exhibition grounds, served as president, 1866–70; but normally, as was the case with Colby, the position was held only for a year.

14 The tension in Whig thought is succinctly summarized in Daniel Walker Howe, *The Political Culture of the American Whigs* (Chicago: University of Chicago Press 1979), 218.

15 Even in 1891 when he finally suffered defeat, his Liberal opponent T.B. Rider squeaked by with only a majority of 102 votes, and Rider was defeated in 1896 by the Conservative candidate.

16 A survey of biographical dictionaries and compendia reveals that of the 181 members of the House of Commons of the first dominion parliament, 112 (or 61.8%) are known to have been Protestant, 53 (or 29%) were Roman Catholic, and 16 (or 8%) have left no indication of religious affiliation. Only 42 of the 112 Protestants were able to be identified by denomination: 19 were Church of England, 12 were Presbyterian, 5 Methodist, 3 Baptist, 1 Unitarian, 1 Disciple of Christ, and 1 Quaker; for the list of members, see N. Omer Coté, *Political Appointments, Parliaments and the Judicial Bench in the Dominion of Canada, 1867–95* (Ottawa: Thoburn & Co. 1896), 184–9. John Webster Grant has noted that "a striking proportion of Protestant churchmen who actively supported Confederation were Presbyterian"; John W. Grant, *The Church in the Canadian Era*, new edn. (Burlington: Welch 1988), 26. Colby's efforts on behalf of his denomination included in 1872 tapping the pockets of a number of Ottawa politicians for subscriptions for Stanstead Wesleyan College, as well as preparing and presenting its charter for parliamentary ratification. When he could, he also tried to advance the cause of individual Methodists, such as young Duncan Campbell Scott, whose educational trajectory had been adversely affected by the dismissal of his father as Stanstead's minister in 1878, but who was able to begin a lengthy career in the Bureau of Indian Affairs thanks to Colby's success in arranging a personal interview with the prime minister; see CCC to John A. Macdonald, 16 June 1879, Macdonald Papers, 87522–4, MF 1127, LAC.

17 His speech on the National Policy in 1876 received high praise in R.S. White's "Parliament and Personalities," *Dalhousie Review*, n.d.; see CCC Papers, Series 2:F, Box 5:8, FC. High praise for his record was also noted in the *Stanstead Journal*, 3 July 1872. Colby's own favourable self-assessment as a speaker can be found in CCC to HCC, 9 March 1870, CCC Papers, Series 4:A, Box 2:4, FC.

18 Colby wanted the repeal of the 1869 law (which would have naturally lapsed in 1874) because in his view it encouraged excessive legal costs and fraudulent claims. His bill, debated in April and May 1872, was passed in the Commons but failed in the Senate. See "Debate on Insolvency Laws," *Parliamentary Debates*, 23 April–31 May 1872, 120–3, 134–41, 156–64, 281–7, 466, 663–9, 715–18, 743–51 783–9, 909–12.

19 House of Commons, *Debates*, 7 and 11 March 1876, 474–6, 640–4. The reference to Webster is on p. 641.

20 Pointing out his own familiarity with American ways and beliefs, CCC emphasized that without such a national policy, the Liberal government's hopes of gaining reciprocity with the United States would be futile. "So long as Americans continue to possess all the advantages they now enjoy, they will not give us reciprocity of trade. The sound

and politic course then, to adopt, is to put up our duties to where they were before the Reciprocity Treaty [of 1854] was framed; to place ourselves in a position where we can pinch some classes in the United States and deprive them of some of those advantages which they now freely enjoy"; *Mr. C.C. Colby's Speech on Tariff Revision, House of Commons, March 1878* (privately published), 39.

21 Jean-Pierre Kesteman, "Une bourgeoisie et son espace: industrialisation et développement du capitalisme dans le district de Saint-François (Québec), 1823–1879" (PH D thesis, Université du Québec à Montréal, 1985), 714–19.

22 Howe, *The Political Culture of the American Whigs*, 219.

23 CCC Papers, Series 2:A, Box 1:3, FC.

24 Ben Forster, *A Conjunction of Interests: Business, Politics, and Tariffs, 1825–1879* (Toronto: University of Toronto Press 1996), 201.

25 Quoted in Robert Kelley, *The Transatlantic Persuasion: The Liberal Democratic Mind in the Age of Gladstone* (New York: Knopf 1969), 390. This study, which assumes a congruence of interests between Evangelicals, Liberals, and Democrats, fails to take into account the strong evangelical support for the Whig Party in the antebellum United States.

26 Carwardine, *Evangelicals and Politics in Antebellum America*, 105.

27 *Mr. C.C. Colby's Speech on Tariff Revision*, 8.

28 Daniel Walker Howe, "Religion and Politics in the Antebellum North," in *Religion and American Politics*, ed. Mark A. Noll (New York: Oxford University Press 1990), 130.

29 Prince Edward Island, which joined in 1873 and had had its own divorce laws, chose not to establish divorce courts. It was not until 1925 that the Canadian parliament removed the double standard. For a succinct description of the social and legal nature of divorce in Canada prior to the 1968 overhaul of divorce legislation, see D.C. McKie et al., *Divorce in Canada: Law and the Family in Canada* (Ottawa: Minister of Supply and Services Canada 1983), and Robert Pike, "Legal Access and the Incidence of Divorce in Canada: A Sociohistorical Analysis," *Canadian Review of Sociology and Anthropology* 12, no. 2 (1975): 115–33. The Canadian parliament entered the divorce business ten years after the British parliament had abandoned it; Roderick Phillips, *Untying the Knot: A Short History of Divorce* (Cambridge: Cambridge University Press 1991), 138.

30 The evidence and the debate can be found in Senate, *Journals*, 29 May 1872, 1, 17, 21–23, and vol. 5: 59–61, 88–91, 96–7, 101–15, 127–35. See also *Parliamentary Debates*, 30 April, 1 May, 17 May, 3 June, 6 June 1872, 218, 254, 647, 944, 1018; and House of Commons, *Journals*, 3 and 6 June 1872, vol. 5: 204, 205, 240.

31 Of 48 Protestant senators, 13 were known to be Church of England, 6 Presbyterian, 4 Methodist, 2 Congregationalist, 2 Baptist, and the remaining 21 were unknown. Nineteen senators were found to be Roman Catholic, and the affiliation of 6 others could not be discerned. The Select Senate Committee to examine the evidence consisted of Senators Dickey, Dickson, Odell, Botsford, Allan, Sanborn, and Wilmot. Dickey, Odell, Allan, and Botsford were Church of England, Sanborn was Congregationalist, and Wilmot was Methodist.
32 CCC to HCC, 4 June 1872, CCC Papers, Series 4:A, Box 3:1, FC.
33 CCC to HCC, 9 June 1872, CCC Papers, Series 4:A, Box 3:1, FC.
34 "If I should happen to be in the library or smoking room when the division bell rings I may not go in to vote upon this case but shall take strong ground hereafter against divorces for this cause"; CCC to HCC, 6 June 1872, CCC Papers, Series 4:A, Box 3:1, FC.
35 "I see Mr. John Martin has begun again in the Senate for his divorce ... Is there no such thing as *finality* about it?" HCC to CCC, 27 March 1873, HCC Papers, Series 1, Box 1:3, FC.
36 Although it was incumbent on the Senate and Commons committees to verify that Martin had not fabricated the evidence in order to support his request for divorce, any questions to the servants of possibly improper behaviour by him were at best perfunctory.
37 CCC to HCC, 7 June 1872, CCC Papers, Series 4:A, Box 3:1, FC.
38 Senate, *Journals*, 24–26 March, 17, 18, and 23 April 1873, vol. 6: 53–9, 99–130; and CCC to HCC, 30 April 1873, CCC Papers, Series 4:A, Box 3:2, FC.
39 Pike, "Legal Access and the Incidence of Divorce in Canada: A Sociohistorical Analysis," 115–33.
40 CCC to HCC, 6 June 1872, CCC Papers, Series 4:A, Box 3:1, FC.
41 This argument would not hold true in cases where the wife was the petitioner, for example, "Donigan, Ada: – Petition ... J.A. Donigan" and "Harrison, Hattie – Petition ... H.B. Harrison"; House of Commons, *Votes and Proceedings, Nos. 1–87*, 1892, xiv.
42 See, for example, P.B. Waite, *The Man from Halifax: Sir John Thompson, Prime Minister* (Toronto: University of Toronto Press 1985), 183–4.
43 Senate, *Journals*, 18 April 1872, 108.
44 Nancy Cott, *Public Vows: A History of Marriage and the Nation* (Cambridge: Harvard University Press 2000), 53–5. The quotation is on p. 54. See also the analysis of the distinction between rhetoric and reality regarding the sacred nature of marriage in Constance Backhouse, "'Pure Patriarchy': Nineteenth-Century Canadian Marriage," *McGill Law Journal* 31 (1985–86): 265–312.
45 The nineteenth-century Roman Catholic understanding of marriage is briefly elaborated in Serge Gagnon, *Mariage et famille au temps de Papineau* (Sainte-Foy: Presses de l'Université Laval 1993), 188–93, and

the implications for sexual relations are examined in Serge Gagnon, *Plaisir d'amour et crainte de Dieu: sexualité et confession au Bas-Canada* (Sainte-Foy: Presses de l'Université Laval 1990), 85–93. See also the succinct but informative discussion in Mark McGowan, *The Waning of the Green: Catholics, the Irish, and Identity in Toronto, 1887–1922* (Kingston/Montreal: McGill-Queen's University Press, 1999), 104–7.

46 See, for example, the speech by Senator Robert Gowan during the 1888 debates on divorce legislation revision, cited in Christina Burr, "Letters to Mike: Personal Narrative and Divorce Reform in Canada," in *Family Matters*, ed. Lori Chambers and Edgar-André Montigny (Toronto: Canadian Scholars' Press 1998), 397.

47 Gagnon, *Plaisir d'amour*, 72–8, examines the efforts of clergy to impose their sacred time on rural rhythms of life.

48 "Sabbath Observance," in House of Commons, *Journals*, 27 March 1876, 850.

49 The rhetoric has received sustained attention in Mariana Valverde, *The Age of Light, Soap, and Water: Moral Reform in English Canada* (Toronto: McClelland & Stewart 1991).

50 Kelley, *Transatlantic Persuasion*, 376, and J.M.S. Careless, *Brown of the Globe*, vol. 1 (Toronto: Macmillan 1959), 231–2.

51 For Mackenzie's unsuccessful efforts to combat patronage while in power, see Dale Thomson, *Alexander Mackenzie: Clear Grit* (Toronto: Macmillan 1960), 218–20.

52 The memorial was signed by representatives of the Wesleyan Methodist Church, Baptist Missionary Convention of Canada, Methodist Episcopal Church of Canada, Primitive Methodist Church of Canada, Congregational Union of British North America, Methodist New Connexion Church, and Bible Christian Church; but it did not have the official endorsement of the Roman Catholic and Episcopal churches. See House of Commons, *Journals*, 27 March 1876, 845.

53 Ibid., 851.

54 Ibid., 855.

55 Paul Laverdure, "Canada's Sunday: The Presbyterian Contribution," in *The Burning Bush and a Few Acres of Snow*, ed. William Klempa (Ottawa: Carleton University Press 1994), 83–99.

56 CCC to HCC, 22 September 1867, CCC Papers, Series 4:A, Box 2:3, FC; and CCC to daughters, 19 March 1870, CCC Papers, Series 4:A, Box 2:4, FC.

57 CCC to HCC, 22 April and 6 May 1872, 1 May 1875, CCC Papers, Series 4:A, Box 2:5, Box 3:3, FC.

58 For example, "Grandma Colby wondered a little about accepting a Sunday night invitation at the O'Connors. But it seemed to be then if at all"; HCC to girls, 10 March 1883, HCC Papers, Series 1, Box 2:1, FC.

59 The move towards sophistication in Ottawa's social life is described in Sandra Gwyn, *The Private Capital: Ambition and Love in the Age of Macdonald and Laurier* (Toronto: McClelland & Stewart 1984).
60 Kevin Kee, "'The Heavenly Railroad': An Introduction to Crossley-Hunter Revivalism," in *Aspects of the Canadian Evangelical Experience*, ed. George Rawlyk (Kingston/Montreal: McGill-Queen's University Press 1997), 327. Macdonald entered the Church of England in 1875.
61 John W. Grant, *A Profusion of Spires: Religion in Nineteenth-Century Ontario* (Toronto: University of Toronto Press 1988), 123–6, 190.
62 P.B. Waite, "Sir Oliver Mowat's Canada: Reflections on an Un-Victorian Society," in *Oliver Mowat's Ontario*, ed. Donald Swainson (Toronto: Macmillan 1972), 31.
63 Charles Colby's letters home describing similar social events managed to keep a critical distance. Knowing the interest his wife and daughters had in the modest balls which marked social life in the earliest years of the capital, he took pains to describe these in letters home, but ambivalence about the decorum of such events and about his own situation as a married man is evident. In 1869, for example, just before going off to attend the annual Ottawa Citizens' ball, he noted, "I am not much inclined to amusements while my wife is drudging at home and I have plenty of private and public cares to occupy my mind"; CCC to HCC, 5 May 1869, CCC Papers, Series 4:A, Box 2:4, FC. In 1878, as Ottawa entered a glittering new era with the arrival of the Marquess of Lorne and Princess Louise at Rideau Hall, social invitations increased, and as his political star began slowly to rise with his appointment as Deputy Speaker in 1887, they became even more numerous. As the Colby daughters began to make their entry on the capital's social stage for extended periods, his participation became more wholehearted. "They are likely to take a leading place in society," he confided to his wife, offering as evidence of their popularity a full social calendar for the week: all three were to have dinner with the Speaker of the House on Monday; Abby and he to dine with the Macphersons, dinner at Sir John's on Wednesday, the Convent concert on Thursday, and the McLelan's [sic] on Friday"; CCC to HCC, 7 March 1883, CCC Papers, Series 4:A, Box 4:5, FC.
64 For a brief discussion of Tilton's many reform efforts on behalf of women, see Sharon Anne Cook, "To 'Bear the Burdens of Others': the Changing Role of Women in the Diocese of Ottawa, 1896–1996," in *Anglicanism in the Ottawa Valley*, ed. Frank A. Peake (Ottawa: Carleton University Press 1997), 131–41 passim.
65 HCC to girls, 20 and 21 March 1884, HCC Papers, Series 1, Box 2:2, FC. The importance of the new "scientific" approach of the WCTU is discussed in Sharon Cook, "'Earnest Christian Women, Bent on Saving

Our Canadian Youth': The Ontario Woman's Christian Temperance Union and Scientific Instruction, 1881–1930," *Ontario History* 86, no. 3 (1994): 249–68.
66 The member was Murray Dodd; HCC to girls, 15 March 1884, HCC Papers, Series 1, Box 2:2, FC. The comment on Pope is in 21 March 1884; on McMaster, 11 March 1884; HCC Papers, Series 1, Box 2:2, FC.
67 House of Commons, *Debates*, 5 March 1884, 1:656–65. For a report of Tilley's remarks, see *Stanstead Journal*, 3 April 1884.
68 See Acheson, "Evangelicals and Public Life in Southern New Brunswick," in *Religion and Public Life in Canada: Historical and Comparative Perspectives*, ed. Marguerite Van Die (Toronto: University of Toronto Press 2001), 55–60, 65–6.
69 HCC to girls, 17 February 1883, HCC Papers, Series 1, Box 2:2, FC.
70 *Stanstead Journal*, 23 October 1884.
71 HCC to JMC, 10 October 1884, HCC Papers, Series 1, Box 2:8, FC; and *Stanstead Journal*, 9 October 1884.
72 Letter of J.T. Pitcher, "The Triumph in Stanstead," *Stanstead Journal*, 16 October 1884.
73 House of Commons, *Journals*, 9 May 1873, 6:1–9; House of Commons, *Debates*, 10 April 1876, 1162–4; 4 April 1877, 1126–38; and 5 March 1884, 1:656–65.
74 For the prevalence of drink among parliamentarians, see Waite, "Reflections," in *Oliver Mowat's Ontario*, ed. Swainson, 21–8.
75 *Good Templarism: An Address. Delivered at Stanstead, P.Q., September 8th, 1870, by C.C. Colby, Esq., M.P.*; CCC Papers, Series 4:B, Box 5:7, FC.
76 For the religious and political background, see Acheson, "Evangelicals and Public Life in Southern New Brunswick, 1830–1880," in *Religion and Public Life*, ed. Van Die, 50–68; and Peter M. Toner, "New Brunswick Schools and the Rise of Provincial Rights," in *Federalism in Canada and Australia: The Early Years*, ed. Bruce W. Hodgins et al. (Canberra: Australian National University Press 1978), 125–36.
77 CCC to HCC, 29 May 1872, CCC Papers, Series 4:A, Box 2:5, FC. The letter has been printed in Charles W. Colby, ed., "From the House of Commons: 'Look Out for the Speaker's Eye,' Letters of the Hon. Charles C. Colby, Part II: 1870–1887," *Stanstead Historical Society Journal* 9 (1981): 69–71.
78 CCC to HCC, 29 May 1872, CCC Papers, Series 4:A, Box 2:5, FC.
79 CCC to HCC, 31 May 1872, CCC Papers, Series 4:A, Box 2:5, FC.
80 Where in 1852 francophones comprised 26.8% of the total population of the Eastern Townships, by 1881 they constituted 55%; Jean-Pierre Kesteman, Peter Southam, and Diane Saint-Pierre, *Histoire des cantons de l'Est* (Sainte-Foy: Presses de l'Université Laval 1998), 258–9, 264–6.

81 Brian Young, "Federalism in Quebec: The First Years after Confederation," in *Federalism in Canada and Australia: The Early Years*, ed. Hodgins et al., 97–108.

82 H.M. Rider to CCC, 11 January 1887, CCC Papers, Series 2:B, Box 2:1, FC. See also fragment of the speech directed against Mercier and any government founded on nationalism [no title], CCC Papers, Series 2:B, Box 2:1, FC.

83 The definitive study of the religio-political meaning of the controversy is J.R. Miller, *Equal Rights: The Jesuits' Estates Act Controversy* (Montreal/Kingston: McGill-Queen's University Press 1979). For a succinct survey of anti-Catholicsm in nineteenth-century Canada, see also his "Anti-Catholic Thought in Victorian Canada," *Canadian Historical Review* 66 (1985): 474–94.

84 *A Complete and Revised Edition of the Debate on the Jesuits' Estates Act in the House of Commons, Ottawa, March, 1889* (Montreal: Eusebe Senecal & Fils 1889), 56.

85 Ibid., 150.

86 Ibid.

87 Such an irenic view was also totally at variance with the criticism that Alexander Galt voiced on the negative impact on church and state relations in Canada of the new militant ultramontanism he saw emerging after Vatican 1; see Sir Alex. Galt, *Church and State* (Montreal: Dawson Brothers 1876); see also *Montreal Witness*, 27 March 1889. For Mowat's very different position, see A. Margaret Evans, "Oliver Mowat: Nineteenth-Century Liberal," in *Oliver Mowat's Ontario*, ed. Swainson, 44–5. Letters in support of Colby's position are in CCC Papers, Series 2:B, Box 2:1, FC. Tom White had died suddenly on 21 April 1888; see W. Stewart Wallace, *The Memoirs of the Rt. Hon., Sir George Foster* (Toronto: Macmillan 1933), 64.

88 CCC to HCC, 27 March 1889, CCC Papers, Series 4:A, Box 4:8, FC.

89 Charles William Colby used the term *in loco parentis* to characterize his father's relationship with his constituency; address on CCC1, CWC Papers, Series 1:C, Box 11:1, FC.

90 Macdonald to CCC, 17 November 1871, Macdonald Papers, 1202, LB 16, 447, LAC. A similarly reassuring note to ease Colby's "scruples" was sent in 1873: "Private," Macdonald to CCC, 5 October 1873, CCC Papers, Series 2:B, Box 2:3, FC.

91 He shared his favourable self-assessment as a speaker with his family in CCC to HCC, 9 March 1872, CCC Papers, Series 4:A, Box 2:5, FC. Upon his spirited defence of his insolvency bill, and its passing in the House in 1872, he exulted, "I do not think the judgeship or any other reasonable thing would be denied me now. Of course anything in that way would be kept back until after the session"; CCC to HCC, 26 April

1872, CCC Papers, Series 4:A, Box 2:5, FC. Though he had secretly expected that such triumphant moments as his speech on the New Brunswick school legislation and his much-acclaimed address on the National Policy would be rewarded by preferment, or at the least a judgeship, his movement through the ranks had been agonizingly slow.

92 CCC to HCC, 2 May 1887, CCC Papers, Series 4:A, Box 4:7, FC.

93 J.A. Chapleau to CCC, 10 June 1889, CCC Papers, Series 2:1, Box 2:1, FC. Chapleau's ambitions are mentioned in Waite, *The Man from Halifax*, 317–18.

94 What was not mentioned, however, was that though the honour bestowed on Colby was considerable, Macdonald had rewarded him with only half of Pope's portfolio. The other half, minister of railways, a coveted source of patronage, Macdonald had assumed himself. Never one to forget opportunities for family advancement, Colby was already, on the day of his swearing-in as a privy councillor, busy trying to persuade Macdonald to make an appointment, "possibly the Indian Office," to his new son-in-law, Somerset Aikins of Winnipeg. A little later, he mooted the possibility that as a co-religionist, Aikins might be appointed to fill the Senate vacancy left by the recent death of Toronto Methodist businessman, John Macdonald. According to Hattie Colby, "Sir John thinks highly of Somerset," but neither materialized. See CCC to HCC, 27 November 1889, CCC Papers, Series 4:A, Box 4:8, FC, and CCC to JMC, 5 February 1890, CCC Papers, Series 4:A, Box 1:6, FC.

95 Congratulatory letters and telegrams are in CCC Papers, Series 2:B, Box 2:9, FC.

96 Since 1884, these had branched out to include regular visits to England, in order to sell stock on a variety of ventures, including by 1890 shares in a typewriting company, which eventually ensured the family's financial well-being. On his varied business concerns during this period, see, for example, the detailed accounts of the silver mine in Mineral Point, Colorado [1888], and P. Alex Peterson to CCC, 20 April 1890, CCC Papers, Series 3:A, Box 1, FC. The latter letter is an offer by William Van Horne "to put his name down for $10,000 of stock in your Typewriter Co." CCC detailed his subsequent involvement in the Silent Typewriter Company in CCC to CWC, 31 October 1898, CCC Papers, Series 4:A, Box 1:9, FC

97 Letterbooks 1889–90 and 1890, CCC Papers, Series 3:B, Box 10:1, 2, Box 11:1, FC. He was also on a number of parliamentary committees: Privileges and Elections, Railways, Canals and Telegraph Lines, Public Accounts, and Banking and Commerce; and in April and May 1890, in the absence of Charles Tupper, he was acting minister of marine and fisheries.

98 H.M. Rider to CCC, 11 January 1887, and CCC to H.M. Rider, n.d., CCC Papers, Series 2:B, Box 2:1, FC.
99 1889–90 Letterbook, 56, 68, 343–4, CCC Papers, Series 3:A, Box 10:2, FC; and 1890 Letterbook, 83, CCC Papers, Series 3:A, Box 11:1, FC.
100 William Smith to CCC, 27 March 1890, CCC Papers, Series 2:D, Box 4:6, FC.
101 The extensive correspondence on the appointment is in Letterbook, 1890, CCC Papers, Series 3:A, Box 11:3, FC, and in "Appointment of Coaticook Collector of Customs, March–July 1890," CCC Papers, Series 2:D, Box 4:6, FC.
102 This was exacerbated by the fact that the editor of the *Coaticook Observer*, a longtime Conservative supporter, did not hold back his outrage, leading the party to consider establishing a rival pro-Conservative paper in the town; see W.L. Burtiff to CCC, 10 and 13 March 1890, CCC Papers, Series 2:D, Box 4:6, FC.
103 Melvina Colby to Mary Colby, 29 March 1889, and Melvina Colby to Martha Colby [1890], WBC Papers, Box 1:1, FC.
104 CCC to the Reverend Father Macaulay, 17 October 1890, Letterbook 1890, 343–4, CCC Papers, Series 3:A, Box 11:1, FC.
105 The purpose was to float stock for the phosphate mining company in Quebec; see CCC to Francis Wyatt, 8 November 1890, 1890 Letterbook, 453, CCC Papers, Series 3:A, Box 11:1, FC.
106 CCC to unidentified correspondent, n.d., and CCC to Macdonald, 14 October 1890, CCC Papers, Series 2:B, Box 2:3, FC. The 14 October letter is also in Macdonald Papers, 87570–3, LAC. On receiving the letter, Macdonald sent Colby a telegram to arrange a meeting with him immediately, "and meanwhile keep your counsel"; 15 October 1890, Macdonald Papers, 87575, LAC. Colby sent a telegram in return, stating that he was unable to leave Ottawa until the evening of 16 October; Macdonald Papers, 87574, LAC. Macdonald distanced his party from Colby's stance on the issue; Macdonald to J.A. Chapleau, 4 December 1890, Macdonald Papers, MF 1294, LB 272, 377, LAC.
107 CCC to W.E.C. Eustis, 13 February 1891, Letterbook 1891, CCC Papers, Series 3:A, Box 11:2, FC.
108 Macdonald to CCC, 25 March 1891, CCC Papers, Series 2:B, Box 2:3, FC. During the campaign he tried to distinguish between the Liberal policy of "Unrestricted Reciprocity" and the new Conservative approach of "Fair Reciprocity"; see "To the Electors of Stanstead County," *Stanstead Journal*, Extra Issue, 16 February 1891.
109 His opponent in the 1887 election, H.M. Rider, had unexpectedly died. He was succeeded as the county's Liberal candidate by his brother, T.B. Rider, who now won in 1891. See Stephen Alexander Moore, "T.B. Rider and the Rider Family of Fitch Bay, 1850–1960:

Enterprise and Entrepreneurship in a Rural Quebec Village" (MA thesis, Bishop's University, 1992), 132-9.
110 Through an intermediary, Shipley Snow, "a Conservative hack," Colby contested the election count; Moore, "T.B. Rider and the Rider Family," 139. See also CCC to William White, 6 March 1891, CCC Papers, Series 2:B. Box 2:1, FC. A decision against Colby was given by the Supreme Court in November, with all costs to be carried by the plaintiff; William White to CCC, 21 November 1891, CCC Papers, Series 2:B, Box 2:1, FC. Colby had earlier submitted his resignation; CCC to Macdonald, 23 April 1891, Macdonald Papers, 87579, and Macdonald to CCC, 4 May 1891, Macdonald Papers MF 1294, LB 28-1, 39.
111 Melvina to Matt [Martha Stoddard Colby], 8 March [1891], WBC Papers, Box 1:1, FC.
112 The defeat was by 102 out of 3,208 votes cast; see "Election results, 1867-1896," CCC Papers, Series 2:D, Box 4:3, FC. Hattie's perspective is presented in great detail in HCC to ALCA, 6 March 1891, HCC Papers, Series 1, Box 2:5, FC. Macdonald expressed his concern about Colby's defeat and about the capabilites of his expected successor, William Ives, in a letter to Rufus Pope; Macdonald to Pope, 7 April 1891, Macdonald Papers, MF 1294, LB 28-1, 23-4.
113 Shock and amazement at the defeat are expressed in the *Stanstead Journal*, 12 and 19 March 1891. Colby's earlier expressed desire to withdraw from politics because of the demands of his "private affairs" is mentioned in *Stanstead Journal*, 16 April 1891.
114 W.L. Shirtliff to CCC, 13 March 1891, CCC Papers, Series 3:A, Box 1. FC. Letters asking Colby to re-enter politics (e.g., Hugh Graham to CCC, 7 October 1900) are in CCC Papers, Series 2:B, Box 2:1, FC. In 1904 his son Charles William considered entering politics, and his father suggested that he would offer his own candidacy and, once received by acclamation, would then decline and offer his son's name as a substitute. This seems not to have been put into effect. See CCC to CWC, 12 January 1904, CWC Papers, Series 1:A, Box 1:2, FC.
115 Michael Bliss, "The Protective Impulse: An Approach to the Social History of Oliver Mowat's Ontario," in *Oliver Mowat's Ontario*, ed. Swainson, 174-88.
116 HCC to CWC, 4 June 1888, HCC Papers, Series 1, Box 3:2, FC.
117 For a brief overview of some of the literature of social control and a response, see Valverde, *The Age of Light, Soap, and Water*, ch. 1, and Daniel Howe, *Making the American Self: Jonathan Edwards to Abraham Lincoln* (Cambridge: Harvard University Press 1997), 114-28.
118 Valverde, *The Age of Light, Soap, and Water*, 33.
119 Howe, *Making the American Self*, 115.

CONCLUSION

1 In 1892 he had secured control of the foreign patents on the "Wellington" typewriter, developed by Wellington Parker Kidder, which under his auspices became the "Empire" for the British Empire and Western Europe, and the "Adler" in Germany and Eastern Europe. To this in 1905 was added another of Kidder's inventions, a noiseless typewriter, which was further developed by the Parker Machine Company, based in Buffalo, New York. In 1907, shortly after Charles Carroll Colby's (CCC's) death, the Noiseless Typewriter Company was organized, and in 1924 it merged into the Remington-Noiseless Company, with Charles William Colby (CWC) serving for some time as its president; CCC Papers, Series 3:B, Box 12–13, Fonds Colby (FC), and CWC Papers, Series 3:B, Box 8–12, FC. Charles William Colby discusses his father's relationship with Kidder in "Garrulities of an Octogenarian" (typescript), 111–13, CWC Papers, Series 1:C, Box 11:3, FC.

2 While in Germany he contracted TB, which necessitated a visit from his sister Jessie. His brother John, who was with him at the time, accompanied him on a walking tour of the Swiss Alps after his recovery; "Garrulities of an Octogenarian" (typescript), 70–3, CWC Papers, Series 1:C, Box 11:3, FC.

3 "Yesterday was a Field Day – Easter Sunday – and we went to 6 services!" These were divided among Anglican, Roman Catholic and Methodist churches in the company of his son Charley, who was studying at McGill. See Hattie Child Colby (HCC) to Abby Lemira Aikins (ALCA) and Jessie Maud Colby (JMC), 14 April 1884, HCC Papers, Series 1, Box 2:2, FC. For an account of the trip to England, see Diary 1892, HCC Papers, Series 2, Box 1, FC.

4 1891 Diary (2 vols.), JMC Papers, Series 2, Box 1, FC.

5 "In the evening we had a jolly visit from our Stanstead friends David Mansur, Will Butters and Louis McDuffy who sold their cattle very well in Liverpool"; Diary, 19 June 1892, HCC Papers, Series 2, Box 1, FC. Prominent among home contacts were their former Methodist minister Charles Hanson and his family. Hanson, after his departure from Canada in 1890, became a partner in the firm Coates, Son, and Co., a London alderman, and in 1917-18 served as Lord Mayor of London; see William Lamb, "Sir Edward Augustin Hanson: Canadian Circuit Rider, Stock Broker, Lord Mayor of London," *Hay Bay Guardian* 6 (1998): 3–6.

6 In 1894, for example, thirty nights of special services resulted in twenty-five conversions, including nine female Stanstead College students, whose names were immediately listed on the traditional class meeting rolls; HCC to ALCA, 14 April 1894, HCC Papers, Series 1, Box 2:6, FC.

7 In addition to her extensive papers, see "Entire Community Mourns the Passing of Miss Jessie M. Colby, O.B.E.," *Stanstead Journal*, 9 January 1958.
8 "A Community Calamity," *Stanstead Journal*, 2 September 1926.
9 The wedding is described in detail in 1897 Diary, CWC Papers, Series 1:C, Box 12, FC.
10 CWC to Emma Colby, 27 February 1897, CWC Papers, Series 1:A, Box 2:5, FC.
11 According to his memoirs, he was asked to let his name stand on the promise (confirmed by William Osler, who was then at Oxford) that "the Chair was definitely mine"; see "Garrulities of an Octogenarian" (typescript), 98–9, CWC Papers, Series 1:C, Box 11:3, FC.
12 Charles William lists his father at death leaving Carrollcroft and $53,000 to his mother, $15,000 to Jessie, and $8,000 to each of the other three children. The primary assets consisted of shares in a Wire Rope Company and the Imperial Writing Machine Company, and a $20,000 Life Insurance Policy; "Garrulities of an Octogenarian" (typescript), 105–6, CWC Papers, Series 1:C, Box 11:3, FC. An inventory of the estate on 5 April 1907, on the other hand, listed the assets at $67,609.31 and the liabilities at $14,806.66. A will dated 19 December 1903 left a $1,000 bequest to the trustees of the Stanstead Methodist Church; CCC Papers, Series 4:B, Box 5:9, FC.
13 "Mrs. J. Somerset Aikins," *Stanstead Journal*, 10 June 1943.
14 Hattie's final passport, showing her in the heavy black lace veil she assumed at Charles's death, bears the stamp of a visit to Morocco four years before her own death in 1932 at age 92; HCC Papers, Series 2, Box 3, FC.
15 Clifford Geertz, *The Interpretation of Cultures* (New York: Basic Books 1973), 89–90. Cited also in William G. McLoughlin, *Revivals, Awakenings, and Reform* (Chicago: University of Chicago Press 1978), 15–16. McLoughlin's insights have been suggestive in shaping the conclusions that follow.
16 See, for example, her note to Moses Colby thanking him for his wedding gift of a "Sacred Text"; WBC Papers, Box 1:1, FC.
17 Russell E. Richey, *Early American Methodism* (Urbana: Indiana University Press 1991), 82–97.
18 Helpful in recognizing the varieties of evangelical religion is the account of how the movement splintered into fundamentalist, moderate, and liberal forms in the early twentieth century; see George M. Marsden, *Fundamentalism and American Culture: The Shaping of Twentieth-Century Evangelicalism, 1870–1925* (Oxford: Oxford University Press 1980), esp. 11–39, 124–38.

Index

Adventists, Stanstead County, 30, 132, 248n24
Aikins, Abby Lemira. *See* Colby, Abby Lemira
Aikins, Carroll, 181
Aikins, Sir James Cox, 12–13, 122
Aikins, Sir James M. Albert, 12, 228n73
Aikins, Lady Mary. *See* Colby, Mary French
Aikins, Somerset, 12–13, 122, 181, 228n73, 244n105
Amaron, Calvin, 79, 120, 228n73; pension at Berthier-en-Haute, 120, 146
Amaron, Daniel, 228n73
Anderson, Benedict: *Imagined Communities*, 126–7
Anglican Church, 6, 17, 30, 48, 59, 71, 116, 122, 132, 142, 184
Arminianism: theology of, 205n35; shift from Calvinism, 23, 43

Baconian science, 22
Bailey, Mrs, 66, 78
Ball, A.P., 92
baptism: theological views on, 104–5
Baptists, 6, 17, 30, 132
Beecher, Catharine, 80, 81
Beecher, Henry Ward, 186, 221n68; influence of writings, 57–8, 71, 80, 84, 98–9, 106; model of the Christian businessman, 98–9; scandal of, 58

Bendroth, Margaret, 105, 124
benevolent societies. *See* voluntary societies
Bibles: as family gifts, 108–9, 115
Blumin, Stuart, 64
Borland, Rev., 208n64
Bradbury, Bettina, 35
Braude, Anne, 54
brick church. *See* Wesleyan Methodist Church (Stanstead, pre-1866)
Briggs, Mahala Pratt. *See* Child, Mahala Pratt
British American Land Company, 32
Brooks, Edward, 43, 46–7
Brooks, Phillips, 181
Brown, George, 163, 165
Burwash, Nathanael, 245n3
Bushman, Richard, 110
Bushnell, Horace, 105, 106, 109–10
"businessmen's revivals." *See* revivals

Calvinism, 22, 23, 25–6, 43, 106, 205n35
Canada Temperance Act (1878), 167, 168, 179
Carman, Albert, 245n3
Carroll, Charles (of Carrollton, 1737–1832), 11, 199–200n44, 246n10
Carroll, Rev. John, 125–7, 128, 147

Carrollcroft, 85–6, 93, 122, 184, 185, 212n99; loss of, 61, 76, 91–2, 102; origin of name, 11, 86, 199; repurchase of, 94
Cartier, Sir George, 170
Carwardine, Richard, 10, 129, 155
Catholicism, Roman, 5, 63–7 *passim*, 71, 104, 127, 132, 150, 157–62, 169–72 *passim*, 180, 188; and baptism, 104; divorce in, 157–62; education of children, 104, 169; family life, 8; marriage in, 71, 161–2; theology, 104
Caughey, James, 54–5, 220n55
Chalmers, Thomas, 92, 97
Chapleau, Joseph, 173
Child, Andrew Jackson (Jack), 49, 50, 59, 66, 90, 217n27, 218n37
Child, Dan, 79
Child, Harriet (Hattie) Hannah. *See* Colby, Harriet Hannah
Child, John A., 59, 90
Child, John (f. of Harriet H. Colby), 48, 50–1, 53, 60, 72
Child, Lizzie (w. of Andrew Jackson Child), 66
Child, Mahala Pratt (née Briggs), 48–9, 52, 55, 57, 68
Child, Marcus, 32, 138, 209n74, 215–16n18, 256n8
Child, Sarah L., 59
Child family: settlement in New England, 103–4
children: and character formation, 106, 107, 239n21; discipline of, 106, 107, 239n2; leisure activities, 112–13; moral formation, 110–12, 123; religious instruction, 104, 107–8; role of community, 111; role of education, 102–10, 123; role of self-formation, 102–3, 110, 123
Chown, Edwin, 141
Civil Code of 1866 (Quebec), 63
Cobb, Emma (Kitty) Frances (w. of Charles W. Colby). *See* Colby, Emma
Colby, Abby Lemira (d. of Charles C. Colby), 12, 68, 79, 94, 102, 115–16, 118, 120, 121–2, 123, 181; conversion to Anglican, 116; engagement of, 121–2, 244n103; marriage to Somerset Aikins, 123, 244n107; social formation of, 102, 118, 120, 121–2

Colby, Anthony, 17, 202n10
Colby, Carroll Child (s. of Charles C. Colby), 69
Colby, Charles Carroll (s. of Moses F. Colby), 11, 12, 15–16, 17, 27, 33, 36, 37, 42–60 *passim*, 135, 257n13, 262n63, 265n94, 266n106; academic and moral formation, 43–5, 105, 153; assumes Methodist membership, 99, 127, 232n31; as college trustee, 140–1; as Congregationalist, 47, 68, 232n31; contributions to Methodist church, 47, 89, 125–6, 134, 135, 138, 140, 258n16; conversion of, 52, 54–7, 58, 60, 71, 84, 103, 116, 135, 220n57; and electoral defeat in 1891, 150, 170, 178–9, 181, 234n59, 257n15, 265n112, 267n110; eulogy of, 96; in federal election (1867), 141, 146–7, 149–54, 256n11; final years, 181, 184; financial situation, 12, 89, 102–3, 106, 118–19, 123, 124, 140, 149, 181, 211n90, 234n62; fundraising for Wesleyan Methodist Centenary Church, 133; and the Imperial Writing Machine Company, 96, 181; as Independent, 12, 149, 151; influence of Whigs and Daniel Webster, 43–4, 154–5, 172; and insolvency legislation, 91, 154, 258n18; insolvency of (*see also* Carrollcroft, loss of), 12, 61, 76–7, 90, 91–4, 96, 100, 108, 140, 142, 154, 234n58, 252n67; investments, 12, 37, 88–9, 90–1, 93, 97, 101, 173, 235n72, 265n96, 268n1; involvement in Stanstead Seminary, 117–18; and Jesuits' Estates Act, 170–2, 175, 176, 177–8; joins Conservative party (1872), 12, 153; last will and testament, 269n12; as lawyer, 12, 47, 87, 88; legal apprenticeship, 34; marriage of, 48; and Martin case (1872), 157–62; as MP, 12–13, 79, 93, 96, 149–51, 167; and National Policy, 154–5, 156, 179, 258–9n20; and New Brunswick Schools Act (1872), 169–70; and party spirit, 153, 154, 256–7n11; and patronage, 151–3, 176–8, 256–7n11; promoted to deputy speaker, 173; promoted to president of Privy Council, 174–7; and Sabbath observance, 164–5; sale of

Ascot Township mines, 90, 94; as schoolteacher, 45, 47, 215n11; and temperance, 166, 168–9; views on education, 105–6; views on revivalism, 54–5; on social life in Ottawa, 262n63
Colby, Charles William (s. of Charles C. Colby), 12, 69, 107, 181, 184–5, 201n10, 241n61, 268n2; academic formation of, 102, 119–20, 122, 123, 184–5; conversion to Anglican, 116, 184; at McGill University, 12, 119, 184–5; and politics, 267n114
Colby, Emily (d. of Moses F. Colby; d. 1832), 27, 165
Colby, Emily Stewart (d. of Charles C. Colby), 69
Colby, Emily Strong (d. of Moses F. Colby; d. 1866), 12, 27, 35, 39, 54, 66, 70, 72; views on revivals, 54–5
Colby, Emma (née Cobb), 184, 241n61
Colby, Harriet Alice (d. of Charles C. Colby), 69–70, 95
Colby, Harriet (Hattie) Hannah (née Child), 12, 42–82 *passim*, 158–62 *passim*, 165, 173, 178–9, 181, 218n43, 269n14; as consumer, 73–4, 227n49; crisis of faith, 81; education of, 48–9, 216n21, 217n29; financial worries, 101–3, 106, 142; health of, 79, 122, 125, 146; involvement in Stanstead Wesleyan College, 141–2; as Methodist adherent, 68; Methodist membership, 68, 99, 127, 135; and religious nurture, 103, 106, 108, 109; role in local church life, 141–4; romantic poet, 49, 52–4, 71, 106; social network, 66–7; teacher at Stanstead Seminary, 47, 49, 51, 52–3, 67, 75; and temperance movement, 166–8
Colby, Jessie Maud (d. of Charles C. Colby), 12, 69, 79, 94, 107, 118–19, 120, 181–4, 189, 244n100, 244n105, 268n2; academic formation of, 102; role in local church life, 115, 117, 181–2, 183; social formation of, 121
Colby, John Child (s. of Charles C. Colby), 12, 70, 119, 181, 184; academic formation of, 102, 119, 120
Colby, Lemira (née Strong), 11, 12, 14, 17–18, 35, 39, 66, 68, 72, 76–7, 107, 185; marriage to Moses Colby, 23, 24–7 *passim*; role in bankruptcies, 72, 76–7
Colby, Martha Stoddard (d. of William B. Colby), 77
Colby, Mary French (d. of William B. Colby), 12, 77
Colby, Mary Spafford (née Williams), 184
Colby, Melvina (née Wallingford), 12, 65, 76, 77, 91, 114, 167, 177–8, 186
Colby, Moses French, 11, 12, 14–41 *passim*, 44, 66, 72, 77, 91, 96, 161, 180; academic formation of, 18–19, 205n42; and Badger Place farm, 35; business partnership, 38, 207n51; as Congregationalist, 18, 21, 25, 213n106; as Conservative MLA, 11, 32–3, 43, 199n44; at Dartmouth College, 21–2, 204n33; election (1841), 32; electoral defeat, 256n8; financial situation, 33–4, 208n63, 212n96; at Harvard, 25, 204n33; land transfer, 212n99; last will and testament, 34–6, 37, 47, 51, 66, 88–9, 102, 210n81, 211n90, 223n16; lawsuit, 32–3, 34, 209n74, 210n81, 210n86, 212n96; marriage to Lemira Strong, 23–5; as physician, 16, 20–1, 25, 27, 31–2, 40, 68, 208n64; position on land tenure reform, 209n71; publications in medicine, 40; religious views and experience, 20–3, 25, 26–7, 31, 34, 39–41, 84, 185; on revivals, 20–1; Stanstead tavern purchase, 33, 37–8, 208n68; on women, 23–4; at Yale College, 16, 18, 19, 20, 39, 40, 204n33
Colby, Nehemiah (s. of Samuel Colby), 18, 33
Colby, Ruth (née French), 18
Colby, Samuel (f. of Moses F. Colby), 18; settlement at Thornton Township, 202n13
Colby, Stoddard B. (s. of Nehemiah Colby), 33, 50
Colby, William Benton (s. of Moses F. Colby), 12, 27, 33, 35, 36, 37, 46, 59, 65, 66, 72, 77, 166; alcoholism, 38, 76, 77, 88, 91, 114; bankruptcy of, 91, 233n48
Colby family: settlement in New England, 17–18, 103–4; settlement in Stanstead Plain, 11, 17, 27–9

common-sense philosophy: influence of, 10, 22, 44–5
Confederation (1867), 10, 256n3
Congregationalists: as evangelicals, 7, 21, 57. *See also* Methodist Church, and Congregationalism; Stanstead Plain, Congregational Church in
"Congregational way," 16, 18
consumerism, 72–4; religious, 108, 181–2
conversion, 22, 53, 54, 56, 58, 85, 180; childhood, 238n13; and gender, 54, 55; male resistance to, 219n54; shift to Christian nurture, 104–5
Cooke, Martha Stoddard (née Colby). *See* Colby, Martha Stoddard
Cowles, Dr Cecil P., 47, 67, 141, 208n64
Cowles, Emma, 166, 167

Daly, John, 177, 178
Dartmouth College, 21–2, 33, 43–5, 58, 105, 120, 153, 214–15n8
Darwinian evolution: impact on evangelical Protestants, 7, 41
Davidoff, Leonore, 5, 53
death: changing attitude to, 39, 72, 106–7
Derby, Vt, 11, 16, 17, 18, 21, 30, 47
Dickerson, Silas, 29
divorce, 150, 157–62, 180, 186, 259n29
Dixon, Matthew, 36
domesticity: and Hattie Colby, 72–9, 80; paternal, 98–9, 101–2; as Victorian construct, 62–3
Dorion, A.A., 170
Dwight, Timothy, 40

Eastern Townships, 16, 43, 73, 87, 91, 118, 128, 170, 173; development of mail system, 29, 72–3; development of railway system, 36, 38, 72–3; early settlement, 15–18; economy, 27–9, 31–2, 33, 34, 36–8, 43, 87, 90–1, 131, 154–5
Eastern Townships Bank, 87, 94
economy: and religious change. *See* Stanstead County, economy; Stanstead Plain, economy
Edwards, Jonathan, 18, 26
Elder, Hugh, 33, 209–10n78
Episcopals. *See* Anglican Church
evangelicalism, liberal. *See* Protestantism, liberal

evangelicals, 5, 6, 9, 10–11, 13–14, 42, 44, 46, 52, 56, 84–5, 98–9, 111, 144, 150, 155–6, 162–4, 180, 185, 198n40; definition of, 6; and domesticity, 103; and economics, 38–9, 84–5, 91–2, 98–9, 150, 155–6, 198n35; and education, 44, 46, 111; and female spirituality, 52–4; and free trade, 155–6; and moral reform, 10, 156–7; and party spirit, 152; and polite culture, 144; and politics, 10, 151; prescriptive nature, 10–11; and romanticism, 53; and Sabbatarianism (1873–78), 162–5; and temperance, 165–9; and theology of atonement, 38, 161

factionalism. *See* Stanstead County, factionalism in
family: and birth control, 27, 206n49; and Christian domesticity, 123–4; as religious institution, 106, 188; and; religious rituals, 4–5, 59–60, 67–8, 94–5, 115, 142–3, 147; sacralization of, 5, 124, 188–9; Victorian, 4–5, 103
Farrar, Frederic, 71
Ferrier, James, 256–7n11
First Church of Christ Congregational Meeting House, East Haddam, Conn., 29
First Great Awakening. *See* revivals, First Great Awakening
Fisk, Wilbur, 22
Fort Edward Institute, 49, 50
Fort Plain Seminary and Female Collegiate Institute, 49
Foster, George, 167, 168
free trade: evangelical position on, 155–6
Free Will Baptists, 30, 130
French, Ruth. *See* Colby, Ruth
fundraising. *See* voluntary societies; Wesleyan Methodist Centenary Church, fundraising

Galbraith, William, 255n92
Galt, Sir Alexander T., 173, 256–7n11, 264n87
Geertz, Clifford, 185–6
Gillis, John, 5, 42
Gordon, Adam, 163–4
Graham, Dougall, 141
Greven, Philip, 18

Index

"half-way covenant," 26
Halttunen, Karen, 91
Hanson, Charles, 255n92, 268n5
Harvard: School of Practical Anatomy, 25
Hatch, Nathan, 23
Hempton, David, 140
"higher criticism": impact on evangelical Protestants, 7, 71
Hilton, Boyd, 38, 99
home: market influence on, 102–3; naming of, 86; role of evangelical family religion, 103; sacralization of, 5
House of Commons: religious affiliation of members (1867), 258n16
Howe, Daniel Walker, 10, 144, 156, 180; and self-construction, 20, 50, 203n21
Hoyle, Robert, 209n74
Hughes, Hugh Price, 182
Hunter, W.S., 92

Ignatieff, Michael, 150
Imperial Order Daughters of the Empire, 183
Imperial Writing Machine Company, 96, 181
infant depravity: debate about, 107
inheritance practices, nineteenth-century, 27
Insolvency Act of 1869. *See* Colby, Charles Carroll, and insolvency legislation

James, William, 186; and the psychology of religion, 40
Jesuits' Estates Act. See Colby, Charles Carroll, and Jesuits' Estates Act
Johnson, Curtis, 140
Johnson, Rev. Hugh, 255n92

Kerr, William, 245n3
Kesteman, Jean-Pierre, 37, 131
Kingston College (Royal Military College), 120
Kirk, Edward, 107
Knight, Albert, 92, 151–2, 256n11, 257n12
Knight, Jonathan, 22

lay influence: on appointment of ministers, 144–7; on church fundraising, 125–7
Legislative Assembly of Lower Canada, 11
liberal evangelicalism. *See* Protestanttism, liberal
liberal theology. *See* Protestantism, liberal
Lincoln, Abraham, 132
Little, Jack, 128
"lived religion," 8–9, 188–9
Long, Kathryn T., 84
Lount, William, 158
Lucas, Daniel Van Norman, 255n92

Macaulay, Father, 93, 168, 178
Macdonald, John, 134
Macdonald, Sir John A., 114, 154, 155, 165, 169, 173, 178, 234n59, 265n94, 266n106; visit to Stanstead, 114
MacDonald, Malcolm, 39
McFee, K.N, 244n103
McGill University, 120, 122, 123
Mackenzie, Alexander, 155, 163–4
McLellan, Archibald, 228n73
McLellan, May, 228n73
McMaster, William, 166
Mann, Horace, 105
marriage, 3, 16–17, 23–7, 49, 56, 58, 59, 60, 61–3, 64–5, 67, 80, 157, 186, 218n41, 221n75; companionate, 16–17, 23–7, 49, 56, 58, 59, 60, 61–3, 67, 80; and middle-class women, 64–5
Martin, John Robert, 157–62, 180, 186, 260n36
Martin, Sophia (née Stinson), 157–62, 180, 186
Masons, 30–1
Matthews, Glenna, 53
Medical Board of Lower Canada, 27
Mercier, Honoré, 170–1
Methodist Church, 5–6; and Congregationalism, 13–14, 21, 29–31 *passim*, 132; construction of new centenary church at Stanstead Plain, 99, 125–40; and dancing, 113; denominational stationing committee, 113; egalitarian roots of, 129; moral community, 147–8; New Connexion Methodists, 132; political support in 1867 election, Stanstead County, 151–3, 256n11; and prohibition/intemperance, 113,

167-8, 113-14, 167-8; sesquicentenary of, 125-7; at Stanstead, 17, 30, 31, 47, 85, 92, 199n40; shift to middle class, 123-4, 126, 137, 242-3n84; united with Wesleyans, 255n94. *See also* revivals; Wesleyan Methodist Centenary Church, Stanstead Plain
Methodist Young People's Association, Stanstead. *See* societies for young people
Millerism, 17, 30, 84, 132, 248n24
Mills, Mary Ann (w. of Carlos Pierce), 126
mining, 87-8, 90-1, 94, 101; Ascot Township Mines, 88, 90-1, 94; Belden's Falls, 90-1; Canadian Copper Mines, 88; Middlebury, Vt, 90-1; Potton Township, 88; Stowe, Vt, 88
Montreal Witness, 171, 186
moral philosophy, 44-6
Morrill, Ozro, 88, 92, 133, 233n39
Mowat, Oliver, 165, 172

Nelson, Robert, 32-3, 209n74
Nelson, William, 32-3
new birth: as evangelical conversion, 20-1, 52-7
New Light. *See* revivals, First Great Awakening
Noll, Mark, 10, 84

Old Union Meeting House, 147
Orange Order, 171
Orsi, Robert, 9, 96

Palmer, Phoebe, 56-7, 84
Palmer, Walter, 56
Papineau, Louis-Joseph, 29, 32
Parker, Rev. W.R., 126
Parti national, 170-1
patriarchal household: transition of, 17, 25-6, 102, 108, 124
Pawlet, Vt, 24
pew rents, 47, 137-9, 188
Pierce, Carlos, 92, 126, 132-4 *passim*, 138, 139, 144, 152, 249n29, 249-50n39; benefactor of Stanstead's Wesleyan Methodist church, 132, 133-4, 138, 250n47, 252n66; Crystal Lake Cemetery, 132, 188; fundraising for church, 133

Pierce, Charles Wilder, 132, 140
Pierce, George, 134
Pierce, Martha (Butters), 66, 86, 134
Pierce, Mary, 135, 136
Pierce, Wilder, 66, 92, 129-30, 132, 133, 184
Pomroy, Benjamin, 92, 135, 136
Pope, John Henry, 166, 173
Porter, Noel, 23
Prohibition. *See* temperance
Protestant Ministerial Association of Montreal, 171-2
Protestant, evangelical. *See* evangelicals
Protestantism, liberal: definition of, 7-8, 196n237; and evangelical doctrine of new birth, 52; and fundraising, 9; hegemonic influence of, 127; sacraments, 71; theology of incarnation, 58, 60, 97, 99; transition to, 42, 52, 57, 58, 60, 71, 98-100, 104-8, 127, 135, 150, 185, 186, 187, 189, 194n17, 195n21, 195n22, 232n33; and the Victorian family, 82
Protestants, "mainline." *See* Protestantism, liberal
Punshon, Rev. Morley, 136-7, 255n92
Puritans, 8, 11, 16-18, 20, 26, 103-4, 108

Rack, Henry, 92
railways. *See* Stanstead Plain, and development of railway
Rebellions of 1837-38, 32
Reciprocity Treaty (1854), 37
Registry Ordinance (1841), 35, 63
religion, domestic, 103-4, 196n24, 254n81; and consumerism, 145, 146; as form of social control, 9; and socio-economic impact, 186-7; Victorian domestic and secularization, 5-10, 124, 188-9, 196n24
republican individualism: construct of, 16
revivals, 6, 20-1, 23, 43, 54-5, 80-1, 97, 116-17, 127-8, 135-6, 245n3, 219n54; "businessmen's revival" (1857-58), 56-7, 83-5, 98-9, 135, 187, 236n86; First Great Awakening, 21, 26; Methodists' revival in Stanstead Plain (1826), 128; (1835), 128, 129; (1867), 116, 130, 135-6; in Ottawa (1889), 165; role of women, 56, 80-1; Second Great Awaking, 17. *See also*

Stanstead County, radical revivals; Wesleyan Methodist Centenary Church, Stanstead Plain; Wesleyan Methodist Church, Stanstead Plain, pre-1866.
Richey, Russell, 186
Rider, H.M., 176
Rider, T.B., 257n15
Riel, Louis, 170
Ryckman, Edward, 255n92

Sabbath observance, 67–8, 115, 150, 156, 162–5, 187
St Francis District, Que.: settlement of, 11, 18; investments in, 235n78. *See also* Eastern Townships; Stanstead County; Stanstead Plain
Sanborn, John, 34, 46
Schleiermacher, Friedrich, 57
Schmidt, Leigh Eric, 40, 127–8
Schneider, A. Gregory, 140, 212n95
school: as institution of socialization, 117–18; parental influences, 117–18
Scott, Duncan Campbell, 258n16
Scott, Rev. William, 145–6, 175
Second Great Awakening. *See* revivals, Second Great Awakening
secularization of Western society, 5, 8, 189
self-identity, 42, 49
self-improvement, middle-class, 19–20, 24, 43–4, 110
Sellers, Charles, 129
Senate: religious affiliation of members (1872), 260n31
Silliman, Benjamin, 22
Smith, Ichabod, 129–30, 133
social change: impact on Calvinism, 23
societies for young people, 117
Stanstead College. *See* Stanstead Wesleyan College
Stanstead County, 3, 13, 27, 93, 117; Adventists in, 30, 132, 207n57; commercial capitalism, 50–1; economy, 36–7, 87–8, 126–7, 149–54 *passim*; economy and religious change, 130–1; factionalism in, 151–3; politics, 151–3, 175–6, 178–9; radical revivals, 130; settlement of, 11, 29–31; social life in, 48, 117–18
Stanstead Historical Society, 11

Stanstead Journal, 40, 57, 84, 152
Stanstead Plain (village of), 11, 16, 17, 27–30, 31, 33, 47, 66–7, 74, 84, 87, 94, 97, 112-13, 136, 137; church construction, 132; Colbys settle in, 27; Congregational Church in, 31, 136, 142, 147, 188; and development of mail system, 51, 87; and development of railway, 36–8, 87, 106, 130, 211n91, 215n18; and development of roads, 69, 131; economic change (post-1860), 87–9, 141, 149–50, 153; economic change (pre-1860), 19, 20, 23, 24–34, 40–1, 153; economy of, 73–4, 87–8, 94, 153; formation of municipal government, 130–1; Golden Rule Lodge, 38; incorporation of, 130; population and buildings (1861), 112, 117, 131; religious denominations (1861), 131–2, 133, 248n23; religious life in, 126; revival movement in, 56, 84, 116–17, 127–8, 130, 135–6, 140; telegraph at, 87
Stanstead Seminary, 33, 47–8, 49, 51, 117–18, 216n21
Stanstead Wesleyan College, 81, 118–19, 120, 140–1, 182–3, 243n96, 253n75, 253n76; female involvement in, 141–2; transfer of debts to Methodist Church of Canada, 141
Stationing Committee of the Methodist Church, 97
Stevens, Abel, 246–7n11
Stinson, Sophia. *See* Martin, Sophia
Stoddard, Anthony, 17–18
Stoddard, John, 202n11
Stoddard, Solomon, 18, 26
Stoddard family, 24
Stowe, Harriet Beecher, 57, 80, 81
Strauss, D.F., 71
Strong, Elder John, 17
Strong, Josiah, 202n11
Strong, Lemira. *See* Colby, Lemira
Strong, Timothy (f. of Lemira Colby), 24
Strong family: settlement in New England, 17–18, 24
Swing, David; controversy of, 71

temperance, 150, 165–9, 188; Band of Hope, 114; Canada Temperance Act, 179; support for Prohibition, 114, 179

Terrill, Hazard Bailey, 47, 215–16n18
Terrill, Timothy Lee, 215–16n18
Tilley, Sir Leonard, 167, 168, 169
Tilton, Roberta, 166
Tompkins, Jane, 80
Tosh, John, 68, 102

Universalists, Stanstead County, 112, 132; voting in 1867 election, 257n12

Valverde, Mariana, 180
voluntarism, 114–15, 137, 147
voluntary societies, 30, 143–4, 188; juvenile involvement in, 114–15

Wallingford, Melvina. *See* Colby, Melvina
Wallingford, Mrs (David), 65
Wayland, Francis, 45, 49
WCTU. *See* Woman's Christian Temperance Union
Weaver, Rev. George S., 65
Webster, Daniel, 43–4, 153–4, 172
Wendell, Rufus, 49, 120
Wesley, John, 92–3, 123, 217n35
Wesleyan Methodist Centenary Church, Stanstead Plain, 125–40 *passim*, 134, 136–8, 139, 144, 145–6, 147, 184; congregational unity, 144–6, 147; construction, 99, 125–40 *passim*, 134, 137, 246–7n11; cornerstone laying, 125–6, 134, 136, 147; dedication, 136–7; fire, 139; fundraising, 133–4, 142, 247n17; insurance, 139; membership, 128, 135; pew rental, 137–8, 188, 251n57, 252n67; rebuilding, 115, 144; revival of 1867, 116, 130, 135–6
Wesleyan Methodist Church, Stanstead Plain, pre-1866, 47: construction of brick church, 31, 128–9; 1826 revival, 128; 1835 revival, 128, 129; pew rental, 129, 137–8; plans for new church, 132, 133
Weybridge, Vt, 12, 47, 51, 59–60
White, Charles Colby (s. of William and Emily), 72
White, David, 165
White, Emily Strong (née Colby). *See* Colby, Emily Strong
White, Marianne, 165
White, Tom, 165, 172
White, William T. (h. of Emily Strong Colby), 12, 125, 165, 233n45
Williams, Mary (May) Spafford. *See* Colby, Mary Spafford
Winthrop, John, 17
Woman's Christian Temperance Union (WCTU), 166, 167, 168, 169
women: as converts, 54; and dower rights, 35–6, 63, 76–7, 211n88, 218n41, 227n56; middle-class self-development, 43, 48, 69, 72, 75; motherhood, 5, 17, 68, 69–71, 224–5n29; role of mother as religious instructor, 103, 106, 108–11; self-definition of, 80; social responsibilities, 141–2; spirituality, 52, 81, 225n37; valorization of self, 53, 69, 80, 143, 222n6
Wright, Julia McNair, 111
Wright, Samuel, 59

Yale College, 23, 40
Youmans, Letitia, 167
Young Men's Christian Association (YMCA), 59, 81, 164
Young, Brian, 63